A Digest of 500 Plays

A DIGEST OF 500 PLAYS

PLAYS

PLOT OUTLINES AND

PRODUCTION NOTES

EDITED BY
THEODORE J. SHANK

COLLIER BOOKS
A Division of Macmillan Publishing Co., Inc.
NEW YORK

COLLIER MACMILLAN PUBLISHERS
LONDON

Library of Congress Catalog Card Number: 63-
12787

FIRST COLLIER BOOKS EDITION 1966

FIFTH PRINTING 1977

A Digest of 500 Plays was originally published
in a hardcover edition by Crowell-Collier Press

Macmillan Publishing Co., Inc.
866 Third Avenue, New York, N.Y. 10022
Collier Macmillan Canada, Ltd.
Printed in the United States of America

Contents

CONTRIBUTORS TO A DIGEST OF 500 PLAYS

Claribel Baird
Ronald Edgar Barnes, Jr.
Philip A. Benson
Yvonne Bonsall
Edward W. Borgers
Richard P. Brown
Marvin A. Carlson
James H. Clancy
Wendell Cole
Harriet Ann Deer
Irving Deer
Everard d'Harnoncourt
M. Burton Drexler
Richard A. Duprey
Adele Edling
Stanley L. Glenn
Henry Goodman
Christian P. Gruber
William P. Halstead

Theodore W. Hatlen
Forbes I. Hill
Gerald Kahan
Robert B. Loper
John A. Mills
Lee Mitchell
Jack H. Neeson
Robert O'Brien
William I. Oliver
Richard D. Risso
Alan R. Robb
John R. Robb
Robert I. Schneideman
Theodore J. Shank
Evert M. Sprinchorn
Alan A. Stambusky
Lowell S. Swortzell
Nancy Foell Swortzell
Hal J. Todd

Seth P. Ulman

Sponsored by the
American Educational Theatre Association, Inc.
Production Lists Project

Introduction

This book is intended as a convenient reference guide for those who have an interest in the best drama of all periods and countries. For the director of noncommercial theatre it will serve as an aid to memory as well as a source of ideas for possible productions. For the general reader it provides easily available information on plays with which he may not be familiar or about which he wants to know more. For students and teachers it offers information about many of the significant plays in the history of world drama.

No reference work can be a substitute for the plays themselves; but having brought together in one volume pertinent information on so many important plays, this book should serve to introduce the reader to significant dramas of which he may be unaware. Further, for the theatre artist and the student there is included for each play information on staging requirements and in some instances statements of critical opinion and historical significance.

Doubtless no one will use this book without discovering that at least one of his favorite plays is missing; he will question the inclusion of others. This problem is inescapable when the total selection must be restricted to just over 500 examples. When final work on this digest began in 1959 the select list included more than 1,500 titles which were compiled over a period of more than ten years. Seven Advising Directors, chosen for their extensive experience in college and university theatres, reduced the list to the 528 titles which this book now includes.

An attempt has been made to include good plays not frequently produced as well as those which are often staged. A few, such as *Hernani* and *Uncle Tom's Cabin*, have been included because of their historical importance; others, such as *The Cyclops* by Euripides and Ben Jonson's *Cynthia's Revels*, have been included because they represent unique types. Almost all of the plays are long enough for a full evening's program; the medieval dramas are an exception. Some few other short dramas have been included because they are particularly important works of the dramatists or are the only examples of the dramatists' work—Strindberg's *Miss Julie*, Sartre's *No Exit*, Schnitzler's *The Green Cockatoo*, and Schildt's *The Gallows Man*.

The contributors who wrote the comments on individual titles were chosen because of their directing experience and knowledge of dramatic literature. The generosity of the seven Advising Directors and the thirty-nine Contributors who worked without remuneration must be acknowledged. Especially deserving of commendation is Everard D'Harnoncourt, who prepared the information for approximately 130 plays and whose fluency in French and German made his comparisons of original texts with translations of particular value.

Arrangement of Plays. The plays are arranged by countries in chronological order according to the date of the earliest play included from each. The plays for those countries which have a great many entries are divided into periods; within each period they are arranged alphabetically by dramatist, with the works by each dramatist in chronological order. Medieval plays have been given a separate section following the Roman; Asian plays and miscellaneous European plays have been placed last.

Index. At the end of the guide there is an index which includes the original titles of all plays as well as English titles, dramatists, and countries. (When necessary, the foreign titles have been Latinized or transliterated.)

Royalties. Royalty information obtained from dramatists, translators, and agents has been included for each play when it was available. Fees are subject to change, and each year some plays and translations come into the public domain and royalty payment for performance is no longer required. If a specific play is being considered for production, the best procedure is to write to the agent or publisher indicated. In the text an asterisk (*) after an agent or publisher indicates that the address can be found in the Directory at the end of the book. A large majority of the plays and translations listed which are not in the public domain are controlled by one of the following:

Samuel French, Inc.
25 West 45th Street
New York 36, New York
or
7623 Sunset Blvd.
Hollywood 46, California
or
27 Grenville Street
Toronto 5, Canada

Dramatists Play Service
14 East 38th Street
New York 16, New York

Baker's Plays
100 Summer Street
Boston 10, Massachusetts

NOTE: Samuel French is Baker's representative for the Western United States and Canada.

Although the catalogues published by the above usually indicate a royalty fee for nonprofessional performance rights, a reduction of the stated fee is often possible depending upon the size of the theatre, the admission charge, the expected attendance, the budget for the production, and the purpose for which box-office receipts are used. The director should make certain the required fee has been established before performance.

Texts. Since new editions and new translations of plays are constantly being published and others go out of print, the question of which text to recommend is very complex. For plays originally written in English the contributors have listed editions which in their opinions are most readily obtainable while also giving attention to accuracy and arrangement of the script. Most plays are available in softcover editions, either separately or in collections; it is these that the contributors specially recommend. All inquiries relating to editions should be addressed to the publishers. Translations recommended are those which in the opinions of the contributors are the best available; in some instances these recommendations have been supplemented by those of Robert O'Brien. However, often even the best available translations will still require considerable alteration in order to prepare the play for production. Although a few of the recommended texts are not now in print, they should be obtainable through an interlibrary loan. A helpful reference work for locating other texts that appear in anthologies is John H. Ottemiller's *Index to Plays in Collections* (Scarecrow Press), which is an index of authors and titles of plays which have appeared in collections published between 1900 and 1950.

Whether the reader turns to this volume for production possibilities or to check the basic staging requirements of a play he may be considering for production or for further information on plays contemporaneous with those he is studying or in order to refresh his memory of plays which have not made a lasting impression, those who have worked on this book hope that it will serve its intended purpose of useful reference. They also hope that in some way it may help to broaden the repertoires of noncommercial theatres by introducing directors to good plays which they do not know but which they may be induced to read with a view to possible production.

THEODORE J. SHANK

January 1963

GREEK DRAMA

THE PERSIANS (*Persae;* 472 B.C.)   AESCHYLUS. Tragedy. Outside the imperial palace at Susa the chorus, aged councilors of the Persian Empire, describe the departure of Xerxes' expedition against Greece and speak their anxiety and yearning for news of the campaign. The dowager queen Atossa, widow of Darius and mother of Xerxes, enters, disturbed by an ominous dream. Soon a messenger arrives and recounts the defeat of the Persian fleet at Salamis and the subsequent disastrous retreat of the Persian land forces back to Asia. Atossa prepares a libation which she offers to the shade of her husband while the chorus begs him to appear and give counsel. The ghost of the great conqueror rises from his tomb and is told the dreadful news. He accuses Xerxes of being vain and headstrong, says this impiety has courted ruin for himself and his men, foretells the final Persian defeat at Plataea, and disappears. After the shade has sunk back into the tomb and Atossa has gone to meet her son, the chorus sings of the greatness of Persia under Darius. Xerxes enters, his clothing muddied and torn, his huge army reduced to a few ragged followers. The elders ask about one after another of the Persian warrior-heroes, answered each time by Xerxes' description of his death. Finally the king ordains a period of mourning throughout the Empire and, weeping, moves into his palace.

MEN (*18–27*): 3 principals; chorus of 15 or 24. WOMAN: Atossa (60 or older). SET: Ancient Persian palace courtyard, with provision for altar or tomb for the dead Darius. COSTUMES: Ancient Persian.

ROYALTY: Apply publisher. TEXT: Seth Benardette trans. in *The Complete Greek Tragedies* (Chicago).

THE SEVEN AGAINST THEBES (*Septem Contra Thebas;* 467 B.C.) AESCHYLUS. Tragedy. The citizens of Thebes are in panic over news that a powerful army is about to lay siege to the city. The populace is rebuked by King Eteocles; when he has calmed them he summons his chieftains. Eteocles assigns each of his chieftains a gate. Word comes that the seventh gate is to be attacked by Polyneices, Eteocles' brother and bitterest enemy; Eteocles elects to defend the seventh gate himself. A messenger recounts the struggle in which the invaders are beaten and tells how Eteocles was slain as he killed Polyneices. The bodies of the dead are brought in. A herald enters to announce the decree which forbids burial for Polyneices. The play ends as Antigone, sister of the dead brothers, announces her intention to assure the body of Polyneices the rites due all the dead. Believed to be the third play of a trilogy concerning the Theban legend.

MEN (*9*): 3 are speaking parts. WOMEN (*17*): 2 are 20–25; chorus of 15 Theban women is 25–50. EXTRAS: Soldiers and citizens. SET: A holy place where sacrifices are made. COSTUMES: Ancient Greek; at least 7 warriors in fighting gear. DIFFICULTIES: Little action explicitly indicated.

ROYALTY: Apply publisher. TEXT: David Grene trans. in *The Complete Greek Tragedies* (Chicago).

—— o ——

AGAMEMNON (458 B.C.) AESCHYLUS. Tragedy. The play begins with a watchman looking for the beacon fires that are to announce the fall of Troy. It becomes clear through his speech and that of the chorus that Clytemnestra has been unfaithful to her husband, the absent king Agamemnon. Agamemnon enters with the princess Cassandra captive and is welcomed into his house by Clytemnestra. Agamemnon's transgression of divine command in his prideful manner of returning home as victor sets off the train of retribution to the third generation. Cassandra, reluctantly following her captor into the house, foresees death for him and for herself. Cries are heard. Clytemnestra emerges from the house, her hands and garments bloody, then discloses the bodies of Agamemnon and Cassandra, whom she has trapped in a fowler's net and stabbed to death. When the people protest, Aegisthus, Clytemnestra's lover, enters with a guard of armed men; together they defy the populace. First play of the

Oresteia trilogy in which the subject of justice is treated through choral passages interspersed with acted episodes.

MEN (*about 25*): 15 are members of the chorus of Argive elders; 5–6 are soldiers of Aegisthus; 4 are 30–50. WOMEN (*7*): 1 is about 20; 1 around 40; 4–5 handmaidens. SET: Palace steps. COSTUMES: Ancient Greek.

ROYALTY: Apply publisher. TEXT: Richmond Lattimore trans. in *The Complete Greek Tragedies* (Chicago).

—— o ——

THE LIBATION BEARERS (*Choephoroe*; 458 B.C.) AESCHYLUS. Tragedy. Orestes, son of the murdered Agamemnon, secretly returns home. He lays a lock of his hair on the tomb of his father as an offering. Electra, his sister, coming by night to pray at the tomb, discovers the lock of hair; Orestes comes out of his hiding place and the two are reunited. He tells her his scheme to revenge his father. Orestes and his companions disguise themselves and ask for Clytemnestra, saying they bring news of the death of her exiled son. Clytemnestra is grief-stricken at the news, but she sends for Aegisthus that he may also hear the news. Orestes lures him into the house and stabs him. He then confronts his mother and, despite her pleas for mercy, drives her into the house to die beside her lover. The bodies of the slain are then disclosed. Orestes prepares to depart for the temple of Apollo at Delphi to claim exemption from the crime of matricide, but as he does so he feels the avenging Furies gathering to torment him and rushes out wildly. Second play of the *Oresteia*.

MEN (*4*): 1 is about 20; 1 is about 45; 2 are minor. WOMEN (*18*): 15 are members of the chorus of slave women; 1 is 18–20; 1 is 40–45; 1 is 55–60. EXTRAS: Servants of both sexes. SETS: Tomb of Agamemnon at night; courtyard of the palace of the kings of Argos; three entrances. COSTUMES: Ancient Greek. DIFFICULTIES: Elaborate and complicated choruses carry the main emphasis.

ROYALTY: Apply publisher. TEXT: Richmond Lattimore trans. in *The Complete Greek Tragedies* (Chicago).

—— o ——

THE EUMENIDES (458 B.C.) AESCHYLUS. Tragedy. Orestes is discovered clinging to the altar of the temple of

Apollo at Delphi, where he has taken refuge. Surrounding
him are the Furies, now asleep, waiting to seize him. The
ghost of Clytemnestra appears and rouses the Furies, but they
are prevented from harming Orestes by the intervention of
Apollo. The Furies charge that Apollo has wronged them by
protecting Orestes, an acknowledged criminal, depriving them
of their rightful prey. All finally agree to refer the case to
Athena for judgment. Scene shifts to the temple of Athena
in Athens. Presented with the rival claims, Athena impounds
a jury of Athenian citizens. The vote is taken—it is a tie,
broken when Athena declares for Orestes; he is therefore forever absolved of blame. The disgruntled Furies, at the urging
of Athena, gradually abandon their role of avengers and
become the "Eumenides," protectors and friends of man.
Third play of the *Oresteia*.

MEN (*14*): Orestes; Apollo; and 12 nonspeaking jurors.
WOMEN (*18*): A priestess of Apollo; Athena; the ghost of
Clytemnestra; the 15 Furies, who turn into 15 beautiful
maidens. EXTRAS: Unspecified number of Athenian townspeople. SETS: Temple of Apollo at Delphi; temple of Athena
at Athens (altars for sacrifice, pedestals or thrones for the
deity, entrance for Clytemnestra's ghost). COSTUMES: Ancient
Greek. Means must be provided for the metamorphosis of
the hideous Furies into the lovely Eumenides. DIFFICULTIES:
Long argument between the Furies and Athena after the
climax, the acquittal of Orestes.
    ROYALTY: Apply publisher. TEXT: Richmond Lattimore
trans. in *The Complete Greek Tragedies* (Chicago).

—— o ——

THE ACHARNIANS (425 B.C.) ARISTOPHANES. Comedy.
A hardheaded pacifist farmer, Dicaeopolis, concludes a private treaty with the Spartans when he discovers no Athenian
will accept his plea for peace. Dicaeopolis samples various
treaties from Sparta, like wine, chooses one of thirty years'
duration. Attacked by a chorus of Acharnians who attempt
to stone him, Dicaeopolis persuades them to hear him out.
His high-blown eloquence and comic candor help him win his
cause. Noteworthy are Aristophanes' famous parody of Euripides, his lampoons of the follies of militarists, gullible Athen-
ians, and nearsighted Athenian foreign policy. Peace won
by midplay, Dicaeopolis reaps its fruits in a series of farcical,

hedonistic, nonpolitical scenes. Play ends on a festive note of riotous jollity as it celebrates wine, women, song, and peace. Earliest of Aristophanes' extant plays; may be called the first "antiwar" comedy. Political in theme, rustic in spirit, it satirizes popular Athenian political views.

MEN (*35–60; doubling possible*): 6 are 18–25 (minor); 10 are 20–40 (1 requires an outstanding actor, short in stature; rest are minor); 7 are 40–60; (1 requires an outstanding actor); chorus of 12 to 24 Acharnian elders, age 40-60; several assembly members, ambassadors, slaves. WOMEN (*5*): 4 are 18–25; 1 is 40-60 (all minor). GIRLS: (*2*): 10–15. SET: Street in Athens, meeting place of the Athenian Assembly; in background, 3 houses belonging to Dicaeopolis, Euripides, and Lamachos. Set should be formal, nonrealistic. Unit set is appropriate. Arena production possible but difficult. Houses should be on wagons that can be rolled forward on stage. COSTUMES: 5th-century B.C. Athenian; emphasis on rustic, ragged peasant quality; some conventional Athenian city dress; a few garish Persian costumes; long, ragged cloaks for chorus, 1 with complete battle dress; some wedding-party dress; masks may be utilized. DIFFICULTIES: Some difficult verse; especially long odes chanted by chorus and certain long speeches by Dicaeopolis. Delivery problems in Euripides parody scene, where elevated tragic diction and declamatory rhetoric is utilized for satire. Some archaic language and dated concepts (clarified in recommended translation).

ROYALTY: Apply publisher. TEXT: Douglass Parker trans. in *The Complete Greek Comedy* (Michigan), Vol. II.

— o —

THE CLOUDS (*Nubes*, 423 B.C.) ARISTOPHANES. Comedy. Philosophical satire underlies this sally against the Socratic "new learning" culture of fifth-century Athens. Old Strepsiades, near poverty because of his son's extravagance, enrolls in Socrates' school to learn arguments against his creditors. Socrates, suspended in a basket amid thought-provoking clouds, accepts him as a pupil. A chorus of clouds demonstrates the folly of sophistry and augers Strepsiades' comic fate. The philosopher abandons the incorrigibly stupid Strepsiades, whereupon the old man forces his son Phidippides to replace him. Just and Unjust Discourse vie verbally for Phidippides; Unjust Discourse wins and instructs him within

Socrates' Thoughtery. Returning home with his learned son, Strepsiades rids himself of his creditors without Phidippides' aid. The "new learning" works so well for Phidippides, however, that he beats his father mercilessly and proves through argument his moral right to do so. Enraged, Strepsiades sets fire to the Thoughtery housing Socrates and his disciples, whose allegedly subversive studies have brought about his downfall.

MEN (14): 2 are 20–35 (1 minor, 1 may be played by a boy); 10 are 30–50 (6 nonspeaking roles; 2 minor); 1 is 45; 1 is 60–80 (must be a leading actor). WOMEN (12–24): Chorus of clouds, ages not important. SET: Street in Athens; in background, 2 houses, that of Strepsiades and that of Socrates (the Thoughtery); latter is small and dingy, interior of the former is shown with 2 beds seen. Set should be formal, nonrealistic. Unit set appropriate. Arena staging possible but difficult. Some mechanism needed to suspend Socrates. COSTUMES: 5th-century B.C. Athenian; some suggestion of fantasy needed in dress of chorus of clouds; masks may be used. DIFFICULTIES: Involved choral passages and verse patterns of the cloud chorus require concentrated effort. Argument between Just Discourse and Unjust Discourse requires special attention to vocal range and control.

ROYALTY: Apply publisher. TEXT: William Arrowsmith trans. in *The Complete Greek Comedy* (Michigan), Vol. III.

— o —

THE WASPS (*Vespae;* 422 B.C.) ARISTOPHANES. Comedy. Satirizes abuses of the Athenian judicial system, fostered by the rulers and characterized by the populace's passion for litigation and jury duty. Philocleon, aged litigation addict, is imprisoned at home by his son, Bdelycleon, to prevent his serving on juries. Philocleon makes several abortive attempts to escape. A chorus of wasp-dressed fellow jurymen arrives to accompany him to court. Bdelycleon and his slaves battle the chorus for Philocleon's custody. Matters are resolved by debate between son and father in which Philocleon is convinced he is a tool of the demagogues. Bdelycleon humors Philocleon by allowing a mock trial at home in which a dog is tried for stealing cheese. Tricked into voting for acquittal, Philocleon faints. Afterward he renounces jury duty, vows a life of pleasure, and departs for a banquet. Returning home drunk after insulting the guests and absconding with a flute-girl, Philocleon ends the comedy in a wild dance with three small boys.

MEN (22–34; doubling possible): 2 are 18–25; 5 are 30–50 (3 have lines); 1 is 60–80 (outstanding actor, able to dance); chorus of 12–24 jurymen, dressed as wasps, age 60–80; 2 are undetermined age (disguised as dogs; 1 has no lines, both are minor); some slaves, number may vary. WOMEN (2): 1 is 18–25 (no lines); 1 is 30–45; both minor. BOYS (13–15): 5 or 6 are 7–9 (disguised as puppies; no lines); remainder are 10–15 (1 has lines; 3 must be small in stature and able to dance). SET: Street in Athens; in background, the house of Philocleon, surrounded by a huge net. Set should be formal, nonrealistic. Unit set appropriate. Arena staging possible but difficult. House should have a practical roof so that actors may play on it. Script calls for Philocleon to be brought onstage clinging to an ass; play also calls for actor to swing down from an upper window on a rope. COSTUMES: 5th-century B.C. Athenian; chorus costumed as wasps; 2 actors disguised as dogs; 5 or 6 boys disguised as puppies; 3 boys costumed as crabs; lead actor, in addition to basic costume, must disguise as a threadbare character in a Euripidean play; masks may be used. DIFFICULTIES: Choral passages present some problems. Some dated concepts and references to 5th-century B.C. Athenian legal cases and customs will need to be clarified in production. Topical references to Cleon the demagogue likely to be obscure to the modern audience.
ROYALTY: Apply publisher. TEXT: Douglass Parker trans. in *The Complete Greek Comedy* (Michigan), Vol. VI.

— o —

PEACE (*Pax;* 421 B.C.) ARISTOPHANES. Comedy. Lyricism and a relatively serious tone characterize Aristophanes' second antiwar comedy. Infectious gaiety and warmth reflect a nostalgia for peace and a return to the joys of rural life. A farmer, the vine-grower Trygaeus, strives to end the war between Athens and Sparta by flying to Heaven astride a beetle in search of the goddess Peace. There, War and Tumult have cast her into a pit along with her aides, Opora and Theoria. While War hunts a pestle to grind the warring cities in his mortar, Trygaeus liberates Peace, assisted by farmers and laborers summoned from Greece. Their freedom assured, a feast is prepared to celebrate the peace. Trygaeus rejects the pleas of a soothsayer and armament-makers alike to share in and concludes by singing with the chorus of husbandmen a its fruits. He despatches Theoria to the Senate, weds Opora, festal ode of fertility.

MEN (27–39; doubling possible): 3 are 18–30; 8 are 35–50 (2 have lines); 3 are 40–60 (1 requires an outstanding actor, 2 are minor); 1 is 55–70 (minor); also, chorus of 12–24 husbandmen, some laborers, farmers, and peasants (some women may be used), ages may vary from 18–60; several slaves, etc. WOMEN (3): 2 are 18–25; 1 is 20–40 (none has lines). BOYS (5): All 10–15 (2 have lines; 3 may be cut). GIRLS (2): Both 10–15. SETS: Farm area; farmhouse of Trygaeus; mouth of a cave closed up with boulders; palace of Zeus; a stable, its door closed. Set should be formal, non-realistic. Unit set appropriate. Arena staging possible but difficult. Mechanism needed to have Trygaeus appear astride the huge beetle called for in the script; same must be raised and lowered to the palace of Zeus. COSTUMES: 5th-century B.C. Athenian; should stress rustic, peasant quality, especially among chorus members; military garb needed for at least 2 characters; masks may be used. DIFFICULTIES: Some involved choral passages in the verse. Lead actors must sing—especially Trygaeus and his daughters. Tug-of-war sequence by chorus could present staging problems. Some references, particularly political ones, are archaic.

ROYALTY: Apply publisher. TEXT: William Arrowsmith trans. in *The Complete Greek Comedy* (Michigan), Vol. XI.

— o —

THE BIRDS (*Aves*; 414 B.C.) ARISTOPHANES. Comedy. Pisthetairos and Euelpides are tired of the pests that inhabit Athens and decide to emigrate to the land of the birds. Once they get there they persuade Epops, king of the birds, to set up the city of Cloud-Cuckooland in mid-air. Their purpose is to make men and gods pay tribute to the birds for letting incense smoke pass through the air to the gods. Eventually the gods give in; as evidence of their submission they permit Pisthetairos to marry the goddess Iris. As in most plays by Aristophanes, most of the humor comes in the tangential episodes, such as the scenes with some of the "pests" (the priest, the poet, the prophet); with the messenger; with Prometheus; and a scene in which Herakles learns that he is illegitimate and cannot legally inherit from his father Zeus.

MEN (*21; doubling possible*). WOMAN: Goddess Iris is about 20. Many male roles can be altered to female, e.g., Secretary-bird, Priest-bird, and Herald-bird. Juno is an excellent substitute for Poseidon. CHORUS: Birds, 10 or more, either sex or both. SET: Single complex-platform setting will serve, though changes and moving scenery are possible. COSTUMES: Most productions have used Greek dress and fairly realistic birds. Modern dress possible. DIFFICULTIES: Training the chorus of birds to dance and to sing or speak in unison. Musical background necessary.

ROYALTY: Apply publishers. TEXT: Walter Kerr adap. (Catholic University Press) or William Arrowsmith trans. in *The Complete Greek Comedy* (Michigan), vol. I.

— o —

LYSISTRATA (411 B.C.) ARISTOPHANES. Comedy. To make the men stop the Athens-Sparta war, Lysistrata proposes to all the women of Greece that they go on a sex strike until the men agree to make peace. The women agree, some reluctantly. They capture the Acropolis and lock the gates on the men. When the men start to build a fire to smoke out the women, they get doused with water. Lysistrata has to use a whip hand to prevent some of the women from returning home for short visits, but Myrrhine in a fine scene prepares a bed for her husband with much delay, then leaves him alone in it. Eventually the men capitulate and make peace. Play has a more unified plot than others by Aristophanes.

MEN (*7*): 1 is 20–25; 1 is 25–30; 5 are 45–55. WOMEN (*4*): 3 are 20–25; 1 is 25–30. CHILD: Under 3, either sex. CHORUSES: Young women; old women; old men; Athenian men; Spartan men (some doubling of choruses possible). SET: Before the gates of the Acropolis. COSTUMES: Greek. DIFFICULTIES: Requires imaginative business to help point the humor.

ROYALTY: Apply publishers. TEXT: Gilbert Seldes trans. (Farrar and Rinehart) or Douglass Parker trans. in *The Complete Greek Comedy* (Michigan), Vol. VIII.

— o —

THE FROGS (*Ranae;* 405 B.C.) ARISTOPHANES. Comedy. Dionysus, disgusted at the low standard of tragedy written in Athens, decides to retrieve Euripides from Hades. Remembering that his half-brother Heracles once went to Hades and returned with Cerberus, Dionysus disguises himself in the lion-skin of Heracles and is ferried across the Styx by Charon. People of the underworld who had met Heracles alternately welcome and attack the impersonator, and Dionysus responds by alternately making his servant Xanthius put on the lion-skin or give it back. When, upon meeting Dionysus, Aeschylus insists that Dionysus take him back to earth instead of Euripides, the two take part in a number of contests to prove which is the better poet. The most famous of these contests is that in which they weigh lines of poetry in a pair of scales. Dionysus finally chooses Aeschylus, and Pluto bids them farewell.

MEN (9): plus extras. WOMEN (3): small roles. Choruses of frogs and initiates (male or both sexes) needed. SETS: Hercules' home; bank of the river Styx; the other bank, where the Palace of Pluto is eventually seen. COSTUMES: Greek, except frog chorus.

ROYALTY: Apply translator. TEXT: Richmond Lattimore trans. in *The Complete Greek Comedy* (Michigan), Vol. IV. Music by Gilbert L. Bloom, Television Center, State University of Iowa, or Paul Miller, Milford High School, Milford, Michigan.

— o —

PLUTUS (388 B.C.) ARISTOPHANES. Comedy. Satirizes the effects of unequal distribution of wealth in Athens. Blind Plutus, God of Wealth, regains his vision through the efforts of Chremylus, an Athenian citizen. With Plutus' sight restored, Chremylus sees a solution to the ills of humanity, since Plutus will then be able to discern the deserving and undeserving. Plutus returns, rejoicing in his sight and his new-found ability to distribute his riches justly. A series of comic scenes follows, introducing characters who illustrate the various unhappy social effects of the Utopia brought about by Plutus' cure. Finally, Plutus is led in ritual procession to be installed on the Acropolis.

MEN (22–34; doubling possible): 3 are 18–25 (1 is major,

requires agility and singing ability; 2 are minor); 4 are 35–50 (minor); 2 are 55–70 (1 must be an outstanding actor, 1 is minor); 1 is 60–80; chorus of 12–24 rustics (some women may be used); ages may vary from 35–60 (all must have some ability at dance). WOMEN (3): 1 is 18–25 (tall and robust, must suggest by stature the superhuman); 1 is 30–45 (minor); 1 is 60–80 (minor; must disguise convincingly as a young girl and be able to walk in a youthful and alluring manner). BOY: Age is 10–15 (no lines). SET: Public square in Athens; background, the house of Chremylus. Set should be formal, nonrealistic. Unit set is appropriate. Arena staging possible. COSTUMES: Early 4th-century B.C. Athenian; some conventional city dress; chorus should be costumed in thread-bare rustic cloaks and robes; Plutus wears ragged costume of blind beggar; Poverty must be outfitted in robes reflecting her squalor; masks may be used. DIFFICULTIES: Some singing and dancing ability may be required of chorus members.

ROYALTY: Apply publisher. TEXT: William Arrowsmith trans. in *The Complete Greek Comedy* (Michigan), Vol. VII.

— o —

ALCESTIS (438 B.C.) EURIPIDES. Though destined to die, Admetus, King of Pherae, with the aid of his friend Apollo, cajoled the Fates into postponing their sentence. They agreed on condition that some other die in his place. Admetus asked all his relatives to die for him, but only his wife Alcestis was willing to make the sacrifice. The dialogue between Death, who has come for her, and Apollo forms the prologue. In the first episode, Alcestis' dying speeches are self-controlled; Admetus is almost maudlin. Admetus' father, Pheres, arrives for an episode of characteristic Euripidean argument, full of glittering rhetorical devices: Admetus charges the old man with being too cowardly to die; Pheres replies that his son struck the more cowardly bargain, letting a woman die for him. Admetus in rage drives Pheres off but, left alone, reflects that it would have been better to die than live this life of shame. Heracles comes as guest, and the overhospitable Admetus deceives him into thinking he is welcome. A humorous episode occurs between the gluttonous Heracles and a grieving servant. Heracles, undeceived, produces the comic ending by outwrestling the death-god for Alcestis.

MEN (6): 2 are 60–70 (Death is a minor character); 1 is

40–45; 3 are 25–35. WOMEN (2): Both 25–30. CHILDREN
(1 or 2): Male child, perhaps 5; baby girl, with no lines, can
be cut. CHORUS (6–18): Elders of Pherae. EXTRAS: Bier-
carriers; guards; servants. SET: Courtyard of Admetus' palace; door necessary, columns and walls desirable. Arena
production possible. Considerable room required for chorus
to move. Levels desirable. COSTUMES: Ancient Greek. Might
be done in modern dress. DIFFICULTIES: Choral lyrics, long
and somewhat difficult to understand, are more interesting
sung and danced.

ROYALTY: Apply publisher. TEXT: Richmond Lattimore
trans. in *The Complete Greek Tragedies* (Chicago) or Philip
Vellacott trans. in *Euripides: Alcestis and Other Plays* (Penguin).

—— o ——

MEDEA (431 B.C.) EURIPIDES. Tragedy. Medea, a barbarian, had sacrificed everything to help her lover, Jason, steal
the golden fleece from her father. Now, although Medea has
been his wife for some years, Jason has arranged to marry
the daughter of Creon, King of Corinth. Fearing that Medea
will take revenge, Creon exiles her. She takes vengeance by
sending her children with gifts—a poisoned robe and crown
—to Jason's bride. The gifts burn the princess, as well as
Creon, to death. Medea wants to destroy Jason totally by
killing their children. Her desire to hurt Jason becomes
stronger than her love for her children; she goes into the
palace; the children's dying cries are heard. When Jason arrives, Medea appears in a dragon-drawn chariot. She will not
even let Jason bury the children, but flaunts the full horror
of her deed. (No play exhibits better the ambiguity of Euripides' vision. Jason's cynical moral blindness alienates the
audience; Medea's brutal revenge alienates them perhaps
more.)

MEN (5): 1 is 45–55; 2 are 40–50; 2 are 30–35. WOMEN
(2): 1 is 30–35 (requires outstanding actress); 1 is 40–50. CHIL-
DREN (2): Probably 4 and 6. CHORUS (6–14): Women of
Corinth. SET: Temporary palace of Jason at Corinth. Door
necessary, columns and some suggestion of walls desirable.
Arena production possible. Considerable room required for
chorus to move. Medea gives the impression of floating in air
at the play's end, perhaps behind a scrim. COSTUMES: Ancient

Greek. DIFFICULTIES: Choral lyrics, long and somewhat obscure, are more interesting sung and danced.

ROYALTY: Apply publisher. TEXT: Rex Warner trans. in *The Complete Greek Tragedies* (Chicago) or in *Three Great Plays of Euripides* (Mentor).

—— o ——

HIPPOLYTUS (428 B.C.) EURIPIDES. Tragedy. Hippolytus, son of King Theseus, scorned sexual love and the worship of Aphrodite to devote himself to chaste Artemis. To punish him, Aphrodite inspires in Phaedra, Hippolytus' stepmother, an overpowering lust for him. Phaedra fights it by starving herself, but, at the point of death, is coaxed into revealing the shameful passion to her nurse. The nurse goes to tell Hippolytus. Hippolytus' reaction is so violent that Phaedra can hear him rage, even though she is outdoors. In despair she makes herself the instrument of his destruction. Leaving Theseus a message that Hippolytus has violated her, Phaedra hangs herself. Theseus arrives, hastily pronounces a curse on his son, and exiles him. The curse is soon fulfilled; a messenger rushes on to say that Hippolytus has been dragged to death by his terrified horses when they were chased by a god-sent monster. Too late, Artemis reveals to Theseus that his son was honorable and his wife chaste. Sharpest dramatic interest focuses on Phaedra. Alone and weakened, she still has a conscience which prompts her to battle the sophistical arguments of the nurse. (Compare with Racine's *Phaedra*, on the same theme; page 181.)

MEN (4): Hippolytus must be young, not over 18 or 19; Theseus is 40–45; 2 others are 20–30 (both minor, 1 with a long speech). WOMEN (4): 1 is 25–30; 1 is 50–60; 2 are goddesses, perhaps 25–35. MALE CHORUS (6–12): Huntsmen. FEMALE CHORUS (6–12): Women of Troezen. EXTRAS (2–7): Servants and attendants. SET: Courtyard of Theseus' temporary palace in Troezen; suggestion of walls; pillars and a door desirable. Arena production possible. Considerable room required for chorus to move; steps on one side desirable to give levels. Goddesses give the impression of floating in air, perhaps behind a scrim. COSTUMES: Ancient Greek. DIFFICULTIES: Goddesses' appearances constitute a production problem. Choral lyrics, long and somewhat obscure, more interesting when sung and danced, but appropriate music is necessary.

ROYALTY: Apply publisher. TEXT: David Grene trans. in *The Complete Greek Tragedies* (Chicago) or Philip Vellacott trans. in *Euripides: Alcestis and Other Plays* (Penguin).

— o —

ANDROMACHE (*ca.* 426 B.C.) EURIPIDES. Tragedy. Andromache, Neoptolemus' slave, has incurred the hatred of his lawful wife Hermione because she bore Neoptolemus a son while Hermione remained barren. Neoptolemus has journeyed to Delphi. Andromache has fled to Thetis' shrine to escape Hermione's murderous intent. She has a debate with Hermione and one with Menelaus, who coaxes her from the shrine, using her son's life as bait. Menelaus then allows Hermione to order Andromache and her child killed, but the arrival of Neoptolemus' grandfather Peleus halts the slayings; Menelaus is too cowardly to act against Peleus' opposition. Rather than face her husband's wrath, Hermione flees with Orestes (who claims her father Menelaus promised her to him). A messenger arrives to tell that Orestes has had Neoptolemus murdered.

MEN (*4*): 1 is 65–75; 1 is 40–50; 2 are 20–30. WOMEN (*5*): 1 is 35–40; 2 are 20–30; 1 is 45–55; 1 a goddess of indeterminate age. CHILD: 5–6, speaks 12 lines. CHORUS (*6–18*): Maidens of Phthia. EXTRAS: Servants and attendants. SET: Before the temple of Thetis, a lean-to sheltering an outdoor shrine. Levels desirable. Arena production possible. Considerable room required for chorus to move. Goddess must give the impression of floating in air, perhaps behind a scrim. COSTUMES: Ancient Greek. DIFFICULTIES: Goddess' entrance constitutes a production problem. Choral lyrics, long and somewhat obscure, more interesting sung and danced.

ROYALTY: Apply publisher. TEXT: Moses Hadas and John McLean trans. in *Ten Plays by Euripides* (Bantam) or John Frederick Nims trans. in *The Complete Greek Tragedies* (Chicago).

— o —

THE CYCLOPS (*ca.* 425 B.C.) EURIPIDES. Satyr play. Odysseus and his sailors are driven by a storm to the island of the Cyclops, one-eyed cannibal monsters. The Cyclops who captures them eats two sailors. Odysseus gives him some wine for dessert and he becomes drunk; while he is stupefied, Odysseus and the sailors bore out his single eye with a red-hot pointed stake. The Cyclops blinded, all make their escape. To fulfill the satyr play's conventions, Euripides adds a chorus of satyrs with their father, Silenus. These provide bawdy humor; by and large, however, Odysseus and the Cyclops are serious Euripidean tragic characters, the one a tricky politician, the other a boastful tyrant.

MEN (3): 1 is 50–60; 1 is 40–45; 1 is a giant, perhaps 35. CHORUS (6–24): Satyrs and members of Odysseus' crew. EXTRAS: Slaves; sheep. SET: Before the Cyclops' cave; door necessary; levels desirable. Arena production possible. COSTUMES: Ancient Greek. Satyrs wear goatskin vests, otherwise as near nude as modern standards permit. DIFFICULTIES: Giving the impression that the Cyclops is vastly bigger than the sailors is a problem. The satyrs' lyrics, long and somewhat obscure, should be sung and danced.

ROYALTY: Apply publisher. TEXT: William Arrowsmith trans. in *The Complete Greek Tragedies* (Chicago).

— o —

THE TROJAN WOMEN (*Troades;* 415 B.C.) EURIPIDES. Tragedy. The play unfolds the sorrows of Hecuba, aged queen of conquered Troy. Troy is to be razed; she is made the slave of Odysseus, the Greek she hates more than any other; one of her daughters, Polyxena, is killed; the other, the inspired Cassandra, becomes the mistress-slave of brutal Agamemnon. Cassandra rejoices like a maniac in her terrible nuptial. Andromache, Hecuba's daughter-in-law, enters in a chariot full of armor; she is to go to Achilles' son. The Greeks vote to hurl Andromache's little son Astyanax from the towers of Troy. Menelaus comes to claim Helen. He encounters Hecuba, who urges him to avenge his honor by killing Helen at once. Andromache's master's ship must leave; Astyanax' burial rites fall to Hecuba; the old queen binds the tiny corpse in linen as Troy's huge fire is seen in the background. The Greek victory is cut down to a stupid quarrel over a good-for-nothing woman who has caused untold misery. Each character sees her catastrophe from a different point of view: Hecuba's griefs are so many they make her numb; Andromache wishes for death; Cassandra welcomes with perverse pleasure the role she will play in Agamemnon's destruction; the other women show varying degrees of grief, anxiety, and hysteria.

MEN (*3*): 2 are 40–45; Poseidon, perhaps a vigorous 60. WOMEN (*5*): 1 is 60–70; 2 are 30–35; 1 is 19; Athena perhaps 30–35. CHORUS (*6–18*): Trojan women. CHILD: 2–3 years old. EXTRAS: Greek soldiers. SET: Plain before the beach near Troy; doors to several huts needed. COSTUMES: Ancient Greek. DIFFICULTIES: Some stage effects needed for the burning of Troy. Choral lyrics, long and somewhat obscure, are more interesting sung and danced.

ROYALTY: Apply publisher. TEXT: Richmond Lattimore trans. in *The Complete Greek Tragedies* (Chicago).

— o —

ELECTRA (413 B.C.) EURIPIDES. Tragedy. The story of the revenge of Electra and her brother Orestes upon Clytemnestra and Aegisthus for their father's murder. Aegisthus and Clytemnestra have married Electra to a farmer, thus disposing of the danger of vengeance from a noble son. The farmer announces in the prologue that out of loyalty to the royal house he has not touched his royal wife. When Orestes appears, urged by Apollo to revenge, he and Electra send for their mother on the pretext that she is needed to be Electra's midwife. Aegisthus arrives in the neighborhood to perform a sacrifice, invites Orestes to take part; Orestes, striking from behind, slays him at the altar. His body is borne on for Electra to revile. This tirade is cut short by the arrival of Clytemnestra, who shows herself so amiable that she all but disarms the avengers. She enters the house; her cry is heard; Orestes and Electra throw open the doors and reveal the bodies of Aegisthus and Clytemnestra. They stand giving voice to their repentance until Castor and Pollux tell them how to get on with the funeral and the rest of their lives. Here the characters of the legend are presented with all the complexities and failings of contemporary citizens. Clytemnestra resembles a housewifely matron, Orestes a frightened youth sent on an errand he has no wish for. Electra is basically a materialist, but she has been made lunatic by a short lifetime of brooding on her wrongs and dreaming revenge. (Compare Sophocles' treatment; see page 37).

MEN (*7*): 2 are 20–25 (1 minor); 2 are 35–40 (minor); twin gods perhaps 30–40. WOMEN (*2*): 1 is 18–22; 1 is 40–50. CHORUS (*6–18*): Argive peasant women. EXTRAS: Attendants to Clytemnestra. SET: Hut of the Argive farmer; door and walls are needed, levels desirable. Arena production possible. Considerable room required for chorus to move. Gods give impression of floating in air, perhaps behind a scrim. COS-TUMES: Ancient Greek. DIFFICULTIES: Gods' entrances constitute a production problem. Choral lyrics, long and obscure, are more interesting sung and danced.

ROYALTY: Apply publisher. TEXT: Emily Townsend Vermeule trans. in *The Complete Greek Tragedies* (Chicago).

—— o ——

HELEN (412 B.C.) EURIPIDES. Euripides accepted a version of the Trojan legend designed to rehabilitate Helen's character (which could not be too bad since she had become a divinity). In the prologue, Helen reveals that Paris only carried a phantom to Troy; the real Helen has been in Egypt all the time. The new king, Theoclymenus, seeks to force her to marry him; she remains faithful to Menelaus. A mariner tells her that Menelaus has been lost at sea; full of anxiety, she consults Theonoe, the king's prophetess-sister, who says that he is alive and will be shipwrecked nearby. Menelaus knocks on the palace gates; in a hilarious episode a strapping Egyptian doorkeeper rebuffs him. An exciting and complex recognition follows; then husband and wife plot their escape. First they must persuade Theonoe not to reveal to her brother that Menelaus is here. Then Helen tells Theoclymenus she will consent to the wedding but must first bury an effigy of her husband with proper rites by throwing it into the waves. Deceived, Theoclymenus agrees to have the mariner stranger (Menelaus) direct the rites: Menelaus and Helen take a swift ship and, overpowering the Egyptian crew, make their escape. A messenger swims ashore and tells the tale; the Dioscuri prevent their pursuit by announcing that all has been settled by the will of the gods. The play is a moderately exciting romantic comedy, somewhat a parody of other Euripidean plays, and outspoken antiwar propaganda.

MEN (7): Menelaus is 40–45; Theoclymenus is 20–30; mariner is 35–45; messengers are 30–40; Dioscuri (twin gods) 30–40. WOMEN (3): Helen, a young-looking 37–39; Theonoe is 30–35; doorkeeper is 50–60. CHORUS (6–18): Greek women captive in Egypt. EXTRAS: Sailors; huntsmen; attendants. SETS: Tomb; monument of Theoclymenus' father Proteus; outside gates to the Egyptian palace. A marker, gate, and suggestion of a wall are necessary. COSTUMES: Ancient Greek. DIFFICULTIES: Choral lyrics, long and somewhat obscure, are more interesting sung and danced.

ROYALTY: Apply publisher. TEXT: Richmond Lattimore trans. in *The Complete Greek Tragedies* (Chicago) or Philip Vellacott trans. in *The Bacchae and Other Plays* (Penguin).

— o —

THE BACCHAE (405 B.C.) EURIPIDES. Tragedy. Dionysus was born of Zeus and a maiden of Thebes' royal line, but his mother's sisters never believed his divine origin. Pentheus, King of Thebes, forbids Bacchic rites because he believes them obscene. As punishment, Dionysus has inspired the sisters and other Theban women with Bacchic frenzy and they are reveling on the hills. Pentheus arrests some of the women and seeks to imprison the god himself. Dionysus escapes; he seizes on Pentheus' weakness, an unnatural desire to be a *voyeur* at the obscenities he believes take place during the women's rites. Under Dionysus' influence, the king goes mad; disguised as a woman, he dances wildly out over the mountains to where the women now rest from their orgy. His own mother, Agave, discovers him; the frenzied women see him as a lion and tear him apart with their hands. Agave returns to Thebes bearing Pentheus' head as trophy, boasting how she and her comrades have bested the lion. Her aged grandfather, Cadmus, awakens her slowly from the trance to horrible fact. Dionysus appears and pronounces banishment on all remaining of Cadmus' line. This weird and awesome play, which seems in ways as contemporary as that of an expressionist, creates a mood of mysterious excitement and exhilaration and contains some of Euripides' best poetry.

MEN (7): 2 are 70–90; 2 are 20–35; 3 are 20–30 (minor). WOMAN: She is 40–45. CHORUS (6–18): Asiatic (Near-Eastern) women. EXTRAS: Soldiers and servants. SET: Before the palace of Pentheus in Thebes. Door necessary, columns and some suggestion of walls desirable. Arena production possible. Considerable room required for chorus to move. Dionysus, at the play's end, gives the impression of floating in air, perhaps behind a scrim. COSTUMES: Ancient Greek. DIFFICULTIES: Dionysus escapes from the palace in the midst of an earthquake. Choral lyrics, long and somewhat obscure, require frenzied singing and dancing.

ROYALTY: Apply publisher. TEXT: William Arrowsmith trans. in *The Complete Greek Tragedies* (Chicago).

— o —

IPHIGENIA AT AULIS (*Iphigenia ad Aulis; ca.* 405 B.C.)
EURIPIDES. Agamemnon, unable to sail from Aulis because of contrary winds, has been told by the oracle that he could not capture Troy unless he makes human sacrifice of his daughter Iphigenia. Under pressure from his brother Menelaus and the army, he has sent for her on the pretext she is to marry Achilles. He has a change of heart and sends word to his wife Clytemnestra to keep Iphigenia home. Menelaus intercepts the message and the two brothers are quarreling when Clytemnestra and Iphigenia are announced. Menelaus now also has a change of heart; he will spare Iphigenia. However, Agamemnon has now resolved that she be sacrificed. Agamemnon gives his wife and daughter a long welcome full of allusions to the coming sacrifice. No sooner is he gone than Achilles appears, and Clytemnestra hails him as son-in-law. Amid the confusion a slave tells Agamemnon's plan. Achilles is outraged and promises to save the girl. Clytemnestra and Iphigenia plead with Agamemnon, and he almost breaks under the conflict of his duty to Menelaus and country and his fear of the army. The not-so-heroic Achilles reports that he has met abuse and violence while pleading Iphigenia's cause to the soldiers. The emotional tangle is shattered by Iphigenia, who announces that she is resolved to die for Greece. She marches off alone toward the altar. The plot line is clear and direct, the characters profound and complex. The characters project rather than a noble image the most intense neurotic conflicts as they are gripped by their fearful situation. Iphigenia is deliberately used to exploit the sentimental. Her decision is sudden and wondrous.

MEN (*6*): 2 are 40–45; 1 is 18–22; 1 is 60–70; 2 are 25–30. WOMEN (*2*): 1 is 14–16; 1 is 33–36. CHORUS (*6–18*): Women of Chalcis. EXTRAS: Attendants of Clytemnestra and Iphigenia; nurse for Orestes; soldiers; sentinels; 2 armor-bearers attendant on Achilles. SET: Greek camp at Aulis in front of Agamemnon's tent; levels desirable. Arena production possible if theatre is large enough. Considerable room is required for the chorus to move. COSTUMES: Ancient Greek. DIFFICULTIES: Choral lyrics, long and somewhat obscure, are more interesting sung and danced.

ROYALTY: Apply publishers. TEXT: Moses Hadas and John McLean trans. in *Ten Plays by Euripides* (Bantam) or Charles R. Walker trans. in *The Complete Greek Tragedies* (Chicago).

—— o ——

DYSKOLOS (317–316 B.C.) MENANDER. Comedy. Noteworthy as the sole entirely preserved example of Greek New Comedy. Filled with raucous clowning, the comedy is nevertheless typically Menandrian in its sympathetic tone and natural style, treating realistically the basic conflict between country folk and city dwellers. Cnemon, a misanthrope, lives in seclusion on a farm with his daughter and an aged woman servant. Irascible by nature, Cnemon has been deserted by his wife and stepson Gorgias. Sostratus, a rich city youth, is repulsed by Cnemon when he seeks the daughter's hand in marriage. Sostratus enlists Gorgias' aid to win the testy farmer over. Fate intervenes and Gorgias rescues Cnemon from a well into which he has fallen. Cnemon thereby realizes his need for fellow man; he is reconciled to his wife, consents to his daughter's marriage with Sostratus, and approves Gorgias' betrothal to Sostratus' sister.

MEN (*11*): 6 are 18–30 (2 minor, 1 has no lines); 2 are 35–50; 3 are 50–60 (1 requires an outstanding actor, 2 are minor); several male slaves and guests. WOMEN (*6*): 3 are 16–20 (2 have no lines); 2 are 50–60 (no lines); 1 is 65–80 (minor); several female guests. A chorus of revelers (male, female, or both), though not essential to the play, may be added to dance and sing the interludes. SETS: Wooded mountain country outside Athens; a cave representing the shrine of Pan and the nymphs of Phyle in Attica; a poor farmhouse, home of Cnemon; another poor farmhouse, home of Gorgias. Set should be formal, nonrealistic; simultaneous staging may be employed. Unit set appropriate. Arena production possible. COSTUMES: Late 4th-century B.C. Athenian; emphasis in majority of characters on rustic, ragged, peasant quality; wealthy, luxurious dress for characters identified with the city; some suggestion of fantasy in costume of Pan; masks may be used. DIFFICULTIES: Though the language is conversational, some of the verse passages allotted certain characters are long and require much vocal flexibility to sustain properly the meaning and mood.

ROYALTY: Apply publisher. TEXT: William Arrowsmith trans. in *The Complete Greek Comedy* (Michigan), Vol. XII.

—— o ——

AJAX (*ca.* 447 B.C.) SOPHOCLES. Tragedy. During the Trojan War, Ajax, seeking to revenge himself for a wrong, sets out to murder Odysseus and Menelaus, but Athena frustrates his plan by making him insane. He mistakes some sheep for his enemies and slays them instead. When his reason returns, the humiliation is more than he can endure. He withdraws into some bushes and falls on his sword; his mistress, Tecmessa, finds him dead. One of the men Ajax had sought to murder, Menelaus, orders the body left unburied, but the other intended victim, Odysseus, insists that appropriate rites be performed. The funeral is agreed upon and orders for burial given.

MEN (6). WOMEN (2). CHORUS (15): Warriors. EXTRAS: 1 child; attendants. SETS: Before the tent of Ajax in the Greek camp; a lonely place on the seashore. DIFFICULTIES: Both the question of the burial of Ajax and the subject of his humiliation are much less interesting to modern audiences than to the ancient Greeks.

ROYALTY: Apply publisher. TEXT: John Moore trans. in *The Complete Greek Tragedies* (Chicago).

—— o ——

ANTIGONE (*ca.* 441 B.C.) SOPHOCLES. Tragedy. A great battle has just been fought in which the city of Thebes has triumphed but lost its king. Creon, the new king, decrees as his first action that the body of Polyneices, the unsuccessful invader, shall remain unburied. The edict has scarcely been made public when word comes that an attempt has been made to bury the corpse by the princess Antigone, sister of the dead Polyneices and niece of Creon. She makes no attempt to conceal her deed but goes further and challenges Creon's right to promulgate an edict plainly at odds with the will of the gods. Creon sentences her to be entombed alive. When Creon's son, betrothed to Antigone, hears of the sentence he comes to Creon to plead for her life, but Creon is adamant and the boy finally rushes out distraught. Next comes the old prophet Tiresias. At first he urges Creon gently to reconsider the decree concerning Polyneices and the sentence upon Antigone;

then he describes to the king the frightful consequences about to befall him. Terrified, Creon yields and hurries out to bury Polyneices and set Antigone free. Too late, he finds Antigone, who has killed herself. With her is his son; as his father watches he kills himself also. Returning with his son's body, Creon is greeted with the news that his wife, hearing of her son's death, has stabbed herself. Repentant and broken in spirit, Creon is led into his house. (See Anouilh's play, page 196.)

MEN (3): 1 is old; 1 middle-aged; 1 a youth. WOMEN (3): 2 youthful; 1 middle-aged. BOY: About 10. CHORUS (16): Theban elders. EXTRAS: 4 soldiers; handmaidens. SET: Unlocalized. Arena production possible. COSTUMES: Ancient Greek. DIFFICULTIES: Antigone may not attract as much sympathy as she warrants.

ROYALTY: Apply publisher. TEXT: Elizabeth Wyckoff trans. in *The Complete Greek Tragedies* (Chicago).

— o —

OEDIPUS THE KING (*Oedipus Rex; ca.* 430 B.C.) SOPHOCLES. Tragedy. The play opens with the people of Thebes, stricken by a terrible plague, gathering in prayer. Oedipus, their king, assures them he has already moved to discover the cause of their affliction by sending his brother-in-law, Creon, to the oracle at Delphi to learn what should be done. Presently Creon returns with the word that the plague will vanish as soon as Thebes finds and casts out the murderer of the late king, Laius. Oedipus consults the prophet Tiresias, who tells him that he is himself the unclean creature and that he is furthermore guilty of both incest and patricide. Enraged, Oedipus accuses Creon of plotting with Tiresias to discredit him and is saved from further rashness only by the intervention of his wife Jocasta. Alone with Jocasta, Oedipus confesses to her his secret fear that he might indeed be Laius' murderer, for he had once killed a man, and he had also had a prophecy from Delphi that he would one day kill his own father and marry his own mother. Jocasta quiets his fears by pointing out that Laius had been reported slain by a band of robbers. To prove this, she sends for an old herdsman, the only survivor of the fray in which Laius died. The old man reveals that the death of Laius was not as rumored and that Oedipus is in fact the murderer. He tells Oedipus that the prophecies have come true; not only is he the murderer of his father but also the husband of his father's widow, his own mother. Upon hearing this, Jocasta kills herself and Oedipus puts out his own eyes. Then he comes before the people and begs them to exile him in fulfillment of the curse he had laid upon the killer of Laius. The most famous of the ancient tragedies, this is generally acknowledged to be one of the most skillfully plotted plays ever written.

MEN (6): 4 elderly; 2 about 35. WOMAN: Past middle age. GIRLS (2): Young (no lines). BOY: About 10. CHORUS (15): Theban elders. EXTRAS: Soldiers, suppliants, and handmaidens. COSTUMES: Ancient Greek. SET: Unlocalized. DIFFICULTIES: Many of the choral passages are obscure to an audience unfamiliar with classical mythology. The final scene between the blinded Oedipus and his little daughters, although moving, is rather long.

ROYALTY: Apply publisher. TEXT: David Grene trans. in *The Complete Greek Tragedies* (Chicago).

— o —

ELECTRA (ca. 418 B.C.) SOPHOCLES. Tragedy. Accompanied by a small band of friends, the exiled Orestes returns in disguise to the house of his murdered father determined to wreak revenge upon his faithless mother Clytemnestra and her treacherous lover Aegisthus. To throw the murderers off their guard, one of the band is sent ahead with the false word that Orestes has died in exile. The news is joyfully received by Clytemnestra and sorrowfully by her daughter Electra, who has lived for years sustained only by the hope that Orestes would one day return to right the wrong done their father. Encouraged by Clytemnestra's unquestioning acceptance of the news, Orestes himself next ventures into the court disguised as a messenger bringing an urn supposedly containing the ashes of the dead prince. The first person he meets is Electra; because they have been separated since childhood neither recognizes the other. When she learns what he brings, she asks to hold it; as she embraces the urn and weeps over it, Orestes realizes that she is the sister he left behind. Recognition and joyful reunion ensue. Then, united in purpose, the two move swiftly to their revenge. First they kill Clytemnestra. When Aegisthus comes in, asking to see the remains of the dead Orestes, a body is brought in, wrapped in a shroud. Exultantly, Aegisthus lifts the cover and is confronted with the corpse of his wife. He collapses in grief and is dragged away to die at the hand of Orestes. (Compare the Euripides play on the same theme; see page 30; and Giraudoux's, page 217.)

MEN (7): 1 is about 45; 1 is about 60; the others are youthful. WOMEN (3): 1 is about 45; 2 are youthful. CHORUS (15): Women, ranging from youth to middle age. EXTRAS: 4 men; 1 handmaiden. SET: Unlocalized. The palace is nearby but need not be seen. COSTUMES: Ancient Greek. DIFFICULTIES: Although this is one of the most thrilling of Greek tragedies, most of the excitement comes in the final 10 minutes. The earlier part of the play is mainly preparation for one of the most dramatic moments ever devised—the uncovering of Clytemnestra's corpse by Aegisthus. The scenes between Electra and her sister, Crysothemis, as well as some of the scenes between Electra and the chorus, are somewhat long.

ROYALTY: Apply publisher. TEXT: David Grene trans. in *The Complete Greek Tragedies* (Chicago).

——o——

THE WOMEN OF TRACHIS (*Trachiniae; ca.* 413 B.C.) SOPHOCLES. Tragedy. Deianera, the wife of Heracles, describes her loneliness because of her husband's long absence. A messenger comes with word that Heracles has completed his final labor and is returning home. The messenger is followed by one of Heracles' men, Lichas, bringing a train of captives. One of the captives is the beautiful Iole, whom Heracles has taken as his mistress. When Deianera learns this, she sends Heracles a robe which has been anointed to prevent Heracles' love from straying from herself. After the garment has been sent on its way, Deianera wonders whether she has done properly, remembering that the man who gave her the ointment was a bitter enemy of Heracles. Then her son Hyllus comes in, cursing her, and tells her that Heracles has been poisoned by the robe and is dying. Deianera leaves the stage and kills herself. Heracles is brought in, dying. He reviews his great achievements, describes his agony, and then wrings from Hyllus a promise to care for the captive Iole.

MEN (5): 1 is old; 1 youthful; others are middle-aged. WOMEN (3): 1 young; 1 old; 1 young and beautiful. CHORUS (15): Women of Trachis. EXTRAS: Attendants and captives. SET: Unlocalized; somewhere in the environs of Heracles'

home in Trachis. COSTUMES: Ancient Greek. DIFFICULTIES:
The play consists entirely of actions recounted and feeling
described. There is little plot movement and no really high
dramatic moments.

ROYALTY: Apply publisher. TEXT: Michael Jameson trans.
in *The Complete Greek Tragedies* (Chicago).

— o —

PHILOCTETES (409 B.C.) SOPHOCLES. Tragedy. Odysseus
and Neoptolemus have come to the island of Lemnos to get
the archer Philoctetes, of whom it has been prophesied that
only through him and his magic bow can the war with Troy
be brought to a successful conclusion. Philoctetes has been
marooned here for many years because of a wound the smell
of which rendered his presence unendurable to his comrades.
By allowing him to believe that he is finally being removed
to his homeland, Neoptolemus is able to get Philoctetes to
give up his weapons and come with him. Then, unable to endure the thought of the deception, Neoptolemus confesses to
Philoctetes that their destination is Troy, not home. Philoctetes refuses to leave. Odysseus appears with soldiers, orders
Neoptolemus to take the magic bow and arrows to Troy and
let Philoctetes remain on the island, unarmed, to starve. When
Odysseus is gone, Neoptolemus returns the weapons to Philoctetes. They defy Odysseus' orders and agree to return home
and give up the Trojan War. As they start to leave, the demi-
god Heracles appears and commands them to go to Troy so
that the war can be ended as prophesied. They depart to do
his bidding.

MEN (*approx. 20*): 5 principals, plus the chorus of 15 warriors. SET: Entrance to Philoctetes' cave on the island of
Lemnos.

ROYALTY: Apply publisher. TEXT: David Grene trans. in
The Complete Greek Tragedies (Chicago).

— o —

OEDIPUS AT COLONUS (*Oedipus ad Colonus; ca.* 404 B.C.)
SOPHOCLES. Tragedy. The exiled, blind Oedipus, attended by
his daughter Antigone, stops to rest at the edge of a sacred
grove near Colonus. Learning the identity of their visitor, the
inhabitants of Colonus are alarmed and send for their king,
Theseus. Meanwhile Oedipus' other daughter arrives with the

news that Creon, king of Thebes, is coming to take Oedipus back, having just learned that the spot on which Oedipus dies is to be forever after sanctified. When Oedipus refuses to accompany him, Creon seizes the two daughters as hostages. At this point Theseus enters, stops Creon, and sends soldiers to recover the daughters. Presently Oedipus' son Polyneices, who is marching against Thebes with an army, stops to ask his father's blessing. Instead he receives a curse and departs to his death. A great storm arises, at the height of which Oedipus makes his way unaided into the sacred grove and disappears. From the grove comes a priest who describes Oedipus' final moments. Theseus then declares the spot forever hallowed and takes the sisters Antigone and Ismene into his care.

MEN (*20–30*): 2 are elderly; 1 middle-aged. WOMEN (*2*): Young. CHORUS (*15*): Elders of Colonus. EXTRAS: Soldiers and attendants. SET: Entrance of a shrine. Statuary or similar indication of the nature of the place is desirable. DIFFICULTIES: Some obscure passages.

ROYALTY: Apply publisher. TEXT: David Grene trans. in *The Complete Greek Tragedies* (Chicago).

ROMAN DRAMA

ROMAN DRAMA

THE CAPTIVES (*Captivi;* late 3rd century B.C.) PLAUTUS. Comedy. To recover his son Philopolemus, who has been captured in the Elean War, Hegio buys two Elean captives, hoping to make an exchange for his son. One of the captives, Tyndarus, turns out to be Hegio's other son, stolen many years before by a runaway slave. Philocrates, the second captive, arranges for the return of Philopolemus. With its emphasis on the devotion of a servant to his master rather than upon the generally more usual love affairs, this play is more serious in tone than other Plautine comedies.

MEN (*9*): 5 are 20–30; 4 are 40–60. SET: Street in front of the house of Hegio, in a city of Atolia. COSTUMES: Classical Greek. DIFFICULTIES: Appeal may be limited.

ROYALTY: Apply publisher. TEXT: Loeb Classical Library (Harvard).

— o —

THE TWIN MENAECHMI (*Menaechmi;* late 3rd century B.C.) PLAUTUS. Comedy. Menaechmus II (Sosicles), of Syracuse, comes to Epidamnus in search of his twin brother. The action and situations stem from his being mistaken for Menaechmus I by the cook Culindrus (Cylindrus), the courtesan Erotium, the parasite Peniculus (Sponge), and Menaechmus I's wife and father-in-law. In this play is the earliest surviving example in Roman comedy of the quack doctor who is a standard stock figure in later farces. Shakespeare's *The Comedy of Errors* (p. 68) is the most famous of many later adaptations.

MEN (*7*): 5 are 25–35 (additional slaves and sailors may be cast); 2 are 50–60. WOMEN (*3*): 3 are 25–35. SET: Street in Epidamnus between the houses of Menaechmus I (left) and

Erotium (right). COSTUMES: Classical Greek; can be stylized. DIFFICULTIES: Director must devise and integrate much comic business to maintain rapid pace throughout. Music is also needed.

ROYALTY: Apply publisher. TEXT: Liberal Arts.

—— o ——

THE BRAGGART WARRIOR (*Miles Gloriosus; ca.* 205 B.C.) PLAUTUS. Comedy. Pyrgopolynices, the braggart warrior, carries off a young courtesan, Philocomasium, to Ephesus and holds captive Pleusicles' slave Palaestrio, the girl's lover. Palaestrio digs a hole in the wall of the house next door so that the two lovers may meet secretly, and another courtesan is brought in to deceive the braggart warrior. Pyrgopolynices is eventually caught in a compromising situation and punished.

MEN (9): 5 are 25–30; 2 are 50–60; 2 are boys, 12–15. WOMEN (3): All 25–30. SET: Street in Ephesus in front of the houses of Pyrgopolynices and Periplectomenus. COSTUMES: Ancient Greek or Asia Minor. DIFFICULTIES: Expert direction and carefully paced, skillful acting required to bring off farce scenes successfully. Music should be used.

ROYALTY: Apply publisher. TEXT: Loeb Classical Library (Harvard).

—— o ——

THE POT OF GOLD (*Aulularia; ca.* 194 B.C.) PLAUTUS. Comedy. The miser Euclio discovers a pot of gold; when he becomes frightened and reburies it, the gold is stolen by a slave. Lyconides, the slave's owner and lover of Euclio's daughter, returns the money. Delighted to be released from the need to guard his gold, Euclio gives it to his daughter as a dowry. *Aulularia* is one of the early studies of miserliness in Western drama; Molière used it as a basis for his *L'Avare* (*The Miser, q.v.*); and Fielding, Shadwell and Wycherley are likewise indebted to Plautus for the plays each wrote and called *The Miser.* The director planning to stage any one of these plays can profitably compare all of them in his preparation.

MEN (9): 2 are 20–30 (additional slaves possible); 7 are 50–60. WOMEN (5): 3 are 18–25 (2 music girls, minor); 2 are 50–60. SET: Street in Athens with the houses of Euclio and

Megadorus and the Temple of Faith. COSTUMES: Classical
Greek. DIFFICULTIES: Role of Euclio requires a talented and
experienced character actor.

ROYALTY: Apply publisher. TEXT: Loeb Classical Library
(Harvard).

—— o ——

AMPHITRYON (*ca.* 186 B.C.) PLAUTUS. Comedy. Jupiter
is in love with Amphitryon's wife Alcumena. While Amphitryon is away at war, Jupiter assumes his form and appears in
Thebes, accompanied by Mercury in the guise of Sosia, Amphitryon's slave. (Mercury, as Sosia, speaks the prologue,
explaining in detail everything that is going to transpire
throughout the play. He notes that Jupiter and Amphitryon
will be indistinguishable from each other except for a gold
tassel on Jupiter's hat, and that he himself will seem Sosia
except for a tiny plume on his helmet.) Amphitryon returns
unexpectedly from the wars, having sent the real Sosia ahead
to notify Alcumena. The ensuing farce scenes conclude somewhat seriously when Amphitryon, unaware of Jupiter's deception, suspects Alcumena of unfaithfulness. At the end
Jupiter reappears with an explanation for Amphitryon. (Compare Giraudoux's *Amphitryon 38*, see p. 214.)

MEN (5): All 30–40. WOMEN (2): 25–35. SETS: Near the
harbor in Thebes and before the house of Amphitryon. COS-
TUMES: Classical Greek; sets and costumes may be stylized.
DIFFICULTIES: For a successful modern staging of this version, the roles of Jupiter/Amphitryon, Mercury/Sosia, and
Alcumena must be filled by actors who are both capable and
experienced.

ROYALTY: Apply publisher. TEXT: Loeb Classical Library
(Harvard).

—— o ——

THE HAUNTED HOUSE (*Mostellaria;* early 2nd century
B.C.) PLAUTUS. Comedy. Philolaches and his mistress Phi-
lematium have been using his father's house for wild drinking
parties during the old man's absence. When father Theopropides returns home unexpectedly, Tranio, the clever slave,
convinces him that his house is full of frightful apparitions
and that Philolaches has been forced to move out. Although
Philolaches has been squandering his property, Tranio tells

Theopropides that the money has been spent to buy the house next door. In the end Tranio's lies are found out, but the angry Theopropides is finally appeased and all ends happily.

MEN (*10*): 6 are 20–30 (additional slaves or attendants possible); 4 are 50–60. WOMEN (*3*): All 20–30. SET: Street in Athens on which the houses of Theopropides and Simo front; altar center stage. COSTUMES: Greek. DIFFICULTIES: The latter part of the play is theatrically weaker than the opening act.

ROYALTY: Apply publisher. TEXT: Liberal Arts.

— o —

THE WOMAN OF ANDROS (*Andria;* 166 B.C.) TERENCE. Comedy. Pamphilus has seduced Glycerium, a girl from Andros, but his father Simo wishes him to marry Philumena, the daughter of Chremes. When Pamphilus is about to be forced into marriage with Philumena (in love with Charinus), Glycerium is revealed as also the daughter of Chremes, who had secretly married a second wife.

MEN (*9*): 5 are 20–35; 4 are 50–60. WOMEN (*3*): 2 are 18–25; 1 is 40–50. SET: Street in Athens in front of the houses of Simo and Glycerium. COSTUMES: Ancient Greek. DIFFICULTIES: The plot of mistaken identities holds few surprises for modern audiences.

ROYALTY: Apply publisher. TEXT: Liberal Arts.

— o —

THE SELF-TORMENTOR (*Heauton Timorumenos;* 163 B.C.) TERENCE. Comedy. Menedemus torments himself with regret that his severity has driven away his son Clinia, in love with Antiphila. Clinia is secretly staying next door with Clitipho, son of Chremes. Clitipho loves Bacchis, a courtesan, who arrives at Chremes' house with Antiphila disguised as her maid. Clitipho deceives his father with the aid of Syrus, an intriguing slave. Antiphila at the end is discovered to be the sister of Clitipho. (Like other comedies by Terence, this is taken from Menander's play with the same title; it involves one of the most complicated deceptions in Roman comedy.)

MEN (*6*): 3 are 20–25; 3 are 50–60. WOMEN (*5*): 3 are

20–25; 2 are 40–50. SET: Country road in Attica; houses of Menedemus and Chremes, separated by a field. COSTUMES: Classical Greek. DIFFICULTIES: For modern audiences, the plot complications are likely to prove more confusing than comic.

ROYALTY: Apply publisher. TEXT: Loeb Classical Library (Harvard).

—— o ——

THE EUNUCH (*Eunuchus;* 161 B.C.) TERENCE. Comedy. Phaedria is in love with a courtesan, Thais; his younger brother Chaerea is charmed by her supposed sister Pamphila. Chaerea gains entrance to Thais' house disguised as the eunuch Dorus to seduce Pamphila, who is subsequently revealed to be an Athenian citizen. Stock characters include a boastful soldier, Thraso, and the parasite Gnatho. (This was Terence's most successful play.)

MEN (*10*): 7 are 20–30; 3 are 40–60. WOMEN (*4*): 3 are 18–25; 1 is 50–60. SET: Street in Athens on which the houses of Thais and Laches front. COSTUMES: Classical Greek.

ROYALTY: Apply publisher. TEXT: Loeb Classical Library (Harvard).

—— o ——

PHORMIO (161 B.C.) TERENCE. Comedy. Phormio (Churchmouse) is a penniless young adventurer who engineers the intrigues and cleverly solves the difficulties in this farce. Phaedria, son of Chremes, is in love with a slave girl, Pamphila, but does not have the money to buy her. His cousin Antipho, son of Chremes' brother Demipho, loves Phanium, a poor but beautiful orphan. Through the machinations of Phormio, Antipho obtains Phanium in a false lawsuit and Demipho is tricked into purchasing Pamphila for Phaedria. Phanium is then revealed as the lost daughter of Chremes. (Compare Molière's free adaptation, *Les Fourberies de Scapin;* see p. 177.)

MEN (*11*): 4 are 20–30; 7 are 40–60. WOMEN (*2*): Both 40–60. SET: Street in Athens in front of the houses of Demipho, Chremes, and Dormio. COSTUMES: Classical Greek. DIFFICULTIES: Particularly inventive direction is necessary for successful modern production. Much of the humor depends also on the characterization implicit in the names of the *dramatis personae.*

ROYALTY: Apply publisher. TEXT: Liberal Arts.

— o —

THE BROTHERS (*Adelphi;* 160 B.C.) TERENCE. Comedy. Two opposing systems of education and their results are illustrated in the contrasts between the two old brothers and the sons of one of them. Micio, a bachelor, rears his brother's son Aeschinus permissively; his brother Demea raises his other son Ctesipho with harshness and restraint. Both sons have been guilty of wrongdoing. Aeschinus has seduced a poor but respectable Athenian girl, Pamphila, and Ctesipho loves a girl musician who has been abducted from the slave-dealer and pimp Sannio. Aeschinus and Ctesipho are forgiven as Micio and Demea realize each has been too extreme in his treatment of the young men. (Compare Molière's *L'ecole des maris,* which is based on this play, see p. 172.)

MEN (*9*): 4 are 20–30; 5 are 50–60. WOMEN (*3*): 1 is 18–20; 2 are 50–60. SET: Street in Athens on which the houses of Micio and Sostrata front. COSTUMES: Greek. DIFFICULTIES: The 2 old brothers require casting of experienced character actors.

ROYALTY: Apply publisher. TEXT: Liberal Arts.

— o —

THE MOTHER-IN-LAW (*Hecyra;* 160 B.C.) TERENCE. Comedy. Pamphilus has married Philumena against his will and leaves her without consummating the marriage. Upon his return he finds that his wife has left her mother-in-law, Sostrata, to give birth to a child. He refuses to accept her as his wife, but the play ends acceptably when Bacchis, a courtesan Pamphilus had loved, discovers that he had in fact ravished Philumena while he was intoxicated. (This is the most serious extant Roman comedy and is much less conventional in technique than the other plays of Plautus and Terence.)

MEN (*5*): 2 are 20–30; 3 are 40-60. WOMEN (*5*): 2 are 20–30; 3 are 40–60. SET: Street in Athens in front of the houses of Laches, Phidippus, and Bacchis. COSTUMES: Greek. DIFFICULTIES: For modern tastes, the play has little humor and lacks dramatic action.

ROYALTY: Apply publisher. TEXT: Liberal Arts.

MEDIEVAL DRAMA

ADAM (*Le Jeu d'Adam;* mid-12th century) ANONYMOUS. (French or Anglo-Norman) Mystery play. Adam and Eve are led into Paradise by the Figure of the Lord. After Eve is tempted by the Devil and she and Adam eat of the forbidden fruit, they are cast out. They reproach themselves bitterly, but are driven to Hell by devils. In a subsequent episode Cain slays Abel. The extant portion of this play concludes with a procession of prophets and a scene with Nebuchadnezzar foretelling the coming of the Son of God. This is the earliest existing medieval play of genuine dramatic worth. Apparently originally intended to be performed outside a church, it is suitable for modern outdoor production.

MEN (*18 plus devils and ministers; doubling possible*): 6 are 20–30; 12 are 40–60. WOMAN: Eve. CHORUS: Variable size if music is used. SETS: Stage directions, unusually complete for a medieval play, specify a Paradise with an apple tree, a Hell scene, and a church door. COSTUMES: Biblical or medieval. DIFFICULTIES: Plays less than 2 hours.
ROYALTY: Apply publisher. TEXT: Edward Noble Stone trans. in *World Drama* (Dover), Vol. I.

— o —

ABRAHAM AND ISAAC (14th century; manuscript 15th century) ANONYMOUS. (Brome manuscript [English]) Mystery play. God sends an angel to command Abraham to sacrifice his son Isaac. In a touching scene of great suspense, Abraham prepares to slay Isaac but is stopped by the angel. The characterizations of Abraham as a tender father and Isaac as a trusting child are exceptionally human. This play concludes with the appearance of a learned doctor who expounds the moral for the audience. A short play considered the masterpiece among serious English medieval plays.

MEN (*4*): 3 are 40–60; 1 is 30–40. BOY: 12–15. SET: Countryside with hill; suitable for outdoor performance. Properties include faggots for building sacrificial fire and a live ram. COSTUMES: Biblical or medieval English. DIFFICULTIES: Both Abraham and Isaac call for capable actors.

ROYALTY: Public domain. TEXT: *Religious Drama* (Meridian), Vol. II.

—— o ——

THE SECOND SHEPHERDS' PLAY (*Secunda Pastorum*; mid-15th century) ANONYMOUS. (Townley manuscript, Wakefield Cycle [English]). Three shepherds grumble about their hard lives as they watch their flocks on the moor. After they go to sleep, Mak steals one of their sheep, carries it to his hut, and with the help of his wife Gyll, hides it in a cradle. The shepherds search Mak's hut without success and are about to leave when they decide to offer gifts to the new baby in the cradle. When the "baby" is discovered to be their lost sheep, Mak is tossed in a blanket for punishment. An angel appears to the shepherds to announce the birth of Christ, and the play concludes with their visit to the manger. This short play is regarded the masterpiece of medieval English farce.

MEN (*4*): All 30–40. WOMEN (*2*): 1 is 30–40; 1 is the Virgin Mary. BOY: 14–18. SETS: Mak's hut on the moors; the manger. Action is laid in Palestine but characters and setting are late-medieval English. Scenery may be simple, nonrealistic, with some indication of 3 different areas. COSTUMES: Biblical or medieval English.

ROYALTY: Apply publisher. TEXT: *Religious Drama* (Meridian), Vol. II.

—— o ——

EVERYMAN (15th century) ANONYMOUS. (English; source may be Dutch *Elckerlijk* by Peter Dorlandus, published 1495) Morality play. God calls Death and orders him to take Everyman. Seeking someone to accompany him to the grave, Everyman turns to Fellowship, Kindred, Cousin, and Goods, but is rejected by each. At first it appears that Knowledge, Confession, Discretion, Strength, Beauty, or Five-Wits may agree to go with him, but all forsake him on the last journey. Only Good-Deeds is prepared to enter the grave with Everyman. At the conclusion the very obvious moral is interpreted for the spectators by a doctor. Most typical and best of all the moralities, this drama has been performed frequently and continues to retain its power. (Compare Hofmannsthal's play on the same theme; see page 431.)

MEN (*11*): Abstractions, although Everyman probably should be middle-aged and God elderly. WOMEN (*6*): All abstract. SET: Simple background, suggestion of grave or tomb. Could be presented in church or outdoors. COSTUMES: Medieval. DIFFICULTIES: Plays less than 1 hour.

ROYALTY: Apply publisher. TEXT: *Religious Drama* (Meridian), Vol. II.

ENGLISH DRAMA

Elizabethan and Jacobean

THE KNIGHT OF THE BURNING PESTLE (*ca.* 1607-10) FRANCIS BEAUMONT and JOHN FLETCHER. Comedy. A spirited satire on plays, players, and public of the Jacobean theatre that features a play within a play. A citizen-grocer and his wife interrupt a performance of *The London Merchant* with a demand for a play "notably in honor of the commons of the city," in which their apprentice shall play a heroic grocer. As The Knight of the Burning Pestle, equipped with armor, horse, and two squires, Ralph—the apprentice— makes a shambles of a conventional plot which details how the merchant Venturewell is thwarted in his effort to marry his daughter Luce to the wealthy Humphrey rather than to Jasper, the apprentice she loves. The citizen and his wife sit on stage, cheer, comment, and generally misinterpret what is happening, while Ralph, after several quixotic misadventures, slays a "giant" and dies a tragic death. The plot is lively, the characters broadly amusing, the language a mixture of verse and prose.

MEN (*20; doubling possible, some can be cut*): 1 is 12–16, most can be 18–30 (1 should sing; 1, Ralph, should be a clever clown); 10 are minor, 1 should be 30–50, 2 are over 50 (1 must sing). WOMEN (*5; 1 can be cut*): 2 are 18–25 (1 should sing); 2 are 35–50. SETS: Platform stage where an inner stage is practicable. A few stylized set pieces or props can suggest the varied locales of the play within the play. COSTUMES: Jacobean actors, merchants, soldiers, etc.; Ralph is costumed in comic armor. DIFFICULTIES: Passages of deliberate parody of heroic style of the period.

ROYALTY: Public domain. TEXT: *English Drama, 1580-1642* (Heath).

THE SHOEMAKERS' HOLIDAY (1599) THOMAS DEK-
KER. Comedy. This warm, happy play about the tradesmen
of Elizabethan London chronicles how the Earl of Lincoln,
to discourage the love between his nephew Lacy and Rose,
daughter of the Lord Mayor of London, has him ordered to
France on military duty. Instead, Lacy comes "disguised like
a Dutch shoemaker to the house of Symon Eyre... who
served the Mayor and his household with shoes." Amid much
merriment in the shoemaker's house, Eyre becomes Mayor of
London and Lacy gets his love. A second conflict, presented
somewhat more seriously, concerns Eyre's apprentice Rafe,
who returns crippled from the French war to find his wife
Jane, believing him dead, on the point of remarrying. With
the king's blessing, Simon, Hodge, Firk, and the other honest
shoemakers help set affairs right.

MEN (*15, plus 6 or 8 extras; doubling possible*): Most
can be 18–35 (3 should sing); 4 should be 50–60. WOMEN
(*4*): 3 are 18–25; 1 is 45–50. SETS: "The City of London
and the Adjacent Village of old Ford." A number of locales,
including streets, garden, shops and halls, can be staged simply by alternating scenes originating in an inner stage and
on a forestage. COSTUMES: Elizabethan tradesmen (shoemakers), soldiers, a few noblemen, and the king. Could be
set in early 1400s.
ROYALTY: Public domain. TEXT: *Four Great Elizabethan
Plays* (Bantam).

—— o ——

A WOMAN KILLED WITH KINDNESS (1603) THOMAS
HEYWOOD. Tragedy. Gentle John Frankford is married to
sweet Anne Acton, but their domestic bliss is destroyed when
Master Wendell betrays the trust of his friend and host by
seducing Anne. Discovering their guilty relation, Frankford
puts aside his revenging sword and banishes Anne to another
manor house. Dying of a contrition made unbearable by consciousness of his kindness, she at last earns Frankford's forgiveness. A second plot line follows Anne's brother's contrasting
career. At first, Sir Francis Acton is merely a young ruffian
harassing Sir Charles Mountford and his virtuous sister Susan.
Then he learns to respect and love her. Finally he learns to
act nobly and wins Susan's hand. The rapid succession of
contrasting scenes (marriages and quarreling, crime and con-

trition, revenge and forgiveness) are psychologically sound and theatrically effective.

MEN (*18 plus extras; doubling and tripling possible*): 5 major. All except 1 minor character can be 18–30. Most minor characters and extras could be 18–60 (3 must do country dance; musicians can be off stage). WOMEN (6): 2 major 18–25. Others 18–60. CHILDREN (2): Toddlers or babes in arms; dolls can be used. SETS: The 17 scenes shift among public rooms, a study, manor yard, open field, road, bedroom, dungeon, and jail. Rapid shifts make a modified Elizabethan unit set almost a necessity. Arena production possible; servants used to shift furniture on and off. COSTUMES: Elizabethan; ranging from lower class to smartly dressed landed gentry; include ordinary and special-occasion attire. Costumes and properties, more than architecture, create the sense of place.

ROYALTY: Public domain. TEXT: *Eight Famous Elizabethan Plays* (Dutton).

— o —

EVERY MAN IN HIS HUMOUR (1598)   BEN JONSON. Comedy. Five acts of complicated intrigue among vivid London types. The follies and frolics of city folk and those of their newly arrived country cousins are revealed in considerable detail. This is Plautus Elizabethan style, full of sons against fathers, shrewd servants countering masters, jealous husbands versus wives and lovers. Many characters' names reveal their "humor"——Kno'well, Down-right, Well-bred, Formal. Even those without revealing names possess splendid obsessions——Captain Bobadill, swaggering; Master Matthew, poetic plagiarizing; Kitely, shuddering fear of constant cuckoldry. The crafty servant Brain-worm's scheme to help Kno'well, Jr., elope with Mistress Bridget is the slim plot framework. The complications are myriad.

MEN (*16*): 2 are 18–25 (minor); 4 are 20–35 (1 must swordfight); 4 are 35–50 (1 must swordfight, 2 are minor); 3 are 40–60 (1 must swordfight, 1 must disguise as 3 different characters); 2 are 60–75; 1 is Prologue (age not important). WOMEN (*3*): 1 is 18–25; 1 is 20–35; 1 is 35–50 (minor). EXTRAS: Several servants, either sex. SETS: Rooms in 4 houses; a merchant's shop; Moorfields; a tavern; and 16th-century London streets. Multiple or modified Elizabethan staging is appropriate. Unit set and arena staging feasible. COSTUMES: Elizabethan; fashionable city dress, some country dress; magistrate's robes; armor; police sergeant's uniform; some servant garb; a few disguises. DIFFICULTIES: Play is in verse, often complicated; some archaic language.

ROYALTY: Public domain. TEXT: *Ben Jonson: Complete Plays* (Dutton), Vol. I.

— o —

CYNTHIA'S REVELS, OR THE FOUNTAIN OF SELF-LOVE (1600) BEN JONSON. Comedy-Masque. This highly allegorical play satirizes aristocratic fashion among fops and dandies of the Elizabethan English court. Idle court votaries imbibe their fatal folly in a "Fountain of Self-Love." Cupid and Mercury come to Cynthia's court disguised as pages and observe ladies and gallants who personify self-love, wit, folly, and so on. Learning of the fountain's magic waters, courtiers send their pages for some. The pages return; all, except one, drink of the water (and so increase self-love). Revels are ordered to entertain royal Cynthia (Queen Elizabeth I), who will arrive shortly. A masque is chosen, and each participant assumes as his mask a Virtue opposite the Vice he personifies with which to conceal his true self. After the performance, Cynthia unmasks each and orders them at once to the "Well of Knowledge" where, purged of their maladies, they may report "the grace of Cynthia, and her court."

MEN (*16; doubling possible*): 3 are 18–25 (all must sing, 1 sing and dance, 1 speak some French, 1 minor); 5 are 20–35 (2 must sing and dance, 1 dance, 1 speak some Italian, 1 minor); 7 are 30–45 (minor); 1 is Prologue (age not important; may be doubled). WOMEN (*13; doubling possible*): 8 are 18–25 (1 must sing, 1 dance, 6 minor); 2 are 20–35 (1 must sing and dance, 1 dance); 3 are 30–45 (1 must dance; 2 minor). BOYS (*4*): All 10–15 (3 double as children for the Induction; 1 must sing). GIRL: 16–18. SETS: Pastoral vale and rooms at court at an unspecified period. Multiple or modified Elizabethan staging appropriate. Unit set possible. Arena staging very difficult. COSTUMES: Elizabethan; highly fashionable court dress; some pageboy, servant, and citizen garb indicated. DIFFICULTIES: Actors must capture the courtly style of the work, in combination with expert direction and setting that maintain the elaborate, graceful yet bitingly satirical mood absolutely necessary to hold a modern audience. If uncut, plays more than 3 hours.

ROYALTY: Public domain. TEXT: *Ben Jonson: Complete Plays* (Dutton), Vol. I.

—— o ——

VOLPONE, OR THE FOX (*ca.* 1605)   BEN JONSON. Comedy. From Volpone's opening lines, "Good morning to the day; and next my gold," to the final speech of the Venetian magistrate, "Let all that see these vices thus rewarded, take heart," the play moves against a backdrop of greed. The sordid underside of Renaissance man's lust for life is revealed as Volpone, with Mosca's help, feigns mortal sickness and so tricks Voltore, Corbaccio, and Corvino into pledging him their wealth (Corvino even pledges his wife) in the hope of inheriting Volpone's estates and fortune. Celia and Bonario, innocent victims of this inheritance game, are finally saved —not by their virtue but because Mosca and Volpone overreach themselves so far that they expose themselves to the justice of a Venetian court. A subordinate plot satirizes the political, social, and moral folly of the Englishman Sir Politic Would-Be and Lady Would-Be.

MEN (*17; doubling possible*): 3 are 20–35 (1 must be an outstanding nimble actor who can sing); 11 are 40–60 (8 minor; some can be cut or doubled); 1 is 60–80 (requires accomplished actor who can sing); 1 is 80–90; 1 is Prologue (age not important). WOMEN (*4*): 2 are 18–25 (minor); 1 is 20–35; 1 is 25–40. BOYS (*4*): All 16–20 (1 must be graceful and small enough to play a dwarf; 2 should be rather stocky); the roles can be played by men 18–25. EXTRAS: Bailiffs, officers of justice, workmen, servants, and crowd. SETS: Private rooms in 3 houses, city street areas and the Senate House in Venice, time unspecified. Multiple or modified Elizabethan staging appropriate. Unit set may be used. Arena staging possible but extremely difficult. COSTUMES: Elizabethan or Italian Renaissance; majority fashionable, some popular crowd and servant garb needed; Venetian magistrates' robes and police uniforms. Special costumes needed for the dwarf, fool, and eunuch. DIFFICULTIES: Play is in verse; language frequently archaic; a few long speeches require much vocal sustaining power; staging sometimes highly complicated.

ROYALTY: Public domain. TEXT: *Ben Jonson: Three Plays* (Hill and Wang), Vol. 1.

—— o ——

EPICOENE, OR THE SILENT WOMAN (1609) BEN JONSON. Comedy. Old Morose, obsessed with silence, is tricked by his nephew, Sir Dauphine Eugenie, into marrying Epicoene, the silent woman. Epicoene finds a permanently wagging tongue and Dauphine's friends manage to have the noisiest and most frivolous representatives of London society invade Morose's once quiet home. Morose is driven desperate by the constant idle chatter of the "Ladies Collegiate" (Lady Haughty, Lady Centaur, and Doll Mavis), by the railing of the termagant Mistress Otter, by the roof-raising toasts of Captain Otter, and by the boastful competition between Sir John (Jack) Daw and Sir Amorous La Foole. Morose finally pledges his nephew £500 a year and the right of inheritance if he will free him of wife and her "friends." Revealing that Epicoene is really a boy actor, Dauphine simultaneously secures his future, frees his foolish uncle, and exposes each social pretender to the ridicule of his fellows.

MEN (*11; doubling possible*): 1 is 18–25 (no lines); 3 are 20–35 1 must be an outstanding actor); 2 are 35–40; 3 are 40–60 (2 must speak Latin fluently; 1 minor); 1 is 60–80 (must be an outstanding actor); 1 is Prologue (age not important; can be doubled role). WOMEN (5): 1 is 18–25 (minor); 2 are 20–35 (1 minor); 1 is 35–50; 1 is 40–60. BOYS (2): 1 is 16–20 (title role; must be an outstanding actor, must disguise and speak convincingly as a young woman for most of the play); 1 is 10–15 (must sing). EXTRAS: Pages, servants, and musicians. SETS: Rooms in 4 upper-class houses in early 17th-century London, a long narrow lane or gallery in 1 house. Multiple or modified Elizabethan staging appropriate. Unit set may be used. Arena staging possible but difficult. COSTUMES: Elizabethan; majority quite fashionable, should reflect social strata of knights, gentlemen, and ladies; some pageboy and servant garb required. DIFFICULTIES: Numerous Latin phrases (almost 1 entire scene) form the dialogue for 2 important characters.

ROYALTY: Public domain. TEXT: *Ben Jonson: Three Plays* (Hill and Wang), Vol. 1.

—— o ——

THE ALCHEMIST (1610) BEN JONSON. Comedy. His
master away, Jeremy the butler plays the dual roles of Face,
the false police captain, and Lungs, an alchemist's assistant.
He joins in the get-rich-quick schemes of Subtle the Alchemist, and his colleague Dol Common. Blackfriars neighbors
soon observe half of London patronizing their quiet district.
Sir Epicure Mammon gives the trio money and old family
silver in hope of possessing the philosopher's stone; cautious
Abel Drugger gives his lucky gold piece to learn how to succeed in the tobacco business. From abroad come the miserly
Puritans, Tribulation Wholesome and Ananias; from upcoun-
try England come Kastrill, a would-be gallant, and his widowed sister Dame Pliant; from nearby "Holburn at the Dagger"
comes Dapper, a lawyer's clerk. By quick wit, disguises, and
deft tongues, the schemers line their pockets while managing
to keep their gullible clients rich only in hope. When Master
Lovewit returns, the cozeners are cozened. With Jeremy's
repentant help, Lovewit even takes over one unfinished scheme
and gets Dame Pliant for his wife.

MEN (*14; doubling possible*): 1 is 18–25; 1 is 21 (minor);
2 are 20–35 (1 must be an outstanding actor, quite agile, who
can disguise well as 3 different characters); 2 are 30–40 (1
must speak some Spanish; 1 has no lines); 3 are 40–60 (1 is
major); 1 is 60–70; 3 are police officers (minor, ages not important); 1 is Prologue (age not important; can be doubled).
WOMEN (*2*): 1 is 19 (attractive); 1 is 20–35 (must be versatile
and able to disguise well). EXTRAS: At least 6 neighbors (men
and women, various ages, minor) and various attendants.
SETS: House in London's Blackfriars district, autumn of 1610.
Majority of scenes take place in 1 room within the house
(outfitted to look like an alchemist's laboratory), others in an
adjoining outer room, and in the street in front of the house.
Multiple or modified Elizabethan staging appropriate. Unit set
may be used. Arena staging possible. COSTUMES: Elizabethan;
some fashionable, some fanciful, others lower-class London
and peasant; police captain's uniform; Puritan religious; Spanish. DIFFICULTIES: Elizabethan blank verse with some long,
involved speeches. Some disguises are changed more than
once, requiring great versatility in acting and variety in
makeup.
ROYALTY: Public domain. TEXT: *Ben Jonson: Three Plays*
(Hill and Wang), Vol. 1.

— o —

THE STAPLE OF NEWS (1625) BEN JONSON. Comedy. The induction to this semi-allegorical play presents a quartet of ladies—Mirth, Curiosity, Expectation, and My Lady Censure—who comment between each act of the main play, in which Frank Pennyboy pretends death in order to observe how Pennyboy Junior will behave. Subsequent scenes depict the social, economic, and moral follies of the emerging London middle class. From Lickfinger of the Devil Tavern to Uncle Richer Pennyboy, all London seeks the favor of Lady Pecunia. Both the usury of the old generation and the prodigal luxury of the new are condemned. Only the prodigal father combines virtue and wit enough to protect Lady Pecunia from becoming the plaything of the age's vice and folly.

MEN (26; doubling possible): 1 is 21 (must be an outstanding actor); 5 are 18–25 (3 minor, 2 have no lines); 8 are 20–35 (6 are minor); 5 are 35–50 (2 are minor); 2 are 40–60; 1 is 50–65 (must sing); 1 is 65–75; 1 is Prologue (age not important); 2 tiremen (minor). WOMEN (10): 1 is 16–20 (minor); 2 are 18–25 (1 minor); 3 are 20–35 (minor); 3 are 30–45 (minor); 1 is 60–80 (minor). BOY: 10–15 (must sing; minor). EXTRAS: Crowd of customers; fiddlers; 2 dogs. SETS: Rooms in 2 London houses, an office, and a tavern dining room. Multiple or modified Elizabethan staging appropriate. Unit set may be used. Arena staging feasible. COSTUMES: Elizabethan; upper-middle class, majority rather fashionable; some peasant, beggars' garb.

ROYALTY: Public domain. TEXT: Ben Jonson: Complete Plays (Dutton), Vol. II.

— o —

THE TRAGICAL HISTORY OF DOCTOR FAUSTUS (ca. 1589) CHRISTOPHER MARLOWE. Tragedy. The play's 15 scenes trace the "hellish fall" of Faustus, the man who sold his soul to the Devil. Acknowledged master of liberal arts, pride and curiosity lead Faustus to turn a deaf ear to the Good Angel. The ever-ingratiating Mephistophilis persuades Faustus to pledge his soul in exchange for 24 years of earthly power and delight. In a kind of tragicomic counterpoint, Faustus' servant Wagner follows a similar cause. Scenes of tragic intensity (the brooding opening scene, the first three scenes with Mephistophilis, and the final scene, with the terrified Faustus waiting out his doom) are interspersed with scenes of parody, farce, black magic, and pageantry. No other Elizabethan drama so fully blends the ethical focus and dramatic intensity of the medieval mystery play with the psychological preoccupation and high poetry of Elizabethan drama.

MEN (36; doubling possible): 4 are 18-25 (3 minor; 1 has no lines); 12 are 20–35 (all minor; 1 has no lines); 12 are 35–50 (11 minor; at least 5 sing); 3 are 40–60 (minor); 1 is 50–65 (outstanding actor also able to speak Latin); 3 are 60–80 (minor); 1 is Chorus, who speaks Prologue and Epilogue (age not important; can be doubled). WOMEN (6; doubling possible): 5 are 18–25 (all minor, devils in disguise; only 1 has lines); 1 is 20–35 (minor). BOY: 16–18 (minor). EXTRAS: Devils and attendants (devils must dance). SETS: The study of Doctor Faustus; a grove; an inn; the Pope's privy chamber at Rome; the courts of the Emperor and the Duke of Vanholt. Multiple or modified Elizabethan staging appropriate. Unit set may be used. Arena staging possible but extremely difficult. COSTUMES: Elizabethan or late Renaissance; suggestion of fancy or allegory in costumes of devils, angels, 7 deadly sins, other spirits; some fashionable German 16th-century court dress, religious habit, and peasant garb; 1 dragon. DIFFICULTIES: Play is in verse and prose. Complex technical effects required for conjuring sequences; appearance and disappearance of devils, shapes, and spirits, turning of 2 characters into animals; and Faustus being borne away to Hell.

ROYALTY: Public domain. TEXT: *Doctor Faustus* (Washington Square).

— o —

THE JEW OF MALTA (*ca.* 1590) CHRISTOPHER MARLOWE. Tragedy. The "Ghost of Machiavel" is prologue to this drama of vicious intrigue. The Jew of Malta is the most unscrupulous among those who, motivated by ruthless self-interest and devoid of "compassion, love, . . . hope, and . . . fear," plot and counterplot. Jew, Turk, or Christian, the major characters are almost equally guilty of gross inhumanity. The Turks impose a ruthless tribute on the Maltese, who in turn confiscate Jewish property. Barabad, the richest Jew, betrays the Maltese Christians to the Turks and the Turks to the

Christians. Along the way he poisons any, including his daughter, who thwart his maniacal lust for possession. Finally he falls into the boiling cauldron he had set as a trap for others. In such an atmosphere, the innocent love of Abigail, the Jew's daughter, and Don Mathias cannot survive. Everything becomes tainted in this land that has lost all vision of love and charity.

MEN (*26; doubling possible*): 4 are 18–25 (2 minor); 5 are 20–35 (3 minor); 9 are 35–50 (1 is Prologue; all minor); 7 are 40–60 (5 minor); 1 is 55–70 (must be outstanding actor); knights, bassoes, officers, slaves, carpenters, Turks. WOMEN (5): 3 are 20–35 (2 have no lines); 2 are 40–60. GIRL: 14 (may be played older). SETS: Rooms in 4 houses, a market place, a courtyard, and several public areas within and outside the city on the island of Malta in the 16th century. Multiple or modified Elizabethan staging appropriate. Unit set may be used. Arena staging impractical. Upper level needed, rigged so floor will give way, causing 1 character to fall into a boiling cauldron. COSTUMES: Elizabethan; majority fashionable, wealthy mercantile class; some colorful Turkish and Spanish court dress; military uniforms; ragged slave garb; religious habit, peasant dress. DIFFICULTIES: Main portions of the play are verse; some long and involved speeches by the title character. Five characters die on stage (1 within a boiling cauldron after lengthy death speech), presenting technical problems.

ROYALTY: Public domain. TEXT: *Christopher Marlowe: Five Plays* (Hill and Wang).

— o —

EDWARD THE SECOND (1591-92) CHRISTOPHER MARLOWE. Tragedy. Fortune's turning wheel provides the underlying dramatic metaphor which holds together the swift succession of scenes depicting the successful rebellion of Mortimer and Queen Isabella, the killing of Edward II and such venal favorites as Gaveston, and the ultimate defeat of the rebels upon the ascent to power of the child-king Edward III. Whether they are "proud, overdaring" Mortimers, the crude Warwick, ambitious Lancaster, vacillating Kent, gentle Isabella, or such weaklings as Edward II and Gaveston, all become victims of base Fortune—all "tumble headlong down" from her ever-turning wheel.

MEN (*39; doubling possible*): 2 are 18–25 (minor); 11 are 20–35 (6 minor); 9 are 35–50 (7 minor); 12 are 40–60 (minor); 3 are 50–70; 2 are 70–80; monks, lords, guards, soldiers, attendants. WOMEN (*4*): 1 is 18–25; 2 are 20–35 (1 has no lines); 1 is 35–50 (no lines); ladies of the court. BOYS: (*2*): 1 is 15; 1 is 16–18 (minor). SETS: Rooms in 2 houses, 3 castles, Westminster Palace, and an abbey; city streets, open country, and battlefields in England and early 14th-century Paris. Multiple or modified Elizabethan staging appropriate. Unit set may be used. Arena staging possible. COSTUMES: Elizabethan or early Gothic; fashionable court dress, appropriate dress for clergy, some armor and battle dress; some peasant and servant garb. DIFFICULTIES: Play is in verse, much of it fluent. Staging problems created by onstage battle scenes, swordfighting sequence, and 2 onstage murders. Expert production and direction mandatory.

ROYALTY: Public domain. TEXT: *Christopher Marlowe: Five Plays* (Hill and Wang).

—— o ——

THE CHANGELING (1623) THOMAS MIDDLETON and WILLIAM ROWLEY. Tragedy. Proud Beatrice-Joanna, conceiving a passion for Alsamero and seeking to rid herself of her undesired betrothed, Alonzo, turns to her father's ugly servant De Flores, whom she has hitherto scorned. De Flores willingly undertakes the charge and kills Alonzo, but refuses gold and jewels and demands she submit to him in payment. Though appalled, Beatrice sees no other choice. "Vengeance begins; Murder, I see, is followed by more sins." Her loathing for De Flores turns to a kind of fascination, but they arouse suspicion and, though they kill again, are apprehended. The scenes between Beatrice and De Flores provide strong drama and some memorable lines, but both the verse and the plot are uneven. Much of the action is taken up with a loosely connected comic subplot, credited to Rowley, which gives the play its name. Set in a madhouse, it concerns the efforts of two counterfeit patients to seduce Isabella, the wife of their doctor-keeper and, ironically if crudely, echoes the main theme.

MEN (*11, plus 6 or 8 extras who can be doubled, some eliminated*): 15 can be 20–35 (1 should be a strong actor); 2 are 50–70. WOMEN (*3, some extras could be women*): All

20–25 (1 must be a strong actress). SETS: Style of the period, chiefly within a castle and a madhouse. COSTUMES: Jacobean or Spanish, chiefly court; ragged or outlandish for the madhouse scenes.

ROYALTY: Public domain. TEXT: *English Drama, 1580–1642* (Heath).

—— o ——

THE COMEDY OF ERRORS (*ca.* 1591) WILLIAM SHAKESPEARE. Comedy. This comedy of mischance and mistaken identity begins with a death sentence on the aged Syracusan merchant Aegeon, whose family had been split many years earlier in a shipwreck in which Aegeon's wife and one of his twin sons (both named Antipholus) had been carried away, lashed to a spar. Although Syracuse and Ephesus are at war, the family is once again—unknown to each other at first—gathered in the same city. Possibilities for confusion are increased by the presence of the two Dromios, twin servants of the twins Antipholus (the "lost" Antipholus has married and lives in Ephesus). Shakespeare exploits the situation in a dizzying series of farce maneuvers that involve a jealous wife, her moralizing sister, a befuddled courtesan, and a schoolmaster-wizard who proffers a religious cure for the city's madness. Under the succession of improbable action runs the theme of loss and recovery—Aegeon is saved from death, identities are discovered, and the family closely united with bonds strengthened by adversity and long separation. (Compare Plautus' *Menaechmi*; see p. 43.)

MEN (*11, plus attendants*): 6 are 40–60 (4 minor); 5 are 20–30 (twin brothers and twin servants should have similar builds). WOMEN (*5*): 1 is 40–60, 4 are 20–30 (2 minor). SET: A single setting in the fashion of the Roman comedy with maximum space for physical action. COSTUMES: Pre-Christian Roman; Elizabethan; or variants of either. (Has been successfully transplanted to a half-dozen periods and places.) Freedom and boldness more important than accuracy. DIFFICULTIES: Maintaining the spontaneity of the script means painstaking directional planning.

ROYALTY: Public domain. TEXT: Pelican.

—— o ——

RICHARD III (*ca.* 1593) WILLIAM SHAKESPEARE. History. The physically deformed Richard is determined to seize the English throne from his brother Edward IV. He rouses Edward's hatred against their brother Clarence, who is arrested; then, assuring Clarence of a quick release, he gives the orders for his murder. This is the first of the many deceitful actions that mark Richard's rise. He succeeds in wooing Anne, widow of a son of Henry VI whose death he has caused, in the presence of the corpse. After the king's natural death, Richard has the young heir to the throne and his brother murdered in the Tower. Richard unscrupulously removes all who stand between him and the throne, stopping at nothing. He is finally brought to account and killed, at the battle of Bosworth Field, by the future Henry VII.

MEN (*35*): 2 are 10–20 (minor); 23 are 20–40 (1 requires an outstanding actor; others minor); 10 are 40–60 (2 require outstanding actors; others minor). WOMEN (*3*): 2 are 20–40 (1 requires an outstanding actress); 1 is 50–60 (minor). SETS: A street in London; the Tower; the king's palace; Lord Hastings' house; Bosworth Field. Sets need not be realistic. Arena production possible. COSTUMES: Late 15th-century court and military costumes. DIFFICULTIES: Act V, scene iii calls for the appearance and disappearance of several ghosts.

ROYALTY: Public domain. TEXT: Cambridge.

— o —

KING JOHN (*ca.* 1594) WILLIAM SHAKESPEARE. History. The plot of *The Life and Death of King John* is concerned with his attempts to make his throne secure, against a French claimant, the young Arthur of Bretagne, and dissident elements inside the country. John sends an army to Angiers in France to enforce his claim, but the citizens refuse to accept either John or Arthur. Both French and English kings decide to settle their differences by arranging a marriage between the Dauphin and John's niece, Blanch of Spain, and by a cession of some of John's territory in France. This peace is abhorrent to patriotic Englishmen. On another count, John is excommunicated by the Pope and the French are authorized to take up arms once more against England. They are defeated, and Arthur of Bretagne falls into John's hands. Arthur escapes being blinded by John but leaps to his death, thus bringing suspicion on the king. There is another battle with the French and revelations of further duplicity on both sides, before the Pope mediates. Meanwhile, however, John has died, apparently poisoned.

MEN (*19*): 2 are 14–18 (1 minor, other requires an outstanding young actor); 10 are 20–40 (4 require outstanding actors, 6 minor); 7 are 40–60 (1 requires an outstanding actor, 6 are minor). WOMEN (*4*): 2 are 20–40 (1 requires an outstanding actress, other is minor); 2 are 40–60 (minor). SETS: King John's palace; before Angiers; the French tent; the Dauphin's camp; the orchard at Swinstead Abbey. Sets for 2nd act must have practical gates which open revealing Angiers. COSTUMES: Late-12th and early-13th century, including fashionable court and military costumes.

ROYALTY: Public domain. TEXT: Cambridge.

—— o ——

RICHARD II (*ca.* 1594) WILLIAM SHAKESPEARE. History. Bolingbroke, cousin of Richard II and later to be King Henry IV, accuses Mowbray of plotting the death of an uncle of the king. Richard permits the adversaries to arrange to settle their differences in trial by combat at Coventry, hoping they will destroy each other, then capriciously stops the contest and banishes both men. Richard takes speedy advantage of the death of John of Gaunt (his own uncle and Bolingbroke's father) by seizing his property. When news of Richard's action reaches Bolingbroke, he returns from exile with an army to claim what is rightfully his. The nobles, hearing rumors of Richard's death in combat in Ireland, desert the king and he is forced to take refuge in Flint Castle, where he is soon discovered by Bolingbroke. Richard, weak and pitiable yet sensitive and intelligent, is captured and is forced to surrender his crown to Bolingbroke at Westminster Hall. Deposed, he is murdered at Pomfret Castle by Exton, who considers his deed a favor to the new Henry IV. Richard's corpse is brought before Henry, who rewards Exton with banishment. Henry repents Richard's death and promises to do penance by voyaging to the Holy Land.

MEN (*21*): 13 are 20–40 (2 require outstanding actors, 11 are minor); 8 are 40–60 (3 require outstanding actors, 5 are minor). WOMEN (*3*): 1 is 20–30 (minor); 2 are 40–60 (1 requires an outstanding actress, 1 is minor). SETS: King's palace; Duke of Lancaster's palace; the lists at Coventry; Gloucestershire; Flint Castle; Westminster Hall; Pomfret Castle. Walls of Flint Castle must support 5 men. COSTUMES: Early 15th-century Italianate for Richard's court; the more conservative English fashion worn by all others. DIFFICULTIES: Lacks overt specified physical action.

ROYALTY: Public domain. TEXT: Pelican.

— o —

THE TAMING OF THE SHREW (*ca.* 1594). WILLIAM SHAKESPEARE. Comedy. The play opens with an Induction in which a drunken tinker, Christopher Sly, is thrown out of a tavern by the irate hostess and falls asleep in the street. Discovering him, a merry lord dresses him in fine clothing, brings him to a sumptuous apartment, furnishes him a wife (a disguised page), and convinces him he is a nobleman who has suffered amnesia for 15 years. The main action of the play is now performed in order to prevent Sly (who is scarcely mentioned again) from falling back into his supposed madness. The madcap Petruchio woos Katherina, the perfect wife in every respect but one—she is an intolerable shrew. From their first explosive meeting, Petruchio subjects Kate to a series of verbal and physical indignities under the pretext of kindness. Despite her superb resistance, she is finally ready to swear that the sun is the moon or that an old man is a fair virgin if Petruchio says so. Contrasted to this direct clash is the elaborate wooing of the demure sister Bianca by the disguised Lucentio and Hortensio. At the end, Kate defends marriage as hotly as she denounced it in the beginning.

MEN (*17, plus servants*): 9 are 18–30 (3 minor); 8 are 35–50 (1 minor). WOMEN (*4; 2 minor*): 3 are 18–25; 1 is 35–50. SETS: Unit setting should allow for quick change from exterior (house with upper window) to interior, but can be very simple, especially if Induction is used. COSTUMES: Exaggerated Elizabethan or Italianate; nobility and servants. Special madcap costume for Petruchio. Entire effect should be bold.

ROYALTY: Public domain. TEXT: Pelican.

— o —

LOVE'S LABOUR'S LOST (*ca.* 1595) WILLIAM SHAKE-SPEARE. Comedy. Prompted by the ascetic King of Navarre, three young lords sign an oath to close themselves away from worldly pleasures and study for three years in dedicated austerity. They resolve to fast, sleep only three hours a night, and, above all, neither see nor speak to a woman. The merry Biron has grave doubts about the possibility of keeping such an oath, but his wise counsel about the dangers of arid study is scorned and he joins the bargain. The ink is scarcely dry on the parchment when news comes of the arrival of the Princess of France. The king concedes that formalities must be observed, but he insists that the princess remain outside the gates of his palace. But the king and the lords are smitten by the beauty of the princess and her three attending ladies. Each in turn composes a sonnet and attempts to deliver it secretly to the woman of his heart. Discovering that they are mutually traitors to their vow, they plunge, disguised as Russians, into direct wooing of the ladies. They meet surprising resistance and eventually discover that they must do penance before they are worthy of offering love. In the subplot are satiric portraits of a schoolmaster, a curate, a constable, and a Spaniard.

MEN (*13, plus attendants*): 9 are 20–40 (3 minor, 1 should be very small and have a singing voice); 4 are 40–60 (1 minor). WOMEN (*5*): All 20–40 (1 minor). SET: Whole of action in King of Navarre's park, preferably formal rather than realistic. COSTUMES: 15th- or 16th-century French court costumes; gowns for schoolmaster and curate; rustic clothing for clowns; a Spanish suit of fantastical cut.

ROYALTY: Public domain. TEXT: Pelican.

—— o ——

A MIDSUMMER NIGHT'S DREAM (*ca.* 1595) WILLIAM SHAKESPEARE. Comedy. Defying parental authority and official edict, Hermia and Lysander affirm the strength of their love by escaping into the enchanted wood outside Athens. In hot pursuit comes the jealous Demetrius, pursued in turn by lovesick Helena. This wayward human quartet is suddenly beset by fairy mischief in the shape of Puck, who, attempting to cure love's torments with drops from a magic flower, turns pursuer into pursued. Puck is emissary for Oberon, king of the fairies, who is piqued with his queen, Titania. The hapless instrument of Oberon's revenge is Bottom the Weaver; he and his fellow "mechanicals" have come to the wood to rehearse the "lamentable comedy" (a play within a play) of Pyramus and Thisbe. Marvelously incompetent in the role of the lover Pyramus, Bottom is transformed by Puck into the donkey-headed favorite of Titania. But midsummer madness evaporates with the dawn. The lovers are magically and happily paired and return to Athens for a dual wedding, the festivities of which will feature a triumphant performance of the mechanicals' play.

MEN (*13, plus attendants*): 6 are 20–40 (1 minor); 7 are 40–60 (1 minor). WOMEN (*7, plus fairies and attendants*): All 20–40 (4 minor; Puck should be sprightly; some must sing). SETS: Duke's palace; Quince's rustic home; magic wood (including bower for Titania). Unit setting desirable. COSTUMES: Classic Athenian; Elizabethan; or a careful blending of both periods.

ROYALTY: Public domain. TEXT: Pelican.

—— o ——

ROMEO AND JULIET (*ca.* 1595) WILLIAM SHAKESPEARE. Tragedy. Among the most famous of love stories, this is a tragedy of circumstance as well as character, in which love is sacrificed to the ancient enmity between the houses of Montague and Capulet. The lyric passion of Romeo and Juliet is "star-cross'd," beset with accident, disastrous coincidence, and foolhardy plans from those normally wise. Some of the play's sense of pressure comes from the combination of exquisite verbal fancy with the swift and shocking turn of events. The mood is unusually high-spirited for a tragedy, not only with the brilliant portraits of Mercutio and the Nurse, but also with the youthful joking of the lovers in both balcony scenes. Their radiance is so vital and their deaths so needless that the play's final effect is one of numbed shock as the ancient quarrel of the Montagues and Capulets dissolves forever in mutual grief.

MEN (*17, plus citizens and relatives*): 7 are 40–60 (2 minor); 10 are 18–30 (5 minor, 1 must have exceptional feeling for language). WOMEN (*4, plus attendants*): 1 must look very young yet possess enormous vocal and dramatic skill; 1 must be physically heavy and middle-aged; 2 are relatively small, middle-aged. SETS: Verona and Mantua. A street; hall of noble house; orchard with wall; exterior with balcony; Friar Laurence's cell; bedchamber; churchyard with tomb. Unit setting strongly recommended. COSTUMES: Elizabethan or 15th-century Italian; some visual means to distinguish Montagues and Capulets; Franciscan habits; apothecary, officers, and masquer's clothing. DIFFICULTIES: Leading roles must have youthful exuberance and technical proficiency. Dancing should be formal, authentic. Fencing must be carefully rehearsed to suggest the unpredictable violence of the quarrel between the houses.

ROYALTY: Public domain. TEXT: Pelican.

—— o ——

THE MERCHANT OF VENICE (*ca.* 1596) WILLIAM SHAKESPEARE. Comedy. Antonio, a merchant, to assist his friend Bassanio's wooing of the heiress Portia, is forced to borrow money from the Jewish usurer Shylock. Because he nurses a grudge against all Christians and against Antonio in particular, Shylock forgoes his usual interest and asks for a pound of flesh in the event the 3,000 ducats are not repaid in three months. Outfitted with the Jew's money, Bassanio sets off in the company of his boisterous friend, Gratiano, to press his suit of Portia. This witty lady is protected from fortune-hunters by three caskets—of gold, silver, and lead. Her father's will has decreed that she shall marry whoever chooses the right casket. Although she declares her love to Bassanio before he chooses, Bassanio shows his worthiness in distrusting outward splendor and chooses the right casket. Happiness is short-lived, as Antonio's ships are lost and his bond forfeit. His hatred fed by the elopement of his daughter, Jessica, to marry a Christian, Shylock prepares to take his pound of flesh. Though Shylock is entreated to be merciful, first by the Duke and later by Portia disguised as a judge, he is adamant. Portia then forbids Shylock to spill a drop of blood in exacting his rights; this, of course, makes the exaction of a pound of flesh impossible. Shylock is defeated and punished appropriately; the play ends with Portia's mock test of Bassanio's love in forcing him by a trick to relinquish his wedding ring.

MEN (*17, plus magnificoes, officers, servants; doubling possible*): 6 are 35–60 (1 is Moroccan, 2 minor); 11 are 18–30 (6 minor, but 1 must sing). WOMEN (*3, plus attendants*): All 18–25. SETS: Venice—street and forecourt of Shylock's house; a court; Belmont—interior and exterior of Portia's house. Because of rapid change of scene, unit setting desirable. COSTUMES: Elegant 16th-century Venetian, contrasting with the plain gabardine of Shylock and Tubal. Rustic garments for Old Gobbo and livery for Launcelot Gobbo. Special national costumes for Aragon and Morocco. Masks needed for men and women. DIFFICULTIES: Greatest single problem is modern audience attitude toward Shylock. While he has sympathetic stature and motivation, he must still be sufficiently villainous to give point to the comedy.

ROYALTY: Public domain. TEXT: Pelican.

— o —

HENRY IV, Part 1 (*ca.* 1597) WILLIAM SHAKESPEARE. History. Henry's insecure throne is being threatened from several sides at once. Warring on the Scottish border, Henry Percy (Hotspur), son of the Earl of Northumberland and a model youth, refuses to surrender to the king his Scottish prisoners. In the west, Owen Glendower is disturbing the peace of the Marches with his raids. To his disappointment, Henry's own son, the future Henry V, is dissipating his youth in carousals and adventures on the highway with the "fat old knight" Sir John Falstaff and other boon companions.

Danger is precipitated when fiery Hotspur and the superstitious Glendower ally to oust the king. At Hotspur's audacity, Prince Hal is galvanized to join his father's army against the rebels (whose uneasy alliance is by this time disintegrating). At the battle of Shrewsbury, Prince Hal shows his quality, redeeming himself in his father's eyes; he kills Hotspur (whose valor is parodied by the unwillingly present Falstaff) and defeats the remainder of the rebel force.

MEN (*17*): 8 are 20–40 (6 minor, 2 require outstanding actors); 9 are 40–60 (5 minor, 4 require outstanding actors). WOMEN (*3*): 2 are 20–40 (outstanding actresses); 1 is 40–60 (minor). SETS: The London palace; an innyard; Boar's Head Tavern; the Archdeacon's house; the King's camp; the Rebel camp. Sets need not be realistic. COSTUMES: Early 15th-century court and rustic costumes; armor used throughout by the majority of characters. DIFFICULTIES: The final scene of Act II has 6 characters on the stage with only 2 carrying the dialogue; the other 4 remain almost silent but must be in-

cluded in the action for the effectiveness of the scene.
ROYALTY: Public domain. TEXT: Cambridge.

—— o ——

HENRY IV, Part 2 (*ca.* 1597) WILLIAM SHAKESPEARE. History. When the Earl of Northumberland receives news of the death of his son, Hotspur, he joins forces with those of the Archbishop of York; together they prepare to advance against the king's army, led by Prince John and the Earl of Westmoreland. Seeking his own profit, Falstaff leads a band of his ragged and frivolous cronies from the Boar's Head Tavern as recruits to the king's army. Less humorous is the action of Prince John who, giving his word that he will listen to rebel grievances, immediately orders their execution. Caught in the tumult of the civil war that surrounds him, Henry continues to look forward to his long-delayed pilgrimage to the Holy Land. His reign, marked by thirteen years of factious rebellion, closes with this death. His heir, Prince Hal, immediately eschews the dissipation and irresponsibility of his earlier youth when he becomes Henry V.

MEN (*36*): 23 are 20–40 (12 minor, 3 require outstanding actors, 8 require competent actors); 13 are 40–60 (11 minor, 2 require outstanding actors). WOMEN (*5*): 4 are 20–40 (require good actresses); 1 is 40–50 (minor). SETS: The Archbishop's palace; a London street; the Boar's Head Tavern; Justice Shallow's house; Gaultree forest; a room in Westminster Abbey. Proscenium and Elizabethan staging methods have been used successfully in recent productions. COSTUMES: Early 15th-century court and military costumes with an assortment of rustic costumes for lesser characters. DIFFICULTIES: The director should treat the Hal-Falstaff relationship so that the banishment of Falstaff by the newly crowned Henry is neither totally unexpected nor unjustified.
ROYALTY: Public domain. TEXT: Pelican.

—— o ——

HENRY V (*ca.* 1598) WILLIAM SHAKESPEARE. History. Henry seeks to divert his rebellious subjects' attention from their grievances at home and prepares to invade France. From a dissolute youth he has developed into a purposeful monarch, and in France proves his ability as a soldier and a skillful leader. At the siege of Harfleur he unites the dissident factions in the English army and goes on to crush the French, against heavy odds, at Agincourt. The play ends with the marriage of Henry to the French king's daughter, the crowns of England and France united and the succession assured. Action is interspersed throughout with scenes of notable comedy. Fluellen, Jamy, and Macmorris represent the Welsh, Scots, and Irish factions in Henry's army who, together with the beguiling rogues Nym, Pistol, and Bardolph (holdovers from the king's wild youth) provide constant humorous diversion.

MEN (*34*): 19 are 20–40 (10 minor; 3 must speak with Welsh, Scotch, and Irish accents); 15 are 40–60 (12 minor, 3 require outstanding actors). WOMEN (*4*): 3 are 20–40 (1 requires an outstanding actress; 2 minor); 1 is 45–50. SETS: An antechamber in the King's palace; before Harfleur; English and French camps outside Agincourt; the French palace. Sets need not be realistic. COSTUMES: Early 15th century; assorted armor, including helmets, breastplates, and gauntlets. DIFFICULTIES: The cast needs many extras to double as lords, officers, soldiers, citizens, messengers, and attendants; dialect passages important to dramatic balance of the play.

ROYALTY: Public domain. TEXT: Cambridge.

— o —

JULIUS CAESAR (*ca.* 1598) WILLIAM SHAKESPEARE. Tragedy. The commoners of Rome rejoice in Caesar's "triumph over Pompey's blood"; the patricians, fearing his growing ambition, conspire against him. Cassius leads the intriguers; with Casca and Cinna they engage the noble Brutus in their cause to assassinate Caesar. Their plotting is successful and Caesar ventures out of his house to the Capitol in spite of bad auguries, to be stabbed by Brutus. Mark Antony, desiring to stir the rabble against the conspirators, pretends to submit to the reasoning of the assassins; and, in the marketplace, delivers an oration which sets the mischief afoot. He then joins the forces of Octavius Caesar and Lepidus. Octavius' army triumphs and Cassius and Brutus take their own lives with the swords used to defeat Caesar.

MEN (*31*): 2 are 10–20 (minor); 19 are 20–40 (2 require outstanding actors, 17 are minor); 10 are 40–60 (1 outstanding actor is required, 9 are minor). WOMEN (*2*): 2 are 20–40 (minor). SETS: A street in Rome; a public place; Brutus' garden; Caesar's house; the Forum; Brutus' tent; Phillipi. Sets need not be realistic. Arena and proscenium production possible. COSTUMES: Authentic costumes of period (1st-century B.C.). DIFFICULTIES: Vocal reactions of the crowd during the orations of Brutus and Antony are sparsely indicated in the text. Select appropriate vocal interjections which will activate the individual members of the crowd into a spirited unit, in turn heightening the effectiveness of the scene.

ROYALTY: Public domain. TEXT: Penguin.

—— o ——

MUCH ADO ABOUT NOTHING (*ca.* 1598) WILLIAM SHAKESPEARE. Comedy. Claudio, returned from the wars, is deeply in love with Hero, but steps aside when he believes Don Pedro is wooing her, because he has a prior allegiance to Don Pedro as both friend and subject. Benedick, a confirmed woman-hater, laughs mercilessly at the changes love has wrought in his friend Claudio, transforming him from a plain soldier into a fashion-conscious wooer. Beatrice, Hero's cousin, heaps mockery upon Benedick but demonstrates deepest feeling when Hero is slandered by the malicious intrigue of Don John, Don Pedro's base-born brother. The plot is also concerned with the high comedy of tricking the witty Beatrice and Benedick into each other's arms and with the bumbling of Dogberry and his Watch who, with agonizing deliberateness, brings villainy to light before tragedy has destroyed the courtship of Hero and Claudio. (Much of the action devolves on the Elizabethan pronunciation and meaning of *nothing*— "noting," i.e., overhearing or eavesdropping.)

MEN (*14, plus attendants*): 5 are 20–30 (1 must sing, 1 must be gifted in verbal comedy); 8 are 35–60 (2 minor); 1 is a boy (minor). WOMEN (*4*): 1 is 18–20; 1 is 20–22; 2 are about 22. SETS: Courtyard of Leonato's house; rooms of house; orchard; church interior; prison; garden. Unit setting highly desirable. Orchard scene must permit hiding places for Beatrice and Benedick. Decor Italian Renaissance. COSTUMES: Elegant Elizabethan or 16th-century Italian. Must permit dancing and graceful movement. Commoners' clothing for Dogberry and Watch. DIFFICULTIES: Language requires great care to maintain both pace and clarity. Balancing of moods, particularly in the church scene and the challenge scene, re-

quires careful preparation to avoid confusing audience.
ROYALTY: Public domain. TEXT: Pelican.

—— o ——

AS YOU LIKE IT (*ca.* 1599) WILLIAM SHAKESPEARE.
Comedy. The wicked Duke Frederick has wrested power
from his brother. The exiled Duke Senior has found refuge
in the Forest of Arden, where a new court has been established under nature's laws. Duke Senior has found, instead of
flattery and corruption, "tongues in trees, books in running
brooks, /Sermons in stones and good in everything." At Duke
Frederick's court Orlando sees Duke Senior's daughter Rosalind and they fall in love. Duke Frederick exiles Rosalind from
court, and she flees with her friend Celia to join her father
in the forest. The girls disguise themselves for the trip——Celia
as a country girl and Rosalind as a boy. They take Touchstone, a jester, with them. In the idyllic setting of the Forest
of Arden Rosalind finds the love-struck Orlando and, while
still disguised as a boy, offers to "cure" him of his passion,
thus allowing herself the double pleasure of mocking her lover
and teaching him to love by turns. In contrast to this romance
are the cynical Touchstone, doubtful of pastoral delights, and
Jaques, doubtful of the joys of human society. Love and
loyalty, however, dispel the clouds of envy. The play ends
with the celebration of a triple wedding and the news that
Duke Frederick has reformed and will welcome them back
to court.

MEN (*16 plus attendants, pages; doubling possible*): 10 are
20–40 (2 minor, 1 must sing); 6 are 40–60 (1 is minor).
WOMEN (*5 plus*): All 18–25 (minor character required to
sing; 1 must be outstanding). SETS: Country house; Frederick's
court; the forest. Unit setting advisable. COSTUMES: Modified
Elizabethan; pastoral setting allows considerable freedom.
DIFFICULTIES: The action is charming but meandering, effectiveness dependent on verbal flexibility of actors. Wrestling
match requires skillful staging.
ROYALTY: Public domain. TEXT: Pelican.

—— o ——

HAMLET, PRINCE OF DENMARK (*ca.* 1600) WILLIAM
SHAKESPEARE. Tragedy. Hamlet is a Renaissance prince with
the authority, intelligence, and moral sensitivity likely to make

him the ideal ruler. However, "the times are out of joint" and sin has corrupted the court. With his mother, Queen Gertrude, married to his uncle Claudius, the murderer of his father, no appearance may be trusted. Though sworn to vengeance by his father's ghost, Hamlet's virtues prevent unthinking action. Although he must obey his father, his deeds must be answerable to God. Feigning madness, Hamlet attempts to discover the extent of the guilty conspiracy at court. He is suspicious of the lord chamberlain, Polonius, and even distrustful of Polonius' daughter Ophelia, whom he had formerly courted. King Claudius betrays his guilt at the performance of a play devised by Hamlet, but even then Hamlet cannot bring himself to kill the king. Inadvertently he kills Polonius, a deed which brings exile for Hamlet and madness and death for Ophelia. Laertes, Ophelia's brother and Hamlet's former friend, challenges him to a duel, with the approval of the king and queen, but the tables are turned—Gertrude dies of poison prepared for Hamlet, who avenges himself on the king. Laertes kills Hamlet, and is in turn killed, with a poisoned rapier.

MEN (27, plus attendants; doubling and cutting possible): 3 are 40–60 (1 minor); 24 are 20–40 (9 minor, 1 must be outstanding). WOMEN (2, plus attendants): 1 is 18–23, 1 is 40–45. SETS: Castle battlements; Polonius' room; royal chamber; castle hall; churchyard (with open grave). Unit setting advisable. COSTUMES: Elizabethan, but many adaptations have been used. DIFFICULTIES: Possibly too long; it may be carefully cut. Expert fencing required of 2 actors.

ROYALTY: Public domain. TEXT: Pelican.

—— o ——

TWELFTH NIGHT: OR, WHAT YOU WILL (ca. 1600) WILLIAM SHAKESPEARE. Comedy. Orsino, Duke of Illyria, is blindly in love with his neighbor the Countess Olivia, who will not hear his suit. Orsino sends his page Cesario (the disguised Viola, who has fallen in love with him) to plead his cause; Olivia falls in love with Cesari. Olivia's household includes her uncle, Sir Toby Belch, a sponger and a tippler; his friend, Sir Andrew Aguecheek, a wealthy but preposterous knight who ludicrously hopes to gain Olivia's hand; and Malvolio, her steward, whose ambition causes his downfall. Scenes of intrigue and merriment alternate and interact with the romantic affairs of the aristocrats. Sir Andrew is persuaded, to his terror, to challenge Cesario-Viola to a duel. Viola unwillingly accepts. Meanwhile, her twin brother Sebastian (whom she believes drowned in a shipwreck) arrives in Illyria with Antonio, a sea-captain. Antonio comes upon Viola dueling and, mistaking her for Sebastian, comes to the rescue; Viola cannot render him similar assistance when he is arrested. Olivia now mistakes Sebastian for his disguised sister, and Sebastian falls in love with Olivia. Further complications ensue before identities are unraveled and the play brought to a happy conclusion.

MEN (*11, plus attendants*): 2 are 40–60 (1 is fat, sings; 1 minor); 9 are 18–40 (1 requires an excellent actor, 1 must sing and move very gracefully; 4 minor). WOMEN (*3, plus attendants*): All 18–25 (1 must be fine, boyish comic actress). SETS: Duke's palace; seacoast; Olivia's house; garden; street; exterior of a prison. Unit setting desirable. Realism unnecessary, probably undesirable. COSTUMES: Italian or English Renaissance. More difficult to shift in period than other comedies. DIFFICULTIES: Language highly intricate, needs great care to balance voices and achieve clarity without heaviness. Malvolio may seem to modern audiences badly used and hence gain unintended sympathy.

ROYALTY: Public domain. TEXT: Pelican or Ginn.

—— o ——

ALL'S WELL THAT ENDS WELL (*ca.* 1603) WILLIAM SHAKESPEARE. Comedy. Helena is the daughter of a famous physician who, at his death, left her his prescriptions; she is now the ward of the Countess of Rousillon and has secretly fallen in love with the countess' son Bertram. Bertram is called away to the Court of France. Her melancholy reveals Helena's love to the Countess, who is in favor of the match. Helena believes she can cure the king's illness with a rare prescription, and goes to Paris. The king is indeed cured; in recompense Helena demands the hand in marriage of the courtier of her choice. The king agrees, and Helena chooses Bertram. In spite of Bertram's objection, the king forces him to comply. Immediately after the ceremony Bertram flees to the Italian wars. He then imposes conditions which would seem to make it impossible for Helena to regain him; but he has not reckoned with her ingenuity. The success of Helena's scheme is apparent only after she is believed dead and Bertram has repented.

MEN (*10, plus attendants, soldiers*): 5 are 18–25 (1 minor); 5 are 40–60 (1 minor, 1 should sing). WOMEN (*6*): 2 are 18–25; 4 are 40–60 (2 minor, 1 should be exceptional character actress). SETS: Rousillon; Paris; Florence; Marseilles. A rampart is needed for Florentine scene, a throne room in Paris. Rapid shifts of action suggest a unit setting that can be quickly modified. COSTUMES: Elizabethan, with simple modifications to distinguish Italian and French. Soldiers are dressy, not battle-scarred. DIFFICULTIES: Language sometimes difficult enough to obscure sense. Plot is elaborate but amusing. Unless Bertram is very young and high-spirited, Helena's pursuit will seem absurd.

ROYALTY: Public domain. TEXT: Pelican.

—— o ——

MEASURE FOR MEASURE (*ca.* 1604) WILLIAM SHAKESPEARE. Comedy. Because he wants a firsthand view of the workings of justice in his own domain, the Duke Vincentio assigns the governing power of the city of Vienna to the deputy Angelo, a man who is scrupulous in administering the law. Angelo's first official act is to decree death for Claudio, guilty of sleeping with a woman he is unable to marry. When this is followed by a proclamation to raze all the brothels in the city, the prosperous world of bawds, pimps, and whores—represented by Mistress Overdone, Pompey, and Lucio—is threatened by ruin. A much more serious threat faces the novice Isabella when she pleads with Angelo to save the life of her brother Claudio. Angelo's adamant moral stand crumbles as he discovers he desires Isabella, and he offers her brother's life in exchange for possessing her. Aghast at this choice, Isabella tells her brother he must die and is even more horrified when he suggests his death might be a more fearful thing than her dishonor. Resolution of the dilemma comes from the ever-present figure of the Duke in disguise. Though Angelo deserves the death he has ordered for Claudio, the beneficent Duke manages to prevent Angelo's wicked intents from becoming wicked deeds; justice based on measure for measure must be tempered with mercy. The play ends in a triple marriage.

MEN (*17, plus attendants*): 3 are 40–60 (minor); 14 are 20–40 (1 must be a highly competent actor, 1 a capable clown, 4 are low comedians, 5 minor, 1 boy sings). WOMEN (*5, plus attendants*): 1 is 40–60; 4 are 20–30 (1 must be exceptional actress, 3 minor). SETS: Interior of Duke's palace; the street; a monastery; a nunnery; hall in Angelo's house; a prison, interior and exterior; moated grange; city gate. Unit setting strongly recommended. Vienna is specified but exact locale relatively unimportant. COSTUMES: Jacobean; period can be shifted in both place and time. Modern dress not advisable. DIFFICULTIES: Extremely delicate balance of comedy and seriousness. Play tends to fall into 2 parts unless carefully held together by the figure of the Duke.

ROYALTY: Public domain. TEXT: Pelican.

— o —

OTHELLO, THE MOOR OF VENICE (*ca.* 1604) WILLIAM SHAKESPEARE. Tragedy. Iago, passed over for promotion in the Venetian army in favor of a younger man, Cassio, determines to avenge himself on his commander, Othello, a Moorish nobleman. Iago's evil knows no limits in his plot to destroy the generous-hearted and unsuspecting general. Othello has secretly married Desdemona, whom he loves, and Iago chooses to play upon a weakness he discerns in his master—jealousy— with all his resources of cunning and insinuation. He uses as his pawns Cassio and Roderigo, a nobleman who was formerly a suitor of Desdemona, to besmirch her reputation. Othello falls into the trap Iago sets for him, becoming obsessively jealous and ready to believe anything he is told about his wife's reputation. To cover himself, Iago now sets his dupes against each other, causing the deaths of all but Cassio. Meanwhile, Othello has smothered Desdemona, and the revelation of Iago's wickedness and his own credulity compels him to suicide. Discovered, Iago is put to death.

MEN (*8*): 6 are 35–50 (2 require outstanding actors, 4 minor); 2 are 60–70 (minor). WOMEN (*3*): 2 are 20–30 (1 is minor); 1 is 45 and must be outstanding. SETS: Settings need not be realistic (ramps and pylons can be used to suggest expansiveness and restriction in space which would complement the dramatic action). Not readily adaptable to arena staging. Street in Venice; council chamber; seaport in Cyprus; hall in a castle; bedchamber. Brabantio's house must have a practical upper-story window. COSTUMES: 16th-century Italian court and military costumes.

ROYALTY: Public domain. TEXT: Cambridge.

— o —

KING LEAR (*ca.* 1605) WILLIAM SHAKESPEARE. Tragedy. King Lear is a headstrong and arrogant old man who decides to divide his kingdom among his three daughters, reserving the largest share to the one who loves him most. Unable to distinguish between eloquent flattery and sincere love, he banishes the honest Cordelia, his youngest daughter, and awards the realm to Goneril and Regan. These two "gilded serpents" now combine to strip him of every dignity and possession, making no more pretense of affection. Lear is gradually struck by madness, but in his complete destitution begins to know himself as a human being. Like Lear, Gloucester is also blind to the evil he has fathered—in his bastard son Edmund; he perceives the truth only after he has been literally blinded and later saved from despair and suicide by his son Edgar, disguised as a madman. Evil does its worst to both Lear and Gloucester, but in the wake of physical destruction comes spiritual regeneration.

MEN (*20, plus attendants; doubling possible*): 14 are 20–40 (6 minor, 1 must sing); 6 are 40–60 (1 must be an exceptional actor; 3 minor). WOMEN (*3*): All 20–40. SETS: Lear's palace; Gloucester's castle; Albany's palace; adjoining courtyard; open heath and hovel; Dover fields; British camp. Unit setting almost essential. DIFFICULTIES: Heavy dependence on a magnificent actor for title role. Great care necessary in setting Lear's real insanity against Edgar's feigned Poor Tom and the Fool's professional foolishness. The blinding of Gloucester must be carefully placed to keep physical horror from revolting audience.

ROYALTY: Public domain. TEXT: Pelican.

— o —

ANTONY AND CLEOPATRA (*ca.* 1606) WILLIAM SHAKESPEARE. Tragedy. Antony, the "triple pillar" of the Roman world, is bewitched by the charms of the Queen of Egypt. Stung by the news of his wife's death and rebellion in Rome, he determines to break with Cleopatra and returns to make an uneasy peace with Lepidus and Octavius Caesar. But even marriage to Caesar's sister, Octavia, cannot long keep Antony from Egypt and his pleasure. The enraged Octavius moves his fleet swiftly to Egypt; Antony's ill-advised decision to fight at sea brings disaster at Actium. Ultimate defeat, however, comes not from superior military power but from Antony's moral disintegration and consequent loss of his powers as general and leader. Deserted by his men, betrayed by the queen, his suicide is a long agony. Cleopatra chooses to die rather than submit to the shame of being led through the streets of Rome. (See Dryden's play on the same theme; page 92.)

MEN (30, plus attendants; doubling possible): 5 are 40–60 (1 requires an exceptional actor); 25 are 20–40. WOMEN (4, plus attendants): 1 is about 40 (must be exceptional actress); 3 are 18–25 (comparatively minor). SETS: Various places in the Roman Empire. Unit setting desirable because of swift changes of scene. Must have shipboard set and a monument with playing area above. COSTUMES: Roman and Egyptian or Elizabethan with Roman ornamentation. DIFFICULTIES: Technical problem of lifting the dying Antony up to the monument. Rhythm of the last 2 acts is extremely complicated. ROYALTY: Public domain. TEXT: Pelican.

—— o ——

MACBETH (ca. 1606) WILLIAM SHAKESPEARE. Tragedy. With full knowledge of the consequences, Macbeth murders King Duncan, an honored guest in Macbeth's castle. Though tantalized by the Witches and goaded savagely by Lady Macbeth, Macbeth himself takes the fatal steps that lead to Duncan's chamber, the murder, and to the living hell of the days that follow. The crown is his, but Macbeth has murdered his own conscience. Haunted by his act, Macbeth keeps a spy in every noble house. Suspected by Banquo, a fellow general in the Scottish army, Macbeth murders him, but is unmanned when he sees Banquo's bloody ghost. Guilt and despair drive Lady Macbeth to suicide, but Macbeth must play out his damnation to the end. Macduff, a nobleman, together with Malcolm, Duncan's son, at last lead the ravaged Scots to victory. Macbeth, deserted by his followers and bereft of the belief in his vulnerability, is killed.

MEN (21, plus attendants; doubling difficult): 10 are 30–50

(1 requires exceptional talent and energy, 7 are minor); 10 are 20–30; 1 is a boy. WOMEN (*6, plus attendants*): 3 are 20–40 (1 must be strong); 3 witches of indeterminate age; men may be used. Hecate usually cut as later interpolation. SETS: 12th-century Scottish or Elizabethan. Open heath; interior of Duncan's palace; interior of Macbeth's castle; courtyard; park; English courtyard; interior and exterior at Dunsinane Castle; field for battle. Unit setting strongly recommended for rapid action of the play. Floor trap and special lighting for witches, apparitions, and Banquo's ghost. COSTUMES: Ancient Scottish or Elizabethan; assorted rags for witches; swords should be carefully selected for fighting. DIFFICULTIES: All fighting should be carefully planned and rehearsed to make credible Macbeth's physical prowess. The tension of the play seems to relax drastically after the banquet scene, but the major focus of play's action is on last part.

ROYALTY: Public domain. TEXT: Pelican.

—— o ——

THE WINTER'S TALE (*ca.* 1610) WILLIAM SHAKESPEARE. Comedy. Leontes, King of Sicilia, unreasonably suspects his wife Hermione of infidelity with Polixenes, Leontes' boyhood friend. Leontes' passion is unreasonable and obsessive, and he seeks to poison his friend. Polixenes escapes, and the king's jealousy is concentrated on Hermione, whom he throws into prison. A child now born to Hermione is disowned by the king, who commands that it be abandoned. The Delphic Oracle proclaims Hermione's innocence. Leontes is not convinced until the death of his heir and the reported death of his wife. The abandoned child, Perdita, survives and is, years later, courted by Prince Florizel of Bohemia; the King of Bohemia opposes the supposedly unequal match. The lovers flee to Sicilia, and a happy solution occurs.

MEN (*13*): 2 are 10–20 (minor); 7 are 20–40 (3 require outstanding actors, 4 are minor); 4 are 40–60 (1 requires an outstanding actor, 3 are minor). WOMEN (*5*): 1 is 10–20 (minor); 3 are 20–40 (1 requires an outstanding actress, 2 are minor); 1 is 50–60 (minor). SETS: Leontes' palace; a prison; a seaport in Sicilia; Bohemia; a shepherd's cottage; a chapel. Sets should not be realistic. Production demands an imaginative use of setting and lighting because of the fairy-tale charm of the play; for this reason it is best suited to proscenium staging. COSTUMES: Elizabethan court costumes; rustic costumes for the pastoral scenes. DIFFICULTIES: The verse is extremely complicated and difficult to phrase.

ROYALTY: Public domain. TEXT: Pelican.

—— o ——

THE TEMPEST (*ca.* 1611) WILLIAM SHAKESPEARE. Comedy. Prospero, banished from power in Milan by his scheming brother, the King of Naples, establishes dominion over an enchanted island. His deep absorption in study, the cause of his downfall as a worldly ruler, has ironically enabled him to wrest control of the island, through benign magic, from the witch Sycorax. Serving Prospero and his daughter, Miranda, are the delicate spirit Ariel and the monstrous son of Sycorax, Caliban. By raising a tempest, Prospero succeeds in wrecking on the shore of the island a ship carrying his old enemies. Though tempted to revenge his wrongs, Prospero uses his art to heal old wounds, effecting a match between his daughter and Ferdinand, son of his enemy. Caliban, in league with a drunken butler and a jester, attempts to kill Prospero. His plot is foiled. Prospero breaks his staff, casts his books into the sea, promises to free Ariel and return to the world of men.

MEN (*14, plus attendant spirits and dancers, mariners*): 7 are 40–60 (1 must be an extraordinary actor); 7 are 18–35 (Ariel must move with grace—girl can be cast, if necessary). WOMEN (*4*): All 18–30 (the 3 goddesses are minor, but they should sing). SETS: First scene on board ship, which sinks. All other scenes on the magic island, including Prospero's cell. Special effects for masquelike entertainment. COSTUMES: Great latitude in period and imagination for Ariel, Caliban, magic shapes. Court costumes Italian Renaissance. Clowns need butler and jester garments. DIFFICULTIES: Magnificent but difficult language, ornate but seldom directly dramatic. Long expository scene between Prospero and Miranda inherently static. Magic disappearances and dance must be smoothly managed.

ROYALTY: Public domain. TEXT: Shakespeare, *Comedies* (Random), Vol. I.

—— o ——

RALPH ROISTER DOISTER (*ca.* 1540) NICHOLAS UDALL. Comedy. The braggart soldier Ralph Roister Doister attempts to woo wealthy widow Dame Custance, although she is already affianced to someone else. Roister Doister is convinced (wrongly) that Dame Custance secretly loves him. He sends her a letter of proposal, which his friend, Mathewe Merygreeke, reads to her in such a way as to convey a meaning directly opposite the original intention. Merygreeke then suggests that Roister Doister take a more forceful approach in his wooing, since Dame Custance is sure to be impressed by his manly prowess. In the struggle that ensues, Roister Doister and his company are repulsed by Dame Custance and her servants; Merygreeke aids the widow while pretending to help his friend. The play ends with Dame Custance still firmly affianced to her merchant but reconciled to Roister Doister, who is now regarded merely as a source of amusement.

MEN (*11; some can be cut*): 5 are 30–40 (1 is minor); 3 are servants of indeterminate age (2 minor); 3 are musicians of indeterminate age (no lines but should be able to play musical instruments). WOMEN (*4*): 2 are 20–30 (minor); 1 is 30–40; 1 is 40–60. SET: Area or street in front of Dame Custance's house. Platform stage or arena staging appropriate. Set need not be realistic. COSTUMES: Medieval or Elizabethan English; 1 military uniform of the period. DIFFICULTIES: Rhymed verse. Talky.

ROYALTY: Public domain. TEXT: *Minor Elizabethan Drama* (Dutton), Vol. II.

— o —

GAMMER GURTON'S NEEDLE (*ca.* 1575) ANONYMOUS. Farce. While patching the breeches of Hodge, her manservant, Gammer Gurton loses her precious needle. Prankster Diccon the Bedlam hears of the loss and mischievously tells Gammer Gurton that her neighbor, Dame Chat, has found the needle but won't return it. Diccon meanwhile tells Chat that Gammer Gurton believes Chat has stolen a rooster from her and cooked it. A fight ensues and the curate is called in to mediate. Diccon succeeds in confusing the curate and having him beaten by Chat and her servants, who mistake him for Hodge. Gammer Gurton suspects various people in turn of having stolen the needle, which is painfully found (in the fifth act) by Hodge, in the seat of the breeches themselves, when he receives a blow.

MEN (*6; some can be cut*): 3 are 15–25 (2 minor, 1 has no lines); 3 are 30–45 (1 minor). WOMEN (*4*): 2 are 16–25 (1 minor); 2 are 30–50. SETS: Street or area before the houses of Gammer Gurton and Dame Chat. Proscenium, platform stage and arena staging are appropriate. Sets need not be realistic. COSTUMES: Medieval or Elizabethan English. DIFFICULTIES: Archaic language and rhymed verse.

ROYALTY: Public domain. TEXT: *Anthology of English Drama Before Shakespeare* (Rinehart).

—— o ——

THE WHITE DEVIL (1611) JOHN WEBSTER. Tragedy. Visiting the home of Camillo and Vittoria Corombona, the famous Venetian courtesan, the Duke of Brachiano falls in love with Vittoria; aided by Vittoria's pandering brother, Flamineo, he engages in an illicit intrigue with her. The duke's wife Isabella attempts a reconciliation with her husband at the home of her brother, the Duke of Florence, but paid assassins go into action and the torturous revenge tragedy careens from murder to murder (involving broken necks, poison, stabbings, and strangulation) until Brachiano, Vittoria, Flamineo, Isabella, and several others lie dead. This melodramatic story is filled with mental and physical horror, corruption, and both amorous and political intrigue. *The White Devil* has the fascination of a first-rate psychological thriller, told in Elizabethan poetry that is cold, taut, and brilliantly nightmarish.

MEN (*20*): 1 boy of about 10, the rest 20–40. Requires at least 4 excellent actors. Others must be able to move well and handle difficult verse. Good voices and agile bodies an absolute necessity. WOMEN (*5*): 1 character role, age perhaps 50, the rest 20–40 (including a Moorish maid). 3 excellent actresses needed—1 goes mad, the others have long, difficult scenes to carry and theatrical death scenes to negotiate. EXTRAS: Mostly male; females needed for ladies-in-waiting, guests, and so on. Several important nonspeaking roles. Some doubling possible. Pantomime important in several scenes involving minor characters. SETS: Venetian palaces; courtrooms; halls; unspecified areas. Unit setting best. COSTUMES: Lavish gowns, robes, monks' habits, ecclesiastical vestments. DIFFICULTIES: Verse is difficult; special properties and weapons required for spectacular effects; requires many live sound effects.

ROYALTY: Public domain. TEXT: *Webster and Tourneur* (Hill and Wang).

—— o ——

THE DUCHESS OF MALFI (1612)   JOHN WEBSTER. Tragedy.   An especially powerful study of unconventional virtue, suffering, and fantastic revenge within a single family. Motivated by avarice and family pride, the Cardinal and the Duke of Calabria do not want their widowed sister, the Duchess of Malfi, to marry again. They persuade her to hire Daniel de Bosola, a murderous spy, as her purveyor of cavalry. The Duchess and Antonio, master of the household, have a secret alliance, and in time a child is born. Bosola informs the absent brothers of the birth but cannot give the name of the father. The brothers resolve to avenge their family honor. Several years later the brothers kill the Duchess, her maid, and two of the three children she now has from her secret marriage with Antonio. Both Bosola and the Duke of Calabria suffer extreme pangs of conscience. The Duke goes insane; the Cardinal plots Bosola's murder; and in a final melee, Antonio and the three villains all receive death wounds. A bloody but fascinating study of evil, darkness, perversion, corruption, horror, and suffering—a true nightmare reflecting a strange, uncharted side of human relationships in a decaying society.

MEN (*20*): 1 young boy; rest 20–50 (3 excellent actors with some knowledge of weapons). WOMEN (*4*): All 20–50. (1 very sympathetic actress for the role of the Duchess). EXTRAS: As needed. SETS: Early 16th-century Italian. Unit set preferable. COSTUMES: Early 16th-century Italian.

ROYALTY: Public domain. TEXT: *Webster and Tourneur* (Hill and Wang).

Restoration and Eighteenth Century

LOVE FOR LOVE (1695) WILLIAM CONGREVE. Comedy. The prodigal son Valentine agrees in a misguided moment to relinquish his inheritance to his brother Ben if their father, Sir Sampson Legend, will pay off his debts. Ben has been brought back from the sea to marry the naïve Miss Prue, daughter of the superstitious and illiterate Foresight. Ben wants no part of her or of the fashionable society of London. Valentine, in love with Foresight's wealthy niece Angelica, pretends madness to forestall his father's attempts to disinherit him. The amusing byplay between the lovers is resolved as Angelica, pretending to agree to marry Sir Sampson, accepts Valentine when he proves his devotion to her. A number of other interesting characters elaborate the plot. Witty dialogue and sparkling characterizations result in an entertaining play.

MEN (*10*): 7 are 20–35 (2 must sing); 3 are 45–60. WOMEN (*6*): 4 are 18–25; 2 are 30–45. EXTRAS: Several walk-ons, including sailors who dance, and a singer. Some doubling possible. SETS: Valentine's lodgings; Foresight's house; Miss Prue's bedchamber and an adjoining gallery; some combining possible. Wing and drop; shutters; unit, arena productions possible. COSTUMES: Late Restoration, mostly fashionable; sailor dress.

ROYALTY: Public domain. TEXT: *William Congreve, Complete Plays* (Hill and Wang).

—— o ——

THE WAY OF THE WORLD (1700) WILLIAM CONGREVE. Comedy. This intricately plotted play concerns the wooing of Millamant by Mirabell and the resulting compromise achieved in face of the way of the world in which they live. The dramatic high point is the famous "bargaining" scene wherein the lovers set forth the conditions that will make their union mutually tolerable. Fainall's love for Mrs. Marwood and the amorous relationships of Mrs. Marwood, Mrs. Fainall, and Millamant to Mirabell greatly complicate the plot. This play is considered by many the high-water mark of Restoration comedy; it is, in any event, one of the masterpieces of English dramatic literature. The prose style is dazzling and the wit brilliant.

MEN (6): All 20–30. WOMEN (9): 8 are 18–25 (4 minor; 1 is a singer); 1 is 40–50. EXTRAS: Footmen; attendants; dancers of both sexes. SETS: A chocolate house; St. James's Park; a room in Lady Wishfort's house. Wing and drop or shutters most effective. Unit, box, arena production also possible. COSTUMES: Late 17th-century English, highly fashionable; riding habit for Sir Wilfull. DIFFICULTIES: Requires consistently high level of stylized acting.

ROYALTY: Public domain. TEXT: Barron's.

— o —

ALL FOR LOVE (1667) JOHN DRYDEN. Tragedy. One of the landmarks of blank-verse Restoration tragedy. The plot is substantially the same as that of Shakespeare's *Antony and Cleopatra* (see p. 84), with action restricted to a single locale and a single day. Despite major limitations, a loftiness of writing and integrity of conception lift the play to some moments of grandeur.

MEN (6): All 30–60. WOMEN (4): All 20–40. EXTRAS: 2 very young daughters of Antony; priest; servants; gentlemen; musicians; soldiers; Egyptians; dancers (many can be doubled). SET: The Temple of Isis. Style would depend on manner of production. Arena unsuitable. COSTUMES: Historical Roman and Egyptian, or Restoration stage version of this period. DIFFICULTIES: Casting and costume problems; requires dancers and musicians.

ROYALTY: Public domain. TEXT: Barron's.

— o —

THE MAN OF MODE, OR SIR FOPLING FLUTTER (1676) GEORGE ETHEREGE. Comedy. Man-about-town Dorimant is in the process of replacing his mistress, Lady Loveit, with Bellinda. He is interested to learn that he is loved by a rich country woman, Harriet Woodvill. Dorimant's friend, Young Bellair, loves Emilia but is being pressured by his father to marry Harriet. Old Bellair then meets Emilia and, not knowing who she is, falls in love with her himself and wants to marry her. Harriet and Young Bellair meet and realize they do not love each other, but they put on a convincing scene to disarm the parents. The foolish Sir Fopling Flutter, the play's most interesting character, accuses Lady Loveit of infidelity and thus enables Dorimant to break off their affair. Dorimant comes to a party, disguised, to woo Harriet. In the early hours of the morning Dorimant hurries home for a rendezvous with Bellinda, who is later mistakenly carried by sedan chair to Lady Loveit's lodgings. When Dorimant arrives he announces his intention to marry Harriet, Young Bellair and Emilia are subsequently married, and everybody is reconciled by the final curtain. The play's faults are redeemed by its wit, realistic portrayal of contemporary manners, and delineation of the Restoration fop.

MEN (*14–18*): 4 are 20–30; 2 are 40–60 (8–12 extras are 20–60). WOMEN (*9*): 4 are 18–25; 2 are 40–50 (3 extras of various ages). SETS: 11 separate locations, involving 5 interiors and 1 exterior. Wing and drop; shutters; unit. Arena production not recommended. COSTUMES: Fashionable Restoration. DIFFICULTIES: Disciplined, stylized acting required.

ROYALTY: Public domain. TEXT: *Six Restoration Plays* (Houghton Mifflin).

—— o ——

THE BEAUX' STRATAGEM (1706) GEORGE FARQUHAR. Comedy. Aimwell and Archer, in a scheme to marry into money, disguise themselves as master and servant. At an inn run by Bonniface and his daughter Cherry they learn of Lady Bountiful, her daughter Dorinda and son Sullen. Aimwell woos Dorinda, wins her, and learns later that he has inherited a fortune from the viscount brother he has been impersonating. Meanwhile, Archer carries on flirtations with Cherry and Mrs. Sullen. The plot is further complicated by the presence of a French prisoner and several highwaymen. A good example of the so-called transition play, this one wavers between the cynical attitude toward sex and marriage of the earlier Restoration and the sentimental one of the later 18th century.

An exuberant, lusty, and refreshing piece. The suggestion of a separation or divorce as a solution for the unhappily married Sullens strikes a modern note.

MEN (*11*): 9 are 20–30 (2 must sing); 2 are 40–60. WOMEN (*5*): 4 are 18–25; 1 is 40–60. EXTRAS: 4–6 walk-ons, male and female; some doubling possible. SETS: Scenes alternate between an inn, a gallery, and a bedchamber in Lady Bountiful's house. Wing and drop; shutters; unit. Arena production possible. COSTUMES: Late Restoration or Queen Anne; fashionable and rural; some wigs; riding habit.

ROYALTY: Public Domain. TEXT: *Farquhar, Four Plays* (Hill and Wang).

— o —

THE CLANDESTINE MARRIAGE (1766) DAVID GARRICK and GEORGE COLMAN. Comedy. Sterling, an avaricious merchant, is the father of Fanny and Miss Sterling. He hopes to match Miss Sterling with Sir John Melvil and realize a handsome settlement. Sir John, however, falls in love with Fanny—who is secretly married to Lovewell. The elderly and foppish Lord Ogleby, Sir John's uncle, also falls in love with Fanny. Each suitor offers Sterling increasingly better financial terms for Fanny's hand, and he is prepared to sacrifice his daughters' happiness for social position. Fanny is closeted with her husband, while the principals enter the hall, outside, in turn, convinced that Fanny is dishonoring herself with Sir John. There is general astonishment when Sir John himself enters, but the mystery is dispelled when Fanny and Lovewell appear and reveal their clandestine marriage. The elders quickly forgive the couple and the play closes on an indulgent and happy note.

MEN (*9*): 2 are about 60 (1 has a French accent); 2 are about 40; 1 is 25; 4 are 25–40. WOMEN (*6*): 1 is 40; 5 are 18–25 (2 are minor). SETS: Various locations in and about Sterling's house, involving 10 changes. Can be handled simply with wing and drop, shutters, or unit set. COSTUMES: Fashionable dress of the period.

ROYALTY: Public domain. TEXT: *Famous Plays of the Restoration and Eighteenth Century* (Random).

— o —

THE BEGGAR'S OPERA (1728) JOHN GAY. Ballad Opera.
In a colorful low-life London, peopled with thieves and trol-
lops, the dashing highwayman Macheath flirts with the ladies
and the law. Macheath, secretly married to Polly Peachum, is
wanted by the police. Polly's parents, greedy for the reward,
arrange his capture. He escapes but is recaptured. Lucy
Lockit, the prisonkeeper's daughter, is also in love with Macheath, and he promises to marry her to escape hanging. His
plan goes awry and he is led off to the gallows. At the last
moment the beggar-author rewrites the ending and Macheath
is reprieved. This witty satire on public corruption and Italian
opera makes use of popular folk tunes but is essentially dramatic rather than musical in form.

MEN (*14*): All 25–60 (3 major; 1 is 25–30; 2 are 50–60).
WOMEN (*12*): All 18–50 (3 major; 1 is 40–50; 2 are 18–25).
EXTRAS: Various children, men, and women as desired. SETS:
7 different locations; can be suggested very simply. Wing and
drop; unit. Arena not recommended. COSTUMES: Early 18th-
century English, 1 fashionable; others middle-class and rags.
DIFFICULTIES: Requires a cast of good actor-singers. There
are 69 songs, some very short, which should be done simply.
Can be sung without accompaniment, with piano, or with a
small instrumental ensemble. An overture is called for. Several dances required.
ROYALTY: Public domain. TEXT: *Famous Plays of the Restoration and Eighteenth Century* (Random).

—— o ——

SHE STOOPS TO CONQUER (1773) OLIVER GOLDSMITH.
Comedy. Young Marlow and Kate Hardcastle, matched by
their parents, have never met. Marlow and his friend Hastings,
on their way to the Hardcastles, are directed to the house by
the prankster Tony Lumpkin, Mrs. Hardcastle's son by an
earlier marriage. They are deceived into thinking the house
an inn and treat Hardcastle as landlord and Kate as a maid.
Kate takes advantage of the misunderstanding to break down
Marlow's reserve. Hastings and Miss Neville, Mrs. Hardcastle's niece, plan an elopement and are abetted by Tony. A
covey of inept servants adds to the merriment, and the mistakes of the night are pleasantly corrected at the final tableau.

MEN (*13–15*): 3 are 20–25; 2 are 40–60; 8–10 are 20–60

(servants, landlord, etc. Most minor; some doubling possible).
WOMEN (4): 3 are 18–25 (1 minor); 1 is 40–60. SETS: Scene
rotation includes a room in Hardcastle's house; a tavern; the
back of the garden. Sets may be semirealistic or stylized. Wing
and drop; unit. Has also been effective in arena. COSTUMES:
Late 18th-century English; generally rural dress; several wigs.

ROYALTY: Public domain. TEXT: Barron's.

—— o ——

THE LONDON MERCHANT (1731)   GEORGE LILLO. Tragedy.   George Barnwell, a young London merchant, falls prey
to the wiles of the villainous seductress Millwood, and at her
urging robs his master and kills his uncle. Justice asserts itself
when, after various exhibitions of remorse and defiance,
George and Millwood are apprehended and sentenced to
death. The characters are conventional, stilted, and include
such types as Thorowgood, the noble merchant; his long-
suffering daughter Maria, in love with George; Trueman, the
faithful friend; and Lucy, the evil confidante turned honest.
Sentimentality of character, situation, and language steep the
play in bathos, making it difficult for modern audiences to
take seriously.

MEN (13): 2 are 18–20; 2 are 40–60; 9 are 20–40 (most
minor; some doubling possible). WOMEN (3): 1 is 16–20; 2
are 20–25. SETS: Various rooms in houses of Thorowgood
and Millwood; a walk; a prison room; a dungeon. Settings
need not be realistic. Wing and drop most suitable. Unit set
possible; proscenium recommended. COSTUMES: Early 18th-
century English; middle-class. DIFFICULTIES: Temptation to
burlesque the text. The play would probably fare best in the
advanced educational theatre.

ROYALTY: Public domain. TEXT: *Eighteenth-Century Plays*
(Random).

—— o ——

COMUS (1634)   JOHN MILTON. Masque.   Dramatization in
the form of a moral allegory of the conflict between sensuality and chastity. Comus, offspring of Bacchus and Circe,
discovers a lady lost in a wood. Enchanted by her song, he
disguises himself as a villager and leads her to his castle under
the pretext of helping her find her brothers, who meanwhile
search in vain in the forest. The Attendant Spirit enters and

tells them how the lady is to be saved. The brothers and the Attendant Spirit disrupt a moral debate at the castle and save the lady, as Comus escapes. The principals are taken to Ludlow Castle and presented to Neptune and his queen, played by the Earl and Countess of Bridgewater. Probably the greatest English masque.

MEN (*4*): All 20–30. WOMEN (*2*): Both 18–25. EXTRAS: Various men and women, singers and dancers (some doubling possible). SETS: Wild wood; palace; the Lord President's castle at Ludlow. Settings should be fanciful and elaborate. Wings and painted drops most easily adapted. COSTUMES: Classical, allegorical; see the design reproductions of Inigo Jones, Jacobean stage designer, for this work (available in larger-library collections). DIFFICULTIES: Elaborate scenic effects; play not full length; nature of material unfamiliar and stylistically difficult.

ROYALTY: Public domain. TEXT: Penguin.

— o —

THE RIVALS (1775) RICHARD BRINSLEY SHERIDAN. Comedy. Lydia Languish, the wealthy, sentimental heroine whose fortune is dependent upon the whims of her aunt, Mrs. Malaprop, is in love with Captain Jack Absolute, alias Ensign Beverley. Sir Anthony Absolute meets with Mrs. Malaprop in an attempt to match his son with Lydia. The elders agree but confusion of identities leads to many comic incidents. Parallel plots involve the bumbling Bob Acres, in love with Lydia; the tempestuous Irishman Sir Lucius O'Trigger, who carries on an amorous but mistaken correspondence with Mrs. Malaprop; and a sentimental second pair of lovers, Faulkland and Julia. The play vacillates between high comedy and farce as it pokes not always gentle fun at excessive sentimentality. Mrs. Malaprop's ludicrous distortions of the language make her one of the most famous characters in English drama.

MEN (*9*): 2 are 20–25; 2 are 40–60; 4 are 20–60 (3 minor); 1 boy is 6–10 (has 2 lines). WOMEN (*4*): 3 are 16–25; 1 is 40–60. SETS: 12 scenes: 3 streets in Bath; the lodgings of Mrs. Malaprop, Captain Absolute, Julia, and Bob Acres; King's Mead-Fields. Simple stylized sets most effective; set pieces, wing and drop, unit. Best in formal theatrical frame, but can be done in an arena if set changes managed efficiently.

COSTUMES: Late 18th-century English; fashionable and military; some wigs. DIFFICULTIES: Some obscure topical material; Irish dialect.

ROYALTY: Public domain. TEXT: Barron's.

—— o ——

THE SCHOOL FOR SCANDAL (1777) RICHARD BRINSLEY SHERIDAN. Comedy. Lady Sneerwell and her entourage of scandalmongers set the early tone. Charles Surface, the likable prodigal, is portrayed as a libertine while his brother Joseph is held up as a model of prudence and virtue. Both pursue Maria, ward of Sir Peter Teazle—Charles for her love, Joseph for her money. When uncle Sir Oliver Surface arrives, the brothers are shown in their true light. Charles is redeemed through his sentimental attachment to Sir Oliver's portrait, and Joseph is caught in an embarrassing intrigue with Lady Teazle in a celebrated scene. Charles is rewarded with Maria's hand, and the Sneerwell clan is unmasked. The play has superb characterizations, brilliant dialogue, and skillful plot.

MEN (*12*): 8 are 20–30 (1 must sing); 4 are 40–60. WOMEN (*4*): All 20–30. EXTRAS: 3–4 men; a maid. SETS: 7 different interiors require 10 changes but can be handled simply with wing and drop or unit arrangement. Revolving stage or wagons useful. Stylization effective. Arena not recommended unless changes unusually easily managed. COSTUMES: Fashionable late 18th-century English; wigs.

ROYALTY: Public domain. TEXT: Barron's.

—— o ——

THE CRITIC (1779) RICHARD BRINSLEY SHERIDAN. Comedy. A short play divided into two parts. The first takes place in Dangle's house, where a group of theatre people pass judgment on the current state of the drama and dramatic criticism. Mr. Puff, an author, invites Dangle and Sneer to attend a morning rehearsal of his tragedy, *The Spanish Armada*. In this play-within-a-play Sheridan satirizes the bombast and flamboyance of contemporary tragedy and directs sharp thrusts at well-known theatrical figures. Far more good-natured than vitriolic, the play is filled with highly entertaining bits of dialogue and stage business. It opens with a clock striking "to beget an awful attention in the audience," Tilburnia enters to an accompaniment ("nothing introduces you a heroine like soft music"), and so on to the splendiferous ending.

MEN (20): All 20–60 (1 speaks French, 1 Italian). WOMEN (9): All 18–30 (3 speak Italian and sing). EXTRAS: Knights; guards; constables, sentinels; servants; chorus; "rivers"; attendants; musicians; scene men. Cast according to available personnel (doubling possible). SETS: 2 rooms in Dangle's house, and the stage at Drury Lane set for the tragedy. Dangle's house should be simple; the tragic setting theatrically elaborate. Arena not recommended. COSTUMES: Late 18th-century English and Elizabethan theatrical. DIFFICULTIES: Not full-length. Topical references difficult to cut. Music required (recordings can be used). Large cast.

ROYALTY: Public domain. TEXT: Barron's.

— o —

THE PROVOK'D WIFE (1697)   JOHN VANBRUGH. Comedy. The play opens with a soliloquy in which boorish, bored Sir John Brute complains of his married state. As the plot develops we watch Lady Brute encourage the attentions of her admirer, Constant. Simultaneously, a relationship develops between Lady Brute's niece Bellinda and Constant's friend Heartfree. An affected neighbor, Lady Fancifull, is also in love with Heartfree and tries to force her attentions on him. Her lady-in-waiting, Mademoiselle, adds considerable humor in a farcical amorous scene with Sir John's valet, Rasor. Although Lady Brute is involved in a number of compromising situations, Sir John is not cuckolded and husband and wife are presumably reconciled at the final curtain. The chief merits of the play are in the vitality of the writing and characterization.

MEN (10): All 20–40 (3 required to sing). WOMEN (6): All 18–30 (2 minor); 1 servant sings. EXTRAS: 8–10 men needed as servants, footmen, and the like (some doubling possible). SETS: 10 different locations involve 14 set changes. These should be suggestive and handled simply. Wing and drop or unit set effective. Arena not advisable. COSTUMES: Fashionable late 17th-century English; wigs.

ROYALTY: Public domain. TEXT: *Twelve Famous Plays of the Restoration and Eighteenth Century* (Random).

— o —

THE PLAIN DEALER (1666) WILLIAM WYCHERLEY. Comedy. Manly, the rough and outspoken captain, has returned from sea. Bitterly disillusioned by the dishonesty and infidelity he has found in London, he places his last measure of trust in his friend Vernish and his mistress Olivia. When they deceive him by marrying, Manly's fury drives him near madness. He turns to practicing the very evils he had previously scorned as he plans to seduce Olivia in disguise and announce her infidelity to the world. Manly's faith in mankind is somewhat restored through the devotion of his page, Fidelia, who has been disguised as a boy throughout the play. The subplot concerns Freeman, Manly's lieutenant, and his relationship with the litigious Widow Blackacre and her son Jerry. Although much in this play has been borrowed from Molière and Shakespeare, its individuality lies in the author's mordant wit and bitterness.

MEN (*20–25*): All 15–60 (15 minor; considerable doubling possible). WOMEN (*5*): 4 are 18–25 (1 dressed as a boy); 1 is 40–60. SETS: The respective lodgings of Manly, Olivia, and Eliza; Westminster Hall; a tavern and a room in the same. Scenes involve 8 changes. Wing and drop; shutters; or unit. Arena not recommended. COSTUMES: Fashionable Restoration; occupational clothes for servants, sailors, and so on.

ROYALTY: Public domain. TEXT: *British Plays from the Restoration to 1820* (Little, Brown).

— o —

THE COUNTRY WIFE (1675) WILLIAM WYCHERLEY. Comedy. Margery Pinchwife, a naïve country girl, has recently been married and brought to London by her aging, jealous husband who is determined to protect her from the rakes of the town. Horner, an ingenious philanderer, spreads the unfounded rumor that he is a eunuch. Before long, unsuspecting husbands practically throw their wives at him, relieved to know the ladies are having affairs that cannot compromise their honor. Horner, having seen Margery at the theatre, plans a new conquest. Pinchwife, unaware of the rumor, goes to great lengths to have Margery rebuff Horner and gets himself cuckolded for his pains. At the close, Margery almost gives away Horner's secret, but the other ladies present are careful to preserve it and their reputations. This play has great directness and vigor.

MEN (9): 5 are 20–30; 3 are 30–60 (1 has no lines); 1 is a boy, but may be played older. WOMEN (7): 6 are 18–25 (1 must sing); 1 is 60–80. Dancers optional. SETS: Horner's lodging; rooms in Pinchwife's house; the New Exchange; the piazza of Covent Garden. Wing and drop; shutters; or unit. The 10 changes difficult in arena. COSTUMES: Fashionable Restoration; wigs.

ROYALTY: Public domain. TEXT: *Four Great Comedies of the Restoration and Eighteenth Century* (Bantam).

Nineteenth Century

THE MAGISTRATE (1885) ARTHUR WING PINERO. Farce.
A second wife must inform her husband that she had lowered
her age by five years when she married him because her son,
who can be only fourteen years old in the false chronology, is
showing an unusual interest in girls, developing a mustache,
and playing the horses. By a series of improbable circumstances, the new husband—a bumbling but likable magistrate
—finds himself led into a compromising situation by his stepson. The magistrate escapes, but the new wife is involved
quite innocently in a raid on a hotel that sells drinks after
hours, and appears before her husband in court. The family
is reunited happily; when the hirsute fourteen-year-old is told
his real age, he leaves for Canada with a fine new wife, £1000
as a wedding gift (or bribe), and the blessing of his stepfather.
Two scenes in the farce are exceptionally funny: one in which
the husband and wife, unknown to each other, visit in adjoining rooms of the questionable hotel; the other in which
the magistrate, after a night of running from the police, attempts to pull himself together to deliver judgment on the
"criminals" captured in the raid on the hotel. Oscar Wilde
called The Magistrate "the best of all modern comedies."

MEN (12): 2 are 45–50; 2 are 35–40; 1 is 19–20; 7 are of
indefinite age. WOMEN (4): 2 are 19–20; 2 are 30–35. SETS:
Drawing room of the magistrate's house, interior of the hotel,
and the magistrate's room at the police station. COSTUMES:
Late Victorian, but the play could be done in modern dress
with only a few script changes.
ROYALTY: Public domain. TEXT: In From the Modern
Repertoire (Indiana), Ser. III.

THE SECOND MRS. TANQUERAY (1893) ARTHUR WING PINERO. Aubrey Tanqueray, a widower with a daughter, marries Paula Ray, a woman of questionable reputation. They retire to Aubrey's country home and are ostracized by his neighbors. Paula regrets her lurid past, and is dedicated to the daughter Ellean. Mrs. Tanqueray is visited by an old friend and the friend's aristocratic but decadent husband. While this couple is present, Ellean's suitor arrives. Paula recognizes him as a paramour of hers. He leaves, nobly, but Ellean guesses the reason and is horrified by this aspect of her stepmother. Faced with the knowledge that the Tanqueray home is hopelessly divided, Paula kills herself. The shock of her death reveals to Ellean her own responsibility in the affair: "Killed herself? So everybody will say. But I know—I helped her. If I'd only been merciful."

MEN (7): 6 are 50–60; 1 (the young suitor) is 20–30. WOMEN (4): 1 is 50–60; 2 are 35–45; 1 (the daughter) is 20. SETS: Bachelor apartment in The Albany; drawing room in a country house. COSTUMES: Late Victorian.

ROYALTY: Public domain. TEXT: In *An Introduction to Drama* (Macmillan).

—— o ——

CASTE (1867) THOMAS WILLIAM ROBERTSON. Comedy. More accurately described as a "lachrymose" comedy with a strong message, this play deals with the question of social position and its implications. The Honorable George D'Alroy marries an honest actress, Esther Eccles, in spite of the objections of his friend Captain Hawtree and social disapproval of such a misalliance. Soon after the wedding, George leaves for military duty in India and is reported killed. His young wife, who has borne him a son, is victimized by her disreputable father and ignored by her aristocratic mother-in-law, the Marquise de St. Maur. In the last act George suddenly reappears from the war and finds his wife living in poverty but dedicated to raising the boy properly. In the joy of seeing her son still alive, the Marquise suddenly appreciates Esther's virtues, and the aristocratic Hawtree even shakes the hand of a plumber. Neither the aristocratic nor the humble escapes satiric comment in the play. "Caste," says George in the last act, "is a good thing if it's not carried too far. It shuts the door on the pretentious and the vulgar; but it should open the door very wide for exceptional merit. Let brains break through its barrier, and what brains can break through, love may leap over."

MEN (5): 1 is 50–60; 4 are 20–30. Cockney dialect required for plumber role. WOMEN (3): 2 are 20–25; 1 is 60–70. SETS: The humble room of the Eccles family; the elegant Mayfair home of the D'Alroys. COSTUMES: Mid-19th century with 3 in rich and 3 in shabby attire; 2 military uniforms required. DIFFICULTIES: Some dated dialogue.

ROYALTY: Public domain. TEXT: In *Representative British Dramas, Victorian and Modern* (Little, Brown).

—— o ——

THE TICKET-OF-LEAVE MAN (1863) TOM TAYLOR. Melodrama.   Robert Brierly, victim of bad habits and worse companions, helps a starving singer named May Edwards and is about to be redeemed when he is tricked into passing counterfeit bills. Hawkshaw, one of the earliest of stage hero-detectives, arrests him. Brierly serves his time and is released with his ticket-of-leave. May is waiting for him. He gets a job with a Mr. Gibson, and once again is on the edge of redemption when his old companions reveal his prison record. Job after job is lost. In the last act, Brierly tips off the disguised Hawkshaw that Mr. Gibson is to be robbed. The hero and the detective join forces, the criminals are brought to justice, and the pure gold of Brierly's heart is disclosed to all. Music underlines the prevailing mood of the scene, in some cases explicitly in music-hall terms. Most of the characterization is oversimplified, but some of the types who weave in and out are drawn well for comic effect. One of the most successful 19th-century melodramas.

MEN (9): 1 is 20–25 (Brierly); 1 is a "nipper" of 15; 7 are of unspecified ages. WOMEN (3): 1 is 20–25; 1 is 30–35; 1 is 45–55. Some extras. SETS: The Bellevue Tea Gardens; the "humble but neatly furnished" room of May Edwards; Mr. Gibson's brokerage office; the Bridgewater Arms (beer garden); a street in the city; the Churchyard of St. Nicholas. Settings require practical doors, traps and hidden passages.

ROYALTY: Public domain. TEXT: In *Representative British Dramas, Victorian and Modern* (Little, Brown).

—— o ——

CHARLEY'S AUNT (1892) Brandon Thomas. Farce. This still-delightful play concerns two college boys who dress a friend in woman's clothes to impersonate a rich aunt from Brazil. The aunt was to chaperone a tea for the boys and their lady loves, but was delayed. Then, unexpectedly, the real aunt arrives, accompanied by her beautiful ward. The father of one of the boys, Sir Francis Chesney, and Spettigue, the girls' guardian, both attempt to improve their fortunes by proposing to the false aunt while the real aunt looks on. The unmasking finally occurs; the widowed aunt turns out to be an old love of Sir Francis; her ward is the missing love of the suffering masquerader; and the two young ladies admit they are anxious to wed the hosts.

Men (7): 3 are 18–21; 2 are 45–55; and 2 others have no age specification. Women (4): 3 are 17–22; 1 is 40–45. Sets: The college quarters of Jack Chesney; drawing room of the Spettigue house; the garden outside the college rooms. Costumes: Upper class Victorian; liveried servants.

Royalty: $25, Samuel French. Text: Samuel French.

—— o ——

LADY WINDERMERE'S FAN (1892) Oscar Wilde. Comedy. Lady Windermere believes that there is an absolute standard of morality and that anyone who even has the appearance of evil should be avoided. She suddenly finds that her own husband has been seeing a Mrs. Erlynne, a woman of tarnished reputation, and after he insists on having the strange woman invited to the house, Lady Windermere decides to leave him and go away with Lord Darlington. The explanatory note she has left for Lord Windermere falls into the hands of Mrs. Erlynne, who hurries to Darlington's apartment to save the young wife. At this point it is revealed that Mrs. Erlynne is actually Lady Windermere's mother, who herself had made just such a sudden decision. Lady Windermere is persuaded to flee before the return of Darlington and his friends, but leaves her fan behind. The fan is discovered by the men, who draw the obvious conclusion. Mrs. Erlynne appears and tells them that she had borrowed Lady Windermere's fan, plausibly explains her presence in the bachelor's apartment, and receives a proposal from a likable but blundering aristocrat. Lady Windermere has learned that morality and the appearance of morality are not the same. This play contains brilliant examples of Wilde's sparkling dialogue, repartee, and epigrams.

MEN (7): All mature and aristocratic (except Parker, the butler). WOMEN (8): All mature, with enough age difference to make it credible for Mrs. Erlynne to be Lady Windermere's mother. COSTUMES: Late 19th century. SETS: Three Victorian interiors specified, but easily playable in two.

ROYALTY: Public domain. TEXT: Samuel French.

—— o ——

THE IMPORTANCE OF BEING EARNEST (1895) OSCAR WILDE. Comedy. A witty and satirical comedy in which two young men seek the hands of two young ladies in spite of social obstacles. The obstacles are no more serious than the young men: one has very little family background, having been found in a handbag in Waterloo Station; the other has lived a life of indolence for so long that there is some doubt that he has the energy to fall in love. Both face an additional obstacle—their chosen loves can only cherish a man named Ernest, and neither qualifies. A baptism is planned to overcome one of the obstacles, and the others are resolved in a revelation scene in the last act.

MEN (5): 2 are 20–30; 1 is a 50-year-old clergyman; 2 can be any age. WOMEN (4): 2 are 20–25; 1 is 40–45; 1 is 30–40. SETS: Interior of Moncrieff's London flat; exterior of the Worthing garden in Herefordshire; morning room of the Herefordshire house. Suitable for arena staging. COSTUMES: Late Victorian. DIFFICULTIES: The mock-classic form and the bright repartee may cause difficulty for actors accustomed to realistic playing.

ROYALTY: Public domain. TEXT: Samuel French.

—— o ——

EAST LYNNE (1865) MRS. HENRY WOOD. Melodrama. Lady Isabel fears that her husband Archibald's clandestine dealings on behalf of Richard Hare, a fugitive from justice, really mask an affair with Barbara, Richard's sister. She is therefore easily led astray by the unscrupulous Levison, the real perpetrator of Richard's "crime." Later, shamed and deserted, she returns to East Lynne disguised as a governess. There she witnesses her son's death and dies herself in her forgiving husband's arms. The characters are more carefully drawn than is customary in melodrama, but all other qualities are subordinated to lachrymose sentimentality. Miss Cordelia, a snappish old maid with a warm heart, provides touches of humor.

MEN (7): 4 are 20–40; 2 are 40–60; 1 is 60. WOMEN (5): 4 are 20–35; 1 is 30–40. BOY: About 5. SETS: Fashionable chamber at East Lynne, former seat of Lord Mount Severn; a landscape; a dismal room, a bedroom at East Lynne. COSTUMES: Fashionable; servant costumes of crinoline period; policeman's costume.

ROYALTY: Apply Samuel French. TEXT: Samuel French.

Twentieth Century

THE ASCENT OF F6 (1935)   W. H. AUDEN and CHRIS-
TOPHER ISHERWOOD.   F6 is a haunted mountain to be climbed
by Michael Ransom's expedition in this allegory of man's
spiritual quest. Ransom—clearly modeled on T. E. Lawrence
—refuses the mission until his mother confesses she withheld
her love for him throughout his childhood in order to make
him strong enough for just such an honor. Action alternates
between stations on the mountain and England, where news
of the climb evokes spiritual and national pride. In a race for
the summit, three of Ransom's men are killed. Ransom discovers that the legendary Demon of the Mountain exists and
dies on the summit before a vision of his mother as a young
woman. As tribute is paid Ransom's memory back in England,
one character remarks, "In the face of this terrible tragedy
one is almost tempted to believe in the grim old legend of the
Demon."

MEN (*12, plus extras and chorus*): 1 is 25–30 (must be
outstanding); 3 are 25–35; 5 are 40–60; others may be any
age. WOMEN (*3, plus chorus*): 1 is 35–50; 2 are 40–60. SETS:
2 permanent stage boxes; offices; council rooms; levels and
stations of F6. Stylized staging essential; arena production
possible. COSTUMES: Fashionable 1930s dress; climbing outfits; monks' habits; complete set of living chessmen. DIFFI-
CULTIES: Extremely difficult script itself; numerous complex
scenic and lighting effects are essential. Ransom is the only
successfully individualized character.
   ROYALTY: Apply Curtis Brown. TEXT: *Two Plays* (Knopf).

—— o ——

THE CHALK GARDEN (1955)   ENID BAGNOLD. Comedy.
After fifteen years in prison, Miss Madrigal answers an ad-
vertisement placed by eccentric Mrs. St. Maugham—less for

the purpose of finding a governess for her 16-year-old grand-daughter Laurel than for the pleasure of seeing what will come of it. Mrs. St. Maugham's household is as unsuited to the proper development of the granddaughter as her chalk garden is for growing flowers. Madrigal, hired because Laurel's mother is due to visit, succeeds in creating both a more appropriate atmosphere for Laurel and better conditions in the garden. A crisis arises when a guest for luncheon turns out to be the judge who sentenced Madrigal; she can no longer remain as governess. But Madrigal has done her work well, and Laurel is now willing to return to her mother. Madrigal remains on as gardener-companion to Mrs. St. Maugham. Ingredients for tragedy are here used effectively for high comedy.

MEN (2): 1 is 60–65 (in 2 acts only); 1 is 27–32. WOMEN (7, *1 can be cut*): 3 are 35–40 (1 requires outstanding actress, 1 minor); 2 are 50–60 (minor); 1 is 60–65 (requires outstanding actress); 1 is 16. SET: Room in a Sussex manor house. Suitable for arena production. COSTUMES: Contemporary British. DIFFICULTIES: Mother-daughter-grandmother age range may present a casting problem. Excellent diction is necessary to make the most of the play's brittle, witty dialogue.
ROYALTY: $50-25, Samuel French. TEXT: Samuel French.

—— o ——

THE ADMIRABLE CRICHTON (1902) J. M. BARRIE. Comedy. Lord Loam, with a show of democratic principle, holds a monthly tea party at which the servants are waited on by members of the family. Suffering as much embarrassment as Loam's guests, Crichton, the butler, stubbornly insists that class distinctions should be maintained, and that only a return to primitive society would determine who is to be master and who servant. Crichton accompanies Lord Loam, his three daughters, and their friends on a long yachting party which suddenly ends in shipwreck on a Pacific island. Primitive society soon determines that those who work will eat. Crichton's ability to cook and his inventiveness eventually bring him leadership of the group as well as the love of Lady Mary. But they are rescued before they are married, and once back in England they resume their former positions. Crichton cleverly protects the reputation of the entire family, then resigns his job.

MEN (*13*): 7 are 20–30; 2 are 30–50; 2 are 50–60 (only 4 of the men have large roles). BOY (*2*): Minor. WOMEN (*12*): 1 is 18–20; 6 are 20–30; 1 is 50–60; 1 is 60–70; 3 servants may be any age. SETS: Loam House, Mayfair, a fashionable turn of the century interior (modern if desired); desert island in the Pacific, enclosed in jungle foliage; living room and kitchen of the large wooden hut on the island. Sets may be stylized. Arena production possible. COSTUMES: Fashionable early 20th century or contemporary; servant uniforms and island improvisations.

ROYALTY: $35–25, Samuel French. TEXT: Samuel French.

— o —

WHAT EVERY WOMAN KNOWS (1908)   J. M. BARRIE. Comedy.   The Wylies make an agreement with poor but ambitious John Shand to finance his study of law and politics if he will ask their plain sister Maggie to marry him. He agrees, Maggie accepts, and he proceeds to a promising public career. When John becomes infatuated with the beautiful Lady Sybil, Maggie remains at his side, gallantly pursuing her duties as his wife. Endeavoring to write a speech by himself, John realizes it lacks his former brilliance and discovers that Maggie has been his indispensable inspiration all along. He reaffirms his love for her and begs to be forgiven. Maggie replies: "Every man who is high up loves to think that he has done it all himself; and the wife smiles, and lets it go at that. It's our only joke." Maggie is one of drama's most incisive tributes to women.

MEN (*5*): 1 is 20–30 (requires an outstanding actor); 2 are 20–40; 2 are 40–60. WOMEN (*3*): 2 are 20–30 (1 requires an actress of experience and warmth); 1 is elderly. SETS: Wylie's drawing room; middle-class comfortable sitting room and library; Shand's committee room; a former beauty salon; "the little room behind the dining room," used as a study, as well as a glimpse into the dining room; Comtesse's "pretty comic" drawing room. All basically realistic, around 1900. COSTUMES: Middle class and fashionable early 20th century; several changes needed for each character. DIFFICULTIES: Success depends on the ability of the actress who plays Maggie to capture the charm of Barrie's style.

ROYALTY: $35–25, Baker's or Samuel French. TEXT: Samuel French.

— o —

DEAR BRUTUS (1917) J. M. BARRIE. Comedy. Old Lob has assembled an oddly assorted group of house guests who, though feeling they have something in common, cannot determine what it is. All agree to venture into a mysterious wood which Lob says offers them what they need most: a second chance. In the forest "what might have been" takes place with typical Barrie whimsy and sentiment. Dearth, a disillusioned artist, meets the daughter he never had in the person of the tender Margaret ("She is as lovely as you think she is, and she is aged the moment when you like your daughter best"). Back at Lob's house, the various couples return to their former relationships, but with a new understanding of themselves and each other.

MEN (5): 2 are 20–30; 1 is 30–40; 1 is 40–60; 1 is 70–80 or older. WOMEN (5): 4 are 20–40; 1 is elderly. SETS: Lob's living room, a large, fashionable room, early 20th century or contemporary; mysterious wood may be highly stylized. Arena productions have been given. COSTUMES: Fashionable upper-class attire of 1920s or contemporary; butler's uniform. DIFFICULTIES: The play must be exceedingly well acted, particularly by Lob, Dearth, and Margaret, to sustain its charm. Some audiences may find Barrie's optimistic outlook rather unrealistic and somewhat dated.

ROYALTY: $35–25, Baker's or Samuel French. TEXT: Samuel French.

— o —

THE BARRETTS OF WIMPOLE STREET (1930) RUDOLF BESIER. Elizabeth Barrett, an invalid too weak to leave her room, receives her family and a few friends from her sofa. Her Victorian father, Edward Moulton-Barrett, a tyrant, has imposed his will on her. With equal dominance, he restricts the lives of his other children, and they live in terror that he will discover their limited experiences outside the house on Wimpole Street. Into this atmosphere bursts Robert Browning, filled with admiration for Elizabeth's poetry, and in a very short time for Elizabeth herself. Their love renews her health, and she is eventually well enough to marry Browning and escape her father for a life of happiness in Italy. The roles of Elizabeth's cousin and sister add a light touch to the play.

MEN (*12*): 9 are 20–40; 3 are 60–70. WOMEN (*5*): 4 are 20–30; 1 is 30–40 (requires an outstanding actress). SET: Elizabeth's bed-sitting room, London, 1845. Although pleasantly comfortable, need not be elaborate. Easily adaptable to arena staging. COSTUMES: Well-to-do Victorian dress, several changes for leading characters; maid's dress and 1 full-dress military uniform. DIFFICULTIES: The play requires an actor of considerable ability to make Edward Barrett credible.

ROYALTY: $50–25, Dramatists Play Service. TEXT: Dramatists Play Service.

— o —

HAY FEVER (1925) NOEL COWARD. Comedy. The bohemian Bliss family consists of an actress mother, Judith, a novelist father, David, and their two eccentric children, Sorel and Simon, all of whom live in an untidy madcap world. Each member of the family invites a week-end guest each of whom turns out to be ill-prepared for the unconventional hospitality that greets him. Judith plays several improvised scenes of sacrifice without any cause whatever—she is neither the injured wife she pretends to be nor the noble mother she enacts. The guests are so shocked by the treatment they receive from the whole family they decide to leave in a group. While the family bickers in its usual self-absorbed way, the guests drive off. (Long a favorite stock play, *Hay Fever* offers several attractively outlandish characters and good roles for young actors.)

MEN (*4*): 2 are 40–60; 2 are 20–30. WOMEN (*5*): 3 are 20–30; 1 is 30–40; 1 is 40–50. SET: The hall of the Bliss house at Cockham in June; must be both extremely comfortable and untidy. Realistic setting. Arena production possible. COSTUMES: Modern evening, day, and sports wear; unkempt dress of the Blisses. DIFFICULTIES: Lack of substance makes the comedy difficult to sustain throughout.

ROYALTY: $50, Samuel French. TEXT: Samuel French.

— o —

PRIVATE LIVES (1930) NOEL COWARD. Comedy. Elyot
Chase, on a honeymoon with his second wife, Sybil, discovers
his balcony adjoins that of Amanda, his first wife, also honey-
mooning. Reminiscing in some of Coward's most pointedly
polished lines, they decide to leave their new spouses and depart together for Paris. Once there, the old quarrels again
outweigh romance; as they are scuffling on the floor in a
pugnacious effort to settle their differences, their deserted
mates walk in and join this comic scene of domestic relations.
The women at first pair up against the men, but soon Victor
and Sybil are resorting to the same verbal fisticuffs as Elyot
and Amanda. Realizing at last that this is a sign of true love,
Elyot and Amanda steal off together once more.

MEN (2): Both are 20–40 (1 must be an attractive high
comedian). WOMEN (3): All are 20–40 (1 must be the equal
of the actor playing Elyot, in both style and personality).
SETS: 2 balconies of a hotel in southern France; living room
of a fashionable Paris flat. Arena production possible. COS-
TUMES: Modern in excellent taste. DIFFICULTIES: The success
of the play requires two extraordinarily capable leads. The
required worldliness may make production difficult on some
college and university stages.

ROYALTY: $50, Samuel French. TEXT: Samuel French.

——o——

BLITHE SPIRIT (1941) NOEL COWARD. Comedy. Concerns the two wives of Charles Condomine: one living (Ruth),
one dead (Elvira) but nevertheless kicking. After a madcap
seance, Elvira's spirit—summoned by the eccentric Madame
Arcati—refuses to leave. When a vase moves about the room,
even Ruth believes her husband's report that Elvira has come
back, but neither knows of her scheme to make Charles a
spirit too. There is a slip-up, however, and Ruth instead of
Charles joins Elvira. Charles, thinking he is rid of both of
them, prepares for a trip but, as the spirited ending of the
play proves, he is not unescorted. (*Blithe Spirit* offers several
of Coward's best characters and most hilarious scenes in addition to a good measure of his typical satire.)

MEN (2): Both are 20–40 (1 must be an excellent farceur).
WOMEN (5): 4 are 20–40 (2 must be expert comic players);
1 is 40–60. SET: Modern living room, comfortably and taste-

fully furnished. Arena productions have been given; play was also successfully presented in Restoration comedy style. CosTUMES: Fashionable modern: evening gowns; outlandish outfit; 1 maid's uniform. DIFFICULTIES: Technical problem of rigging vases and picture frames to move by themselves at the end of the play.

ROYALTY: $50, Samuel French. TEXT: Samuel French.

— o —

A TASTE OF HONEY (1958) SHELAGH DELANEY. Comedy-drama. Helen, a restless and shiftless semi-prostitute moves into a comfortless Manchester flat with her teen-age daughter Jo, who has learned that she can look to her mother for nothing but the necessities of survival. Peter, one of Helen's customers, looks her up in her new quarters and offers marriage. During the Christmas season Helen goes off with Peter, leaving Jo to fend for herself. She takes up with a Negro sailor; though she knows she will never see him again, she keeps the engagement ring he has given her. A homosexual art student, longing for affection and children, takes care of her during her pregnancy. Peter tires of Helen, who returns to Jo—ostensibly to help, actually, to find a haven.

MEN (3): 1 is middle-aged; 2 are 20–30. WOMEN (2): 1 is 40–45; 1 is 15–20. SET: "A comfortless flat in Manchester and the street outside." COSTUMES: Contemporary; a British sailor suit. DIFFICULTIES: The brutal, anguished humor requires mature actors.

ROYALTY: Apply Theatre Workshop, Theatre Royal, Stratford, London, E 15. TEXT: Grove.

— o —

MURDER IN THE CATHEDRAL (1935) T. S. ELIOT. Verse drama. This solemn verse drama opens with the return of Thomas à Becket to his cathedral after seven years of exile; he is greeted by the chorus of women of Canterbury and the priests of the cathedral. Becket's mind and soul are taunted by Four Tempters, who offer him the choice of different courses of action; he may return to the gaiety of his old life; he may seek power over King and Pope; or (the most tempting), he may aim at martyrdom. He rejects each Tempter in the name of God and righteousness. Following Becket's Christmas sermon, Four Knights arrive to murder him. This accomplished, each speaks directly to the audience, attempting to justify his act from a modern point of view. The play ends with the chorus begging for mercy for having created another saint, finally requesting that Thomas pray for them.

MEN (*13 speaking roles; attendants and extras*): 1 is 40–60; ages of the others may vary. WOMEN: Chorus (as large as the director wishes); no individual women's speaking roles. SETS: The Archbishop's Hall and Canterbury Cathedral, 1170. The play is often presented to great advantage in churches. COSTUMES: Clerical; peasant women; medieval armor; need not be realistic. DIFFICULTIES: Production requires extensive spoken and choral emphasis—so much so that a special speech coach may be required.

ROYALTY: $35, Samuel French. TEXT: Samuel French.

— o —

THE FAMILY REUNION (1939) T. S. ELIOT. Verse drama. This story of sin and redemption is about Lord Harry Monchensey, who, in its course, passes from guilt to repentance and, at last, to holiness. He has been away from the family home for eight years, during which his young wife was drowned, and Harry, suffering ever since the burden of responsibility, has been pursued by the Eumenides. It is apparent that it is not his conscience and mind which are diseased by his guilt but his whole world. He has come home to celebrate his mother's birthday in a milieu that differs from his own in its lack of social morality. Harry expiates his guilt when he recognizes that his choice is not to run away or resume his youthful life at Wishwood, but to pursue "the bright angels."

MEN (*6*): 3 are 60–75; 1 is 35–50 (requires an outstanding actor); 2 are 30–45 (both are minor). WOMEN (*6*): 1 is 65–80; 3 are 40–60; 2 are 25–40. SETS: The country house, Wishwood, in the north of England; a stately mansion of the present. COSTUMES: Contemporary dinner clothing; chauffeur's uniform, maid's outfit. DIFFICULTIES: The verse requires experienced actors. The Eumenides are usually depicted as projections or cut-out mobiles seen through transparencies.

ROYALTY: $25, Samuel French. TEXT: Samuel French.

— o —

THE COCKTAIL PARTY (1949) T. S. ELIOT. Comedy. The marriage of Edward and Lavinia Chamberlayne nears divorce. Edward has been having an affair with Celia Coplestone. The pattern of their lives is altered by a guest at a cocktail party, later identified as the psychiatrist Sir Henry Harcourt-Reilly, a mystic priest. In a series of cadenced confessionals he leads these people to an awareness of their possible choices of reconciliation to the human situation: to compromise with life; not to compromise, but seek individual fulfillment; or to seek an unknown destination that comes from "the kind of faith that issues from despair." In the end the couple is reunited. Celia becomes a nun and subsequently is crucified over an anthill in Kinkanja.

MEN (5): 3 are 20–40 (1 is minor); 1 is 30–40; 1 is 40–60 (requires an outstanding actor). WOMEN (4): 3 are 20–40 (1 minor); 1 is 40–60. SETS: The present-day drawing room of the Chamberlaynes' London flat, fashionably and expensively decorated; Sir Harcourt-Reilly's consulting room. Arena production possible. COSTUMES: Fashionable contemporary day and evening clothes. DIFFICULTIES: The play is written in disciplined verse which so masterfully molds the sounds and rhythm of modern speech that when properly spoken it may not be discerned as verse at all.

ROYALTY: $50, Samuel French. TEXT: Samuel French.

—— o ——

THE CONFIDENTIAL CLERK (1953) T. S. ELIOT. Comedy. On the surface, a comedy of manners in which children who have been separated from their parents at birth are reunited in the last act by skillful and convenient discoveries. Sir Claude Mulhammer had wanted to be a potter; realizing that he would only be second-rate he turned to finance. However, he wishes to give the opportunity of becoming first-rate to his new clerk, young Colby, who is a promising organist and whom he suspects is his illegitimate son. As it turns out, this is not so, but there follow other welcome surprises which give this deeply philosophical play about compromise with life its farcical façade.

MEN (4): 1 is 20–30; 1 is 30–40 (minor); 1 is 40–60; 1 is 60–70 (all must be outstanding actors). WOMEN (3): 1 is 20–30; 1 is 40–50; 1 is 50–65 (all must be outstanding). SETS:

The elegant business room on the 1st floor of Sir Claude's present-day London house; an attractively comfortable flat in a mews, with a piano. Arena production possible. COSTUMES: Modern dress, expensive and in the best taste. DIFFICULTIES: While the verse, properly done, sounds like everyday speech, it nonetheless requires special preparation.

ROYALTY: $50, Samuel French. TEXT: Samuel French.

—— o ——

THE FIRSTBORN (1946) CHRISTOPHER FRY. Verse drama. At once a study of liberty opposed by sadistic despotism and the story of Moses' personal struggle before the great Exodus. Anath, sister of the powerful Pharaoh, Seti the Second, cannot forget Moses. He had been her adopted son until he discovered his Hebraic birth and abruptly left the Egyptian court. Even though happy as a child and successful as a young general in Egypt, he has put past glories behind to help his enslaved people. Abhorring the cruel treatment of the Jews, Moses refuses to help the Pharaoh repel the Libyan invasion. Rameses, son of the Pharaoh, looks upon Moses as an uncle and offers to help him. Although fond of the boy, Moses reminds him that they must go separate ways in life. The Pharaoh keeps none of his promises to Moses, and darkness comes over the land. When the plague of the Death of the Firstborn comes, Moses summons his people. Now he realizes that since all Egyptian firstborn must die, Rameses will be included. He attempts to save the boy by warning the court of the impending doom, but Rameses crumples before him. Anath, sending Moses out to find liberty for his people, bids him farewell.

MEN (*10*): 3 are 30–55; 2 are 18–20; 5 are 20–50 (minor). WOMEN (*3*): 2 are 35–50; 1 is 15. SETS: Terrace of the palace of the Pharaoh; a room in the palace; interior of a tent. Sets need not be realistic. Suitable for arena production. COSTUMES: Biblical, Egyptian royal and peasant dress of 1200 B.C. DIFFICULTIES: The verse requires experienced actors.

ROYALTY: $50–25, Dramatists Play Service. TEXT: Dramatists Play Service.

—— o ——

THE LADY'S NOT FOR BURNING (1947) CHRISTOPHER FRY. Verse comedy. Jennet Jourdemayne is an enchanting young creature who admits speaking French to her poodle but denies having turned old Matthew Skipps into a dog. Thomas Mendip, a disillusioned, life-weary soldier, claims to have killed Skipps, but the older people, like Mayor Hebble Tyson, his sister Margaret, the Judge, and the Chaplain, cannot be bothered with this voluble murderer as long as there are witches to be burned. Margaret's sons are interested in the physical attributes of Jennet and compete for her favors, which gives Humphrey's pure fiancée, Alizon, a chance to elope with an equally pure clerk, Richard. The appearance of Matthew Skipps, neither dead nor bewitched but very drunk, promises a happy ending.

MEN (8): 3 are 18–25; 1 is 25–35; 4 are 40–60. WOMEN (3): 1 is 17; 1 is 20–28; 1 is 40–60. SET: Room in the mayor's house in a small English market town around 1400. Set should reflect the poetic atmosphere and suggest the changing April weather outside. Arena production possible. COSTUMES: Fancifully stylized apparel of medieval townsfolk. DIFFICULTIES: Fry's complex yet graceful verse will lose much of its sparkle if rendered by inexperienced actors.

ROYALTY: $50–25, Dramatists Play Service. TEXT: Dramatists Play Service.

— o —

VENUS OBSERVED (1949) CHRISTOPHER FRY. Verse comedy. The autumnal, urbane Duke of Altair, amateur astronomer and connoisseur of women, has invited three of his past mistresses to watch an eclipse of the sun from his observatory. Jessie is an amiable, homely woman; Hilda a reserved British country lady; and Rosabel a hot-blooded, high-strung actress. They ignore the Duke's intention to have his son Edgar choose his future stepmother from among them. Then Perpetua, youth itself, enters; both the Duke and his son wants her for himself. The Duke is a good loser who has learned from the sun how to decline gracefully. With the generosity of the nobleman of leisure who never earned and always spent, he pardons his land-agent, Reedbeck (Perpetua's father), for having embezzled vast sums. He also forgives Rosabel for having set fire to his mansion in an attack of jealousy; he even decides to marry the lady arsonist once she gets out of jail.

MEN (6): 2 are 20–25; 2 are 40; 2 are 50. WOMEN (4): 1 is 18–24; 3 are 30–40. SETS: The Duke's observatory; the Temple of Ancient Virtues in the ducal park. In the fire scene, flames are seen through the open door of the observatory. Perpetua descends through the window. Play calls for a poetic, nonrealistic setting, but effective staging in arena is scarcely possible. COSTUMES: Elegant contemporary British. DIFFICULTIES: More than any other of Fry's plays, this verse comedy requires subtle taste, culture, and maturity. Plot is loosely knit.

ROYALTY: $50–25, Dramatists Play Service. TEXT: Dramatists Play Service.

—— o ——

A SLEEP OF PRISONERS (1951) CHRISTOPHER FRY. Verse drama. Four soldiers, locked in a church being used as a prison, bicker and squabble about playing the organ and using the pulpit as a place to express their boredom and general disgust with themselves, each other, and a world that allows useless wars. When they go to sleep the Biblical dream of each prisoner is enacted by all four. Private Tim Meadows, the oldest, sees Adam and then Cain and Abel, who fight over a dice game. Cain is called to account for Abel's death. Private David King, dreaming of David and Absolom, enacts King David receiving the news of Absolom's death. Private Peter Able sees the figure of Abraham, and the story of the sacrifice of Isaac unfolds. Corporal Joe Adams dreams of Shadrac, Meshac, and Abednego bound for the fire.

MEN (4): 1 is 60; the others may be 20–30. SETTING: While the play was written to be performed in a church and usually is, it can be produced on a regular stage or in arena. Altar of a church must be suggested, with pulpit, organ loft, memorial tablets, choir stalls, and chancel steps. Double bunks required. COSTUMES: 3 well-worn privates' uniforms and 1 of a corporal. DIFFICULTIES: Requires expert direction and acting.

ROYALTY: $25, Dramatists Play Service. TEXT: Dramatists Play Service.

—— o ——

JUSTICE (1910) JOHN GALSWORTHY. It is discovered that William Falder, junior clerk in a law firm, has embezzled

£90 to buy a passage from England for a married woman whose husband cruelly mistreats her. Falder is turned over to the police in spite of pleas for mercy from various junior members of the firm. The middle section of the play depicts the debilitating life in British prisons and the well-intentioned but stern administrators of the system. In the final act, Falder is released from prison; unable to stand the humiliation of admitting he is an ex-convict, he begs for a job with the old firm. The head of the company offers him a job, but only if he will promise to break off with the woman he loves. However, the police now falsely accuse Falder of another crime, and he commits suicide in the office of the firm. At last he is beyond the reach of human justice—"No one'll touch him now! Never again! He's safe with gentle Jesus."

MEN (*17*): 4 are 60–65; 4 are 30–35; the age of the others immaterial. Only 5 run through the whole play, although almost all have at least 1 good scene. Some doubling possible. WOMEN (*1, plus courtroom extras*). SETS: Law office; warden's office at the prison; prison corridor; Falder's cell. COSTUMES: Middle class, early 20th century; three convict uniforms. DIFFICULTIES: Quick set changes required.

ROYALTY: $25, Samuel French. TEXT: Samuel French.

—— o ——

THE VOYSEY INHERITANCE (1905) HARLEY GRANVILLE-BARKER. Young Edward Voysey's "inheritance" from his father turns out to be an investment firm whose funds Mr. Voysey, senior, has been skillfully embezzling. The son has a choice of leaving the firm and thus allowing the family's name to be destroyed when the father dies, or of staying in partnership with his father and carrying on in a manner to avoid detection. Edward decides to stay. When his father dies, he begins to straighten out the firm's accounts. He plans to make appropriate restitution as far as possible until the inevitable day when some client's large withdrawal forces the affair into the open. Edward's success is not assured, nor is it certain that he will not be tempted to follow his father's unethical example in order to succeed, but in the course of the play he is seen gradually to acquire a new maturity and sophistication.

MEN (*9, one can be cut*): 4 are 55–65 (1 minor); 5 are 25–45 (1 requires an outstanding actor, 2 minor). WOMEN

(*8, 1 can be cut*): 1 is 60–65; 2 are 40–50 (1 minor); 5 are
20–35 (2 minor). BOY (*1, can be cut*): 10–14 (no lines). SETS:
Mr. Voysey's office, the inner office, in the best part of Lincoln's Inn; the Voysey dining room at Chislehurst. Suitable
for arena. Sets should be realistic. COSTUMES: Fashionable
early 20th century.

ROYALTY: $50, Samuel French. TEXT: *Masterpieces of
Modern Drama*, Vol. I, edited by Pierce and Matthews (1915,
out of print).

— o —

THE LIVING ROOM (1953) GRAHAM GREENE. Rose
Pemberton is desperately in love with Michael Dennis, an
older married man. At her mother's death, Rose comes to
live with her two maiden aunts and an uncle—a crippled
priest. Rose is forced to use the living room as her bedroom,
since the sisters have closed every room in the house in which
there has been a death. Aunt Helen prevents Rose from running away with Michael but later discovers she is meeting him
secretly every day. Rose does not feel that loving the man of
her choice is wrong, and is willing to leave the Catholic
Church to become his mistress. Michael's hysterical wife
visits Rose, threatens suicide, and begs the girl to give up her
husband. Rose realizes that Michael can never divorce his
wife and that she must not become his mistress. In despair,
Rose turns to her uncle, who says she must choose between
suffering her own pain or suffering the pain of other people.
Rose believes she cannot forget Michael. She finds herself
unable to pray and commits suicide.

MEN (2): 1 is 40–45; 1 is 65 (invalid priest in a wheel-
chair); WOMEN (5): 2 are 45 (1 minor); 2 are 65–70; 1 is 20.
SET: The second-floor living room of an ordinary town house.
The furniture is musty and old, but good. Set should be fairly
realistic. Suitable for arena. COSTUMES: Modern everyday
dress.

ROYALTY: $50, Samuel French. TEXT: Samuel French.

— o —

THE POTTING SHED (1957) GRAHAM GREENE. After a
long estrangement, John Callifer comes home at the time of
his father's final illness. His mother receives him coldly, will
not allow him to see his father, and refuses to explain what in

John's past caused the separation between the two. Callifer, determined to find the solution, attempts to reconstruct the events of the earliest day he can remember, a day when he was fourteen years old. Something happened in the gardener's potting shed; he must find out what it was. His mother will not help him, and the widow of the gardener appears afraid to tell him. But a visit to his uncle, now a drunken priest, reveals the dark secret that John hanged himself in the potting shed that day and was resurrected. The impact of this miracle destroyed the atheistic convictions of his scientist-father and, likewise, the faith of his uncle.

MEN (6): 1 is 30 (minor); 2 are 40–50; 3 are 50–60. WOMEN (5): 1 is 13; 1 is 30–40; 1 is 50–60 (minor); 2 are 70–80 (1 major). SETS: Comfortable, well-furnished English living room; a small bachelor's flat, poorly furnished; sitting room in a provincial presbytery. Sets should be realistic. Arena production possible. COSTUMES: Modern middle-class English dress; 1 clerical outfit. DIFFICULTIES: The anticlimactic last act is weak, although the detective-story nature of the play holds and even fascinates many audiences.

ROYALTY: $50–25, Samuel French. TEXT: Samuel French.

— o —

THE DREAM OF PETER MANN (1960) BERNARD KOPS. Peter Mann stands apart from the other hard-working money-minded merchants of the London market place, where he lives with his mother, Sonia. He is too spirited and unrealistic for the conventional Sylvia, whom he loves. When Jason the Undertaker bribes Alex (a tramp) to take Peter away, Peter decides to leave and search for uranium. But while Peter is taking money from his mother's safe it falls, knocking him unconscious. During the dream which follows, Peter sees his mistakes before he makes them. Alex, Peter, and Penny (whose love Peter does not return) come back after twelve years of fruitless searching. Jason and his henchmen now rule the trench-ridden market place. Only Jason recognizes the travelers, and he meets no opposition when he suggests that they kill Peter to discourage strangers from trespassing on their uranium land. About to be killed, Peter realizes that he loves Penny. Sonia stops Jason from killing her son, but when the danger is past, Peter forgets Penny and Sonia refuses to recognize him. With persuasive oratory, Peter convinces the people that they will make greater progress if they unite under him. Peter plans to marry Sylvia, and Penny goes to live with the man who once wanted to marry her but now doesn't recognize her.

The dream continues, five years later, the day the bomb will be dropped. The people work in Peter's prosperous shroud factory, which is managed by Jason. Peter wants to go down into his shelter but Sonia, who is dying, refuses to leave the world. After a grotesque and magnificent dance with Alex, Sonia dies. Sylvia, now fat and vulgar, runs into the house to gather valuables. Peter asks Penny to come down into the shelter with him; she refuses and leaves with Alex. Peter goes down alone, telling the workers not to worry, their shrouds will protect them. Sylvia arrives, loaded with riches, and finds herself locked out. There is a flash of light and a rumble. Peter Mann comes out into the silence. Everything is covered with a huge shroud. After a voice tells him he is dying, Sonia appears and sings an ironic lullaby promising greatness to the baby Peter. Peter Mann dies. The dream ends with Alex shaking him. Peter still wants to go uranium-hunting—but without stealing his mother's money and with Penny whom he now loves. Before he and Penny leave, Peter Mann tells the merchants: "Don't you see—you can always make money, but you can't always make merry. You're saving up for nothing . . ."

MEN (*10, plus extras*): 4 are 20–25 (2 minor); 2 are 30–40; 4 are 40–60 (3 minor). WOMEN (*6, plus children's voices singing off stage*): 2 are 20–25 (must age during play); 4 are 40–60 (3 minor). SET: A London market place with several stalls. Unit set. COSTUMES: Contemporary lower-class; one expensive dress; some threadbare. DIFFICULTIES: An air of innocence and lightness must underlie the grim events of the play. A fast-moving, lively play which presents both the good and the bad of humanity; weaknesses must not overshadow strengths.

ROYALTY: Apply Evans Brothers Ltd., Montague House, Russell Square, London WC 1. TEXT: Penguin.

— o —

THE CIRCLE (1919) W. SOMERSET MAUGHAM. Comedy. Thirty years after Lord Porteous and Lady Kitty have abandoned their respective spouses to live with each other as outcasts of a staid and conventional society, they return to England to visit Lady Kitty's son by her former marriage and his wife. Lady Kitty discovers that the wife is about to leave her son, as she left her husband, to live with a man who can give her affection and consideration. Clive, Lady Kitty's former husband, advises his son unsuccessfully on the measures he should take to preserve his marriage. Lady Kitty's vivid example of what her life has become is not enough to dissuade her daughter-in-law from action. The humor lies in the juxtaposition of the characters within and between the two love triangles.

MEN (5): 3 are 20–40 (1 minor); 2 are 50–60. WOMEN (3): 2 are 20–40; 1 is 50–60. SET: Stately Georgian drawing room. Arena productions have been given. COSTUMES: High fashion of the 1920s, including sports clothes, everyday attire, and evening dress. DIFFICULTIES: Preservation of wit and style of the English 1920s upper class.

ROYALTY: Apply Doubleday. TEXT: *The Collected Plays* (Doubleday or Heinemann), Vol. II, or *Treasury of the Theatre* (Simon and Schuster), Vol. II.

— o —

THE CONSTANT WIFE (1926)   W. SOMERSET MAUGHAM. Comedy.   Constance is happily married but feels that the role of the wife in an upper-middle-class household can be only that of a prostitute, since the regular household duties are performed by the servants. When her husband has an affair with her best friend, she quietly does all she can to prevent it from becoming public gossip. In the final act, Constance has assumed an honest role in society by performing successfully a job as an interior decorator. She has earned not only her economic independence but also her sexual independence. Moreover, in her opinion she has achieved the right to be called *wife*.

MEN (4): All are 40–50 (1 minor); WOMEN (5): 4 are 30–40; 1 is 50–60. SET: Tasteful drawing room. Arena productions have been given. COSTUMES: Fashionable everyday 1920s clothing. DIFFICULTIES: The independent woman in society is no longer a phenomenon.

ROYALTY: Apply Samuel French. TEXT: Samuel French.

— o —

THE ENTERTAINER (1956) JOHN OSBORNE. The Rices
are a family of English music-hall entertainers—impoverished, brashly humorous, vulgar, quarrelsome, faithless, and
sentimental. Father Archie, witty and bawdy, badgers both his
second wife, Phoebe, and his grandfather, Billy. He discusses
with his daughter Jean his plan to chuck Phoebe and marry a
girl about Jean's age. When he hears that his son Mick has
been killed overseas, he interrupts his planning to sing a religious blues song. The funeral over, the family resumes its
squabbles. Billy breaks up his son's affair by informing the
new girl's parents of Archie's status as husband and father.
Billy dies; Archie goes on singing until the lights go down.

MEN (5): 1 is elderly, 2 are middle-aged, 2 are 20–30.
WOMEN (2): 1 is middle-aged; 1 is 20–30. SETS: Early 20th-
century mansion, now dirty and dilapidated. Brief external
scene, followed by living-room interior. Spotlight on dark
stage represents music-hall stage. COSTUMES: Billy's clothes
"are probably 25 years old . . . but well-pressed and smart."
Rest are clothes of the period. DIFFICULTIES: Requires considerable acting skill.

ROYALTY: $50, Dramatic Publishing Company.* TEXT:
Dramatic Publishing Company.

—— o ——

LOOK BACK IN ANGER (1956) JOHN OSBORNE. A
cycle in the love life of four members of the English "beat
generation." Jimmy Porter lives in a one-room flat with his
wife Alison and his young business partner, Cliff Lewis.
Jimmy's steady abuse of Cliff and Alison is interrupted only
when one of them turns on him or when Jimmy and Alison
are distracted by momentary outbursts of physical passion.
Actress Helena Charles comes to live with them while she is
playing a local engagement. Affecting moral indignation at
Jimmy's treatment of Alison, Helena induces a quarrel between husband and wife that results in Alison's leaving Jimmy.
Helena then takes over. Several months later she finds herself
as exhausted by the rancor as was Alison. When Alison returns, untidy and ill, having lost Jimmy's baby by miscarriage,
Helena leaves. Neither Alison nor Jimmy now has anything
to offer the other except need, and this is enough to reunite
them. An angry protest against postwar English life.

MEN (*3*): 2 are 20–30, 1 is 60–70. WOMEN (*2*): Both 20–30. SET: Realistic interior: "The Porters' one-room flat in a large Midland town." COSTUMES: Contemporary. DIFFICULTIES: The brutality of 1 character and the spinelessness of the others make difficult the sympathetic and compassionate over-all portrayal implied by the words of the closing scene.

ROYALTY: $50, Dramatic Publishing Company.* TEXT: Dramatic Publishing Company.

— o —

THE BIRTHDAY PARTY (1958) HAROLD PINTER. Action takes place in a drab seaside rooming house maintained by motherly Meg and her taciturn husband Petey. The main character is Stanley, an indolent pianist who has sought refuge from the world. Two sinister men seek lodging in the house; they are clearly after Stanley, although their motives are never named. They suggest having a birthday party for Stanley even though it is not his birthday. During the highly theatrical party scene, they destroy Stanley's individuality. Though Petey makes a feeble attempt to stop the men from taking the broken and speechless Stanley away with them, he backs down, afraid. The two men lead Stanley out to the big black car and back to conventionality.

MEN (*4*): Adult. WOMEN (*2*): 1 young woman, 1 older woman. SET: Room in a second-rate seaside boarding house. COSTUMES: Contemporary. DIFFICULTIES: Dialects. Oblique style of script requires skillful playing for adequate characterization.

ROYALTY: Apply Methuen's Modern Plays, 36 Essex St., Strand, London, WC 2. TEXT: Methuen.

— o —

THE CARETAKER (1959) HAROLD PINTER. Aston lives in a cluttered, decaying room, which he offers to share with Davie, an elderly tramp. Davie has lost his job and his "papers"—his identity. He is unable to recover his papers because he lacks shoes, and the weather is never good enough to make the trip to retrieve them. When Aston's younger brother, Mick, arrives on the scene, Davie does not resist the temptation to maneuver himself into a commanding position. As a result he alienates the brothers and is evicted, despite his pathetic plea for another chance.

MEN (*3*): 2 about 30; 1 old. SET: A cluttered room in a west London house. Suitable for arena. COSTUMES: Contemporary, shabby. DIFFICULTIES: Requires excellent acting. Much of the feeling and meaning is by implication, demanding skillful and sensitive playing.

ROYALTY: Apply ACTAC (Theatrical and Cinematic) Ltd., Cadogan Lane, London, SW 1. TEXT: Grove.

—— o ——

TIME AND THE CONWAYS (1937) J. B. PRIESTLEY. The Conways are a happy, self-satisfied family. Their villa is one of the social centers of an English industrial town in 1919. Mrs. Conway, a nice although somewhat silly widow, has high hopes for her two sons and four daughters. Perhaps Alan will not go too far since he seems quite contented with his dull job as a clerk; but Robin, the charmer just returned from the Army, is sure to make a quick fortune. Hazel, the family beauty, is on the lookout for a dashing and rich cavalier; Kay's ambition is to become a novelist; Madge will reform the world as headmistress of a famous girls' college; and Carol, a sixteen-year-old bundle of life, is destined to become a great comedienne. All this is exposed in the first act, at the celebration of Kay's twenty-first birthday. During charades, Kay is suddenly struck by a terrifying vision that becomes reality in the second act. It is twenty years later and little Carol has died long ago. Mrs. Conway is as silly as ever, but no longer nice. Hazel is constantly humiliated by her husband, a nasty industrialist. Robin has become a drunkard, Madge an embittered spinster, and Kay a third-rate journalist. Only Alan, still a clerk, has not changed. In the third act, Kay is back at her birthday party in 1919. She is still perturbed but regains hope when Alan makes her realize that time is relative and that the happy moments in our life remain ours, and cannot be undone by the future.

MEN (*4*): 2 are 20–25; 2 about 30. WOMEN (*5*): 4 are 18–25; 1 is 40–45. GIRL (*1*): 16. All characters except the girl appear 20 years older in the 2nd act. SET: Sitting room in Mrs. Conway's house. Arena production possible. COSTUMES: Fashionable 1919 party dresses; everyday clothes, 1939; assorted odd costumes for charade. The play can easily be adapted to take place in 1945 and the present time, respectively. DIFFICULTIES: It is essential that the actors be able to convey equally the freshness of youth and the frustration of disillusioned middle age.

ROYALTY: $25, Samuel French. TEXT: Samuel French.

— o —

AN INSPECTOR CALLS (1945)   J. B. PRIESTLEY.   The continuous action takes place in the house of Arthur Birling, a smug, patronizing factory owner in the English Midlands during the untroubled years shortly before World War I. The Birlings are gaily celebrating the engagement of their daughter Sheila to Gerald Croft, son of an industrial competitor. A police inspector enters to inquire about the background of a girl who has just committed suicide in the hospital. With quiet authority he draws each of them into confessing his share of responsibility for the girl's misfortune. When he leaves, Sheila and her younger brother Eric are deeply shaken. Mr. and Mrs. Birling, however, are concerned only with avoiding scandal. Then, discovering that their interrogator is unknown to the local police and that there has been no suicide at the hospital, they easily manage to dismiss the whole unpleasant incident from their minds and fall back into their pompous complacency. The phone rings. A girl has just killed herself in the hospital and a police inspector is on his way to ask some questions.

MEN (4): 2 are 20–30; 2 are 40–60. WOMEN (3): 2 are 20–25 (1 minor); 1 about 50. SET: Dining room of a large suburban house in an industrial city, England, 1912. Realistic set not necessary. Suitable for arena. COSTUMES: Black-tie dinner clothes, 1912. DIFFICULTIES: Repetitious. Climax must be carefully structured.

ROYALTY: $50–25, Dramatists Play Service. TEXT: Dramatists Play Service.

— o —

THE WINSLOW BOY (1946)   TERENCE RATTIGAN.   A 13-year-old cadet, Ronnie Winslow, has been expelled from the Royal Naval College at Osborne, charged with forging a five-shilling money order. He claims his innocence, and his father believes him. The stern, retired bank official begins a long, costly battle to reestablish his son's good name. He wrecks his health; his older son, Dickie, has to leave Oxford; his daughter Catherine loses her fiancé; yet after two years of stubborn persistence his Petition of Right is granted by the House of Commons, a jury trial is held and the boy is vindicated. The play reaches its early dramatic climax in a scene in which the famous, supercilious, and seemingly emotionless barrister Sir Robert Morton subjects the boy to a ruthless examination and then decides to take the case. Catherine, a suffragette more concerned with principles than with the reputation of her family, is her father's only ally; the weak Mrs. Winslow and the frivolous Dickie falter. A very British play that emphasizes by understatement the decency and integrity of the writer's countrymen.

MEN (5): 1 is 18–25; 3 are 30–50; 1 is about 60. WOMEN (4): 1 is 25–30; 3 are 40–60. BOY (1): 13. SET: Drawing room in the Winslow house. Suitable for arena. COSTUMES: Upper middle-class English, early 20th century.

ROYALTY: $50–25, Dramatists Play Service. TEXT: Dramatists Play Service.

— o —

THE BROWNING VERSION (1948) TERENCE RATTIGAN. Crocker-Harris, once a brilliant classical scholar, is forced by illness to abandon his teaching position in an English public school before becoming eligible for a pension. Betrayed by his wife, discarded by the headmaster, feared and ridiculed by his pupils of the Lower Fifth, the humorless, pedantic schoolmaster quietly faces repeated defeat, but breaks down only when one of his students presents him with the Browning version of Aeschylus' *Agamemnon* as a farewell gift. Though his belief in this single act of kindness is shaken by his wife's insinuation that the present was only to win a passing mark for its donor, Crocker-Harris regains confidence in the boy and in himself and finds the courage to stand up against further humiliation. Millie, the flagrantly unfaithful wife, is a pitiful victim of frustration, desperately clinging to her reluctant lover, Frank Hunter, her husband's younger colleague, who will inevitably walk out on her. Dr. Frobisher, the patronizing headmaster; Taplow, the nice but not brilliant pupil; and Peter Gilbert, Crocker-Harris' young successor are unconventionally drawn characters who contribute to raise this sharp and bitter, yet thoughtfully sympathetic, study of failure beyond mere craftsmanship.

MEN (4): 1 about 22; 1 is 25–35; 2 are 50–60 (1 requires outstanding actor). WOMEN (2): 1 about 20; 1 is 35–40. BOY (1): 15–16. SET: Large, gloomy sitting room of the Crocker-Harrises. Suitable for arena production. COSTUMES: Contemporary English school milieu. DIFFICULTIES: Typically English climate of this 70-minute character play should be re-created.

ROYALTY: $20, Samuel French. TEXT: Samuel French.

— o —

SEPARATE TABLES (1954) TERENCE RATTIGAN. *Table by the Window* and *Table Number Seven* are two short plays, each with different leads but linked by the same setting—a drab English boarding hotel—and the same supporting cast. In the first play, Mrs. Shankland, an elegant divorcée terrified by approaching middle age, has to humble herself in her attempt to regain her first ex-husband, John Malcolm, a tough, hard-drinking former Labour Party leader for whose political and physical ruin she had been responsible. The second play concerns the tender feelings between Major Pollock, a pathetic old faker, and Sibyl Railton-Bell, a wallflower, who sticks to him even when the supposed major is exposed in a petty but humiliating scandal. A sense of loneliness and lack of purpose predominates in most of the other characters. Miss Cooper, the compassionate landlady, has a tragedy of her own. The permanent guest—a towering, censorious matriarch; a timid old widow; an extrovert lady horse-player; and a retired schoolteacher—have nothing in common but hotel food and gossip. A young couple who at first apparently despise the old-fashioned ties of matrimony, is later revealed as conventional to the marrow.

MEN (4): 1 is 18–25; 2 are 40–60; 1 about 70. WOMEN (9): 2 are 18–25; 4 are 30–40; 3 are 50–70. SET: Dining room and lounge in an English boarding hotel. Suitable for arena. COSTUMES: Contemporary British; genteel poverty except for the strikingly chic gowns of 1 woman.

ROYALTY: $50–25, Baker's or Samuel French. TEXT: Baker's or Samuel French.

— o —

ARMS AND THE MAN (1894) GEORGE BERNARD SHAW. Comedy. A double-edged satire on the romantic view of life and romantic melodrama. In this play, nothing works as the romantics say it should. The hero, Captain Bluntschli, a professional soldier considerably more interested in saving his skin than in being a hero, carries chocolates instead of bullets in his cartridge belt. The heroine, Raina Petkoff, has noble bearing and a thrilling voice, but she is an unconscionable liar. The cliché romantic hero, Sergius Saranoff, is a fool in practical situations. The charge he has led was successful only because the enemy had been given ammunition of the wrong caliber. Furthermore, although he pretends the loftiest love for Raina, he makes love to the servants whenever he has the opportunity. Major Petkoff, the commander of the Bulgarian Army, knows so little of military matters that he cannot get his troops home from the war. Bluntschli brings order into the chaos of the Petkoff household, gets the Bulgarian Army home again, and forces Raina to admit both that the romantic Sergius bores her and that her nobility is sham. By the final curtain, Sergius and Major Petkoff and his wife have managed to rationalize Bluntschli into a romantic scheme of things. But Raina has come to grips with a more realistic picture of the world and agrees to marry a real man, not a figure out of a fancy-dress ball.

MEN (*5, plus extras*): 3 are 30–40 (1 minor); 1 is 40–50; 1 about 55. WOMEN (*3*): 2 are 20–30; 1 is 45–55. SETS: Raina's bedchamber in a wealthy Bulgarian home; the garden of the Petkoff home; Major Petkoff's "library." COSTUMES: Highly fashionable 1880s Bulgarian costumes, sufficiently brightly colored to indicate the Oriental tastes of the wearers; military uniforms.
ROYALTY: Public domain. TEXT: Samuel French.

— o —

CANDIDA (1895) GEORGE BERNARD SHAW. Comedy. Eugene Marchbanks, an extravagantly impressionable young poet, shatters the self-assurance of a popular London parson when he lays claim to the affections of Candida, the parson's wife. Though her conduct is unequivocal, Candida seems warmed by the ardors of her youthful suitor—which adds considerable fuel to the flames of her doting husband's disquietude. Forced at last to make a choice, Candida remains with the man she feels needs her most—her husband. A provocative, though somewhat enigmatic, examination of marriage.

MEN (4): 2 are 18–25 (1 demands expert playing); 1 is 40; 1 is 60. WOMEN (2): Both 30–35 (1 requires superior acting). SET: Drawing-room office of a London rectory. Arena productions have been given. COSTUMES: Fashionable 1890s (updating possible); black suits, collars for 2 clerics. DIFFICULTIES: Marchbanks is apt to appear offensively effeminate and improbably callow unless deftly characterized. Candida's character also presents ticklish problems of interpretation.

ROYALTY: Public domain. TEXT: Penguin.

—— o ——

THE DEVIL'S DISCIPLE (1897) GEORGE BERNARD SHAW. Comedy.   The story of Dick Dudgeon, a revolutionary American Puritan who has grown up in the most narrow-minded of Puritan communities. He has concluded that those who stand for God are uncharitable, inhumane, and dedicated to causing misery. Since he believes passionately in human happiness, he considers himself a disciple of the Devil. When the British mistake him for the local Puritan minister and he is arrested, Dick discovers himself incapable of causing another human to suffer; he continues the masquerade as Reverend Anderson and is about to be hanged in the minister's place. Anderson's wife is moved by Dick's actions and mistakenly interprets them as an expression of love for her; in spite of his protestations she finds herself romantically attracted to him. At the last minute Dick is saved from the gallows by Anderson who has put aside his ministerial pursuits to become a revolutionary leader. In his hour of trial, Dick discovers "that it was his destiny to suffer and be faithful to the death." Structurally the play resembles the traditional historical melodrama, but Shaw has turned the melodramatic clichés to fresh and realistic uses.

MEN (11, plus extras): 3 are 20–30; 2 are 30–40; 6 are 45–60. WOMEN (5, plus extras): 1 is 16; 1 is 30; 2 are 45–55; 1 is 60–70. SETS: 1777 New England; parlor of the Dudgeon home; parlor of the minister's home; courtroom; village square. This play can be produced in arena or with minimum scenery. COSTUMES: Puritan; late 18th-century uniforms, British and American (reasonably authentic uniforms necessary).

ROYALTY: Public domain. TEXT: Baker's.

—— o ——

YOU NEVER CAN TELL (1897)   GEORGE BERNARD SHAW. Comedy.   A pleasant comedy about confusion caused by changing ideas. Mrs. Clandon, an aging suffragette, returns to England after a long absence, bringing with her a twenty-year-old daughter and eighteen-year-old twins. She has been living in Madagascar, separated from her husband, almost since the birth of the twins, and has been rearing her children according to the ideas considered "advanced" when she left England. She discovers that her "advanced" ideas have been supplanted by others. Her children realize that their upbringing has not properly prepared them for English life. Gloria, the eldest daughter, learns that intellectual prowess is no protection against old-fashioned love. The twins discover that their lack of inhibition is considered bad manners. Further to confuse matters, they unexpectedly meet their father, an extremely conservative Victorian gentleman. They are helped through their confusion by an elderly waiter who always makes people concentrate on social niceties at trying moments. Finally, the father demands that he be allowed to raise the twins, a suggestion that horrifies everyone. The situation is recalled to common sense by a lawyer who turns out to be the elderly waiter's distinguished son.

MEN (6): 1 is 18; 1 is 30; 2 are 45–55; 1 is 60; 1 is 70. WOMEN (3): 1 is 18; 1 is 20; 1 is 45–55. SETS: Dentist's office, veranda of a seaside hotel; drawing room of a hotel suite. COSTUMES: Fashionable 1890s; masquerade costumes.

ROYALTY: Public domain. TEXT: *Selected Plays of G. B. Shaw* (Dodd, Mead).

—— o ——

CAESAR AND CLEOPATRA (1898)   GEORGE BERNARD SHAW. Comedy.   A balding, middle-aged Caesar, marching into Egypt in pursuit of Pompey, finds Cleopatra, an ineffectual young queen, dominated by her slave Ftatateeta. Caesar attempts to educate Cleopatra to the responsibilities of her position. He is partially successful but is not able to imbue her with his love of humanity. Cleopatra orders Pothinus, the people's favorite, killed because he is plotting against her. The slayer of Pothinus is in turn murdered, and the cycle of revenge and further murder is set in motion. Caesar says that "to the end of history murder shall breed murder, always in the name of right and honor and peace, until the gods are tired of blood and create a race that can understand."

MEN (*16, plus soldiers, attendants*): 1 is 10; 1 is 24; 2 are 25; 2 are 30; 1 is 35; 2 are 40; 5 are 50; 2 are 60. WOMEN (*4, plus extras*): 3 are 16–20 (1 requires an accomplished actress convincing both as a very young girl and a young woman; 2 minor); 1 is 35–45. SETS: The Sphinx; a throne room; a palace room; a quay in front of the palace; a boudoir in the palace; the palace roof garden. Sets need not be realistic. Unit set appropriate, but must accommodate a practical sphinx and lighthouse crane. COSTUMES: Roman and Egyptian military; religious; civilian. Extreme stylization appropriate.

ROYALTY: $25, Baker's. TEXT: Penguin.

— o —

CAPTAIN BRASSBOUND'S CONVERSION (1899)

GEORGE BERNARD SHAW. Comedy.   When Attorney General Lord Howard Hallam arrives in Morocco in the company of his sister-in-law, Lady Cicely Waynflete, he little suspects he is soon to be delivered over to an unknown enemy—a nephew of whose existence he has hitherto been totally unaware. The nephew, Captain Brassbound, has for years nurtured dreams of revenge upon Lord Hallam for supposed injustices inflicted on his mother. Before any serious harm can be done, the irrepressibly charming Lady Cicely shows Brassbound the silliness of his schemes for vengeance and sends him back to sea a wiser man.

MEN (*13, plus extras*): 8 are 25–35 (6 minor); 4 are 50–60 (all minor); 1 is 70–80. WOMAN: 30–40 (requires an outstanding actress). SETS: Garden of a missionary's cottage on the Moroccan coast; interior of a dilapidated Moorish castle; rather large room in the missionary's cottage. Sets need not be realistic. COSTUMES: Fashionable turn-of-the-century; assorted Moorish garments including 2 elegant robes; assorted threadbare seamen's garb; 5 to 7 naval officers' uniforms of the period.

ROYALTY: $50, Baker's. TEXT: Baker's.

— o —

MAN AND SUPERMAN (1903)

GEORGE BERNARD SHAW. John Tanner, a young liberal, is an ideal Shavian superman except for one detail—he is a bachelor, and is therefore resisting his primary function of breeding a better human race. Tanner has so far succeeded in remaining a bachelor because his vaunted sense of morality rebels at the duplicity women employ to ensnare mates. He is named guardian for Anne Whitfield, a young lady as vital as she is devious. John tries to flee from her clutches, attempting among other tactics to escape her designs by motor-racing through Europe. Anne pursues him and finally, despite his protests and disgust, traps him into marriage. Although the play has four acts, the third act, the "Don Juan in Hell" interlude, is almost always performed as a separate piece.

MEN (6): 1 is 20–30; 3 are 30–40; 2 are 60–65. WOMEN (5): 3 are 20–30; 2 are 50–60. (If the Don Juan sequence is included, cast will need a dozen brigands of unspecified ages.) SETS: Edwardian drawing room; exterior of the garage at Tanner's house; garden of a Spanish hotel. COSTUMES: Fashionable Edwardian. DIFFICULTIES: Tanner requires skillful casting.

ROYALTY: Public domain. TEXT: Baker's.

— o —

DON JUAN IN HELL (1903) GEORGE BERNARD SHAW. When Don Juan's celebrated love Dona Ana dies, she turns up in Hell, which turns out to be the place that pleases her best. According to Shaw, Hell is the place dedicated to the gratification of one's selfish pleasures, while Heaven is devoted to those who wish to work for the betterment of the human race. Dona Ana's father is in Heaven, much to his disgust; Don Juan is in Hell, to his great unhappiness—and the unhappiness of the Devil, who cannot convert Don Juan to a pleasure-seeking existence. Originally the third act of *Man and Superman*, it stands alone as a complete dramatic unit without reference to the original frame and is most successfully performed as dramatic reading or chamber theatre.

MEN (3): 1 is 35; 1 is 45; 1 is 60. WOMAN: About 30. SET: May be done with full scenery, which would be a series of rock platforms, a good deal of red light and mist, but is ordinarily done without anything but some stools, benches, and a table. COSTUMES: Ordinarily, for concert reading the actors simply wear evening dress. In fact, the modernity of the ideas is better emphasized with a modern-dress production than with a costumed production. DIFFICULTIES: Four actors are required who handle language exceptionally well.

ROYALTY: Apply Samuel French. TEXT: Samuel French.

— o —

MAJOR BARBARA (1905) GEORGE BERNARD SHAW. Comedy. Undershaft, father of the Salvation Army major Barbara, is a munitions manufacturer who considers poverty the greatest possible evil. He is eventually responsible for Barbara's coming to recognize that men's souls can be saved only if their stomachs are full and they are not tempted to pretend belief so as to be rewarded by a bit of bread and treacle. Much of the action concerns the conflict between Undershaft and Barbara's scholarly suitor, who has feigned an interest in the Salvation Army to be near her. Lady Britomart and Stephen, Barbara's mother and brother, are Shaw's comic presentation of the conventional Britisher. Barbara's mundane sister and her absurd beau contribute to the comedy by their failure to understand the ideas discussed by the other characters. The second act, set in the yard of the Salvation Army shelter, introduces several representatives of the working class and of the Salvation Army.

MEN (9): 6 are 20–40 (1 minor); 3 are 40–60 (1 requires an outstanding actor; 1 minor). WOMEN (6): 3 are 18–25 (2 minor); 3 are 40–60. SETS: Library in Lady Britomart's fashionable house; yard of the Salvation Army shelter; hill near the Undershaft munitions foundry. Sets need not be realistic. Arena productions have been given. COSTUMES: Fashionable early 20th century; 3 Salvation Army uniforms for women; assorted threadbare clothes. DIFFICULTIES: In the last act, dialogue carried by 3 characters while 4 others remain on stage saying almost nothing.

ROYALTY: $25, Baker's or Samuel French. TEXT: Penguin.

— o —

THE DOCTOR'S DILEMMA (1906) GEORGE BERNARD SHAW. A satire on science in general and the medical profession in particular that attacks both the physician's moral problem (when life or death is in his power) and the inexactness of medical science. The play concerns Dr. Ridgeon's struggle to decide whether to cure an honest but poor physician or a brilliant but completely amoral artist. He finally cures the physician, not for morality, but because he has fallen in love with the artist's wife. When he proposes marriage to the artist's widow, he discovers that she has always considered him too old for romance.

MEN (9): 2 are 20–30 (1 minor); 1 is 30–40 (minor); 5 are 40–55; 1 is 70. WOMEN (3): 1 is 20–30 (minor); 1 is 30; 1 is 65–70. SETS: Physician's waiting room; private dining room in a restaurant; artist's garret; another physician's office; the office of an art gallery—all Edwardian interiors. Adaptable to arena. COSTUMES: Fashionable Edwardian.

ROYALTY: $25, Baker's. TEXT: Baker's.

— o —

GETTING MARRIED (1908) GEORGE BERNARD SHAW. Comedy. Bishop Bridgenorth's daughter is about to marry a nice young man when she gets hold of a pamphlet which spells out for her the legal rights she is waiving by marrying. Her young man also gets hold of a pamphlet which explains the overwhelming legal responsibilities he accepts in matrimony. In a panic, both of them refuse to go through with the ceremony. The Bishop is unable to straighten out the conflict. The other members of his household are scarcely in a position to offer advice, since the eldest brother has just been divorced by a young snippet who wants entertainment along with marriage, and his other brother has just proposed unsuccessfully for the tenth time to a vigorously independent old maid who wants children but no husband. The problem is finally taken to the family greengrocer's sister-in-law, a lady of much experience who has visions of universal creativity. No one can offer the young couple very sensible advice. But while the family argue among themselves, the young couple slip out and are married on pure faith in each other.

MEN (8): 3 are 25–35; 4 are 50–55; 1 about 60 (minor). WOMEN (5): 2 are 20–30; 1 is 30–40; 2 are 40–50. SET: Old-fashioned kitchen of the Bridgenorth castle. This play is far better suited to performance in arena or chamber theatre than on a conventional stage. COSTUMES: Fashionable early 20th century; clerical garb for the Bishop and his secretary; military garb for the general; civic robes for the greengrocer and beadle.

Royalty: Apply publisher. Text: Gerald Weaks, ed., in *Edwardian Plays* (Hill and Wang).

— o —

MISALLIANCE (1910) George Bernard Shaw. Mr. Tarleton, a wealthy underwear manufacturer, feels he receives no respect from his children. He believes in practical education, but when his son and a college friend come home for vacation, all they discuss is impractical philosophy. His completely man-crazy daughter laughs at his ideas. Tarleton suspects that even his wife, in her own placid way, is in league against him. He is entertaining the son of his best friend—a spoiled weakling who takes calculated advantage of his puniness to get his own way and throws violent tantrums on the floor when all else fails. Crashing through the conservatory roof comes Lina Szczepanowska, a Polish aviatrix. In her stimulating presence, the audience begins to discover why Mr. Tarleton and his friend receive so little respect from their children: they deserve very little. Both the elderly men try unsuccessfully to make love to Lina, followed by the younger men, equally without success. A young man, who turns out to be the son of a woman with whom Mr. Tarleton once had a mild affair, tries to shoot him; the son is bent on avenging his mother's "wrongs." Between Lina's unsettling presence and the threat of assassination, all the members of the family come to some understanding of their plight, and Tarleton's son finally comes to his father's defense. The would-be assassin is cajoled into submission by Mrs. Tarleton; the daughter finally catches the college friend, proving that she has some good sense about men after all; and Lina decides to carry off the spoiled youth to make a real man of him.

Men (6): 4 are 20–30; 2 are 50–60 (one requires an outstanding actor). Women (3): 1 is about 20; 1 is 25–30; 1 is 45–55. Set: Garden room of a handsome Edwardian home; off stage is a conservatory through which the plane crashes. Costumes: Fashionable 1910.

Royalty: Apply Theatre Guild.* Text: In *Selected Plays*, Vol. IV (Dodd, Mead).

— o —

PYGMALION (1912) George Bernard Shaw. Comedy. The tale of a phonetics professor, Higgins, who coaches Eliza, a Cockney flower girl, in the arts of speech and good manners. Higgins is so successful in his efforts that Eliza is accepted into high society as a duchess. However, the flower girl acquires a heightened sensitivity along with her fine language and new sense of breeding. Higgins offends her deeply by treating her as an object instead of as a human being whose potential was central to the success of the experiment. Eliza deserts her professor to deservedly find appreciation as a human being.

MEN (*4, plus extras*): 1 is 20–30; 1 is 35 (must be outstanding); 2 are 50–60. WOMEN (*5, plus extras*): 1 is 18–20 (must be outstanding); 1 is 20–30; 3 are 50–60. SETS: Exterior of Covent Garden; Higgins' laboratory; Professor's mother's drawing room. Covent Garden set may be a drop. Minimum scenery and arena staging possible. COSTUMES: Fashionable and everyday early 20th century. DIFFICULTIES: The actors who play Eliza, Higgins, and Doolittle must all be adept at dialect.

ROYALTY: $50–25, Samuel French. TEXT: Samuel French.

—o—

ANDROCLES AND THE LION (1915) GEORGE BERNARD SHAW. Comedy. Androcles is a meek little tailor who loves animals and is saddled with a shrewish wife. When he makes friends with a wounded lion, his wife leaves him in disgust. Later, Androcles is caught by the Romans and sentenced with a group of other Christians to be fed to the lions in the arena. In the group of martyrs is a young Roman noblewoman who has bewitched a Roman soldier, a wrestler who struggles to control his temper, a coward, and a number of other Shavian characters. When their hour comes, the martyrs face death singing and laughing. They are saved by the skillful performance of the temperamental wrestler. The Romans still need one Christian for the lions; they choose Androcles. But when the lion emerges from the cage, it waltzes about the Colosseum with Androcles. Naturally, this is the lion Androcles befriended in the forest. Androcles earns his freedom.

MEN (*19, plus extras*): 7 are 25–35; 5 are 35–45; 6 are 45–55; and 1 lion. WOMEN (*2*): 1 is about 25; 1 is 35–40. SETS: Forest; street before the Colosseum; behind the Emperor's box at the Colosseum, where the Christians wait to be fed to the lions. COSTUMES: Roman civil and military dress; gladiatorial costumes; 1 lion suit. DIFFICULTIES: Plays less than 2 hours.

ROYALTY: $25, Baker's. TEXT: Baker's.

— o —

HEARTBREAK HOUSE (1916) GEORGE BERNARD SHAW. Comedy. Ellie Dunn, a poor but proper young lady, arrives for a week-end house party at Hesione Hushabye's country house. Upon arrival she discovers that no traditions or conventions exist there. Hessy's father, Captain Shotover, is an inventor who wants to create, but can sell only destructive inventions. He refuses to recognize his elder daughter, Ariadne, because she has wed an archconservative politician. Hessy herself has an unconventional marriage; her husband Hector often poses as a dashing hero and flirts with young girls. When Ellie discovers that she is Hector's current intended victim, she determines to marry a wealthy middle-aged industrialist, Boss Mangan, because she thinks he is at least respectable. However, she discovers that his fortune is founded on his ability to drive promising new businesses into bankruptcy and that he owes his position to his penny-pinching, not his industrial genius. Totally disillusioned, she determines to marry Captain Shotover, because although neither of them has been able to create anything, both want to find creative values.

MEN (6): 2 are 35–45; 3 are 50–60; 1 is 60–70 (must be excellent). WOMEN (4): 1 is 20–25; 2 are 30–40; 1 is 60–70. SETS: Captain Shotover's drawing room, designed to resemble a ship's cabin; garden. Because the drawing room set needs to be realistic, not well suited for arena. COSTUMES: Fashionable World War I clothing; nautical garb for 1 character.

ROYALTY: $50–25, Samuel French. TEXT: *Four Plays by Shaw* (Samuel French).

— o —

SAINT JOAN (1923) GEORGE BERNARD SHAW. This unsentimental drama depicts Joan as a girl of great naïveté in political and religious matters and great genius in military affairs, a hearty country girl who would be a tomboyish buffoon were she not dignified by her boundless faith. The other characters emphasize her basic honesty and dedication to the cause of France in a world corrupted by grasping politicians. The Dauphin is petulant and childish; the generals jealous of her; the Archbishop fearful that he may lose his political power. Only does the Grand Inquisitor, who fights with fanatical sincerity, in any way match Joan's selfless devotion. In the great debate scene between Warwick and Cauchon, Shaw makes explicit his interpretation of Joan as a victim in the struggle for secular power between the medieval Church and the increasingly nationalistic European states. The pettiness of the characters who engage in this vast struggle gives the whole play a profoundly ironic tone. The Epilogue is a dream sequence in which Joan learns that the twentieth century cannot live with her honesty any better than the Middle Ages could. (See also MacKaye's play on this theme; page 352.)

MEN (*22, plus extras*): 4 are 20–30; 9 are 30–40; 6 are 50–60; 3 are 60–70. WOMEN (*2, plus extras*): 1 is 17 (must be outstanding); 1 is 35–40 (minor). CHILDREN (2): 10–12 (minor). Doubling possible on extras but not on other parts. SETS: Medieval castle chamber; throne room of a palace; river bank at Orleans; tent in an English camp; Rheims Cathedral; courtroom at Rouen; King Charles' bedchamber. Sets need not be realistic; arena production possible. COSTUMES: Medieval military, clerical, and court dress. Authentic detail unnecessary. DIFFICULTIES: The tone is extremely difficult to achieve and maintain. All the characters are comic and must be so interpreted or the play seems verbose. However, many of the characters are also sincere; the effort to convey their sincerity must not result in sentimentality.

ROYALTY: $25, Baker's. TEXT: Baker's.

— o —

JOURNEY'S END (1928) ROBERT C. SHERRIFF. A restrained but forthright depiction of the effect of warfare on a small group of English officers during World War I. Central figure is Captain Stanhope, who commands an exposed post on the front lines. Young Lieutenant Raleigh joins the group and is dismayed to see the changes which have taken place in Stanhope, his school hero. Tension mounts as a German attack is imminent. When the bombardment begins, Raleigh is fatally wounded; as the play ends the entire dugout is destroyed by shellfire. (Although the action may seem a bit dated, this play remains strong because of its rich interplay of human reactions caught in moments of crisis.)

MEN (*10*): 2 are 40–50; 2 are 30–40; 6 are 18–30. SET: Interior of a dugout; should be realistic. COSTUMES: World War I English uniforms; 1 German uniform. (Could be updated to World War II.) DIFFICULTIES: Require quiet but thoroughly convincing acting. Sound effects of shellfire need to be credible. Set must be designed so that destruction at the end is effective.

ROYALTY: $25, Samuel French. TEXT: Samuel French.

— o —

A RESOUNDING TINKLE (1957) N. F. SIMPSON. Comedy. A typical English suburban living room is the commonplace locale in which take place an assortment of dotty hijinks that satirize the vacuity of the dreary, conventional world. Characters become involved in absurd conflicts regarding the size of an elephant, the appropriate name for a serpent, and the desirability of producing spectacles for eagles. Interjected into the action are the sudden arrival of an uncle who has changed his sex and the appearance of a group containing two comedians, the author, a technician, and critics who break through the fourth wall to chat with the audience.

MEN (*10*): Adult (majority middle-aged). WOMEN (*7*): Adult (majority middle-aged). (A shorter version was played in London with 6 men and 4 women.) SET: Suburban living room. COSTUMES: Everyday, contemporary. DIFFICULTIES: Offbeat humor and ramshackle structure require adroit direction.

ROYALTY: Apply Curtis Brown Ltd., 13 King St., Covent Garden, London, WC 2. TEXT: *New English Dramatists* (Penguin), Vol. II.

— o —

THE LOVE OF FOUR COLONELS (1951) PETER USTINOV. Comedy. Play opens in the conference room of a four-power zone somewhere in Germany, with a colonel representing each of the occupying nations—England, France, Russia, and the United States. Each is given a stereotyped character, and then all are transported to a nearby enchanted castle containing the legendary Sleeping Beauty. Transportation must be

provided by the Evil and Good Fairy because none of the
armies has been able to clear a passage to the castle. There,
each of the colonels is challenged to awaken the Sleeping
Beauty, which can only be accomplished by making her fall
in love with him. To aid the colonels, the Sleeping Beauty
becomes the ideal woman as seen by each officer. To the
Frenchman she is an eighteenth-century flirt, to the Englishman an Elizabethan beauty, to the Russian a Chekovian
romantic, to the American a gun-moll of the 1920s. In each
case, the Evil Fairy appears to meddle with the plot but is
counterfoiled by the Good Fairy. Each of the officers fails in
his attempt, and at the end of the play, the Frenchman and
the American decide to stay and sleep for a hundred years to
have another try.

MEN (7): 4 colonels should be of age reasonable to their
rank. The Evil Fairy is by far the outstanding part. Other 2
men can be of any age. WOMEN (2): Good Fairy can be any
age, but should be old enough to contrast with Sleeping
Beauty, who is young. The part of Beauty requires some
ability with dialect. Although the script calls for a live chamber orchestra, music could be recorded. COSTUMES: Army
uniforms; exotic costume for Evil Fairy; a series of period
costumes for the four courting scenes. SETS: Three interiors
(could be two); conference room; court of castle; small theatre
where the scenes with Beauty are played.

ROYALTY: $50–25, Dramatists Play Service. TEXT: Drama-
tists Play Service.

— o —

ROOTS (1959) ARNOLD WESKER. The Bryants, contemporary English agricultural workers, are dirty, shiftless, narrow,
and aware of almost nothing but the rudiments of survival.
Yet they are dogged and courageous in the face of poverty,
frustration, futility, and strange, wracking maladies. They
have a Rabelaisian humor toward their own degradation and
a powerful though barely articulate affection for each other.
Existence has blunted the edge, but each in his own way feels
the prick of hunger for greater awareness, a richer level of
experience, and the ability to communicate. The family is
grumbling and suspicious about Beatie's boy friend, a cook
who reads books, listens to classical music, and has confused
but volatile notions about social justice. Yet they rally around

Beatie when her lover sends a letter breaking off the match. And in Beatie's anguish she finds the articulate tongue she never had in the presence of her beloved.

MEN (5): 3 are 20–30; 1 is 50–60; 1 is 65. WOMEN (4): 3 are 20–30; 1 is 50. SETS: Living room of a ramshackle house in Norfolk; living room and part of kitchen in another cottage. COSTUMES: Contemporary English laboring class. DIFFICULTIES: A reasonable facsimile of Norfolk dialect is important.

ROYALTY: Apply Theatrework Limited, 12 Abingdon Road, London W 8. TEXT: Penguin.

—o—

A PENNY FOR A SONG (1951)   JOHN WHITING. Comedy. Play is set in a restful, almost lyric, garden in Dorset in 1804. In the background is the possibility that Napoleon will invade England. Action is concerned more with the garden atmosphere than the invasion, although the dramatic possibilities of the invasion are a substratum. The play contains two plots, one comic and one somewhat serious. The comic element concerns the eccentric behavior of a group of English country gentlemen when Napoleon is incorrectly reported landing on the nearby beaches. Lamprett Bellboys, who has a burning desire to be a fireman, extinguishes the signal fires lighted by a home guard drilling company, while his brother, Sir Timothy Bellboys, attempts to put into operation his plan to defeat the invasion singlehanded. He proposes to land on the beaches behind the French army and, disguised as Napoleon, give orders in phrasebook French, thus entirely demoralizing the French Army. A chance visit from a blind man and a young boy introduces the second plot, about consideration for fellow human beings and the coming of age of the young daughter of the amateur fireman. She falls in love with the blind man and his visionary purpose, but by the end of the play realizes that he must leave her and continue his absurd journey in order to live. The two plots come together only at the end, when the invasion report is seen to have been only a series of comic errors.

MEN (11): Wide range required, from old and doddering to a young boy 10–12. The blind man, the young boy, and

Hallam Matthews must be serious and sincere; the others need only distinct interpretation, not characterization in depth, because of the semifarcical quality of the main plot. WOMEN (3): 1 old enough to be the mother of the 17-year-old girl, 1 maidservant, and the young girl herself. SET: Single set containing a garden, the front of a house with operative 2nd-floor windows, an alcove or summerhouse, and a practical well. COSTUMES: All late-18th- or early-19th century, but include Napoleon's uniform; British army uniform; firemen's helmets of the period; a brass breastplate. DIFFICULTIES: The effects: a drifting balloon, a series of on-stage and off-stage fire effects, a well deep enough for a man to fall into, and a fire engine discovered on stage, then moved off.

ROYALTY: Apply A. D. Peters.* TEXT: *The Plays of John Whiting* (Heinemann or Samuel French).

—— o ——

SAINT'S DAY (1951) JOHN WHITING. Tragedy. Paul Southman, eighty-three-year-old poet, his daughter Stella, her husband Charles (once a painting prodigy), and their faintly threatening butler Winter make up a vitriolic, impoverished English family. Insulting writings by Southman and abusive paintings by Charles have long since caused both men to be rejected by the art world. Indignities and failure to pay debts have created a smoldering feud with the townspeople. The struggle to survive, plus life with two egomaniacs, has turned Stella into a ruthless materialist. On Southman's birthday a young poet, Robert Procathren, comes to take Southman to a literary dinner in the old man's honor. Procathren finds himself so embroiled in the fierce plottings of Stella and the coarse brutalities of the men that he becomes unhinged. When rioting townspeople descend on the Southman estate, Procathren shoots Stella and joins in the lynching of the men. The butler wanders off to a new job.

MEN (9): 4 are 20–30; 2 are 40–50; 1 is 50–60; 1 is 60–70; 1 is 83. WOMEN (7): 1 is 5–10; the others are 40–50 (all but those named above are minor). SET: Contemporary living room in a 1775 building. The new furnishings are of excellent quality, but neglected and misused. COSTUMES: Contemporary English; special costumes for the Reverend

Aldus, the butler, and the country postman. DIFFICULTIES: Set requires stairways going both up and down from stage level.

ROYALTY: Apply A. D. Peters.* TEXT: *The Plays of John Whiting* (Heinemann or Samuel French).

— o —

THE CORN IS GREEN (1940) EMLYN WILLIAMS. Comedy. Miss Moffat, a middle-aged spinster with a small inheritance, moves to a Welsh village to establish a school. Some of the villagers and an eccentric squire resist educating the poor, but Miss Moffat discovers a local boy of great ability and decides to persevere. She manages to prepare Morgan Evans well enough to compete for an Oxford scholarship, but forgets that he is a human being as well as a clever student. He rebels against her authority and gets involved with a tawdry girl. His Oxford exams have just been successfully completed when Bessie Watty, an example of cupidity and ignorance, gives birth to his child. Bessie already has a "friend" and has no interest in marrying Evans, but her paramour will not accept her *and* the child. Miss Moffat decides to adopt the child, even though it means giving up her friendship with Morgan Evans, so that he may go up to Oxford. Evans reluctantly agrees to the plan, and as the play ends he is leaving for the University and Miss Moffat is beginning another school term.

MEN (*10*): 3 are 40–55; 4 are primarily extras; 3 are 14–18. The role of Evans calls for a young man with much variety in his acting. WOMEN (*5*): 1 is 40–50 (requires an excellent actress); 2 are 50–60; 1 is 15–18; 1 is minor. SET: The living room of a house in Wales. Properties would be a more difficult job than setting, because the growth of the school is shown by changes in the living room. COSTUMES: Contemporary. DIFFICULTIES: Major difficulty is the Welsh dialect.

ROYALTY: $35–25, Dramatists Play Service. TEXT: Dramatists Play Service.

SPANISH DRAMA

Sixteenth and Seventeen Centuries

THE PHANTOM LADY (*La dama duende;* 1629) PEDRO CALDERÓN DE LA BARCA. Comedy. This is Calderón's most charming cape-and-sword comedy. The central mechanism that unifies a complex plot of shadowy complications, mischievous deceptions, and appearances that turn out to be real is a movable glass panel separating the apartment of Doña Angela from that of her brother's gallant and unexpected guest, Don Manuel. Virtually all the action is initiated and managed by Doña Angela, a young widow immured in the Madrid town house of her brothers Don Luis and Don Juan. Veiled, she has slipped out to see the shows at the palace grounds; here she is pursued, unrecognized, by her libertine brother Don Luis. She appeals to a stranger (Don Manuel) for aid; he intercepts Don Luis, and Doña Angela is able to reach home safely. As the two men duel, Don Juan appears, recognizes Don Manuel as his friend and guest, and escorts him home. Doña Angela's curiosity about her rescuer increases; with her maid-confidante Isabel she enters his room when he is out and deposits cryptic love notes and other enigmatic tokens of regard. The prime victim of their mischief is Don Manuel's superstitious servant Cosme, who shares none of his master's interest in solving the mystery of the Phantom Lady's identity. After much confusion and some wrangling about honor, three couples are happily united—Don Manuel and Doña Angela, Don Juan and his spirited fiancée Doña Beatriz, and the servants Cosme and Isabel. Only Don Luis remains alone—frustrated and raging as he is throughout the play.

MEN (5): All 20–30 (1 minor). WOMEN (4): All 18–24 (1 minor). EXTRAS: Servants (can be cut). SETS: Street; Don Manuel's apartment; Doña Angela's apartment. Special attention must be paid to the effectiveness of the secret-panel door between the 2 apartments where, in quick alternation, the action takes place. Revolving stage desirable. Arena production impractical. COSTUMES: Elegant early 17th-century Spanish. DIFFICULTIES: This comedy requires expert direction for pace, graceful acting, and particularly smooth scenery operation.

ROYALTY: Apply Actors and Authors Agency.* TEXT: Edwin Honig trans. in *Calderón, Four Plays* (Hill and Wang).

——o——

LIFE IS A DREAM (*La vida es sueño;* 1635) PEDRO CALDERÓN DE LA BARCA. In an effort to thwart destiny, King Basilio of Poland has thrown his son Segismundo into a tower in the wilderness because of the child's ominous horoscope. Years later, before crowning his nephew and niece Astolfo and Estrella, the king decides to test the character of his legitimate heir. Segismundo is given a sleeping potion, brought into the palace, and installed on the throne. Having been raised like a caged beast, the prince rules as cruelly as the stars predicted. Basilio has him drugged again and returned to the tower where, upon awakening, he is made to believe his ephemeral ascent to the throne had been only a dream. When rebellious soldiers liberate and reinstate him, Segismundo, cured by disillusion from his lust for revenge, reigns with generosity and nobility of spirit. In an adroitly integrated but rather contrived subplot, Rosaura, daughter of Clotaldo, Segismundo's scrupulous guardian-jailer, appears disguised as a young cavalier and manages to restore her honor by marrying her betrayer Astolfo. A particularly grotesque element is introduced with Clarín, the stereotyped *gracioso* (buffoon) whose death is quite unconventional. Probably the most famous passage in Spanish literature is Segismundo's soliloquy about the vanity of earthly existence that ends with ". . . all life, it seems, /Is but a dream, and dreams are only dreams."

MEN (9): 7 are 20–30 (4 minor); 2 are 40–60. WOMEN (2): Both 18–25. EXTRAS: Soldiers; guards; musicians; servants; ladies; attendants. SETS: The court of Poland; a nearby fortress; open country. Nonrealistic scenery. Arena production possible. COSTUMES: Apparel of royalty, courtiers, and soldiers in a legendary kingdom. DIFFICULTIES: Segismundo's character development is abrupt. The Rosaura intrigue should not be overstressed.

ROYALTY: Apply Samuel French or Barron's. TEXT: Roy Campbell trans. in *The Classic Theatre* (Doubleday), Vol. III or William E. Colford trans. in Barron's Educational Series.

—o—

THE SURGEON OF HIS HONOR (*El médico de su honra;* 1635) PEDRO CALDERÓN DE LA BARCA. Don Gutierre has married Doña Mencía, beloved of Prince Henry, the king's brother. The prince returns and attempts to court Doña Mencía but to protect her honor she refuses his advances. The prince continues to try to see her. Suspecting his wife's fidelity, Don Gutierre visits her at night disguised as the prince and proves—to his satisfaction—his suspicions. Acting as the "surgeon of his honor," Don Gutierre has his wife put to death. He is pardoned by the king and married to Doña Leonor, the lady he deserted to marry Doña Mencía.

MEN (9): 6 are 30–50 (2 minor); 1 over 60 (minor). WOMEN (5): 2 are 20–35, beautiful; 3 servants (preferably young; 1 must sing). EXTRAS: Courtiers; suppliants; musicians. SETS: Countryside; room in a country house; room in the Alcazar in Seville; country garden; room in mansion in Seville; street in Seville; street before the mansion. Locales should be suggested to avoid frequent, time-consuming changes. Arena production possible. COSTUMES: Fashionable 14th-century Spanish. DIFFICULTIES: The Spanish code of honor of this period may mystify modern audiences.

ROYALTY: Apply publisher. TEXT: Roy Campbell trans. (Wisconsin).

—o—

LOVE AFTER DEATH (*Los dos amantes del cielo;* 1637) PEDRO CALDERÓN DE LA BARCA. Melodrama of ideal chivalric love and Spanish honor, played against a background of the struggle between the Spanish Christians and the Moors. The action is fast-moving and builds to great emotional heights. Written in poetry, lyrical in quality. The roles of the lovers, Doña Clara and Don Alvaro, are idealized but vividly and appealingly drawn and appropriate to the general style of the complete work. The fat, drunken Alcuzcuz, a Moorish servant who speaks a patois, is a clown in the great tradition and an instrument of comic relief. The use of music and dance indicated by the playwright adds to the color and emotional intensity.

MEN (*10, plus extras*): 3 are 20–35; 4 are 35–45; 3 are 45–60; extras are Christian and Moorish soldiers (Moorish soldiers can also be used as Moorish men in the opening scene); some extras must be able to sing and dance. WOMEN (*4, plus extras*): All 18–30 (2 minor); extras are Moorish women. SETS: 13 different settings: 3 interiors in homes and a palace in Granada; 9 exteriors in the mountains; 1 interior of a guard room in a mountain camp. The number of settings and their constant shifting make representational production inadvisable. Unit set best solution for contemporary production. COSTUMES: Spanish, 1570. All major characters except 1 are aristocratic. Extras playing Moorish men and women can be very simply dressed—men in short jackets and trousers, women in white doublets. The remainder of the extras and most of the major men's roles demand military costume. DIFFICULTIES: Long and rhetorical speeches combined with flamboyant and sometimes violent stage movement will tax the ability of inexperienced actors.

ROYALTY: Apply Samuel French. TEXT: Roy Campbell trans. in *The Classic Theatre* (Doubleday), Vol. III.

— o —

THE MAYOR OF ZALAMEA (*El alcalde de Zalamea; ca.* 1642) PEDRO CALDERÓN DE LA BARCA. Pedro Crespo, a rich peasant, proudly asserts he will yield to no one when his honor is at stake. In his rugged outspokenness he matches even Don Lope de Figueroa, the redoubtable gout-tortured general of the troops quartered in Zalamea. When an arrogant young captain, Don Alvaro, abducts and rapes Crespo's daughter Isabel, the peasant sets out to kill the nobleman. In the meantime Crespo has been elected *alcalde* (mayor) and judge; his office compels him to place justice above revenge. He humiliates himself by begging Don Alvaro on his knees to restore Isabel's honor by marriage and arrests the captain only after his contemptuous refusal. A dispute between the mayor and Don Lope is interrupted by the arrival of King Philip II, to whom Crespo shows the body of the officer he has had garroted in the meantime. The king, impressed by such steadfastness, appoints Crespo *alcalde* for life. Particularly in the first half, the play is laced with humorous scenes. Don Mendo, the impoverished *hidalgo* accompanied complainingly by his unruly servant, Nuño; the braggart soldier Rebolledo and his camp-follower sweetheart La Chispa are important supporting characters who lend variety to a consistently engrossing theatrical social drama.

MEN (*12*): 9 are 20–30 (4 minor); 3 are 40–60 (1 minor). WOMEN (*3*): All 18–25. EXTRAS: Soldiers, peasants. SETS: Fields; streets; forest; veranda and room in Crespo's house; the captain's lodging; a prison. Simple decor must suggest Spain. Quick scene changes mandatory. Unsuitable for arena production. COSTUMES: Apparel of Spanish officers, soldiers, and peasants, in the late 16th century. DIFFICULTIES: Much of the force and beauty of Calderon's language, imagery, and rhetoric invariably sound long-winded and declamatory in English. It will also require a powerful actor to convey believably to a modern audience that Crespo's climactic knee fall before the man he and his daughter loathe is motivated not only by rigid Spanish concepts of honor but also by paternal love.

ROYALTY: Apply Actors and Authors Agency* or Barron's. TEXT: Edwin Honig trans. in *Calderón, Four Plays* (Hill and Wang) or William E. Colford trans. in Barron's Educational Series.

—— o ——

THE GREAT THEATRE OF THE WORLD (*El teatro del mundo;* 1645) PEDRO CALDERÓN DE LA BARCA. A long one-act poetic drama in the morality-play tradition, intensely lyrical and conveying an awareness of man's pathetic situation in his struggle from birth to death. The Author (God) summons World to set the stage for a production of the Play of Life. God is the author-director of this play within a play, World the stage manager, the Law of Grace the prompter, and Man the cast. Mortals are assigned the allegorical roles of Rich Man (Wealth) and Beggar (Poverty), King (Power) and Peasant (Slavery), Beauty and Wisdom (Religion), and a Child. Without previous rehearsal or any indication of when each must make his entrance and exit the play begins. Having been created with free will, each mortal may play his role as he sees fit. After each has played his brief scene upon the stage of Life, the cast is reassembled and God judges their behavior.

MEN (7): All mature; 1 (Death) delivers his lines from backstage. WOMEN (3): All young, attractive; (2 must sing). CHILD: 5–6; few lines. SETS: Unit set with at least 2, preferably 3, levels is the simplest solution. Opening scene's dialogue indicates a garden setting. For the play within a play, Calderón describes two great globes which open, God is seated in one upon a throne of glory. The other opens to reveal a stage with 2 doors; 1 painted to represent a cradle, the other to represent a grave. The Law of Grace is on a platform above the globe in which the Life of Man is performed. The final scene is played before and in the globe in which God appeared upon his throne, but which now contains a banquet table on which are chalice and host. Possibly adaptable to arena production. COSTUMES: Author (God), World, and Law of Grace should be dressed allegorically. The remaining characters can be in either prehistoric, mid-17th century, or contemporary dress. DIFFICULTIES: Length of speeches and the fact that they are in poetry.

ROYALTY: Apply publisher. TEXT: Mack Hendricks Singleton trans. in *Masterpieces of the Spanish Golden Age* (Rinehart).

—— o ——

THE TRICKSTER OF SEVILLE AND HIS GUEST OF STONE (*El burlador de Sevilla y convidado de piedra;* 1630) TIRSO DE MOLINA. This picaresque drama, the first presentation of the rogue-hero Don Juan on stage, is an episodic and chaotic story of the legendary libertine who claims, "my greatest pleasure is to trick women leaving them dishonored." Although one justly accepts the retribution that finally overtakes Don Juan, one is also fascinated by the flamboyance and audacity of the hero. Most of the action involves seduction, but sex is treated on a high moral plane. In Don Juan's last escapade, he kills the maiden's father who has come to rescue her. The father's ghost invites Don Juan to his last dinner, and Don Juan dies in the grip of the ghost. The language is flamboyant and at times overblown. In contrast to Don Juan, Catalinón, his lackey, struggles with his conscience, knowing what is right but doing what his master requires.

MEN (*17, plus extras*): 9 are 20–40 (Don Juan must be able to fence; 6 minor); 6 are 40–60 (1 must fence; 2 minor); 2 are in their 60s; extras are peasants, fishermen, guards, and musicians. WOMEN (*6, plus extras*): 2 are 18–24; 2 are 24–30; 2 are of unspecified age; extras are peasants and wives of fishermen. SETS: 10 different locations: 6 interiors (rooms in homes, palaces, and the nave of a church), 4 exteriors (street scene, 2 countrysides, a seashore). Representational settings impractical because of the necessarily rapid and constant changing of scenes. Unit set is the most satisfactory solution. Not suitable for arena. COSTUMES: Except for the opening scene, which demands Italian dress of 1325–1350 period (1 king in bedroom attire; 1 woman and 3 men in aristocratic clothing; guards), the cast should be costumed in the Spanish style of the same period (royalty, aristocrats, servants, fisherfolk, guards, musicians). DIFFICULTIES: A tomb in the church must be dismantled and become a table set for a meal after which the table, tomb and 1 character sink through the floor. Highly stylized and emotional dialogue. There is 1 make-up and costume problem: 1 character, after he is killed, becomes a stone statue which returns to life.

ROYALTY: Apply publishers. TEXT: Roy Campbell trans. in *The Classic Theatre* (Doubleday), Vol. III, or Robert O'Brien trans. (as *The Rogue of Seville*) in *Don Juan in Literature* (Nebraska).

—o—

THE TRUTH SUSPECTED (*La verdad sospechosa; ca.* 1620) JUAN RUIZ DE ALARCÓN Y MENDOZA. Comedy. Don García, a brilliant though pathological liar, finds upon his return to Madrid that his tutor has informed his father of his untruthful habits. In reply to a paternal lecture on truth, Don García lies so persuasively that his father believes him. Meanwhile, Don García has taken a fancy to the beautiful Jacinta. Congenitally unable to proceed without deceit, he turns his courtship of the lady into an elaborate complex of lies. Unfortunately, he is so busy plotting that he confuses Jacinta's name with that of her friend, Lucrecia. He therefore woos, wins, and is finally forced to marry Lucrecia.

MEN (*11*): 7 are 20–30 (3 minor); 1 is 20–40 (minor); 3 are 50–60. WOMEN (*3*): All 18–25. SETS: Many, interior and exterior. Should be produced in a unit set, allowing fluid, suggestive staging. COSTUMES: Early 17th century. DIFFICULTIES: Similar in style and approach to Moliere's plays.

ROYALTY: Apply publisher. TEXT: Robert Ryan trans. in *Spanish Drama* (Bantam).

—— o ——

PERIBÁÑEZ (*Peribáñez y el comendador de Ocaña;* 1614) LOPE FÉLIX DE VEGA CARPIO. The feudal commander of Ocaña is invited to the wedding of one of his most prominent peasants, Peribáñez. During the festivities he becomes fascinated by the beautiful bride, Casilda, and attempts to seduce her. Unsuccessful, he ennobles Peribáñez and places him in command of a group of soldiers and dispatches him to Toledo. While Peribáñez is away, the commander renews his assault upon Casilda. Peribáñez, aware of the ruse, comes back secretly and kills the commander. The king, in consideration of the circumstances, pardons him.

MEN (*19*): 4 are 25–40; 4 are 40–60 (2 minor); 2 are servants (any age); 9 are peasants (range of ages; 1 must sing). WOMEN (*4*): 1 is young and beautiful; 1 is 20–35; 2 are servants (any age). EXTRAS: Courtiers, musicians, peasants. SETS: Peasant wedding scene; room in a nobleman's house; room in peasant's house; outside Toledo Cathedral; guild room in Ocaña; outside peasant's house; painter's studio; countryside; square in Ocaña; street in Ocaña; gallery in castle of Toledo. Scenes should merely be suggested. Arena production possible. COSTUMES: Fashionable and peasant dress of 15th-century Spain.

ROYALTY: $35–25, Actors and Authors Agency.* TEXT: Jill Booty trans. in *Lope de Vega, Five Plays* (Hill and Wang).

—— o ——

THE SHEEP WELL (*Fuente Ovejuna; ca.* 1614) LOPE FÉLIX DE VEGA CARPIO. Fernando Gómez de Guzmán, commander of the order of Calatrava and a brutal and swinish tyrant, so oppresses the peasantry of Fuente Ovejuna that they rise up against him, invade his castle, and kill him. After the uprising, their Catholic Majesties send a judge to Fuente Ovejuna to discover the leaders of the rebellion and the murderers of the commander. The judge puts the whole town to torture but fails to get a confession. In each case the answer is the same: "Fuente Ovejuna did it." Lacking evidence and impressed by the courage and honor of the villagers, the king takes Fuente Ovejuna under his protection. One of the most exciting and brilliantly written plays in all of Spanish Golden Age drama.

MEN (*21*): Some may double. WOMEN (*4*): Several more needed to play peasant women, dancers, etc. SPECIAL CASTING PROBLEM: This play cannot be properly produced without a group of dancer-singers and some musicians to accompany them in the village dance. SET: *Corral* or Elizabethan staging recommended: COSTUMES: Spanish peasant and court costumes of the late-16th- or early-17th centuries. DIFFICULTIES: Play requires a large cast. All English translations are weak precisely at those moments when the Spanish play is strongest—the torture scenes. These scenes have a rhyme-alliteration-and-assonance complex in Spanish that is completely untranslatable and invests (in this play) this most horrible of scenes with a lyrical dignity very important to the total effect of the play. Directors will do well to have a Spanish-speaking person read passages of the torture scenes aloud in the original in order to sense what is captured in the sound of the words.

ROYALTY: Apply Samuel French or Hill and Wang. TEXT: Roy Campbell trans. in *The Classic Theatre* (Doubleday), Vol. III or Jill Booty trans. in *Lope de Vega, Five Plays* (Hill and Wang).

—o—

THE GARDENER'S DOG (*El perro del hortelano;* ca. 1615) LOPE FÉLIX DE VEGA CARPIO. Comedy. Diana, a countess, falls in love with her secretary, Teodoro, and will neither let him marry Marcela, whom he loves, nor consent to be his wife herself. Her reason for not marrying is, naturally enough, the disparity of their stations. Diana is caught in a struggle between love and pride, a struggle further aggravated by jealousy of Marcela. The conflict is delightfully resolved with a twist of Iberian cynicism when Teodoro is passed off as the long-lost son of Count Lodovico. Teodoro gets Diana, and all the available young ladies in the cast are paired off with suitable husbands in a charmingly ironic finale.

MEN (*14*): 1 is 15–20; 11 are 20–40; 2 are 50–65. WOMEN (*4*): 2 leading and 2 supporting roles, all 20–30. SETS: *Corral* staging, if possible; at least Elizabethan staging. No time can be wasted on scene changes. The actors must have a platform stage from which to speak large enough to accommodate the essential musicians and dancers who entertain between acts and when dance and song are required by the action. Cos-TUMES: Spanish, late 16th or early 17th century. DIFFICUL-TIES: Available translations are not fully satisfactory.

ROYALTY: $35–25, apply publisher. TEXT: Jill Booty trans. (as *The Dog in the Manger*) in *Lope de Vega, Five Plays* (Hill and Wang).

—o—

THE KING THE GREATEST ALCALDE (*El mejor alcalde el rey;* 1635) LOPE FELIX DE VEGA CARPIO. This play deals with the individual vengeance of a peasant, Sancho, upon the dictatorial and barbaric nobleman Don Tello. Don Tello prevents Sancho's marriage to Elvira and then abducts the girl. Elvira defends her honor while Sancho pleads for help from Alfonso VII. The king gives Sancho a written order commanding Don Tello to surrender Elvira, but Don Tello ignores the king's edict, insisting that he will take orders from no one but the king in person. Sancho returns to Alfonso's court. The king is sufficiently angered by Sancho's news to leave court and present himself to Don Tello in person, but in the guise of a royal *alcalde* (mayor). But the king arrives too late; Don Tello has forced himself upon Elvira. However, Don Alfonso contrives a typically Lope conclusion. He commands that Don Tello marry Elvira *before* he is beheaded; that following Don Tello's beheading, Elvira, no longer a woman of lost honor, is to marry Sancho; and finally that Feliciana, Don Tello's sister who is now left without an estate, is to join Don Alfonso at court until a suitable match can be made for her.

MEN (*11*): 9 are 20–40; 3 are 40–65; also servants, peasants, and attendants. WOMEN (*4*): All 20–30. SETS: *Corral* or Elizabethan. COSTUMES: Peasant and court costumes of late-16th or early-17th centuries. DIFFICULTIES: Hyperbolic passages and the problem of cultural distance which separates the play from English-speaking audiences. Don Tello must be made a real and dangerous power.

ROYALTY: Apply publisher. TEXT: John Garrett Underhill trans. (Scribner's, 1936, out of print).

—o—

THE STAR OF SEVILLE (*La estrella de Sevilla; ca.* 1615) ANONYMOUS (perhaps Lope Félix de Vega Carpio). A poetic drama of love, honor, and justice, with a lovely lady, a gallant lover, and an infatuated monarch. The aristocratic gallant (Don Sancho) is required by the king to kill not only his close friend but also the father of the woman he loves. After the murder, Sancho's sense of honor will not permit him to reveal who ordered the killing. A last-minute confession by the king saves Sancho's life and reconciles Sancho and Stella. The lovers realize, however, that marriage is no longer possible, for the death of Sancho's friend would always haunt them. The playwright manipulates the feudal and romantic codes through completely engaging situations.

MEN (*12, plus extras*): 3 are 25–35 (2 must fence); 4 are 35–45 (3 minor); 3 are 45–55 (1 must fence; 2 minor); 2 are 55–65; extras are attendants, servants, musicians, and men of Seville. WOMEN (*3, plus extras*): All young (2 minor); extras are women of Seville. SETS: Room in a palace; room in Tabera's house; street before Tabera's house; street leading to the palace; prison, outside the prison. Unit set best. COSTUMES: Heroic age of the Spanish monarchy. DIFFICULTIES: The speed with which the drama must move; language is highly rhetorical; stage movement requires the grand manner. There are also 2 fencing scenes, which must be done well.

ROYALTY: Apply publisher. TEXT: Henry Thomas trans. (Oxford).

Nineteenth and Twentieth Centuries

THE BONDS OF INTEREST (*Los intereses creados,* 1907)
JACINTO BENAVENTE. "A comedy in a prologue and three
acts" that uses the old *commedia dell'arte* characters and a
plot that strongly resembles its seventeenth- and eighteenth-
century models. By a series of tricks, Crispin, posing as Leander's servant, manages: to beguile an innkeeper into royally
entertaining him and his impecunious "master"; to persuade
the poet Harlequin and the army captain that they should
follow Leander and him; to fleece Pantalone of several good
suits of clothing; to convince the city's marriage broker, Doña
Sirena, that she should force the marriage of Leander to
Silvia, daughter of the rich Polinchinelle; to see to it that the
two young people really do fall in love; and finally to get the
marriage performed by the bewildered Dottore. Rather talky
for a farce, the comedy nonetheless has several merry scenes
and a number of improbable but comic characters. Done with
style, it can be a thoroughly successful production.

MEN (*13*): 8 are important (3 ancient, 4 of unspecified age,
1 young and handsome); the Secretary does not talk but must
pantomime; 2 servants and 2 constables (could be reduced to
1 each); doubling possible. WOMEN (*6*): 2 young charmers; 2
intermediate age; 2 older. SETS: City plaza; Doña Sirena's
garden; Leander's room. Scenery need only set the scene and
provide atmosphere. COSTUMES: Early-17th century, recogniz-
ably those of the *commedia;* anything colorful could serve.
DIFFICULTIES: Some challenging acting problems.
ROYALTY: Apply publisher. TEXT: John Garrett Underhill
trans. in *Chief Contemporary Dramatists* (Scribner's), Ser. II.

— o —

THE PASSION FLOWER (*La Malquerida;* 1913) JACINTO
BENAVENTE. Tragedy. Set in early twentieth-century Castile,

this is a tale of repression, murder, and illicit love. Raimunda, a still beautiful woman of middle age, has married Ésteban, although Acacia, her daughter by her first marriage, bitterly resents her stepfather, despite all his efforts to win her approval. Acacia is to be married to Faustino, having mysteriously broken off with her cousin Norbert. Before the marriage can take place, Faustino is murdered; Norbert is suspected. He is freed because of lack of evidence, but no one—least of all the murdered man's family and that of Raimunda—can rest content with the verdict. As they probe deeper into the crime, it gradually appears that Ésteban and his servant Rubio frightened Norbert away from Acacia and then killed Faustino. The reason is Ésteban's illicit passion for his stepdaughter. In a dramatic climax, we learn that Acacia's hate for Ésteban is really love; as the people of the village come for him, Raimunda forces him to kill her. She dies, knowing that Acacia will never give herself to the murderer of a parent.

MEN (7): 4 are middle-aged; 2 young. WOMEN (9): 2 middle-aged, 1 young (major); of the others, 3 are young, 3 older. EXTRAS: Age unimportant. SETS: Room in the town house; entrance hall in the country farmhouse. Both should suggest Spain. COSTUMES: Early 20th-century Spanish country dress. DIFFICULTIES: Despite the Freudian emphasis, this play has long self-revelatory speeches. Chief problem is to make these effective for a modern audience; some judicious cutting may help. Production should be carefully styled and the acting completely straight.

ROYALTY: Apply publisher. TEXT: John Garrett Underhill trans. in *Contemporary Drama* (Scribner's), Vol. III.

— o —

THE GREAT GALEOTO (*El gran Galeoto;* 1881) JOSÉ ECHEGARAY Y EIZAGUIRRE. Melodrama. Don Julian, an old man, is married to Teodora, a young, lovely, virtuous girl. Don Julian is the patron of a certain Ernesto, an intelligent, good youth. Ernesto lives in Don Julian's house. Rumors begin to circulate concerning the relations between Ernesto and Teodora. In spite of himself and his certainty in the moral rectitude of his bride and his protégé, Don Julian begins to feel jealousy. Ernesto is provoked into challenging a nobleman who has insulted Teodora's honor. Teodora, in an effort to prevent the duel, goes to Ernesto's house. (Ernesto has moved out of Julian's house to stop the rumors.) Julian has also found out about the insult to his wife's honor and fights a duel some time before Ernesto's. Wounded by the nobleman, Julian arrives at Ernesto's house accompanied by his seconds. Teodora is forced to hide in Ernesto's room. The wounded Julian is taken into Ernesto's room to lie down and Teodora is forced to reveal herself. Julian sees her and faints. In the last act Julian is in his home, wounded and in bed. Upon receiving word that Ernesto has arrived, Julian gets out of bed only to find his wife talking to Ernesto. This prompts him to new outbursts of jealousy and invective. In the end, Ernesto and Teodora are forced into love by the stupidities of the world, by gossip, jealousy, greed. The virtuous Ernesto gives Julian's greedy brother, Don Severo, one of the most brutal tongue-lashings imaginable and takes Teodora for his own. (This hyperbolic piece of nineteenth-century melodrama was once a favorite in American theatres.)

MEN (7): 2 are 50–60; 2 are 20–30; 3 are 30–40. WOMEN (2): 1 is 50; 1 is 20. SETS: 3 interiors, late 19th-century Spanish. COSTUMES: Late 19th-century Spanish. DIFFICULTIES: Acting style required is more suited to Renaissance drama than late 19th century "social realism." The play is full of violent situations violently portrayed. If the director takes the time to alter the script to suit the Renaissance, the play works excellently. Set in the 19th century it can prove embarrassingly funny.

ROYALTY: Apply publisher. TEXT: Eleanor Bontecou trans. in *Masterpieces of Modern Spanish Drama* (Appleton).

—o—

THE SHOEMAKER'S PRODIGIOUS WIFE (*La zapatera prodigiosa;* 1930) FEDERICO GARCÍA LORCA. Comedy. One of the oldest of farce situations again demonstrates the conflict which often arises between love and sex. An old shoemaker falls in love with a young, lively girl and marries her. His wife also loves him, but no amount of tenderness can overcome their sexual incompatibility. In spite of herself, the wife becomes so shrewish that the shoemaker decides to run away. In a marvelously comic and pathetic scene, he takes leave of his shoe shop and sneaks off. The wife curses her state, laments her husband's absence, and, in order to make a living, turns the shoe shop into a tavern. Instantly, the tavern is full of men and the town full of gossip. Most ardent in his advances toward the desolate wife is the town mayor. The shoemaker's wife remains faithful to her husband and loves him the more in his absence. He returns, disguised as a puppeteer-storyteller. He has missed his wife as much as she has missed him. In order to test his wife, the shoemaker tells the assembled company a story that parallels his own. The story is interrupted by news that two young men have stabbed each other in a quarrel over the shoemaker's wife. Everyone leaves except the shoemaker and his wife. The two talk and the shoemaker is able to discern how much his wife really loves him. At last he can stand it no longer; he removes his disguise. Instantly, she runs to him in a mixture of joy and anger and begins kissing and beating him simultaneously. The play ends with the suggestion that the couple is no more able to live with each other in peace than to endure separation. The wife will be as frustrated as ever and the shoemaker as henpecked as ever, but they know now that they cannot live without each other.

MEN (7; 3–6 extras): 1 is 50; 2 are 40–50; 4 are 20–30. BOY: 10. WOMEN (10; 3–6 extras): 2 are 50–60; 5 are 40–55; 3 are 20. SET: Interior of rural 18th- or 19th-century Spanish shoe shop. COSTUMES: Andalusian, 18th- or 19th-century. DIFFICULTIES: The play's charming puppetlike quality could tempt a director to aim for coyness and sweetness while ignoring the moving and relentless struggle beneath the comedy surface. In one of the stage directions Lorca says, "If an actor exaggerates this character in the slightest he should be hit over the head by the director. No one should exaggerate. The farce always demands naturalness. The author has drawn the character and the tailor has dressed him. Simplicity."
ROYALTY: $35, Samuel French. TEXT: James Graham-Lujan and Richard L. O'Connell trans. (New Directions).

— o —

BLOOD WEDDING (Bodas de sangre; 1932–33) FEDERICO GARCÍA LORCA. Tragedy. The play centers in the conflict of two feuding families. The groom, the last living male of one of the families, chooses to court a girl in the district who has been implicated in an affair with the one male of the enemy clan not behind prison bars. Against her better judgment, the mother of the groom agrees to let her son marry. The wedding arrangements are made. The bride, on the eve of her betrothal, resumes her relations with Leonardo, the groom's enemy. Leonardo, though married and a father, is no more able to discipline himself than is the bride. The two love and hate each other simultaneously. On the day of the wedding, Leonardo and the bride flee together. They are pursued by the groom and his friends and take refuge in a forest. At this point, the play takes a decidedly expressionistic turn. Allegorical figures of the Moon and Death appear in the forest. The groom and Leonardo fight and kill each other. The bride returns to the house of the groom where there is a confrontation scene between the bride and the mother. The play ends with the two women standing face to face before the mystery of passion and death.

MEN (4): 1 is 60–70; 3 are 20–30. WOMEN (7): 4 are 50–60; 1 is 20; 1 is 25–30; 1 is 60–75. EXTRAS: 3 woodcutters; 4–8 young men (wedding guests); 4–8 young girls. SETS: Granadan. 7 scenes, possible with 4 settings. Unit set recommended. COSTUMES: Spanish, turn of 20th century. DIFFICULTIES: Include requirement that English-speaking actors handle long passages of passionate poetry in the forest scene with rapidity, clarity, and lyricism. Also most important to the play is the singing and dancing, which is dramatic rather than spectacular. The less stylistically foreign to the fabric of the play the Moon and Death appear the better. They are different from the "real" characters, but must not be treated so bizarrely as to appear stylistic intruders.

ROYALTY: $35, Samuel French. TEXT: James Graham-Lujan and Richard L. O'Connell trans. (New Directions).

—— o ——

YERMA (1933) FEDERICO GARCÍA LORCA. A tragedy of sex, love, maternity, and materialism. Yerma [*Wastelands*] is the archetypal mother; she lives for nothing but to conceive and bear children—yet Yerma is condemned to be barren. Her barrenness is not biological; she is condemned to barrenness by the author on ideological grounds. Yerma will not enjoy her husband's love; to enjoy sex is sinful. Yerma understands sex only as it becomes part of the process of making her a mother. "Why, the first day I was engaged to him," she says, "I already thought about our children." Her husband Juan is also sterile; he sees love and sex as facts to be possessed as certainly as one possesses a farm, money, or cattle. Juan is a sensuous man, but also a selfish one who enjoys the advantages of having no children. "Things on the farm go well," he says; "we have no children to use them up." The tragedy comes to its conclusion at a mountain shrine where Yerma has gone to pray for children—a very effective shrine, popular with childless women, well attended by the young males of the vicinity. Yerma is approached by an old woman (The Old Pagan Woman), who offers her an opportunity to escape Juan and become her son's woman. Yerma refuses. Juan, who has been spying on his wife, takes Yerma's refusal of the old woman's proposition to indicate that Yerma has finally come to accept him on his own terms. He tries to make love to Yerma and in the process declares his innermost feelings about love and children. It is as though their natures were crystallized: they are enemies, not lovers. Yerma allows Juan to embrace her.

At this point Yerma strangles her husband. A chorus of pilgrims enters and Yerma holds them back, speaking one of the most terrible speeches in all Spanish drama: "I've killed my son. I've killed my son myself!"

MEN (7): 1 is 10–15; 4 are 20–30; 2 are 25–35. WOMEN (19): 1 is 12; 2 are 16–18; 3 are 20–30; 2 are 25–35; 4 are 35–45; 5 are 50–60; 2 are 60–65 (number of old women may vary with production). SETS: 2 interiors and 3 exteriors; can be done with unit setting. COSTUMES: Spanish peasant costumes. DIFFICULTIES: The music and singing, which are dramatic rather than spectacular.

ROYALTY: $35, Samuel French. TEXT: James Graham-Lujan and Richard L. O'Connell trans. (New Directions).

— o —

THE HOUSE OF BERNARDA ALBA (*La casa de Bernarda Alba;* 1936) FEDERICO GARCÍA LORCA. Tragedy. This most realistic of García Lorca's plays is closely related in its thematic material to his play *Yerma*. Sex and honor are the ingredients of the tragic explosion. Bernarda is a Yerma cursed with the fulfillment of her wishes; she has married twice and has had five children (all daughters) but has loved no one. The play begins with the burial of Bernarda's second husband. She announces that she and her daughters are to go into cloistered mourning for eight years. Bernarda rules her household with an iron hand. She seems to live on her honor; it is her honor that protects her from her own sensuality— and devours her. She seems devoted to the need of restricting, suppressing, and destroying her own sexuality as well as that of her daughters. Her eldest daughter is engaged to one of the village youths. The youngest is in love with the same man. The youngest daughter is unwilling to live by the mother's restrictions and goes to meet her man. A third daughter (the ugly one), also in love with the man, reveals the affair to Bernarda. Bernarda takes a gun, goes to the window of the house, and shoots at the young man who is waiting for the youngest daughter in the yard. She misses him but leads the youngest daughter, Adela, to think she has killed him. Adela hangs herself. The play ends with Bernarda's fierce proclamation that Adela died a virgin and that she and the remaining daughters will "drown in a sea of mourning."

WOMEN (*10*): 1 is 80; the 5 daughters are 20–39; 4 are 50–60. EXTRAS: 10–20 female extras; men's voices for a working song also needed. SETS: 3 interiors; can be produced with 1 setting. COSTUMES: Castilian, rural. DIFFICULTIES: Major problem is to bridge the cultural gap between the English-speaking audience and the world of Bernarda.

ROYALTY: Apply Samuel French. TEXT: James Graham-Lujan and Richard L. O'Connell trans. (New Directions).

— o —

THE CRADLE SONG (*Canción de Cuna;* 1911) GREGORIO MARTÍNEZ SIERRA. Comedy. A prostitute leaves her baby at a convent. The nuns, at first bewildered by the problems of rearing a child, agree to keep the baby. The presence of the child gives them an opportunity to express all manner of affection and tenderness generally suppressed by the strictness of their order. The girl grows up, falls in love, and finally leaves her home in the convent to marry her young man. The characterizations are deft and delightful, the humor is warm, and the pathos genuine.

MEN (*4*): 1 is 60; 1 is 25; 2 are 30–40. WOMEN (*10*): 5 are 18–19; 2 are 30–36; 2 are 40; 1 is 50; extra nuns and a lay sister may be needed. SETS: 2 interiors in 20th-century Spanish convent. COSTUMES: 20th-century Spanish for men; Dominican nuns' habits for the women.

ROYALTY: $50, Samuel French. TEXT: John Garrett Underhill trans. (Samuel French).

FRENCH DRAMA

Seventeenth and Eighteenth Centuries

THE BARBER OF SEVILLE (*Le Barbier de Seville;* 1775) PIERRE CARON DE BEAUMARCHAIS. Comedy. Rosine succeeds in evading the advances of her amorous old guardian, Dr. Bartholo, with the aid of the barber Figaro and young Lindoro (Count Almaviva), with whom she is in love. The plot is moved along chiefly by the intrigues of Figaro and by the devices with which the Count obtains entrance into Bartholo's house. (Because of the dialogue in which Figaro satirizes the aristocracy, performances were banned for a year by the French king. Figaro's attitude toward the nobility is indicative of the coming Revolution. Today, Rossini's comic opera [1816] is better known than Beaumarchais' play, on which it was based, but the play is an amusing comedy in its own right.)

MEN (*12*): 3 are 20–30 (Figaro and the Count sing); 6 are 30–50 (2 servants and 2 policemen have no lines); 3 are 50–60. WOMAN: Rosine is 18–20 (sings). SETS: Street in Seville outside Bartholo's house; reception room in Bartholo's house. Need not be realistic. COSTUMES: Spanish, 18th century.

ROYALTY: Apply Baker's. TEXT: W. R. Taylor trans. in *World Drama* (Dover), Vol. II.

—— o ——

THE MARRIAGE OF FIGARO (*Le Mariage de Figaro;* 1784) PIERRE CARON DE BEAUMARCHAIS. Comedy. For services rendered in *The Barber of Seville*, Count Almaviva has made Figaro major-domo of his castle. On the eve of his marriage to the Countess' spirited chambermaid, Suzanne, Figaro learns that the Count, invoking an old feudal privilege, intends to spend the night with his bride. The ensuing battle of wits between the powerful nobleman and the resourceful ex-barber leads to fireworks of imbroglios and *quid pro quos* and ends with the Count's complete humiliation as he, the dupe of a travesty, makes love to his Countess, whom he mistakes for Suzanne. All through these well-organized confusions stumbles the page Cherubino, one of the most charming characters of French comedy, in love with every female on the stage. Figaro's relationship to the Count changes from accomplice to adversary, and he becomes a more direct critic of rank and privilege than in *The Barber*. The sparkling witty comedy nevertheless does not become rhetorical (except in two historically famous, dramatically isolated monologues), but rather follows Molière's advice that the best way of attack is ridicule.

MEN (*10*): 4 are 20–30 (2 minor); 4 are 30–50 (3 minor); 2 are 50–60 (1 minor). WOMEN (*3*): 2 are 18–25; 1 is 50–60. BOY: 14–15 (the author's request that this part be played by a young and very pretty woman still has validity). GIRLS (*2*): Both 15. EXTRAS: Valets and peasants. SETS: Half-furnished room; the Countess' bedroom; reception room; ballroom; park. Unit set has been used. COSTUMES: 18th-century Spanish.

ROYALTY: $25–20, Samuel French. TEXT: Jacques Barzun trans. in *The Classic Theatre* (Doubleday), Vol. IV.

— o —

THE CID (*Le Cid;* 1636) PIERRE CORNEILLE. Tragicomedy. Despite his love for Chimène, Don Rodrigue, the Cid, challenges her father to a duel and kills him to avenge an insult to his own father. Before the Cid can be brought to justice, he leads the Spaniards to victory against the Moors attacking Seville. He is then forced to duel with Don Sanchez, who is also in love with Chimène. When Rodrigue wins, the king asks him to postpone his marriage to Chimène for a time. A great storm of controversy, the "Quarrel of *The Cid*," broke around this drama because it not only seemed to violate the seventeenth-century neoclassical unities of time, place, and action, but also to sanction dueling in spite of Cardinal Richelieu's prohibition. The French Academy eventually condemned both the subject matter and the dénouement.

MEN (*7*): 2 are 20–30 (The Cid should be an excellent actor); 5 are 40–60. WOMEN (*4*): 2 are 20–30 (Chimène should be a capable actress); 2 are 40–60. BOY: Young page with only a few lines. SETS: King's palace in Seville; the house of Chimène. A single unit setting could serve for all scenes. COSTUMES: Fashionable French court dress of 1630s, or 11th-century Spanish.

ROYALTY: Apply publishers. TEXT: Lacy Lockert trans. in *Chief Plays of Corneille* (Princeton), or James Scheville trans. in *The Classic Theatre* (Doubleday), Vol. IV.

—— o ——

POLYEUCTE (1642) PIERRE CORNEILLE. Tragedy. Pauline, the daughter of the Roman governor Felix, has yielded to her father's command that she marry Polyeucte, an Armenian noble. With the arrival of Severus, the Roman officer whom she loves, she is torn between her duty to her husband and her passion for Severus. Polyeucte, who has become a Christian, suggests that she marry Severus after he himself goes to his martyrdom. When Polyeucte is executed, Pauline recognizes the nobility of her husband and is converted to Christianity in order to be with him in death. This conflict between love and duty is a recurring theme in Corneille's tragedies; in *Polyeucte*, by choosing divine love, both hero and heroine place a high value on human love.

MEN (*10*): 6 are 30–40 (3 are guards with no lines); 4 are 40–60. WOMEN (*2*): Both 25–35 (Pauline should be a capable actress). SETS: Room in the palace of Felix at Melitena in Armenia; can be very simple. COSTUMES: Fashionable French court dress of 1640s, or 3rd-century A.D. Roman.

ROYALTY: Apply publisher. TEXT: Lacy Lockert trans. in *Chief Plays of Corneille* (Princeton).

—— o ——

THE GAME OF LOVE AND CHANCE (*Le Jeu de l'amour et du hasard;* 1730) PIERRE DE MARIVAUX. Comedy. M. Orgon has arranged to marry his daughter Silvia to the nobleman Dorante. Since the young people have never met, their parents, with a leniency exceptional in the eighteenth century, agree to allow them freedom to accept or reject the marriage. To make certain that Dorante is the right choice, Silvia exchanges places with her maid Lisette. At the same time Dorante arrives disguised as his valet, Arlequin, in order to observe Silvia. Thinking Arlequin is to be her future husband, Silvia is horrified by his boorishness, but finds herself fascinated by Dorante, who in turn falls in love with her. Believing her to be a servant, he confesses he is a nobleman and asks her to marry him in spite of their different social positions. Dorante's willingness to cut across social lines was a bold theatrical innovation in 1730. (Marivaux's dialogue gave a new word [*marivaudage*] to French literary criticism.)

MEN (5): 4 are 20–30 (1 minor); 1 is 40–60. WOMEN (2): Both 20–30. SET: Room in Orgon's house in Paris. Could be played in drapes or arena. COSTUMES: Fashionable early 18th century; 1 traditional Harlequin costume.

ROYALTY: Apply publisher. TEXT: Richard Aldington trans. in *French Comedies of the XVIIIth Century* (Dutton).

—— o ——

THE SCHOOL FOR HUSBANDS (*L'École des Maris;* 1661) MOLIÈRE. This comedy has to do with the consequences of mistrust and a too-rigid discipline placed upon young girls. Sganarelle and Aristo are brothers who have been given the responsibility of bringing up two orphaned sisters separately. Aristo believes in freedom and trust; Sganarelle in close watching and strong discipline. Each wishes to marry his ward, but Aristo, the older of the two, will allow her her choice. Sganarelle's ward, Isabella, contrives to send messages of her love to Valère and to arrange a tryst with him, and the unwitting Sganarelle delivers the messages under the impression that he is thwarting the affair. The crisis arrives when Sganarelle moves up his wedding date, but Isabella contrives to be wed to Valère under the nose of Sganarelle, who mistakes her for his brother's ward. The play is based on Terence's *The Brothers*, see p. 48.

MEN (8): 1 is 60; 3 are 40 (2 minor); 4 are 20–30 (2 minor). WOMEN (3): All 20–25. SET: A single setting of a street with 3 houses. Should be stylized; could be staged in arena (with the aisles serving as entrances to the houses). COSTUMES: Fashionable 17th-century French.

ROYALTY: Apply publisher. TEXT: H. Baker and J. Miller trans. in *Comedies of Molière* (Dutton), Vol. II.

—— o ——

THE SCHOOL FOR WIVES (*L'École des Femmes;* 1662) MOLIÈRE. Comedy. Arnolphe is a wealthy middle-aged bourgeois who has remained a bachelor because of his fear of being cuckolded. His solution has been to rear his ward Agnes in complete ignorance of the ways of the world until she is old enough to become his wife. His plans are complicated, however, by Horace, the son of an old friend, who, unaware of Arnolphe's relationship to Agnes, confides to him that Agnes has encouraged his attentions. The play is concerned with Arnolphe's efforts to prevent Horace's success and the way they help bring about the exact opposite. Arnolphe's servants, Alain and Georgette, supply the physical comedy in the play as they are caught between the orders of the master and the desires of the mistress.

MEN (7): 5 are 40–50; 2 are 20–30. WOMEN (2): Both 18–23. SET: A street in front of Arnolphe's house in a 17th-century provincial French town; practicable windows. The setting should be stylized. Arena staging is feasible, although the window action might have to be cut. COSTUMES: Fashionable 17th-century French; wigs. DIFFICULTIES: Lengthy speeches.

ROYALTY: Apply publisher. TEXT: Morris Bishop trans. in *Eight Plays by Molière* (Random).

— o —

TARTUFFE (1664) MOLIÈRE. Comedy. Tartuffe, a mountebank, has worked his way into the confidence and affection of Orgon, a rich bourgeois concerned about his own salvation. Tartuffe moves into Orgon's home, where he gains power over the entire household. He asks for the hand of Orgon's daughter, Marianne, who loves Valère. He wants Marianne's inheritance, but is physically attracted to Elmire, Orgon's beautiful second wife. There are two scenes in which Tartuffe is exposed attempting to seduce Elmire. Orgon refuses to believe the first report, but cannot deny the second attempt which takes place while he is hiding under the table in the same room. In the meantime, however, Tartuffe has attained legal control of Orgon's wealth and possessions. Only the intercession of the king, who recognizes the evil in Tartuffe, saves Orgon and brings Tartuffe his just deserts.

MEN (8): 3 are 45–60; 4 are 20–40 (2 minor); Tartuffe might be played as a younger man, or he could be as old as

Orgon. His role, one of the favorites in French drama, requires great skill. WOMEN (5): 1 is in her 60s; 4 are 20–40 (1 minor). SET: Salon (living room) of Orgon's house. Might be realistic, but would probably be more interesting and appropriate stylized. Arena staging feasible. COSTUMES: Fashionable 17th-century French, with appropriate uniforms for M. Loyal, the constable, and the police officer.

ROYALTY: $25–20, Samuel French or apply publishers. TEXT: Haskell M. Block trans. (Appleton), Morris Bishop trans. in *Eight Plays by Molière* (Random), or Miles Malleson trans. (Coward-McCann).

—— o ——

THE DOCTOR IN SPITE OF HIMSELF (*Le Médecin Malgré Lui;* 1666) MOLIÈRE. Farce.   Martine, wife of the worthless woodcutter Sganarelle, determines to avenge a beating which her husband has just administered to her. She tells two servants who are seeking a doctor to cure their master's daughter, Lucinde, of a sudden inability to speak, that Sganarelle is really a doctor. She warns them that he will probably not admit to his profession unless he is beaten. After several beatings, the two servants finally persuade Sganarelle that he is a doctor, and bring him to their master, Géronte. The cause of Lucinde's malady is revealed by Jacqueline, a wet nurse, whom Sganarelle attempts to seduce in the course of the action. Jacqueline is aware that Lucinde's refusal to speak is the result of her father's objection to Léandre, the man of her choice. Eventually, by means of a trick in which Léandre is disguised as an apothecary, Lucinde's speech returns and Géronte is persuaded to let the lovers unite. The slight romance and Sganarelle's deception are the plot threads upon which Molière builds a number of farcical situations involving cuckoldry and the ridicule of medical practice.

MEN (8): 2 are 50 (1 minor); 5 are 25–40 (2 minor), 1 is 16 (minor). The Sganarelle role demands tremendous vitality and skill. WOMEN (3): All 20–40. SETS: Exterior of Sganarelle's house; a room in Géronte's house; a "sylvan" setting near Géronte's house. The last 2 acts could be played in the same setting. Stylization of setting preferable. A single, simultaneous setting with prop changes is possible. Arena staging possible. COSTUMES: Peasant garb and the well-to-do provincial of 17-century France (although any period and place is possible). Sganarelle's doctor disguise should exaggerate the characteristic medical uniform of the time. DIFFICULTIES: Plays about 1½ hours.

ROYALTY: Apply publishers. TEXT: Morris Bishop trans. in *Eight Plays by Molière* (Random) or John Wood trans. in *The Misanthrope and Other Plays* (Penguin).

—— o ——

THE MISANTHROPE (*Le Misanthrope;* 1666) MOLIÈRE. Comedy. Alceste has become so bitter in his opposition to the superficiality and hypocrisy of society that he wishes to withdraw from the world. Successive scenes reveal his justification in criticizing his society with its slandering gossips, fops, and artificial poets, but at the same time reveal Alceste's excessive intolerance, refusal to compromise, and obsession with the faults of mankind. Alceste is in love with Célimène, who is very much a part of the society which he despises, and who enjoys baiting men with her affection and then pitting them against one another. Éliante, also a member of the hated class, is less a hypocrite than Célimène, and more reasonable than Alceste in her toleration of society's ills. She loves Alceste, but when he offers to marry her to avenge Célimène, she refuses, recognizing that his motive is wrong. Célimène is finally exposed when letters to two of her wooers are revealed. Alceste is willing to forgive her if she will agree to retire with him from the world, but she refuses. Alceste departs at the end, alone and more violently determined to "flee from this dunghill home of every vice."

MEN (*8*): All 20–35 (3 minor). WOMEN (*3*): 2 are 20–30; 1 is 40–50. SETS: The salon (living room) of Célimène. Should be highly fashionable French 17th century, preferably stylized. Probably the most feasible of Molière's plays for arena. COSTUMES: Fashionable 17th-century French, exaggerated to reveal excesses of fashion; wigs. DIFFICULTIES: Since this play contains less farce and is more an intellectual comedy than many of Molière's other plays, it requires a greater degree of maturity and polish for its success.

ROYALTY: Apply publishers. TEXT: Morris Bishop trans. in *Eight Plays by Molière* (Random), Miles Malleson trans.

(as *The Slave of Truth;* Coward-McCann), or Richard Wilbur trans. in *The Classic Theatre* (Doubleday), Vol. IV.

—o—

THE MISER (*L'Avare;* 1669) MOLIÈRE. Comedy. Harpagon, widower and father of a grown boy and girl, allows his miserliness to rule his every action which frustrates his children and makes him the dupe of those who recognize his all-consuming foible. The children scheme to select their own mates rather than those chosen from their father's parsimony. His son, Cléante, is his rival for the affections of Marianne. When Cléante forces Harpagon to choose between the girl and his missing cash box, Harpagon chooses the money. Several farcical episodes in the complicated plot ridicule various aspects of miserliness and include chases, servant beatings, and one hilarious scene in which Harpagon—giving orders to his servants for a party he is planning—carries his miserly tactics to ridiculous extremes. (Compare the same theme in Plautus' *The Pot of Gold;* see p. 44.)

MEN (*11*): 2 are 50–60; 9 are 20–40 (5 minor). WOMEN (*4*): All 20–30 (1 minor). SETS: A room in Harpagon's house, probably a living room. Furnishings are 17th-century French, should suggest sparseness but not poverty. Could be realistic or stylized. Arena staging possible. COSTUMES: Ranges from the stingy dress of Harpagon to the more fashionable dress of the other principals. Servants, lackeys, broker, and officer should be dressed according to class or profession in 17th-century France. DIFFICULTIES: The role of Harpagon is most demanding, particularly during the famous scene in which Harpagon finds his gold missing.

ROYALTY: Apply publisher. TEXT: Sylvan Barnet, Morton Berman, and William Burto trans. in *Eight Great Comedies* (Mentor).

—o—

THE WOULD-BE GENTLEMAN (*Le Bourgeois Gentilhomme;* 1670) MOLIÈRE. Comedy. M. Jourdain, a wealthy bourgeois who wishes to be regarded as a gentleman, hires instructors to teach him the qualities of a gentleman. In succession, we witness his exposure to a music master, a dancing master, a fencing master, and a philosophy teacher, who eventually fight among themselves over the superiority of their respective specialties. Jourdain forbids his daughter to marry Cléante, the man of her choice, because he modestly refuses to be called a "gentleman." This complication is resolved when Covielle, Cléante's servant, persuades his master to disguise himself as a Grand Turk, who will offer to make Jourdain a *mamamouchi*, or high dignitary; there follows an elaborate Turkish ceremony with comic pantomime. The couple marry happily; but Jourdain remains as deluded as ever. Each act is separated by interludes of song or ballet.

MEN (*11*): Most 20–40; Jourdain is a bit older; the ages of the various instructors may vary according to the director's discretion (1 minor). WOMEN (*4*): All 20–40. EXTRAS: Lackeys, singers, dancers, cooks, tailors' apprentices; male and female, any age. SET: Jourdain's house, Paris. The setting, stylized, should be an ornate, overdecorated, drawing room. Arena staging not recommended. COSTUMES: Jourdain's costumes should be lavish and exaggerated. Each of the professionals should wear exaggerated characteristic garb. Turkish scene requires rich-looking 17th-century Turkish costume. All the rest, elegant French 17th century. DIFFICULTIES: Appropriate music (such as by J. B. Lully) and dance for period and style must be created.

ROYALTY: Apply publisher. TEXT: Morris Bishop trans. in *Eight Plays by Molière* (Random).

—o—

THE CHEATS OF SCAPIN (*Les Fourberies de Scapin;* 1671) MOLIÈRE. Farce. Leander and his friend Octavio get into difficulty with their fathers by falling in love with two girls whose family identities are unknown. Action consists of the various tricks Scapin, Leander's servant, plays upon the parents to assure the happiness of the sons. The plot is little more than a framework for the scenes of comic deception, beatings, and horseplay. Molière here deserts his comedy of character and social criticism for farce in the Roman and *commedia dell'arte* style.

MEN (*9*): 2 are 50–60; 7 are 20–40 (3 minor). WOMEN (*3*): 1 about 45; 2 are 20–25. SET: The action takes place in a street in Naples and should be stylized. A setting resembling the scene for comedy in Roman drama would not be implausible. COSTUMES: Costumes of Molière's period or *commedia dell'arte* costumes and masks could be used. DIFFICULTIES: The part of Scapin demands tremendous skill, energy, vocal speed, and physical flexibility. Playing time is about 2 hours.

ROYALTY: Apply publishers. TEXT: H. Baker and J. Miller trans. in *Comedies of Molière* (Dutton), Vol. II or John Wood trans. (as *That Scoundrel Scapin*) in *The Misanthrope and Other Plays* (Penguin).

— o —

THE LEARNED LADIES (*Les Femmes Savantes;* 1672) MOLIÈRE. Comedy. The little clique of pedants with which Molière is concerned is headed by Philaminta, who, with her sister and one of her daughters, entertains shallow poets and philosophers. She is determined that her other daughter, Henrietta, marry Trissotin, her favorite among her entourage of pseudo-poet-philosophers. Henrietta, however, prefers the more down-to-earth Clitandre. The one person who has the power to change this situation is Chrisalus, Henrietta's father and long-suffering husband of Philaminta. Unfortunately he is too weak willed to cope with his domineering wife, and much of the comedy results from the contrast between his determination to assert his authority and his eventual inability to do so. When, by a stratagem, Trissotin's mercenary purposes are revealed, Henrietta is permitted to marry Clitandre. In this play Molière ridicules the excesses of those interested in learning for its own sake who permit pedantry to overcome their essential functions as social beings.

MEN (*8*): 3 are 50–60; 5 are 20–30 (2 minor). WOMEN (*5*): 2 are 45–55; 3 are in their 20s. SET: Salon (living room) of Chrisalus' house. The decor is fashionable 17th-century French and should be stylized. Arena staging possible. COSTUMES: Fashionable French 17th century; wigs.

ROYALTY: Apply publisher. TEXT: H. Baker and J. Miller trans. in *Comedies of Molière* (Dutton), Vol. II.

— o —

THE WOULD-BE INVALID (*Le Malade Imaginaire;* 1673) MOLIÈRE. Comedy. Argan is a wealthy bourgeois who, because of his desire for attention and self-indulgence, affects severe illness. His obsession makes him a perfect target for the medical charlatans of the day and for a grasping second wife who hopes to see him killed off by the doctor's cures so that she may inherit his fortune. To save money, Argan insists that his daughter marry someone in the medical profession and chooses the imbecile son of his doctor. Angélique, however, is in love with another man. Through the efforts of Toinette, a saucy servant, the mercenary wife is revealed to the blind husband and the daughter permitted to marry the man she loves. By disguising herself as a ninety-year-old doctor, Toinette comically carries Argan's obsession to its absurd extreme. The play is filled with Molière's parodies of social types, including M. Bonnefoi, a scheming notary; M. Purgon, an overpowering physician; M. Diafoirus, a pompous physician who rejects all new discoveries in medical science and clings to the superstitions of the "ancients." The original includes ballet interludes, and an elaborate parody of a medical initiation at the end. The ballet can be cut.

MEN (*8*): 5 are 40–50; 3 are 20–30. Argan's role predominates and demands great energy and comic skill. The elder Diafoirus and his son should be comically contrasted. WOMEN (*4*): 3 are 20–35; Louison is about 10. SET: Argan's bedroom. The decor should be stylized and suggest an ornate 17th-century French bedroom with appropriate furnishings. An elaborate bed could contribute strongly to comic business. Arena staging possible. COSTUMES: Fashionable clothing of the period and locale for the nonprofessional characters. Doctors, notaries, and the apothecary should wear comically exaggerated costumes of their professions. Toinette's disguise should be like the doctor's, but very full to cover her regular servant's wear. DIFFICULTIES: The initiation pageant at the finale is delivered completely in mock Latin.

ROYALTY: Apply publishers. TEXT: Morris Bishop trans. (Appleton) or Mildred Marmur trans. (as *The Imaginary Invalid* in *The Genius of the French Theater* (Mentor).

— o —

BRITANNICUS (1669) JEAN RACINE. Tragedy. The central figure is the young Emperor Nero, not Britannicus, the legitimate heir to the crown. In compliance with the French classic's claim for the unities of time, place, and action, Racine chooses the moment of the unchaining of the brute for the unfolding of his tragedy. Agrippina, Nero's mother, who has secured the throne for him through murder and intrigue, now refuses to abandon the reins. But Nero fears her no longer; he avoids her. When he orders the abduction of Junia, the lovely betrothed of Britannicus, Agrippina sides against her son. Britannicus is his first victim; Agrippina may well be his second. The development of Nero's character toward vanity and viciousness is displayed in his gradual breaking away from the restraining hand of his old, honest counselor Burrhus and his surrender to the flatteries of the intriguing Narcissus.

MEN (4): 2 are 18–22; 2 are 45–65. WOMEN (3): 1 is 17–20; 2 are 40. EXTRAS: Guards. SET: Hall in Nero's palace at Rome. Suitable for arena production. COSTUMES: Sumptuous Roman, 1st-century A.D. DIFFICULTIES: The part of Agrippina requires a great actress.

ROYALTY: Apply publishers. TEXT: Robert Henderson and Paul Landis trans. in *Six Plays by Corneille and Racine* (Random) or Kenneth Muir trans. in *Racine, Five Plays* (Hill and Wang).

— o —

BERENICE (*Bérénice;* 1670) JEAN RACINE. Tragedy. The play involves three characters, each supported by a confidant. The Roman Emperor Titus loves Bérénice, Queen of Palestine, but renounces her because a marriage to a foreign princess would offend Roman tradition. Bérénice eventually consents to their separation; she will devote her life to his memory. Antiochus, King of Commagene, who also loves Bérénice, accepts her refusal of his hand with resignation. This scanty theme, with almost no physical action, is sufficient to prove Racine's dramatic genius. The hesitations of Titus and the hopes and fears of Bérénice are displayed in ever new variations; the strong emotional tension of the verse in French makes them dramatic and the revelation of mental suffering makes them tragic.

MEN (5): 4 are 30; 1 is of unspecified age (minor). WOMEN (2): Both 30. SET: Room in the palace of Emperor Titus at Rome, 1st-century A.D. Suitable for arena production. COSTUMES: Roman. DIFFICULTIES: This tragedy resists translation to a greater degree than any other of Racine's plays. Contains almost no physical action.

ROYALTY: Apply publisher. TEXT: Kenneth Muir trans. in *Racine, Five Plays* (Hill and Wang).

—— o ——

ANDROMACHE (*Andromaque;* 1676)   JEAN RACINE. Tragedy.   In his first masterpiece, Racine took great liberties with the Greek legend. Andromache, Hector's widow, has followed Pyrrhus after the fall of Troy, not as a slave and mistress but as a royal captive who refuses his love. Only to save her young son's life does she finally accept Pyrrhus' hand, secretly vowing to kill herself after the ceremony. While Andromache still shows some traits of Cornelian heroism, her rival Hermione, the neglected fiancée of Pyrrhus, is the first in the gallery of Racine's famous paintings of female passion. Hermione dominates the second half of the five-act tragedy; she triggers the action which, according to classic rule, takes place behind the scene. Burning with jealousy, she orders her faithful suitor Orestes to kill Pyrrhus, only to curse him after he has obeyed her. She commits suicide upon the body of Pyrrhus. Orestes goes mad. Andromache, off stage since the beginning of Act IV, survives.

MEN (*4*): 3 are 20–35; 1 is 50–70. WOMEN (*4*): 2 are 20–30; 2 are 20–40. EXTRAS: Soldiers. SET: Hall in the palace of Pyrrhus. Greek classical style. Suitable for arena staging. COSTUMES: Mythological Greece. DIFFICULTIES: Requires 4 exceptional players.

ROYALTY: Apply publishers. TEXT: Robert Henderson trans. in *Six Plays by Corneille and Racine* (Random), or Kenneth Muir trans. in *Racine, Five Plays* (Hill and Wang).

—— o ——

PHAEDRA (*Phèdre;* 1677)   JEAN RACINE. Tragedy.   Phaedra, wife of Theseus and descendant of gods and monsters, is the helpless victim of Aphrodite's hate. The goddess has implanted in her a guilty passion for her stepson Hippolytus. When the false news of Theseus' death is spread, Phaedra's confidante, Oenone, argues that the passion of her mistress would now no longer be adulterous. In a grandiose scene Phaedra entangles herself into confessing her love to Hippolytus. The young hero is shocked and disgusted; he loves Aricia, a captive princess. Then suddenly Theseus returns; Phaedra, desperate, permits Oenone to accuse Hippolytus of her own crime. Theseus invokes Poseidon to punish his son. When Phaedra learns that the god has slain Hippolytus, she takes poison and dies, confessing at the feet of Theseus. Though the manners and mannerisms of the French court can be detected in Hippolytus and Aricia, this barely affects the tragedy as a whole since everything in it is subordinated to the character of Phaedra. Racine succeeded in blending the ancient's claim of mythological heredity with the Jansenistic concept of grace. Phaedra is the great traditional role for every French tragedienne. (See Euripides' *Hippolytus*; page 27.)

MEN (*3*): 1 is 18–25; 1 is 45; 1 is 40–60. WOMEN (*5*): 2 are 17–25 (1 minor); 1 is 30–40 (requires powerful actress); 2 are 40–60 (1 minor). EXTRAS: Guards. SET: Hall in the palace of Theseus; style of Greek mythology, possible barbaric influence. Amphitheatre (open air) is appropriate. Grandeur of theme and style calls for monumental staging. COSTUMES: Greek. DIFFICULTIES: Requires superb actors.

ROYALTY: Apply publishers. TEXT: Robert Henderson trans. in *Six Plays by Corneille and Racine* (Random), Kenneth Muir trans. in *Racine, Five Plays* (Hill and Wang), or Robert Lowell trans. in *The Classic Theatre* (Doubleday), Vol. IV.

— o —

ATHALIAH (*Athalie;* 1691) JEAN RACINE. This play was especially written for performances by the schoolgirls of the convent of Saint-Cyr. Based on the Scriptures, it glorifies the preservation of the house of David. Athaliah, daughter of Jezebel, has killed her progeny and rules in Judah. She does not know that the high priest Joad has saved one child, Joas, from the massacre. For seven years the boy is hidden in the Temple. Haunted by a premonitory dream, Athaliah forces her way into the holy place, speaks to the child, and tries to lure him away. Her ruses fail and Joas is crowned. The Levites defend their new king and slay Athaliah. There is a chorus, in the Greek manner, formed of young Levite girls whose chants, ranging from piety to ecstasy, accentuate an atmosphere of providence and prophecy.

MEN (*7*): All 30–50 (3 minor). WOMEN (*3*): 2 are 25–40

(1 minor); 1 is 50–70 (requires outstanding actress). Boys: (2): 1 is 10; 1 is 13. Chorus: (*6 girls minimum, many more recommended*): All under 18 (6 have considerable speaking parts; in most productions the chorus has to sing canticles). Extras: Athaliah's suite; soldiers; Levites. Set: Vestibule to the apartment of the high priest in the Temple of Jerusalem. Amphitheatre (with *skene*) production recommended. Not suitable for theatre in the round. Costumes: Biblical, 9th-century B.C. Difficulties: Choral passages require considerable experience.

Royalty: Apply publisher. Text: Kenneth Muir trans. in *Racine, Five Plays* (Hill and Wang).

Nineteenth Century

THE VULTURES (*Les Corbeaux;* 1882) HENRI BECQUE.
The sudden death of the wealthy industrialist Vigneron leaves
his financially naïve family at the mercy of a rapacious group
of creditors led by Vigneron's former partner, the aged Teissier, and Bourdon, an unscrupulous notary. Mme. Vigneron
struggles in vain to hold her husband's business. The family
is reduced to poverty. Blanche, the youngest daughter, now
without a dowry, loses her beloved fiancé and goes insane.
Judith, a second daughter, is contemplating a "life of shame"
when Marie decides to marry the detested Teissier to rout the
other vultures. Her sacrifice saves the family. In spite of
Becque's attempts at objectivity, modern audiences may find
the sentimentalization of the helpless women overdrawn. The
attacks on the "old family," represented by Blanche's fiancé
and on the legal profession, represented by Bourdon, seem
hardly revolutionary today, but the play remains harrowing.

MEN (*12*): 1 is 23; 2 are 20–25; 4 are 30–50 (1 minor); 4
are 40–60 (2 minor); 1 is over 60. WOMEN (*6*): 3 are 18–25;
3 are 35–45. SETS: A luxuriously furnished French drawing
room in the 1880s; a shabby, cheaply furnished dining room.
COSTUMES: Fashionable and ordinary costumes of the 1880s
(late bustle period); maid and servant's costumes; lawyer's
gown.

ROYALTY: Apply publisher. TEXT: Freeman Tilden trans.
in *Treasury of the Theatre* (Simon & Schuster), Vol. II.

—— o ——

THE WOMAN OF PARIS (*La Parisienne;* 1885) HENRI
BECQUE. Comedy.   The completely amoral Clotilde ruthlessly
torments her suffering lover, Lafont, who is convinced he is
being deceived but can find no proof. When her husband, Du
Mesnil, seeks a position in the Ministry, she obtains it for him

by taking a new lover, Simpson, and using the influence of his mother and her questionable friends. This affair concluded, she drifts back to Lafont, attracted by the steady respectability of the triangle he offers her. Her trusting husband remains ignorant of all. The opening scene, which leads the audience to assume Clotilde and Lafont are husband and wife, is a stunning *tour de force*, and Becque's merciless portrait of a woman completely unaware of her own degeneracy is a masterpiece of bitter irony. The rigor of her characterization leaves that of the other characters rather weak, however. Lafont's jealousy and suffering are unrelieved, and he receives little development in view of his large role. Other characters receive even less attention.

MEN (*3*): 1 is 20–30; 2 are 30–50. WOMEN (*2*): 1 is 18–25; 1 is 25–35. SET: Fashionably furnished drawing room in Paris. COSTUMES: Fashionable 1880s (late bustle period); maid's costume.

ROYALTY: $25, Samuel French. TEXT: Jacques Barzun trans. (Samuel French).

—— o ——

CAMILLE (*La Dame aux Camélias;* 1852) ALEXANDER DUMAS, FILS. Marguerite Gautier, a beautiful young woman with several lovers, at last falls in love with her shy admirer, Armand Duval. Armand's father begs her to break off their relationship for the sake of the family. She does so although Armand, not understanding, treats her cruelly. When at last he learns the truth it is too late; Marguerite's illness has become fatal and he returns only to see her die.

MEN (*11*): 7 are 20–30 (3 minor); 4 are 30–50 (1 minor). WOMEN (*6*): 5 are 18–30 (2 minor); 1 is 30–40. SETS: Marguerite's fashionable drawing room in Paris; a room looking out on a country garden; an elegantly furnished room in Paris; Marguerite's bedroom, sparsely furnished. COSTUMES: Fashionable mid-19th century; maid and butler outfit. DIFFICULTIES: The minor characters are sketchily drawn; many scenes seem ragged and hastily conceived; the motivations are often intellectually unconvincing.

ROYALTY: $25, Samuel French. TEXT: Edith Reynolds and Nigel Playfair trans. in *Camille and Other Plays* (Hill and Wang).

—— o ——

HERNANI (1830) VICTOR HUGO. Tragedy. The plot, set in 1519 in Spain, concerns Hernani, a nobleman in rebellion against King Charles of Spain, who has caused the death of his father. Hernani is in love with Doña Sol, who is supposed to marry her uncle, Don Ruy. The lady has also won the king's affection, and it is in her room that the two adversaries first come together. They part, agreeing to try to kill each other. In later scenes, Hernani once spares the king; Don Ruy, acting on the principle of *noblesse oblige* toward a guest, saves the brigand from the monarch; all the conspirators are captured and then pardoned by the king, who has just learned of his election as Emperor of the Holy Roman Empire. Hernani is to be allowed to marry his love; then the uncle-fiancé appears demanding that Hernani kill himself as he has promised earlier. The noble Hernani does so; Doña Sol follows suit, and the unhappy lovers are joined in death.

MEN (*21, plus extras*): 1 quite young; 2 are 30–40; 1 old; others may be any age. Doubling possible, but court atmosphere requires a cast of at least 20. WOMEN (*3*): 1 young, 1 old, 1 is any age. SETS: Doña Sol's chamber; a palace square; Don Ruy's gallery; the tomb; palace terrace. These could all be done somewhat suggestively, except for the gallery scene, which requires a number of portraits and a secret panel. COSTUMES: 1519 Spanish dress for courtiers and mountaineers; cloaks for conspirators. DIFFICULTIES: Many consider this the beginning of romanticism in France, but today it lacks both novelty and credibility. Its personages are all conceived in a bigger-than-life style that, to modern audiences, may well seem laughable; the characters are given to flights of fancy, long ranting speeches, dramatic duels, and tragic love scenes.
ROYALTY: Apply publishers. TEXT: Mrs. Newton Crosland trans. (Little, Brown) or Linda Asher trans. in *The Genius of the French Theater* (Mentor).

— o —

THE ITALIAN STRAW HAT (*Le Chapeau de Paille d'Italie;* 1851) EUGÈNE LABICHE and MARC-MICHEL. Comedy. A play that is little more than an extension of one of the characteristics of farce—the chase. The whole story concerns the adventures and misadventures of Fadinard, an excitable young man about to be married, whose horse has innocently eaten the Italian straw hat worn by a lady enjoying an illicit meeting with a "fierce soldier." The soldier demands its replacement at once—very inconveniently—because Fadinard's wedding party, made up of the bride and her unsophisticated country relatives has just arrived in eight carriages. In search of the hat, Fadinard leads the party to a milliner's, a musicale, a stranger's apartment, a police station; they think it all part of the wedding. At length, a duplicate of the hat is found among the wedding gifts. The humor is broad, characterization leans heavily to comic eccentricity, pace is furious. Originally produced with many songs, the play has enough pure comedy to be given without music.

MEN (*11*): Age range is extreme, 20–80, but does not need realistic or type casting, so long as father-son relationships and the like are credible. WOMEN (*6*): 1 is 50; 1 young and innocent; others any age. EXTRAS: Some of both sexes are required. SETS: Fadinard's apartment; milliner's shop; aristocratic salon; upper-class apartment; the court outside Fadinard's house. The settings are important to the plot and must be distinctly descriptive, but could well be done with an arrangement of drops or painted flats. COSTUMES: Either satirically period or satirically modern; play depends primarily on sharpness of characterization. DIFFICULTIES: Mainly technical, though each actor must play with sharpness and broadness. Problems are not serious when weighed against the possible hilarious results.
ROYALTY: $25, piano score $10, Samuel French. TEXT: Lynn and Theodore Hoffman trans. in *The Modern Theatre* (Doubleday), Vol. III.

—o—

A TRIP ABROAD (*Le Voyage de Monsieur Perrichon;* 1860) EUGÈNE LABICHE and EDOUARD MARTIN. Comedy. The plot of this classic farce ("boy meets girl, boy competes for girl, boy gets girl") traces the involved rivalry between two good friends for a young lady's hand. To win her parents' approval one young man follows the pattern of being helpful to the stupid *nouveau riche* father; the other lets the father do *him* favors. Only an overheard conversation, conveniently arranged in the tradition of the well-made play, prevents the sincere young man from losing the girl. Characterization is simplified, but the humor is undeniable. The conclusion is apparent, but the steps leading to it—as M. Perrichon and family travel to Switzerland, pursued by the suitors, become involved with a Zouave Major, a near duel, and continual embarrassment as the head of the family bullies wife, employees, and household in a clumsy attempt to prove his importance—are all extremely amusing. The play depends almost entirely on the acting for success. The fact that this play is still a standard in the Comédie Française repertory is a testimony to its mirth and value.

MEN (*11*): Perrichon and the major must be older than the young suitors; others any age. In the group scenes some extras may be required, even with minor characters doubling. WOMEN (*2*): Mother and daughter, the latter old enough to assist in choosing a husband. SETS: Railway station; hotel lobby; Parisian salon; Perrichon's garden. None of these does more than provide a scenic background and the proper entrance doors. The garden scene could be played in the salon set. COSTUMES: Satiric treatments of the period to strengthen play's intended good-natured comment on human nature.

ROYALTY: Apply publisher. TEXT: R. H. Ward trans. in *Let's Get a Divorce and Other Plays* (Hill and Wang).

—— o ——

A CAPRICE (*Un Caprice*, 1837) ALFRED DE MUSSET. Comedy. Mathilde, having made a purse for her capricious husband, M. de Chavigny, is crushed when he shows her another purse given to him by another woman. She begs him to give it up; he refuses. Her friend, Mme. de Léry, resolves to help. She sends Mathilde away and convinces M. de Chavigny that his wife's purse is hers, and the interest of a new "caprice" leads him to give up the other. Mme. de Léry then reminds him of his wife's love and the pain he has unthinkingly caused. Chastened, Chavigny resolves to mend his ways. The play is a delightful example of Musset's gift for creating light and spirited conversation. The plot is insubstantial, but the characters are well drawn and theatrically effective.

MEN (*2*): Both 30–50. WOMEN (*2*): Both 20–30. SET: Mathilde's bedroom, fashionable French of the 1830s. COSTUMES: Fashionable Romantic period (later in the century, if desired); one manservant's costume.

ROYALTY: Apply publisher. TEXT: George Gravely trans. in *A Comedy and Two Proverbs* (Oxford) or Theatre Arts.

—— o ——

A LOVING WIFE (*L'Amoureuse;* 1891)   GEORGES DE PORTO-RICHE.   Germaine Feriaud, like most women, adores Étienne, but her plight is unique since she is his wife. Étienne tolerates her love but considers it a constant irritation and distraction from his work. He is not without a sense of obligation to her, which makes his suffering even greater. At last his abuse throws her into the arms of their friend Pascal and the marriage seems doomed, but Étienne discovers that they are inseparably bound together by their very suffering. The conclusion suggests Strindberg, but the play has little of the Swede's gloom. Action is slight but compelling, and the couple are fine psychological studies. The dialogue accomplishes the easy naturalness that so many of the naturalistic writers attempted but failed to accomplish.

MEN (*2*): 1 is 43; 1 is 30–40. WOMEN (*5*): 1 is 22; 4 are 25–35 (2 minor). SET: Study in Étienne's home. COSTUMES: *Fin-de-siècle*, fashionable but not rich; maid's costume.

ROYALTY: Apply Librarie Ollendorf, Paris. TEXT: J. W. P. Crawford trans. in *Chief Contemporary Dramatists* (Cambridge, 1921; out of print), Ser. II.

—o—

CYRANO DE BERGERAC (1897)   EDMOND ROSTAND.   Although Cyrano loves his cousin Roxane, the thought of his grotesque nose prevents him from telling her. When she begins to love Christian, a young guardsman in Cyrano's company, the musician-poet-swordsman-philosopher puts all his talents at Christian's disposal. Roxane is won, but when Christian dies in battle, Cyrano resolves never to reveal his part in the wooing. He remains devoted to Roxane, who becomes a nun, and visits her regularly. At last, ambushed by his enemies, he comes to her dying, and the truth comes out—he was the soul behind the man she loved. He falls, still fighting in his imagination his ancient foes. The play presents a great number of colorful characters, but they are all so overshadowed by Cyrano that most are mere dramatic foils. Eternally glorious, dashing, proud, and romantic, Cyrano is one of the theatre's memorable figures.

MEN (*30, plus extras; doubling possible*): 25 are 20–40 (21 minor); 5 are 30–60 (3 minor). WOMEN (*10, plus extras*): 8 are 18–25 (6 minor); 2 are 30–50. (Roxane, Cyrano, De Guiche, and Rageneau all age 15 years between Acts IV and V.

SETS: The Hotel de Bourgogne stage and parterre in 1640; Rageneau's spacious pastry shop; the square beside Roxane's house; a battlefield near Arras; the park of a convent in Paris. COSTUMES: Colorful mid-17th century, great variety required; soldiers, nobility, commoners, clergy, actors, cooks, etc. DIFFICULTIES: The play is carried largely by a single actor. The supporting cast is large and settings called for are detailed and elaborate.

ROYALTY: $25, Dramatists Play Service. TEXT: Brian Hooker trans. in *Treasury of the Theatre* (Simon and Schuster), Vol. II.

— o —

CHANTECLER (1909) EDMOND ROSTAND. Fantasy. A colorful allegory with barnyard inhabitants as characters. The glorious Chantecler is worshiped by the denizens of the barnyard, hated by the creatures of the night (for whom his voice means dawn), and loved by a hen pheasant who flies into the barnyard pursued by a hunter. Chantecler's enemies plot his death and, although they fail, Chantecler's disillusion leads him into the forest with the pheasant. There he finds that the sun will rise without him, but he cannot give up his heralding of the dawn or his concern for the barnyard. He returns, and the pheasant, flying after him, is caught in a poacher's net. A lively array of subsidiary birds and animals provides amusing counterparts of familiar human types, and the play gives a unique opportunity to employ fanciful and colorful costumes. Characters and situations are strongly suggestive of cinema cartoon features.

MEN (*40, plus extras*): 6 or 7 are major; much doubling possible. WOMEN (*14; doubling possible*). SETS: Interior of a farmyard, somewhat magnified; a wild hillside with a ruined wall and a gigantic tree, overlooking a valley; the corner of a kitchen garden; a haven in the forest. COSTUMES: Fantastic, suggesting a great variety of birds and animals—chickens, owls, dogs, a cat, a blackbird, and so on. DIFFICULTIES: Play is long. Sets should be rather elaborate to fit atmosphere the author suggests. Large cast with unusual problems of make-up and costume.

ROYALTY: Apply publisher. TEXT: Gertrude Hall trans. (Duffield, 1910; out of print).

— o —

A SCRAP OF PAPER (*Les Pattes de Mouche;* 1860) VIC-
TORIEN SARDOU. Farce.   Clarisse tries to retrieve the indiscreet
letter she wrote to her lover Prosper before her marriage to the
jealous Vanhove. Her cousin, the free-spirited Suzanne, undertakes to help her. Prosper, meanwhile, still annoyed at Clarisse's
abrupt break with him, decides that he should marry Clarisse's
sister Marthe. Marthe, however, is in love with Paul, a young
student, whose tutor's wife Columba has romantic designs on
him. One thing leads to another, one involvement to its sequel,
one misunderstanding is compounded into two or three. Eventually all ends happily, each lover united to his love, with
Prosper and Suzanne being "forced" by the others to marry
each other. They pretend they don't want to, but actually both
are happy at the results.

MEN (7): 1 is under 20; 2 are 25–35; 2 are over 45; 2
(servants) can be any age. WOMEN (6): 1 is under 20; 2 are
under 30; 1 is 40; 2 (servants) can be any age. SETS: Salon in
the château; Prosper's apartment; the greenhouse at the château. All to be done in an elaborate and finished style, the
salon suggesting wealth, the apartment crowded with curios,
the greenhouse filled with flowers, plants, and garden furniture. It would be difficult to produce without these aids, especially the greenhouse scene in which the actors keep hiding in
the foliage. COSTUMES: Should suggest wealth and fashion,
exact period not important so long as it is not too modern.
ROYALTY: Apply publisher. TEXT: Leonie Gilmour trans.
in *Camille and Other Plays* (Hill and Wang).

— o —

LET'S GET A DIVORCE (*Divorçons;* 1880) VICTORIEN
SARDOU and EMILE DE NAJAC. Comedy.   A light, frothy
comedy, this play concerns a bored young wife, Cyprienne,
who is agonizing her middle-aged husband, Des Prunelles, by
flirting with his young cousin Adhemar. There is much talk of
a projected divorce law. Adhemar fakes a report that it has
passed, hoping thus to assuage Cyprienne's scruples about becoming his mistress. The wily husband encourages the deception, saying he is willing to get an early divorce and see his
wife married at once to his cousin. By so doing, he naturally
switches positions with his rival: the husband becomes the
admired lover, the wanted one, while Adhemar takes on all
the husbandly disadvantages. Cyprienne eventually scorns the

younger man and nestles happily back into her husband's arms several farcical scenes later.

MEN (*13*): 2 are 40–50; 2 are 25–30; 1 is a spry but not specifically aged headwaiter. Others are guests, policemen, and waiters, age unspecified. Some doubling posible. WOMEN: (*5*): 2 are young (major); 1 slightly older; 2 older still (minor). SETS: The Des Prunelles winter garden; the restaurant's private dining room. Both require elegance in furnishings and some workable effects, including fires, lamps, and bells. However, they are not difficult. COSTUMES: Late 19th century. Since some of the attitudes and lines are dated, this play should definitely be done as a period piece. DIFFICULTIES: The acting must be polished, the rhythm staccato, and the characterization authoritative.

ROYALTY: $25–20, Samuel French. TEXT: Angela and Robert Goldsby trans. in *Let's Get a Divorce and Other Plays* (Hill and Wang).

—o—

THÉRÈSE RAQUIN (1873) ÉMILE ZOLA. Thérèse Raquin and Laurent, finding themselves in love, drown Camille, Thérèse's good-natured but colorless husband. Camille's mother blesses their marriage, but the secret slips out and the old lady is completely paralyzed by the shock. Under the unblinking eyes of this living corpse, Thérèse and Laurent grow to hate each other, and even when Mme. Raquin begins to recover, she does not expose the former lovers, but continues to torture them until at last they kill themselves at her feet. This first important drama of naturalism retains a good deal of brutal power, although to current taste it is highly melodramatic. (The evening domino sessions with their colorful minor characters are delightful realistic vignettes.)

MEN (*4*): 2 are 20–30; 2 are 40–60. WOMEN (*3*): 1 is 17; 1 is 20–25; 1 is 40–60. SET: A large bedroom in Paris, rather shabbily furnished, which also serves as a parlor and dining room. COSTUMES: Middle-class attire of the bustle period (action may easily be set earlier or later if desired). DIFFICULTIES: The play is an uneven blend of psychological study and melodrama. Dialogue often stiff and awkward.

ROYALTY: $25–20, Margery Vosper Ltd., 36 Shaftesbury Ave., London W 1, England. TEXT: Kathleen Boutall trans. in *From the Modern Repertoire* (Indiana), Ser. III.

Twentieth Century

PING-PONG (*Le Ping-Pong*; 1955) ARTHUR ADAMOV. The main attraction at Mme. Duranty's cafe, as at other places of leisure, is the pinball machine. A silly, trivial object, yet this "machine at the center of the world" affects man's life in spite of his relative freedom. Mme. Duranty and Sutter, the hard-boiled salesman, depend upon the machine for their living; young Robert, who detests it, finds no other way of using his talents than becoming secretary to the head of the Pinball Corporation; Annette, an usherette, forgoes her enthusiasm for the passive entertainment of the silver screen in favor of the action, conflict, and participation offered by the machine; two men, Arthur and Victor, virtually exhaust their lives in a continuous search for ways to improve the pinball game with gimmicks such as "pleasure through fear" and "death and resurrection." Old and gray, they resort to extreme simplification and finish by playing a kind of ping-pong game with neither net nor paddles. In showing man's vain efforts to attain an inanimate, meaningless object, the playwright sees him as sentenced to solitude because of his failure to communicate. It is debatable whether the machine should be interpreted as a symbol for a mechanized civilization or whether it represents the futile goal of political or religious strife. The characters have no past, no future. Adamov does not analyze their individual development; they act in accordance with the morphological behavior pattern of the human species.

MEN (5): 3 are 18–25 (2 reach old age toward the end of the play); 2 are 40–60. WOMEN: (2): 1 is 18–25; 1 is about 60. SETS: Café; office; foyer of a Turkish bath; shoe store; square; dancing school; bedroom; room. Simple, stylized sets. Everything may be distorted except one genuine pinball machine. Arena production possible. COSTUMES: Contemporary street clothes.

Royalty: Apply publisher. Text: Richard Howard trans. (Grove).

— o —

THIEVES' CARNIVAL (*Le Bal des Voleurs;* 1938) Jean Anouilh. Comedy. The play throws a variety of delightfully interesting people together in a faded resort town. Among them are bored, elderly Lady Huff and her friend, equally bored Lord Edgard, her two attractive, wealthy nieces looking for romance, and a trio of romantic thieves who are past masters at picking pockets and at quick changes of disguise. The younger thieves fall in love with the girls. Lady Huff pretends, for the sake of excitement, to recognize the elder thief (disguised as a Spanish grandee) as an old friend. The "grandee" and his two "sons" become her house guests. The thieves' endeavors to succeed romantically as well as professionally provide a merry runaround. Finally, the younger thief and niece elope, bringing the whole masquerade into the open. A way is found to permit them to marry when Lord Edgard offers to adopt the boy as his long-lost son.

Men (*10*): 6 are 20–30 (2 minor); 4 are 40–60 (1 minor).

Women: (*4*): 3 are 20–25 (1 minor); 1 is 40–60. Girl (can be cut): 6-8. Sets: The public gardens of a once fashionable French watering place; the drawing room of Lady Huff's house, the conservatory of her house. Sets should be stylized. Suitable for arena production. Costumes: Fanciful early 20th century; fantastic masquerade costumes; numerous male and female disguises for 3 male characters; 2 policemen's uniforms. Difficulties: All actors must be light on their feet and know how to move, since the play is essentially a comic ballet with lines and needs to be choreographed. A clarinetist is also needed.

Royalty: $35, Samuel French. Text: Lucienne Hill trans. in *The Modern Theatre* (Doubleday), Vol. III, or Samuel French.

— o —

TIME REMEMBERED (*Léocadia;* 1939) Jean Anouilh. A frothy, padded vehicle, the plot of which revolves around a Cinderella—an attractive milliner's assistant—and an idle Prince Charming who has re-created on his aunt's estate the inn, restaurant and park which he and his lately deceased love had frequented. The aging aunt is the fairy godmother who, in a desperate effort to distract him from mourning his recent loss, arranges for the milliner's assistant to meet Prince Charming. Girl meets boy, girl loses boy, girl gets boy—after much verbiage and make-believe. The play is most delightful and witty when the aunt and her assortment of servants are on stage.

MEN (*15*): 8 are 20–40 (1 very good actor is required, 3 play stringed instruments, 1 sings); 7 are 40–50 (4 minor). WOMEN (*3*): 1 is 60 (should be small); 2 are 18–25 (1 minor). SETS: The study in a château; a clearing in a park; a night club; outside an inn in the park. Scenery may be either realistic or stylized. Arena production difficult. An antiquated taxicab is needed for scene ii. COSTUMES: Fashionable early 20th century; butler's and servants' uniforms; hunting costumes.

ROYALTY: $50–25, Samuel French. TEXT: Patricia Moyes trans. (Samuel French).

—o—

LEGEND OF LOVERS (*Eurydice;* 1941) JEAN ANOUILH. Tragedy. The Orpheus and Eurydice legend used to comment on the ephemeral quality of love and happiness. An actress, Eurydice, and an itinerant musician, Orpheus, meet at a railroad station and fall in love. They elope. She leaves her company and he his father with whom he works. They spend a blissful evening in a third-rate hotel. Eurydice learns that the company manager, one of her former lovers, is on his way to the hotel to take her back. She flees and is killed in a bus collision. A "Monsieur Henri," who has been observing the lovers since their first meeting, arranges to bring Eurydice back from the dead, but Orpheus must not look at her before dawn. They meet. They discuss her earlier affair with the manager. Knowing that if she is telling the truth about the affair and really does love him it will show in her eyes, he looks at her. They part, to be reunited only in death.

MEN (*10*): 2 are 50–60 (1 minor); 4 are 30–50; 4 are 20–30 (1 requires an outstanding actor who can play the accordion; 2 minor). WOMEN (*5*): 2 are 40–50; 3 are 20–30 (1 requires an outstanding actress; 2 minor). SETS: Refreshment room of a provincial French railroad station; room in a Marseilles hotel. Sets should be realistic, in keeping with the play's mood. COSTUMES: Contemporary continental dress; 2 waiters' uniforms.

ROYALTY: $35, Samuel French. TEXT: Kitty Black trans. (as *Point of Departure;* Samuel French).

— o —

ANTIGONE (1944) JEAN ANOUILH. Tragedy. This modern-dress version of Sophocles' play (*q.v.*) follows the plot line of the original closely. Antigone defies the order of her uncle and king, Creon, not to bury the corpse of her rebel brother. Creon offers to spare her and kill the guards who arrested her if she will be silent about the incident and obey his laws in the future. Her refusal results in her death and in the suicide of Creon's son, Haemon, her betrothed. This adaptation of the play focuses on the conflict between man's laws, political expediency, and common sense on one side, and moral law, human dignity, and decency on the other. The common-sense approach of Creon, however, frequently overshadows Antigone's emotional irrationality and tends at the end to make him seem the more tragic figure—alive, but with nothing for which to live.

MEN (6): 1 is 50–60 (must be outstanding actor); 5 are 25–40 (3 minor). WOMEN (4): 1 is 50–60 (much on stage, but no lines); 3 are 25–30 (1 requires an outstanding actress). BOY: 10–16 (minor). SET: Space staging on a formal unit, 3 steps the width of the stage backed by a cyclorama. COSTUMES: Modern formal evening clothes and military uniforms.

ROYALTY: $25, Samuel French. TEXT: Lewis Galantiere trans. (Samuel French).

— o —

RING ROUND THE MOON (*L'Invitation au Château;* 1947) JEAN ANOUILH. Comedy. An Edwardian romp, a turn-of-the-century charade. Hugo, a cynical young man-about-town and his identical twin brother, Frederic, a lovelorn fool, are the focal points of a game that reaches its climax at a ball given by their aunt, Mme. Desmortes, in honor of Frederic's engagement to Diana Messerschmann. Diana, however, is really in love with Hugo, who loves no one but would prefer not to see his brother married to Diana. Hugo carefully plots an elaborate scheme to break the engagement. His plan backfires into success after a series of plots with counterplots involving his aunt, her companion, a ballet dancer, and a multitude of other charming intriguers. The dashing young villain, Hugo, is justly punished by being trapped into marrying Diana himself. The play sparkles with wit and frivolous good humor.

MEN (8): 3 are 50–60 (1 minor); 2 are 30–50 (1 should be a good ballroom dancer); 3 are 20–30 (1 has the dual role of twin brothers; 2 minor). WOMEN (5): 2 are 20–30; 3 are 45–60 (1 performs from a wheel chair). SET: The winter garden of Madame Desmortes' château in Auvergne. A striking but fairly realistic set works well. The dual-role problem makes an arena production difficult. COSTUMES: Extravagant and fashionable early 20th century.

ROYALTY: $50–25, Dramatists Play Service. TEXT: Christopher Fry trans. (Dramatists Play Service).

— o —

ARDELE (*Ardèle, ou La Marguerite;* 1948) JEAN ANOUILH. The piercing shrieks of General de Saint-Pé's madly jealous, bedridden wife mingle with the mating call of the peacock in the park. The aging general simulates the solicitous husband while clandestinely seeking relief by making love to the chambermaids. His daughter-in-law, the personification of purity, is tortured by the sexual satisfaction she derives from a husband she cannot love. The general's sister lives in a triangle with her philandering husband and her peevish lover. They are all miserably trying to keep up appearances in strict acordance with the moral code of upper society as they gather to discuss the shocking news: Ardèle, the general's other sister (who remains off stage), intends to marry the tutor of the general's youngest offspring. Such an alliance would subject the Saint-Pés to ridicule, since both Ardèle and the tutor are hunchbacks; and they prevent it by driving the unfortunate lovers into suicide. Two children, spying on the grown-ups and aping their amorous misbehavior, guarantee that the distorted concept of love will be carried over from generation to generation.

MEN (4): 1 is 18–22; 3 are 40–60. WOMEN (4): 2 are about 20; 2 are 35–50. BOY: About 10. GIRL: About 10. SET: Hall of a French château. 2 flights of stairs lead up to either end of a gallery running the length of the set; a number of doors lead off it. Because of these scenic demands, the play is not suitable for arena production. Lavish neo-Baroque style, early 20th century. COSTUMES: Fashionable 1912 French.

ROYALTY: $35–25, Samuel French. TEXT: Lucienne Hill trans. in *Anouilh, Selected Plays* (Hill and Wang).

— o —

MADEMOISELLE COLOMBE (*Colombe;* 1951) JEAN ANOUILH. Colombe, the naïve young wife of Julien, is left in the care of her actress mother-in-law, Mme. Alexandra, when her husband is drafted. A part is written for her in Mme. Alexandra's new play. The bohemian life suits Colombe, and she realizes how unhappy and restricted she was as the wife of an impoverished, moody, puritanical young pianist. She has an affair with her charming, ne'er-do-well brother-in-law. Confronted with evidence of her infidelity by her husband, she is unabashed. It is he who will have to make the adjustment this time; she will not resume their former way of life. The play's serious moments are skillfully interwoven with comic ones, provided chiefly by a delightful variety of backstage characters, many of whom are part of Mme. Alexandra's retinue and are also Colombe's unsuccessful suitors.

MEN (*10, 1 can be cut*): 3 are 25–30 (1 minor); 6 are 40–55 (2 minor; all character roles): 1 dancer (optional). WOMEN (*5, 1 can be cut*): 1 is 19–23; 2 are 50–60 (1 requires a very good actress); 1 is 30–40 (minor); 1 dancer (optional). SETS: 2 dressing-rooms, 1 elaborate, 1 plain, each with part of a backstage corridor visible; 1 set showing a cross section of Paris theatre stage area, with a portion of a proscenium arch on 1 side on which the final scene of a play in performance can be shown. Sets should be realistic. COSTUMES: Early 20th century; 2 fashionable women's dresses; 4 very fashionable men's outfits. DIFFICULTIES: A fly gallery is needed to strike the set for the play-within-a-play quickly and quietly during 1 scene.

ROYALTY: $50, Samuel French. TEXT: Louis Kronenberger trans. (Samuel French).

— o —

THE WALTZ OF THE TOREADORS (*La Valse des Toréadors;* 1952) JEAN ANOUILH. Comedy. General St. Pé resists growing old. He desires to maintain his reputation as a dashing lover and soldier but he does not want to hurt his invalid wife. He dreams of his bygone affairs of love and honor as he tries to write his military memoirs, while his querulous, bedridden wife continuously shouts at him from her room—accusing him of unfaithfulness in mind if not in body. The unexpected arrival of Mlle. Ghislaine, an aging maiden lady who has been waiting seventeen years for the general to be free, complicates the routine of the ménage. Tragicomic suicidal attempts by both Mme. St. Pé and Ghislaine fail to change the *status quo*. Ghislaine decides to marry the general's secretary, who turns out at the end of the play to be the general's son by an earlier liaison. The general resigns himself to growing old. There are some poignant scenes between the general and his wife, as well as some excellent farce.

MEN (4): 3 are 50–60 (1 requires an outstanding actor); 1 is 22–30. WOMEN (7): 2 are 50–60 (1 requires a very good actress; 1 minor); 3 are 17–20 (1 minor); 2 are 25–35. SETS: The study of General St. Pé and his wife's adjoining bedroom, the interior of which can be seen, when necessary, through a scrim wall. Sets should be realistic. Arena production possible. COSTUMES: Fashionable early 20th century; a general's uniform; a priest's cassock.
ROYALTY: $50–25, Samuel French. TEXT: Lucienne Hill trans. (Samuel French).

—— o ——

THE LARK (*L'Alouette*; 1955) JEAN ANOUILH. Tragedy. This frankly theatrical retelling of the story of Joan of Arc begins with her trial and dramatizes various events in her life through flashbacks. The next to last scene is her execution and the final scene is a flashback to the coronation of Charles VII. The play has been described as an attempt to accent the idea of Joan's and France's triumph over the picayune demands of worldly institutions.

MEN (19): 1 is 50–60; 5 are 40–50; 5 are 30–40 1 (minor); 4 are 20–30 (2 minor); 4 are extras. WOMEN (7): 3 are 18–25; 2 are 40–50; 2 are extras. SET: Bare stage with platform, a cyclorama, a few pieces of 15th-century furniture. Projections on the cyclorama may be used. Suitable for arena production. COSTUMES: Realistic 15th-century court, peasant, military, and clerical dress. DIFFICULTIES: A talented actress is needed to make Joan a fresh character. The flashbacks must be distinct from the trial itself.

ROYALTY: $50–25, Dramatists Play Service. TEXT: Lillian
Hellman trans. (Dramatists Play Service).

—— O ——

BECKET (*Becket, ou l'Honneur de Dieu;* 1959) JEAN
ANOUILH. Anouilh presents a diversified and highly dramatic
chronicle of the love-hate relationship between Henry II of
England and Thomas à Becket. It begins with Henry's peniten-
tial humiliation in the cathedral of Canterbury and then flashes
back to the days when Becket had championed the king's
cause as his loyal chancellor and had shared his royal friend's
pleasures in hunting and wenching. The primary motive for
the historical conflict lies, in Anouilh's interpretation, in the
incompatibility of the two pivotal characters. He makes Becket
a noble and cultivated figure, altruistic and unrelenting in his
dedication; Henry a rough, simple-hearted roisterer, well aware
of his companion's superiority and attached to him with the
faithful affection of a dog. Once Becket, at Henry's insistence,
becomes Archbishop of Canterbury, he serves the Church with
the same uncompromising devotion he had formerly offered to
his worldly sovereign. Henry's hurt and rage cause his henchmen to murder Becket. All is subordinated to the irreconcil-
able power struggle between the implacable archbishop and
the passionate king, leading to Becket's martyrdom and Henry's
despair.

MEN (*20; doubling possible*): 13 are 20–40 (10 minor);
6 are 40–60 (5 minor); 1 is 60–80. WOMEN (*5*): 3 are 16–21;
1 is 25–30; 1 is 40–50. BOYS (*2*): 1 is 3–4 (no lines); 1 is
6–9. EXTRAS: Soldiers; monks; servants; pages. SETS: Numerous exterior and interior locations in England and France,
ranging from palaces and cathedrals to primitive huts. Stylized
scenery, unit set strongly recommended. In an arena production the play is bound to lose many of its spectacular qualities.
COSTUMES: Colorful 12th century. DIFFICULTIES: The character of the king is far more touching than that of the archbishop; every effort should be undertaken to restore the
balance. In 2 important scenes, Henry and Becket appear on
horseback (dummy horses).
ROYALTY: $50–25, Samuel French. TEXT: Lucienne Hill
trans. (Samuel French).

—— O ——

CLÉRAMBARD (*Clérambard;* 1949) MARCEL AYMÉ. Comedy. To save his honor and his château, the impoverished Comte de Clérambard condemns his family to slave labor at the knitting machine. Then, one day, a miracle by St. Francis of Assisi transforms him from a proud eccentric into a humble one who loves his "sister spider" at least as much as his wife. Instead of marrying his son to an ugly bourgeois heiress, he betrothes him to the town trollop. Later, his belief in the miracle is shaken, but not his faith—the faith of those who do not see and yet believe. Now St. Francis really appears, and all those free from vanity see him. Clérambard sells his castle and embarks with his family and friends in a wagon on a beggarly good-will tour. His pathetically self-sacrificing wife, his miserable retarded son, and his valiant mother-in-law are comically contrasted with the proletarian, uninhibited trollop, and with the snobbish middle-class couple and their awkward, silly daughters. The matchmaking priest is the only one who "cannot see a blessed thing."

MEN (7): 2 are 20–25 (1 minor); 2 are 30–40 (1 minor); 3 are 40–60 (1 requires outstanding actor). WOMEN (7): 3 are 16–19; 1 is 30; 2 are 45; 1 is 66. SETS: The Clérambard mansion; the trollop's room; courtyard in the Clérambard mansion. 4 knitting machines must be provided. Sets should accentuate the unrealistic character of the play. Arena production possible. COSTUMES: Upper class, around 1910; 1 priest's soutane and hat; 1 Franciscan monk's habit; 1 soldier's uniform.

ROYALTY: $50–25, Samuel French. TEXT: Norman Penny trans. (Samuel French).

— o —

WAITING FOR GODOT (*En Attendant Godot;* 1952) SAMUEL BECKETT. Early evening on a country road. Estragon and Vladimir wait vaguely and disconsolately for a nebulous Godot. They complain of life, toy with repentance, fall asleep to nightmares, quarrel, make up, consider hanging themselves, and wonder what it is they really expect of Godot when he does come. Down the road struts Pozzo, a pompous taskmaster, with Lucky, whom slavery and unquestioning acceptance have reduced to near-idiocy. Prodded to think, Lucky recites a frenzied jumble of theology and politics, then stumbles off into the darkness with his master. During Act II, in a dreamlike slapstick, Estragon and Vladimir trade funny hats, pretend at slave-and-master, recite humorous poetry, argue over the past, the distant, and the present. Pozzo and Lucky stumble in again, one now blind and the other dumb. Neither remembers who he is or was. Godot sends word he will not come today, but surely tomorrow. Vladimir and Estragon should be moving on, but neither can bring himself to stir.

MEN (5): 2 are probably 40–60; the other 2 are probably older. Boy is about 12 (minor). SET: A country road with a tree. COSTUMES: Fantastic—possibly 20th century. DIFFICULTIES: Allegorical and symbolical, heavily dependent on a strong sense of theatre and comedy to bring it off.

ROYALTY: $50–25, Dramatists Play Service. TEXT: Samuel Beckett trans. (Grove).

—o—

ENDGAME (*Fin de Partie;* 1957) SAMUEL BECKETT. The final stage in chess, when only a few pieces remain on the board and mate is near, is called "endgame." There are only four characters in Beckett's play: Hamm; Nagg and Nell, his parents; and Clov, his servant. The scene is a hollow; the time, zero. Outside are lifeless lands and motionless waters. Hamm is blind and paralyzed, a sardonic tyrant who rules his comatose confines from a wheel-chair throne. The past is worn out and has become garbage: Nagg and Nell vegetate in ash bins. They chatter idiotically and sentimentalize their trivial memories until they finally disintegrate. The future is immobile. Clov, attached to Hamm in a vaguely son-slave relationship, is lame. He repeatedly announces his departure. Hamm seeks to find the significance of his life in sham-philosophical dialogue. But in vain; it leads to an endless, meaningless soliloquy. Though there is a certain playfulness in the sometimes farcical action and in the startling juxtaposition of statements open to various interpretations, this barely alleviates the oppressive mood of futility and inescapable doom: "You cried for the night; it falls: now cry in darkness."

MEN (3): 1 young; 1 middle-aged; 1 old. WOMAN: Old. SET: Bare interior. Gray light. 2 tiny windows, 2 ash bins, a small stepladder; an armchair on casters. Beckett's esthetic requires a walled-in set, seen by the audience from approximately the same angle. COSTUMES: Timeless; unrealistic. DIFFICUL-

TIES: The play requires detailed, imaginative direction and highly nuanced acting.

ROYALTY: $35–25, Samuel French. TEXT: Samuel Beckett trans. (Grove).

— o —

HAPPY DAYS (1961) SAMUEL BECKETT. The first act encompasses a day late in the life of a very ordinary woman, Winnie, imbedded to above her waist in a mound of earth. There is also Willie, presumably her mate, who dwells in a hole nearby. He is able to move somewhat on all fours, but most of the time he keeps quiet and out of sight. Winnie prattles away in an unceasing attempt to establish something like a conversation; and it is a happy day when she succeeds in extracting a monosyllabic retort from her reluctant companion. Her earthly treasures—toiletries, medicines, a little music box, a parasol, and other bric-a-brac—are contained in a shopping bag. Rummaging among her possessions she kills time and does not need to take recourse to the only unnecessary object she owns, a revolver. The second and final act shows another day in Winnie's blissful life. Now she is buried up to her neck and cannot move her head. Her delight is immense when Willie crawls into her field of vision. Though he fails to reach her—or is he trying to take the revolver?—Winnie gaily incants the waltz from *The Merry Widow* as her swan song. Beckett once more presents his grim view of the human condition in crudely humorous, unrhetorical, and strangely theatrical terms. Elusive elements of poetry counteract his ruthless exposure of man trapped in a hostile universe and lend compassion to the pathetically struggling creature.

MAN: About 60. WOMAN: About 50. SET: Expanse of scorched grass rising to a low mound. Maximum of simplicity and symmetry. Unsuitable for arena production. COSTUMES: Woman's bodice; antiquated formal attire of a man; top hat. DIFFICULTIES: In spite of the considerable amount of stage business allotted to Winnie in Act I, her part requires the ultimate in theatrical expression. During the entire play her partner punctuates her 1½–hour monologue with only 43 words.

ROYALTY: Apply publisher. TEXT: Samuel Beckett trans. (Grove).

— o —

DIALOGUES OF THE CARMELITES (*Dialogues des Carmélites;* 1948) GEORGES BERNANOS. An adaptation of Gertrud von Le Fort's novel, *The Last at the Scaffold*, based upon the execution of twelve Carmelite nuns toward the close of Robespierre's reign of terror. Blanche de la Force, an oversensitive young aristocrat, has been tormented since childhood by unwarranted fears. To overcome what appears to her a disgraceful weakness, she seeks admission to the Carmelites. Though the prioress warns her of the illusionless solitude of a true religious, the girl willingly accepts the hardship of the rule and, to conquer her own agony by uniting her will with the passion of the Lord, she chooses as her Carmelite name Sister Blanche of the Agony of the Christ. After the outbreak of the Revolution and the ensuing persecutions, Blanche falters, deserts the order, but eventually gains new strength and follows her sisters to the guillotine. Bernanos treats the themes of death, heroism, and martyrdom in manifold variants as exemplified by the different religious. He shows the characters vividly human in their generosity and pettiness, pride and humility, austerity and humor.

MEN (7): 4 are 20–30 (3 minor); 3 are 30–50 (1 minor). WOMEN (16): 3 are 17–20 (1 minor); 8 are 25–40 (all minor); 3 are 40–60 (1 minor); 2 are 60–80 (1 minor). EXTRAS: Crowd at the guillotine. SETS: Living room and bedroom in the Palais de la Force; parlor, chapel, garden, and various rooms and corridors in the Carmelite convent; the Conciergerie prison; the Place de la Revolution. Sets should be very simple. Unit set highly recommended. Arena production possible. COSTUMES: Garments of the aristocracy and of the people during the French Revolution; 1 priest's habit; habits of 14 Carmelite nuns and 2 novices.

ROYALTY: Apply publishers. TEXT: Michael Legat trans. (as *The Fearless Heart;* The Bodley Head, John Lane Ltd., 10 Eariham St., London, WC 2) or Gerard Hopkins trans. (William Collins, 14 St. James's Pl., London, SW 1).

—— O ——

CALIGULA (1944) ALBERT CAMUS. The unexpected death of his sister reveals a simple truth to Caligula—that men die and they are not happy. Since he is emperor, with seemingly limitless power but still cannot change the cruel order of the universe, Caligula attempts to echo the cruel behavior of the gods as he resorts to torture, blasphemy, and murder. Before he dies he shatters the mirror that reflects only the outer shell of his being, as his actions have reflected only the surface of what he is.

MEN (*11, plus extras*): 17–70. WOMEN (*1, plus extras*). SETS: A state room in the imperial palace; Cherea's dining room. Nonrealistic. COSTUMES: Roman, early Empire.

ROYALTY: Apply A. D. Peters.* TEXT: Stuart Gilbert trans. in *Caligula and Cross Purpose* (New Directions).

— o —

STATE OF SIEGE (*L'État de Siège;* 1948) ALBERT CAMUS. The Plague (personified by a baleful, uniformed dictator) and his female companion, Death, claim possession of Cádiz. The woman carries a notebook containing a list of the inhabitants. One pencil stroke can extinguish life. A brief demonstration and the assurance of a safe retreat persuade the authorities to surrender. The Plague now establishes a totalitarian regime of minutely organized terror. Nada, a drunken nihilist, is put in charge of a vast bureacratic machine aimed at reducing man to a cipher. One man, Diego, finds the courage and the faith to resist. Sacrificing his love for his romantically inclined sweetheart, Victoria, and sacrificing his own life, he saves hers and that of the city. The state of siege is ended. The authorities return. Whether or not freedom will return remains to be seen. The essentially abstract characters, in their interaction of antithetic ideas and ideals, have more intellectual than emotional appeal.

MEN (*24, including chorus*): 14 are 20–40 (12 minor); 10 are 40–60 (8 minor). WOMEN (*10 including chorus*): 3 are 18–25 (2 minor); 4 are 25–40 (3 minor); 3 are 40–60 (2 minor). Many members of the chorus are assigned individual parts. SETS: Exterior and interior locations in an unreal, besieged city. In most productions the sets have been designed in surrealistic style. Several scenic effects, such as the closing of the 5 city gates, cannot be achieved in arena production. Complicated lighting. COSTUMES: Timeless stylized costumes and uniforms.

ROYALTY: Apply publisher. TEXT: Stuart Gilbert trans. in *Caligula and Three Other Plays* (Knopf).

— o —

THE JUST (*Les Justes;* 1949) ALBERT CAMUS. A group of
revolutionaries await the opportunity to carry out their plan
of assassinating the Grand Duke. The year is 1905, the place
Russia. Kaliayev is chosen to throw the bomb into the carriage
of the Grand Duke, but in his first attempt he fails because
the Grand Duke's children are in the carriage, too, and he
does not wish to cause useless suffering. Other members of the
group disagree strongly with his position, but Dora, who loves
Kaliayev, understands his delicacy. His second attempt is a
success; the Grand Duke is killed and Kaliayev is imprisoned.
In the fourth act, Kaliayev is visited by the Grand Duchess
and by the Chief of Police who wish to pardon him if he will
betray his accomplices. Kaliayev knows, however, that his
death is the just price of his righteous assassination.

MEN (*7*): 2 are 20–25; 1 is 25–30; 2 are 35–40; 2 are
40–50. WOMEN (*2*): Both are 25–35. SETS: simple apartment,
looking out on street; prison cell. Selective realism. COS-
TUMES: Early 20th century; 1 uniform.

ROYALTY: Apply publisher. TEXT: Stuart Gilbert trans. in
Caligula and Three Other Plays (Knopf).

—— o ——

BREAK OF NOON (*Partage de Midi;* 1905) PAUL CLAUDEL.
A play of struggle between the Creator and the creature, this
one concerned with the meaning and experience of love between man and woman and with the idea that physical passion
may lead to spiritual passion. Ysé and her husband De Ciz
find themselves on a boat in the Indian Ocean with Amalric,
a former lover of Ysé, and Mesa, a man to whom passion in
any sense is yet to have meaning. Mesa becomes the lover of
Ysé. De Ciz accepts the situation in the hope of profiting from
the new arrangement. Ysé leaves Mesa to return to Amalric,
then returns to die with the injured Mesa, both now accepting
the fuller meaning and use of human passion. The last two
acts take place in China, the final situation being isolated by a
Chinese revolt against the "missionaries." The play is a powerful and richly stated development of the themes of human
and eternal love.

MEN (*3*): All mature. WOMAN: Mature. SETS: Forward
deck of a liner; the Happy Valley Cemetery, Hong Kong; a
Confucian temple in a small Chinese port (trap in floor desir-

able but not obligatory). Selective realism probably best; certain properties and set pieces symbolically important. Cos-TUMES: Turn of the century; colonial tropical in last 2 acts. DIFFICULTIES: The actors must be emotionally and technically mature.

ROYALTY: Apply publisher. TEXT: Wallace Fowlie trans. (Regnery).

—— o ——

THE TIDINGS BROUGHT TO MARY (*L'Annonce Faite à Marie;* 1910) PAUL CLAUDEL. The kiss of charity that Violaine gives to Pierre de Craon, a leper, robs her of earthly love, marriage, and happiness. When her fiancé Jacques discovers that Violaine, too, has leprosy, he marries Mara, Violaine's coarse and evil sister. The years pass, and on the eve of the birth of Christ, Mara brings her dead child to the leper Violaine, demanding a miracle to bring it back to life. The Heavenly Voices speak and the child stirs and sucks at Violaine's breast; Mara repays the gift by pushing the blind Violaine into a sand pit. Violaine is reunited briefly with Jacques before she dies. Through her constant faith, love, and self-sacrifice, she brings salvation to the rest in the spirit and imitation of Christ.

MEN (*4, plus extras*): 1 is 18–25; 1 is 25–30; 1 is 35–45; 1 is 60. WOMEN (*3, plus extras*): 2 are 16–23; 1 is 40–55. EXTRAS: 4 or 5 men. SETS: The barn at Combernon; the kitchen at Combernon; an orchard; the fountain at Adoue; a forest road; the leper's cave. Selective realism might be best. COSTUMES: End of the Middle Ages, "such as the poets of the Middle Ages might have imagined Antiquity."

ROYALTY: Apply publisher. TEXT: Wallace Fowlie trans. (Regnery).

—— o ——

ORPHEUS (*Orphée;* 1926) JEAN COCTEAU. Poetic creation and the poet's relation to death are recurrent themes in the work of Cocteau. In spite of its tragic impact, he presents his modern-dress version of the Orpheus myth in the form of a farce. A horse, whose cryptic hoof-tapping messages fascinate Orpheus but disconcert Eurydice, has been installed in the living room. Heurtebise, a glazier, but also a kind of guardian angel, cannot prevent Eurydice's death when she attempts to poison the horse. Death is a beautiful woman in an elegant evening gown. It is she, rather than the suburban-housewife Eurydice, whom Orpheus follows through a mirror into the Underworld. Having lost his wife a second time, Orpheus provokes the girls of the Bacchantes Club to lynch him. His head rolls into the room and is put on a pedestal. At the forthcoming inquiry it confuses the police inspector—and possibly the audience—by declaring itself to be Jean Cocteau. Death, in the end, unites Orpheus and Eurydice.

MEN (6): 4 are 20–30 (2 minor); 2 are 30–50. WOMEN (2): Both 20–30. SET: Living room in the house of Orpheus; niche in the center of stage for horse in front view; empty pedestal for a bust. Necessary tricks cannot be performed in arena theatre. Set should not be realistic. COSTUMES: Ordinary modern clothes; 1 fashionable evening gown and fur; 3 surgical whites; head and front feet of a handsome white horse. DIFFICULTIES: A certain magic charm must be preserved throughout the play in spite of the dominating farcical elements. Effects of scenery and lighting are very important.

ROYALTY: Apply publisher. TEXT: Carl Wildman trans. (Oxford).

—— o ——

THE INFERNAL MACHINE (*La Machine Infernale;* 1934) JEAN COCTEAU. Thebes is ravaged by pestilence and threatened by the Sphinx. The ghost of Laius appears on the ramparts, but Queen Jocaste cannot hear his warnings. At the same time Oedipus encounters the Sphinx. She has adopted the earthly forms of a young girl and of the jackal-faced death god Anubis. The girl falls in love with Oedipus and reveals to him the answer to her fatal riddle. Disdaining her sacrifice, he triumphantly carries her corpse, combined with the head of Anubis, to Thebes. Now the true nature of the Sphinx is revealed in the clouds: it is Nemesis, the goddess of vengeance. In spite of Tiresias' warning, Oedipus marries the queen. The wedding night turns into a nightmare of premonitory dreams. Seventeen years later, the truth comes to light. Jocaste strangles herself, and Oedipus, no longer blinded by his ambition, pierces his eyes.

MEN (9): 2 about 19 (1 must be 17 years older in the last act); 3 are 25–40 (1 minor); 2 about 50; 2 are 60–80. WOMEN

(3): 1 is 18–25; 2 about 37 (1 must be 17 years older in the last act). BOYS: (2): 1 is 6–8; 1 is 14–16. GIRLS: (2): 1 is 4–6 (no lines); 1 is 8–10. SETS: The ramparts of Thebes; temple ruins and a mutilated statue of a chimera on a hill; Jocaste's bedroom; courtyard in the palace of Oedipus. Stylized, mythical Greece. Production in horseshoe theatre possible. COSTUMES: Greek mythological with modern influence; 1 jackal's head. DIFFICULTIES: After a farcical beginning, the picturesque magic of the 2nd act is succeeded by psychoanalytical denudation in the 3rd. All this must be blended and must lead the modern and quite unheroic characters to tragedy.

ROYALTY: Apply Oxford University Press (Amen House, Warwick Sq., London, EC 4). TEXT: Carl Wildman trans. in *Modern International Plays* (Dutton).

—— o ——

THE KNIGHTS OF THE ROUND TABLE (*Les Chevaliers de la Table Ronde;* 1937) JEAN COCTEAU. The birds in Camelot sing no longer; the sun has ceased to shine. King Arthur and his knights ascribe this to the presence of the Holy Grail which, they think, has put them under a spell. They ignore the fact that they have become victims of the sorcerer Merlin, an evil, negative spirit. The arrival of Galahad, the Very Pure who disenchants, causes the collapse of the forces of artifice. The most captivating character is Ginifer, a puckish sorcerer's apprentice, whose mischievous tricks carry the action forward. Unique in dramatic literature, the little demon has no body of his own but instead posesses the gift of assuming the corporeal appearance of any absent person. In the first act he makes Gawain, the king's virtuous but boring nephew, appear an amusing rascal. In the second, as Queen Guinevere, he shocks Lancelot, her lover for eighteen years, with unladylike frivolities. And in the third, as Galahad, he brags that he is the new lover of the queen. When at last the spell is broken and the truth emerges, it is hard to bear. The queen and Lancelot take their lives. The Very Pure—the poet—cannot stay where he is loved. The birds sing again. Segramor, Lancelot's and Guinevere's son, understands their language. They chirp in concert: "pay, pay, pay . . . you must pay . . ."

MEN (6): 3 are 20–25; 3 are 40–50. WOMEN (2): 1 about 18; 1 about 38. SETS: Hall of the Round Table; hall in the sorcerer's castle; room in Camelot. Several supernatural manifestations, such as the chess game with the invisible Devil, the talking flower, the magic table and others, require trick devices. Production in horseshoe theatre possible. COSTUMES: Fanciful medieval; mythological as well as modern influences. DIFFICULTIES: The character of Ginifer, portrayed consecutively by Gawain, Guinevere, and Galahad, must assume a life of its own, well-rounded and consistent.

ROYALTY: Apply publisher. TEXT: W. H. Auden trans. in *Orpheus and Other Plays* (New Directions).

—o—

THE BALCONY (*Le Balcòn;* 1953) JEAN GENET. The play concerns Madame Irma and the perverted customers who come to her bordello seeking release through the act of role-playing. One is a bishop who enjoys forgiving sins; one is a sado-masochist judge who takes pleasure in punishing thieves before he in turn is humiliated by them; one is a general who finds satisfaction in imagining acts of courage. George, the police chief, seeks Irma's help during an insurrection in which the queen has been killed. Irma consents to accept the role of the queen, which she does successfully with the assistance of three strange customers who serve as cabinet members. The rebellion is put down, but the chief of police is not satisfied because no one aspires to emulate him. Finally, a new client acts out the role and ends up emasculating himself.

MEN (*8*): Adult. Women (*5*): Adult. SETS: 9 scenes including a sacristy, café interior, funeral studio, balcony and Irma's room. Atmospheric, not realistic. Arena production possible. COSTUMES: Decaying military uniforms, contemporary and beggar's clothes, decaying judge's robes, hangman's costume, *cothurni* (laced boots with platform soles). Costumes are from many different periods and are highly exaggerated, such as use of extremely broadened shoulders. DIFFICULTIES: Requires skillful, stylized playing and creation of bizarre atmosphere.

ROYALTY: Apply publisher. TEXT: Bernard Frechtman trans. (Grove).

—o—

THE BLACKS (*Les Nègres;* 1959) JEAN GENET. Characterization by Genet as a "clown show" does not suggest the play's expressionistic, dance dialogue quality. There is no plot in the usual sense of the word, but the progression of the play is based on a series of units, each having a beginning, a middle, and an end. The basic situation is the apparent re-enactment by Negroes of the murder of a white woman, which is being done for the benefit of a queen, her valet, a general, a bishop, and a judge. The court as well as the actors are all Negroes, with the members of the court wearing white masks. (If the audience is all Negro the playwright insists that one white person be invited to the performance.) The progression of the story is not direct; sometimes the actors rebel against their roles, sometimes the court seeks to control the play, and often the details of the re-enactment refuse to follow any narrative form. Near the end, those acting as the court shed their masks and join the actors on the stage to mourn the death of a prisoner whose crimes apparently parallel the re-enactment. The court then remasks to let the play work itself out. The queen explains the ending by saying, "We're actors, our massacre will be lyrical. Gentlemen, your masks." The deaths of the court form a counterpoint to a love scene between two of the actors.

MEN (9). WOMEN (5). No need to consider age or appearance. SET: 1, with levels and communicating ramps. Nonrepresentational. COSTUMES: Court (legal) costumes and a wide range of modern costumes (evening clothes to sweat shirts). The masks are not intended to be realistic. DIFFICULTIES: The acting style runs from realism to lyric expressionism.

ROYALTY: Apply publisher. TEXT: Bernard Frechtman trans. (Grove).

— o —

THE MARVELOUS HISTORY OF ST. BERNARD (*La Merveilleuse Histoire du Jeune Bernard de Menthon;* 1924) HENRI GHÉON. The Devil, encased in a statue of Jove atop Mont-Joux, manages with the aid of his four attendants—Envy, Pride, Gluttony, and Murder—to kill every tenth pilgrim who passes by. The nine who remain from a particular pilgrimage appeal to the Monastery of Aosta for aid in exorcising the Devil. The prior, too old for this work, bids them wait the coming of another who will solve their problem. He is Bernard de Menthon, who has caught a sense of the love of God along with his secular schooling in Paris and who, upon his return home, is forced to choose between his father and his duty to God. His father wishes him to marry the lovely Marguerite de Miolans, and Bernard is strongly attracted to her. But his attraction to God is greater, and with the aid of a miracle (of will as well as of fact) he escapes from his father's castle, abandons his fiancée, and becomes the new prior of the Monastery of Aosta. In this position he travels the road that crosses Mont-Joux and, with a balcony of Heavenly aid, bests the Devil and drives him off—at least from Mont-Joux.

MEN (*22, plus extras*): Youth to old age; some doubling possible, but difficult to give proper effect with fewer than 30 (most minor). WOMEN (*4*). EXTRAS: Several, 4 angels. SETS: 4 areas or localities, most logically all parts of 1 set; unrealistic and simple. COSTUMES: 14th- or early-15th century.

ROYALTY: Apply publisher. TEXT: Barry V. Jackson trans. (Sheed and Ward).

—o—

THE COMEDIAN (*Le Comédien et la Grâce;* 1925) HENRI GHÉON. The aging Emperor Diocletian, seeking diversion in the theatre, is soon bored with the uninspired dramatizations of Greek mythological themes which Polydorus, the official court playwright, offers as a vehicle for the emperor's mistress, Poppaea. For variety's sake he orders Polydorus to write a play about Adrian, a Roman captain who died as a Christian martyr. Chosen to play the lead, Genesius, the emperor's favorite actor, protests in vain his inability to portray such a wretched fanatic. In search for a key to the seemingly absurd character, Genesius secretly contacts members of the forbidden sect and becomes himself a Christian and a martyr.

MEN (*9*): 2 are 20–25 (1 minor); 2 are 30–40; 5 are 40–60 (2 minor). WOMEN (*3*): 1 is 17–22; 1 is 25–30; 1 is 50–60. EXTRAS: Actors; maidens of the chorus; attendants; the crowd. SETS: Rehearsal room in Genesius' acting school; the theatre of Dionysus in Nicomedia. Very simple but spacious setting. Arena production not possible. COSTUMES: Suggestion of local color (Asia Minor during the reign of Diocletian, end of 3rd-century A.D.) is necessary.

ROYALTY: Apply publisher. TEXT: Alan Bland trans. (Sheed and Ward).

—o—

THE TRIAL (*Le Procès;* 1947) ANDRÉ GIDE and JEAN-LOUIS BARRAULT. Tragedy. Adapted from a novel by Franz Kafka, this play is an expressionistic nightmare that tells the story of Joseph K., who is placed under arrest and then released pending trial. He is guilty of no crime that he knows of and never finds out of what he is accused or who his accusers are. K. finds that many others are in his predicament, know less about their crimes, and have waited longer than he for their trials. No amount of bribery or influence gains him any more information. Finally, he gives up the struggle for acquittal and denounces the court. K. is judged guilty and executed. The play bitingly satirizes judicial bureaucracy.

MEN (*38; double and tripling possible*): 9 are 20–23 (most minor); 25 are 35–45 (most minor); 4 are 50–70. WOMEN (*6; doubling possible*): 5 are 20–35 (2 minor); 1 is 50–60. GIRLS (*3*): All 8–12 (1 is a hunchback, all minor). SETS: Numerous fragments of sets needed, including K.'s apartment and a neighboring apartment; various rooms and apartments in and around the law court; K.'s office in the bank; a counselor's bedroom and kitchen; a painter's studio; a cathedral interior. Sets should be stylized. Unsuitable for arena. COSTUMES: Contemporary dress; 1 medieval whipper's costume. DIFFICULTIES: The large cast and kaleidoscopic nature of the scene changes demand expert stage managing and technical direction.
ROYALTY: Apply publisher. TEXT: Jacqueline and Frank Sundstrom trans. (Secker and Warburg Ltd.*).

— o —

SIEGFRIED (1928) JEAN GIRAUDOUX. Siegfried, a democratic statesman, destined to re-establish order in the political chaos of Germany during the Twenties, is a man without a past. Seven years ago he was found in a battlefield, gravely wounded and suffering total amnesia. His name, his language, his fatherland—everything he now owns was given him by Eva, a young German nurse. Baron Zelten, representative of romantic feudalism, has discovered his political opponent's true origin; Siegfried is a Frenchman, Jacques Forestier. When Zelten spitefully introduces Genevieve Prat, Siegfried does not recognize in her the woman he once loved. His identity at last revealed, he must choose between the country of his brilliant future and that of his obscure past. He chooses France. Paraphrasing the main action, Giraudoux uses the supporting characters (among them three German generals, a French philology professor, and a French customs official) ingeniously to compare and oppose the mentalities of the two rival nations. They can, he believes, be harmonized. In the end, Genevieve does not fully regain Jacques, but begins to love Siegfried.

MEN (*17; doubling possible*): 12 are 30–50 (5 minor); 5 are 50–70 (minor). WOMEN (*4*): 1 about 20; 2 are 50–70 (minor); 1 is 30–40. SETS: Waiting room and study in Siegfried's house, German "Secession" style; a frontier railway station. Arena production possible. COSTUMES: Upper-class German 1925; uniforms of 3 German generals, 2 German policemen, 1 German and 1 French customs official.

ROYALTY: Apply Madame Ninon Tallon-Karlweis.* TEXT: Philip Carr adap. (Dial).

—— o ——

AMPHITRYON 38 (1929) JEAN GIRAUDOUX. Comedy. Among the classical legends of Jupiter's amorous exploits, his impersonation of the Theban general Amphitryon is obviously more dramatic than his adventures in animal or mineral disguise (the theme had been used by at least thirty-seven dramatists before Giraudoux). The thirty-eighth Alcmena is not a statuesque, legendary beauty but a warmhearted modern woman who refuses to exchange her conjugal love for a divine love affair. On the first night, as her husband, Jupiter is able to possess her; on the second, as her heavenly lover, he fails miserably and is talked into accepting friendship for love. Mercury, sometimes adopting the appearance of Amphitryon's servant Sosie, is a brilliant and witty though not altogether successful procurer. In a charming boudoir scene, Alcmena's attitude is contrasted with that of Leda, the eternal mistress. (S. N. Behrman's very effective adaptation stresses the comic aspects, slightly obscuring Giraudoux's reflections on the human condition.)

MEN (*6*): 2 are 30–40; 4 are 20–40 (1 minor). With slight adaptation, the parts of Jupiter and Amphitryon and those of Mercury and Sosie can each be played by 1 actor. WOMEN (*5*): All 18–25 (3 minor). SETS: On a cloud; terrace in front of Amphitryon's palace; chamber next to Alcmena's bedroom; roof of Amphitryon's palace. Greek mythological style. Arena production requires *tour de force*. COSTUMES: Fashionable, semi-modern, mythological Greece; 2 identical cuirasses.

ROYALTY: $25, Dramatists Play Service. TEXT: S. N. Behrman trans. (Dramatists Play Service).

—— o ——

JUDITH (1931) JEAN GIRAUDOUX. This unbiblical Judith is rich and pampered, the reigning beauty in Bethulia, who looks with contempt at the discouraged defenders of the besieged city. Sheer pride makes her believe the Lord has chosen her to deliver Israel from its enemy. Disdainfully turning down an offer from the prostitute, Susanna, to share the conqueror's bed in her place, she also rejects a lesson in love and humility. In turn she finds humiliation and love in the tent of Holofernes. She is duped into wasting her grand plea for virginity upon a royally disguised, sadistic pederast, and disgusted with Jehovah's "failure" to make her recognize her true opponent, abandons herself into the arms of the real Holofernes. The next morning she kills him to preserve the unique exaltation of her love. The imaginary appearance of a fallen angel, caused by her returning pride, convinces her that her love-night was only an illusion; and the chanting rabbis glorify her as Israel's heroine.

MEN (20; doubling possible): 12 are 20–40 (6 minor); 8 are 40–60 (3 minor). WOMEN (4): 2 are 18–25; 2 are 40–60 (1 minor). BOY: 6–10 (minor). SETS: Room in the house of Judith, 7th-century B.C.; antechamber in the tent of Holofernes. Arena production possible. COSTUMES: Jewish women's garments; uniforms of Assyrian and Jewish warriors; robes of rabbis and cantors. DIFFICULTIES: The *deus ex machina* appearance of the fallen angel, disguised as a drunken guard, seems somewhat contrived. However, in a congenial production the poet's elegant and imaginative dialogue may compensate for this shortcoming.

ROYALTY: Apply publisher. TEXT: John K. Savacool trans. in *The Modern Theatre* (Doubleday), Vol. III.

—— o ——

THE ENCHANTED (*Intermezzo;* 1933) JEAN GIRAUDOUX. Comedy. What is wrong with the little town? Everyone is gay and happy, does exactly as he pleases. Alarmed by such irregular conditions, the authorities dispatch a plenipotentiary inspector to restore the usual topsy-turvydom He discovers the origin of the town's poetic delirium in the relationship between Isabelle, a young schoolteacher, and an equally young ghost, who tempts the girl with the adventure of death. In the end she is won back to life, not by the machinations of the narrow-minded inspector, but by the very real love of the Supervisor of Weights and Measures, who proves that romance can be found even in his seemingly monotonous profession. The people in the play range from whimsical to poetic. On the funny side are the pedantic inspector, the timorous mayor, the elderly spinsters, and the retired executioners; on the poetic side are Isabelle and her schoolchildren, the tender ghost, the devoted supervisor, and the transcendentally oriented doctor.

MEN (9): 2 are 20–30; 7 are 30–50 (4 minor). WOMEN (3): 1 is 18–25; 2 are 40–60. GIRLS (8): All 8–10. SETS: A clearing in the woods; Isabelle's room. Graceful style of pastoral fantasy. Production in horseshoe theatre possible. COSTUMES: Provincial and slightly bizarre 20th century; 8 schoolgirls' uniforms.

ROYALTY: $50, music $5, Baker's or Samuel French. TEXT: Maurice Valency adap. (Samuel French); incidental music, Francis Poulenc (Samuel French).

—— o ——

TIGER AT THE GATES (*La Guerre de Troie n'aura pas lieu;* 1935) JEAN GIRAUDOUX. Borrowing from the *Iliad* only the basic situation at the outset of the Trojan War, Giraudoux creates an enchanting but resignedly skeptical picture of man in his struggle against destiny. Hector, the young leader of the Trojan forces, has come to realize the baseness and hypocrisy in glorifying war, and intends to return Helen, a beautiful doll without a soul, to the Greeks. He is supported by his loving wife, Andromache, his cynically outspoken mother, Hecuba, and his lucidly reasoning sister, Cassandra, but is opposed by the chauvinistic poetaster, Demokos, and the Trojan elders who adore martial talk and Helen's pretty derrière. Paris, after having caused all the trouble, is unconcerned. In a great debate, Hector and the clever, experienced Greek envoy, Ulysses, come to terms. It seems that the Trojan War will not take place until Demokos unexpectedly succeeds in arousing the slumbering Tiger at the Gates.

MEN (16): 1 is 16–18; 6 are 20–30 (2 minor); 4 are 40–60

(1 minor); 5 are 60–80 (3 minor). WOMEN (6): 5 are 18–28
(2 minor); 1 is 60–80. GIRL: 8–12. SETS: The ramparts of
Troy; a palace enclosure. Modern view of Greek mythology,
not realistic. Unit set can be used. Performance in horseshoe
theatre possible. COSTUMES: Graceful antique Greece, possibly influenced by modern *haute couture*. DIFFICULTIES:
Giraudoux's poetic approach to a tragic theme, interspersed
with scintillating comedy, requires subtle performance in all
parts.

ROYALTY: $50–25, Baker's or Samuel French. TEXT: Chris-
topher Fry trans. (Samuel French).

— o —

ELECTRA (*Electre;* 1937) JEAN GIRAUDOUX. As in the
Greek legend (see pp. 30, 37) Electra incites Orestes to revenge their father's death. Here the similarity ends. Electra
does not know of her mother's guilt, but hates her instinctively. Aegisthus, now ruler of peaceful and prosperous Argos,
senses the danger in the girl's obsession for justice and tries to
marry her to a gardener. An ever present beggar—a god or
just a drunk?—intervenes with poetic, clairvoyant comments
in the manner of the Greek chorus: either Aegisthus must kill
Electra to save his country and himself, or Electra will fulfill
her mission of justice. Fortified by the arrival of Orestes,
Electra wrests an admission from her mother. Disaster overtakes the guilty and the innocent. With the representatives of
the ordinary people, the pompous magistrate, his coquette
wife, and the simple gardener, a touch of humor is added to
the tragedy of ideas. Three insolent children grow up during the
play, and, taking the shape of Electra, pursue Orestes as the
Furies.

MEN (8): 3 about 20 (2 minor); 2 are 30–40 (1 minor);
3 are 40–60. WOMEN (7): 5 about 21 (3 minor, must resemble Electra); 2 about 40 (1 minor). GIRLS (6): 3 are
10–12 (minor); 3 are 13–15 (minor). SET: In front of Agamemnon's palace at Argos; Greek mythological style. Suitable
for arena and amphitheatre production. COSTUMES: Greek
mythological; possibly modern stylized.

ROYALTY: Apply publisher. TEXT: Winifred Smith trans. in
The Modern Theatre (Doubleday), Vol. I.

— o —

ONDINE (1939) JEAN GIRAUDOUX. When the knight-errant Hans von Wittenstein meets the charming little Ondine in a poor fisherman's cottage, he forgets his betrothal to princess Bertha, and carries her away. Ondine is really a water sprite. In a pact with the Old One, king of the waterfolk, she accepts the condition that Hans must die if ever he tries to leave her. And so it happens: the Old One, disguised as a royal magician, evokes at the king's court the scenes of the knight's future betrayal. On the very day of his wedding to princess Bertha, Ondine is tried as an evil spirit. The Old One saves her and makes her forget her earthly life. Hans, having lost his love, dies. The first act is bathed in the magical light of a whispering lake and its enchanting naiads; the second and third are peopled with many picturesque characters—such as the chamberlain, the judges, the opera singers, the trainer of seals, and the king himself. The always present sad undertones dominate again at the end, when Ondine does not recognize the dead knight but knows she would have loved him.

MEN (15; doubling possible): 2 are 20–30; 5 are 20–60 (minor); 8 are 40–60 (3 minor). WOMEN (12; doubling possible): 4 are about 16 (3 minor); 7 are 18–25 (5 minor); 1 is 40–60. EXTRAS: Lords and ladies of the court; naiads; people. SETS: Fisherman's cottage; hall in the king's palace; courtyard in Wittenstein's castle. Fairy-tale Middle Ages; transparent walls; many light and sound effects; music. Several visual illusions cannot be achieved in an arena theatre. COSTUMES: Fairy-tale court; 1 suit of breakaway armor; judges; executioner; fishermen; naiads, appearing as if nude. DIFFICULTIES: Scenic splendor and magical effects are called for to enhance the enchanted character of the play.

ROYALTY: $50, Baker or Samuel French. TEXT: Maurice Valency adap. and incidental music Virgil Thomson (Samuel French); score and orchestral parts rented from G. Ricordi & Co., 1370 Sixth Ave., N.Y., N.Y.

—O—

SODOM AND GOMORRAH (Sodom et Gomorrhe; 1942) JEAN GIRAUDOUX. The Archangel appears to a gardener in Sodom and foretells that the power and riches of the city cannot preserve it from destruction as long as there is war in the heart of man. God seeks not sacrifice but love—one fulfilled couple representing the undivided creation. Sodom's salvation hinges upon John and Leah. Other couples—like Mark and Ruth or Samson and Delilah—are discarded, since their marriages are based on weakness, deceit, and stupidity. But Leah and John have once known complete happiness. Now she charges that with every little change her husband removes himself from past perfection. John is ready to go on pretending, but Leah, in her implacable demand for the absolute, refuses to save the city at the price of a lie. A nameless angel who has been sent to exhort the couple hopes in vain for a human miracle. While the world around them collapses, the men and women confront each other in separate camps and continue their fatal dispute.

MEN (8): 20–40 (3 minor). WOMEN (8): 20–40 (1 requires an actress with a great range of nuances; 5 minor). SET: Terrace overlooking Sodom and Gomorrah. Poetic stylization. Production in a horseshoe theatre is possible. COSTUMES: Stylized sumptuous biblical robes.

ROYALTY: Apply Madame Ninon Tallon-Karlweis.* TEXT: Herma Briffault trans. and music Arthur Honegger, apply Madame Ninon Tallon-Karlweis.

— o —

THE MADWOMAN OF CHAILLOT (*La Folle de Chaillot*; 1943) JEAN GIRAUDOUX. There is a conspiracy against the heart of Paris. A group of financiers, presidents, brokers, and other shady figures suspect oil in the Parisian subsoil and do not hesitate to destroy the beautiful city to exploit it. But they find a formidable opponent in the poor and humble led by Aurelia, the Madwoman of Chaillot, who entices all the greedy businessmen into her cellar and sends them down a secret stairway from which there is no return. Beauty and love now return to earth. The first part of the play abounds with charming episodes of Parisian street life. The peddler, the flower girl, the street-singer, and all the other have-nots are colorful characters. In the second half, the mock trial by Aurelia and her friends, the madwomen of other districts of the city, is highly dramatic. Beneath its humor and whimsical satire is the ironic comment that the one person "sound enough to frustrate all the madness in the world" is a poor old madwoman.

MEN (*24, usually reduced by doubling to about 15*): 4 are 20–25 (1 should be an expert juggler, or else cut); 5 are

30–50 (2 minor); 7 are 40–60 (5 minor). WOMEN (8): 4 are 18–25 (3 minor); 4 are 50–80. SETS: A café terrace in Paris; the Madwoman's residence, a fantastic cellar with access to the sewer. Arena production feasible. COSTUMES: Modern; great variety, including a dozen expensive business suits, a policeman's uniform, colorful rags, and 4 ladies' gowns of past generations.

ROYALTY: $50–25, Dramatists Play Service. TEXT: Maurice Valency adap. (Dramatists Play Service).

—— o ——

DUEL OF ANGELS (*Pour Lucrèce;* 1944) JEAN GIRAU-DOUX. Lucile, wife of the pedantic public attorney, Lionel Blanchard, is not only a provincial nineteenth-century version of Lucrecia, she is purity itself. Her opponent is the amoral Paola, her complete opposite. In an allegorical struggle between the woman who cannot remember and the woman who cannot forget, Paola drugs Lucile and then makes her believe she has been violated by the debauched Count Marcellus. Lucile demands that her presumed rapist commit suicide. He refuses, but is killed in a duel with Paola's husband, Armand. An insurmountable wall will forever separate Lucile and her husband. When Paola finally reveals her cruel hoax, Lucile, disgusted with the baseness of mankind, takes poison. The melodramatic plot abstractly describes the duel of good and evil.

MEN (9): 3 are about 40; 4 are 40–60 (minor); 2 are 20–60 (minor). WOMEN (4): 3 are about 30 (2 require exceptional actresses); 1 is 40–60. GIRL: 14–16 (minor). SETS: Café terrace in Aix-en-Provence; apartment of Count Marcellus; study of Lionel Blanchard. Sets need not be realistic. Arena production possible. COSTUMES: Fashionable French 2nd Empire. DIFFICULTIES: Requires expert acting and direction.

ROYALTY: $50–25; Dramatists Play Service. TEXT: Christopher Fry trans. (Dramatists Play Service).

—— o ——

THE BALD SOPRANO (*La Cantatrice Chauve;* 1950) EU-GÈNE IONESCO. In this long one-act play Mr. and Mrs. Smith, during an evening at home, are visited by the Martins and the Fire Chief. Nothing happens, but this does not prevent a great deal from being said that reflects, as it parodies, the emptiness and absurdity of the lives of the Smiths, the Martins, and perhaps everybody.

MEN (*3*): 1 is 25–30; 2 are 40–50. WOMEN (*3*): 1 is 20–25; 2 are 40–50. SET: Middle-class English living-room interior; realistic; arena production possible. COSTUMES: Contemporary. DIFFICULTIES: Chiefly in letting Ionesco do the distortion.

ROYALTY: Apply Marie Rodell and Joan Daves, Inc.* TEXT: Donald M. Allen trans. in *Four Plays by Eugène Ionesco* (Grove).

—— o ——

THE CHAIRS (*Les Chaises;* 1951) EUGÈNE IONESCO. An Old Man and Old Woman, his wife, hold a reception for those who have come to receive, through the speech of the Orator, the great message that the Old Man is leaving for humanity. When the guests, all imaginary, are at last settled, the Old Man and Old Woman jump out of the window of their tower room, content that the meaning of their life will be safely delivered by the Orator. The Orator is deaf and dumb, and his message, if sensible, is unintelligible.

MEN (2): 1 is about 40; 1 is 60–70. WOMAN: She is 60–70. SET: 1 simple set with a large group of chairs. COSTUMES: Vaguely modern. DIFFICULTIES: The actor and actress who undertake the parts of the Old Man and Old Woman must have great variety, endurance, and especially expressive bodies. It is a short play.

ROYALTY: Apply Marie Rodell and Joan Daves, Inc.* TEXT: Donald M. Allen trans. in *Four Plays by Eugène Ionesco* (Grove).

—— o ——

AMÉDÉE, OR HOW TO GET RID OF IT (*Amédée, ou comment s'en débarasser;* 1958). EUGÈNE IONESCO. Comedy. For years a middle-class, middle-aged French couple, Amédée and Madeleine, have kept a corpse hidden in their bedroom. Neither can any longer remember the fit of passion or greed that caused one of them to kill the victim. Day by day the corpse grows, sprouting mushrooms, pushing at the walls that hold it. The couple shout protests of innocence to uninterested visitors or even the night air. When at last the corpse's feet burst out into the living room, the couple realize that some effort must be made to dispose of it. They push the immense carcass out the window. Outside, Amédée drags it clattering down the street. The noise, however, produces no alarms—only an offer of help. At last Amédée gets tangled in the arms of the body and takes off in the air with him. As he disappears from sight, Amédée shouts apologies to the gendarmes below.

MEN (6): Amédée is 45; soldier presumably young; ages of others unspecified. All but Amédée are minor. WOMEN (2): Madeleine is 45; Mado (minor) is presumably in her teens or early 20s. SETS: An unpretentious dining-drawing room and office; a village square. COSTUMES: Contemporary. Uniforms for postman, 2 policemen. The bizarre story makes possible almost any type of fantastic setting and costumes. DIFFICULTIES: A giant corpse, weird lighting effects, and the balloon-like ascension of Amédée with the corpse all pose unusual staging problems. (A simpler staging is possible with an alternate ending that uses 3 more men and 1 more woman.)

ROYALTY: $25–20, Samuel French. TEXT: Donald Watson trans. (Grove).

—— o ——

THE KILLER (*Tueur sans gages;* 1959) EUGÈNE IONESCO. Man is alienated from the elementary forces of life—a nightmare is provoked by the discrepancy between reality and man's dreams. By taking the wrong bus, Bérenger, an average, simple-hearted citizen, discovers the "Radiant City," constructed by the perfect civil servant, an automated architect. Bérenger is delighted with the amazing housing project, a photographic copy of a mirage, and intends to settle down there and marry the architect's pretty secretary, Dany. Then he learns that the inhabitants of the welfare state live in constant terror; a killer is at large who lures his victims into an artificial lake. Bérenger revolts against the collective apathy of the authorities. Back in the dark, ugly living quarters of his regular life, he finds the sinister Edouard (possibly his alter ego) whose briefcase contains all the paraphernalia of the killer. Bérenger, convinced that now he will be able to track down the evil-doer, makes Edouard accompany him on his quest; on their way, in the midst of a totalitarian rally by Mother Goose and her goose-stepping geese, they lose the material of circumstantial evidence. Then, alone, Bérenger meets the killer. In a long monologue he attempts to outreason him with a deluge of philosophical and religious commonplaces, only to realize the weakness of his arguments and because of his impotence, to offer himself as a victim.

MEN (*11; doubling possible*): 5 are 30–40 (3 minor); 5 are 40–60 (4 minor); 1 is of unspecified age (he, the dwarfish killer, may but need not appear on stage). WOMEN (2): 1 is 18–22; 1 is 40–50. VOICES, SILHOUETTES, and SOUND EFFECTS: "Indispensable around the empty stage in order to continue and intensify the visual and aural atmosphere of city and street." Part of the voices and sound effects can be taped. SETS: The Radiant City; Bérenger's room; streets. "The decor of Act II [Bérenger's room] is heavy, realistic, and ugly; it contrasts strongly with the total lack of decor and the simple lighting effects of Act I [Radiant City]." The author calls for a picture-frame setting. COSTUMES: Contemporary street clothes.

ROYALTY: $35–25, Samuel French. TEXT: Donald Watson trans. in *The Killer and Other Plays* (Grove).

—— o ——

RHINOCEROS (1960) EUGÈNE IONESCO. In a small French town, a rhinoceros suddenly appears bellowing and trampling through the streets. Gradually it is learned that people are being transformed into rhinoceroses. One by one the citizens are caught in the transformation until only one brave individualist remains who defies the mass hysteria: "I'm the last man left, and I'm staying that way until the end." Ionesco's allegory serves as a point of departure for him to turn loose his considerable ingenuity and imagination in satirizing many aspects of the human condition. It is a high-spirited, extraordinarily theatrical play with serious undertones beneath the rambunctious action.

MEN (6): Adult; 2 outstanding actors. WOMEN (4): Adult. EXTRAS: Several men and women. SETS: The town square; a government office; Jean's living room. Scenery may be stylized. COSTUMES: Contemporary clothes. Stage directions call for rhinoceros heads, but the New York production did not use them. DIFFICULTIES: Transformation to rhinoceros requires a skillful performance. The play demands astute direction.

ROYALTY: Apply Eugène Ionesco and Margaret Ramsay,

14 Goodwins Court, London WC 2. TEXT: Derek Prouse
trans. in *Rhinoceros and Other Plays* (Grove).

—— o ——

TIME IS A DREAM (*Le Temps est un Songe;* 1919) HENRI-
RENÉ LENORMAND. Tragedy. A conjectural discussion of
time and space in relation to life and fate. Romée Cremers
walks by a lake on the Van Eyden estate one day and has a
vision of an unknown man drowning there. An investigation
seems to indicate that the vision was of an incident that happened thirty years earlier. But after she meets and becomes
engaged to Nico Van Eyden, Romée confesses to his sister
that in her vision it was he who was drowning. Details in the
vision begin to materialize in fact when the lake is cleaned of
reeds and when, later, a green boat is ordered for it. The
actual drowning occurs at the final curtain.

MEN (*2*): 1 is 25–30; 1 is 50 (Javanese). WOMEN (*3*): 2
are 20–25; 1 is 55-65. SET: The drawing room of an old
mansion in Utrecht, Holland. Set should be realistic. Arena
production possible. COSTUMES: Either contemporary or those
of the 1920s. DIFFICULTIES: Characters poorly drawn.
    ROYALTY: Apply publishers. TEXT: Winifred Katzin trans.
in *Modern Continental Dramas* (Knopf) or in *Chief Contemporary Dramatists* (Houghton Mifflin), Ser. III.

—— o ——

ARIADNE (*Le Chemin de Crète;* 1936) GABRIEL MARCEL.
Ariadne Leprieur, who has married her husband Jerome partly
to save him from the associates his weakness of character has
thrown him with, has succumbed to an illness that prevents
her from living a normal married life. She insists that Jerome
spend most of his time in Paris while she remains in the
mountains, and, upon discovering that he has taken Violetta
Mazargues as his mistress, befriends her. Violetta and Jerome
are soon following the pale thread of Adriadne's directions
through the labyrinthine ways of mutual distrust, thwarted
love, and final separation. Marcel, a Christian existentialist,
does not develop a theme here so obviously as does Sartre;
instead he probes delicately but deeply into the mystery of the
human relationship caught in the trammels of a purely human
love. There is an air of failure that surrounds all of the chief
characters, even Ariadne, but the play as a whole resists this

feeling of failure by creating an atmosphere of infinite possibility and essential vitality.

MEN (*5*): 3 about 35, 2 about 40. WOMEN (*5*): All 35–40. Depth and refinement of characterization are essential. SETS: Violetta's studio apartment; Ariadne's Paris apartment; Ariadne's home in the mountains. Sets should be realistic. COSTUMES: Modern. DIFFICULTIES: British translation must be adapted for American production.

ROYALTY: Apply publisher. TEXT: Rosalind Heywood trans. in *Gabriel Marcel, Three Plays* (Secker and Warburg Ltd.*).

— o —

ASMODÉE (1938) FRANÇOIS MAURIAC. Blaise Couture is a former seminarist who was rejected as a candidate for the priesthood because of his fanaticism and his rebellious obstinacy. Hired by Marcelle de Barthas, a beautiful, wealthy widow, as a tutor for her oldest son, he soon becomes her indispensable guide in secular as well as in spiritual matters. His possessive hold over Marcelle is threatened by Harry Fanning, an English student who has come to spend the summer vacation at the Barthas estate. Indeed, Madame, infatuated with the fresh, healthy youth, sends Blaise away, only to call him back when Harry and her seventeen-year-old daughter, Emmanuelle, fall in love. Blaise cannot and will not prevent the girl from marrying Harry. He makes Marcelle renounce an illusory happiness and resign herself to an austere life under his despotic guidance. Mauriac's style is sober and restrained. He ceaselessly probes into the conscience of his characters, revealing their temptations, their succumbing to sin, and their mental torture by the feeling of guilt. Yet for the author these very weaknesses give testimony of man's freedom of will and of human dignity.

MEN (*4*): 1 is 20; 1 is 40; 2 are 50–60. WOMEN (*3*): 1 is 17; 1 is 30; 1 is 38. SET: Hall in a country house near Bordeaux. A terrace beyond and a stairway to the 2nd floor provide additional acting space. Arena production, even if technically feasible, not recommended. COSTUMES: Fashionable country clothes, 1938 or present. DIFFICULTIES: The play requires exceptional psychological delicacy.

ROYALTY: $35–25; Samuel French. TEXT: Beverly Thurman trans. (Samuel French) or *Port-Royal and Other Plays* (Hill and Wang).

—— o ——

THE MASTER OF SANTIAGO (*Le Maître de Santiago;* 1947) HENRY DE MONTHERLANT. Don Alvaro Dabo, the head of the Order of Santiago, holds a meeting at his home for the last faithful followers of that order. Alvaro's daughter Mariana discovers from one of the members of the order that her father is to be sent to the New World, ostensibly to enlarge the work of the order, actually to help rebuild his broken finances. With this new source of wealth Don Alvaro will be able to marry his daughter to Jacinte, the son of Don Bernal. Don Alvaro refuses to go to America, seeing it as a temptation of evil, and when Don Bernal plans to trick him into his own material salvation by pretending that the king has ordered him to go, Mariana reveals to her father the true state of affairs. She thus sacrifices her marriage for duty to her father, and her father accepts her sacrifice, offering her as well as himself to that severe idea he has of his relationship with God.

MEN (7): 18–60. WOMEN (2): 1 is 18; 1 is 55. SET: The hall of honor in the house of Don Alvaro Dabo. COSTUMES: Spanish, 16th century. DIFFICULTIES: The script is extremely spare, pure, and passionate; the acting must have the same chiseled but incandescent quality.

ROYALTY: Apply publisher. TEXT: Jonathan Griffin trans. in *The Master of Santiago and Four Other Plays* (Knopf).

—— o ——

NOAH (*Noé;* 1931) ANDRÉ OBEY. This retelling of the old biblical story is a generally pessimistic comment on the futility of trying to help most people. Only Noah has implicit faith in God, though even he falters occasionally. His wife is unable to cope with life, having little faith in anything or anybody His children have no respect for their parents and no gratitude toward anyone for being permitted to live and enjoy life. For them, nothing is sacred. Their conduct, while still on the ark, suggests that the flood will have no lasting effect in ridding the world of evil. Noah himself is the story's one redeeming figure and around him are built the play's most poignant scenes. Eight assorted animals lend a whimsical touch to the play, during their "conversations" with Noah and by their general antics.

MEN (*5*): 1 is 50–60 (requires an outstanding actor); 3 are 17–21; 1 is 30–40 (minor). WOMEN (*4*): 1 is 50–60; 3 are 17–21. MEN OR WOMEN (*8*): Assorted animals (no lines). SET: A stylized ark which can be placed in various positions on stage before a cyclorama for the different scenes. Cutout trees and waves may be added for appropriate scenes. Not suitable for arena production. COSTUMES: Simple, colorful costumes of a biblical period; 8 different animal costumes and headpieces. DIFFICULTIES: The play is somewhat overwritten and requires an imaginative director-choreographer.

ROYALTY: $25, Samuel French. TEXT: Arthur Wilmurt trans. (Samuel French).

— o —

DOCTOR KNOCK (*Knock, ou Le Triomphe de Médecine;* 1923) JULES ROMAINS. Comedy. Enterprising Dr. Knock, former department-store clerk and ship's "doctor" who has just gotten his medical degree, takes over the declining small town practice of Dr. Parpalaid. To attract a clientele he engages the town crier to announce free treatment to all comers on Monday mornings. Inconsequential symptoms blossom into major illnesses; the town druggist's business triples; the local hotel is converted into a clinic and hospital with hardly a bed to spare. Even Dr. Parpalaid returns to become his successor's patient. Dr. Knock's tactics are a triumph of quackery, advertising, and applied psychology. The satire of the play, however, is directed more toward the gullible and imitative actions of the populace than toward opportunism or malpractice.

MEN (*9*): 2 are 50–60; 3 are 40–50 (1 must be an outstanding actor); 4 are 25–35 (each appears in 1 act only). WOMEN (*5*): 2 are 50–60; 2 are 40–50; 1 is 20–30 (each appears in only 1 act). SETS: In and around a 1902 motor car (the surroundings may change); Dr. Parpalaid's old consulting room; the front hall of the local hotel, now converted into a hospital. Sets need not be realistic. Arena production possible if removing car in Act I is no problem. COSTUMES: Early 20th-century provincial French DIFFICULTIES: Impression of a car in motion must be given, but this may be achieved effectively without moving scenery.

ROYALTY: $50, Samuel French. TEXT: Granville-Barker trans. (Samuel French) or Marston Balch trans. (Tufts).

——o——

THE WORLD IS ROUND (*La Terre est Ronde;* 1937) AR-MAND SALACROU.

Savonarola provides the force which moves the action of this play, although he does not mix with the other characters. His three conversations with God let us see the power of ascetic dedication and the domination of the spirit as it revolts against the demands of the flesh and the earth. Against this background we see a practical demonstration of such asceticism carried out in the domination of Florence by Savonarola's child followers and in the conversion of the gay Silvio—who abandons his love, Lucciana, first to follow Savonarola, then to die in his place, demanding a miracle that Savonarola dare not ask. Around Silvio and Lucciana swirl a medley of other characters, caught in this struggle between two worlds.

MEN (*12*): Some extras may be used; youth and age are contrasted, but age here is in the 50s. WOMEN (*5*): A few extras may be used, youth and middle age again contrasted. BOYS (*4*): All 10–15 (minor). SETS: A public square; Minutello's home; Savonarola's cell; Lucciana's room; a prison cell. Selective realism. Square, Minutello's room, and Lucciana's chamber may be all 1 unit. COSTUMES: Late 15th century; carnival additions in Act I; 2 Dominican and 1 Franciscan. DIFFICULTIES: Savonarola scenes demand an actor of both power and great variety; they are at once the base and climax of the play and are carried almost alone.

ROYALTY: $35, apply James H. Clancy, Dept. of English, Dartmouth University, Hanover, New Hampshire. TEXT: James H. Clancy trans.

——o——

THE FLIES (*Les Mouches;* 1943) JEAN-PAUL SARTRE. Tragedy.

An existentialist retelling of the Orestes story. Instead of accepting responsibility for his murder of the former king, Aegisthus forces the whole population of Argos to share it. In a weird festival of death, the inhabitants subject themselves to orgies of self-torture and repentance. Electra tries to expose the king, only to get herself banished. Orestes seeks to give meaning to an empty life by what he believes to be a divinely ordered mission of vengeance. But he learns that neither the gods nor the dead exist except in his mind. The revenge-murder of Aegisthus and Clytemnestra can be no one's directive but his own and the furies of remorse can be unleashed only by the killer's own mind. Because Electra is irresolute at the hour of killing, she can escape subsequent torment only by perpetual repentance. Orestes strides off, firm and free. The flies follow him, convinced their hour will come.

MEN (7, *plus menservants, palace guards*): Leads: 1 is 20–30, 1 is 40–50, 1 is 50–60; minor roles: 1 is 10–15, 1 is 30–40, 2 are 60–70. WOMEN (6, *plus extras and furies*): 2 leads are 20–25 and 40–50; minor roles: 3 are 60–70, 1 is 20–30. SETS: A public square in Argos, dominated by a statue of Zeus; a mountain terrace with a cavern on the right; a throne room in the palace; the temple of Apollo. COSTUMES: Classical Greek. DIFFICULTIES: The complexities of existentialist philosophy make this a difficult play to communicate to an audience, in spite of good dramatic construction and exciting characterization.

ROYALTY: $25, Samuel French. TEXT: Stuart Gilbert trans. in *No Exit and Three Other Plays* (Knopf).

—— o ——

NO EXIT (*Huis Clos*; 1944) JEAN-PAUL SARTRE. A play primarily concerned with exposition of a portion of Sartre's existential philosophy, it has as the three principles Garcin, a coward; Estelle, a socialite and adultress; and Inez, a Lesbian. Each has recently died and the action concerns their attempts to alter or relive their earthly lives while confined in an apartment in Hell. Their desires are thwarted by the evolution of a complex triangle in which each is held in check by one of the others. To the existentialist death means the termination both of the activities of the body and of free will; each character must thus follow a determined pattern of action. The realization of this fate becomes the punishment of Hell.

MEN (2): 1 is 30–45; 1 is any age (minor). WOMEN (2): 1 is 26; 1 is 30–35. SET: 2nd Empire drawing room with 3 couches. Need not be realistic. Arena production possible. COSTUMES: Contemporary; 1 fashionable dress. DIFFICULTIES: A long one-act play.

ROYALTY: $25, Samuel French. TEXT: Stuart Gilbert trans. in *No Exit and Three Other Plays* (Knopf).

— o —

DIRTY HANDS (*Les Mains Sales;* 1948) JEAN-PAUL SARTRE. Tragedy. Communist Hugo is a newspaper editor, appointed secretary to Hoederer, a high official in the party. Russians are driving Germans back through the mythical kingdom of Illyria. As a political expedient, Hoederer advocates a coalition with the reactionary Prince Paul against the Germans —a position disapproved by Louis and the majority of the party's inner circle. Since Hoederer is intractable, Louis orders Hugo to assassinate Hoederer. Hugo eagerly agrees. But he finds in Hoederer a selfless wisdom, brilliance, wit, courage, and generosity that not only unnerves him but convinces him that Hoederer is right. Eventually, under the mistaken notion that Hoederer is trying to steal his wife, Hugo shoots him. By this time the party has decided that Hoederer was correct, and it deifies him as a martyr. An unusually subtle, delicately humorous, yet moving picture of individual conscience struggling with persuasive authoritarianism.

MEN (*10*): Ages not specified, but 6 appear about 20–30, 2 about 30–40, 1 about 40–50, and 1 about 50–60. WOMEN (*2*): Both in their 20s. SETS: The ground floor of a small cottage; a summer-house bedroom; an austere but comfortable office. COSTUMES: 1945 European.

ROYALTY: Apply publisher. TEXT: Lionel Abel trans. in *No Exit and Three Other Plays* (Knopf).

SCANDINAVIAN DRAMA

Eighteenth Century

JEPPE OF THE HILL, OR THE TRANSFORMED PEAS-
ANT (*Jeppe paa bjerget;* 1722)   LUDVIG HOLBERG (Danish).
Comedy.   Jeppe is a peasant who likes to drink and sleep.
His wife sends him to the market; instead he ends up drinking
at the inn. The local baron, with his secretary and attendants,
discovers Jeppe drunk, asleep in the street. They decide to play
a joke on him. They take him to the baron's estate, dress him
royally, and when he awakes they pretend he is the baron.
Although he is at first incredulous, at last he believes them and
berates them, orders food, and wields power indiscriminately.
When he is again drunk, they dump him back on the dung-
heap from which they originally removed him. He wakes up,
thinks he has dreamed of paradise, and tries to recapture the
dream on the spot. Instead, his wife comes along and beats
him, after which three armed men come to take him off to
trial for impersonating the baron. The baron's sport continues
as Jeppe undergoes a mock trial and is finally hanged, not by
the neck but under the arms. Imagining himself brought back
to life by the merciful judge, and with a substantial reward in
his pocket, Jeppe proceeds to imbibe again at the inn. This
time, however, he leaves embarrassed when the town gossip
comes in with the true story and makes fun of him.

MEN (*13, plus lackeys and retainers; doubling possible*): 9
are 40–60 (6 minor); 4 are 30–40 (all minor). WOMEN (2):
Both 30–40 (1 minor). SETS: A village road; a bedroom in
the baron's castle; dining room in the castle; outdoor set;
outdoor set with a tree. Sets probably should not be realistic.
COSTUMES: Anything that suggests shoddy Danish peasant
costumes of the period; assorted costumes for the baron's retainers; wigs for the judge and 2 lawyers.
ROYALTY: Apply publisher. TEXT: Reginald Spink trans. in
Three Comedies by Ludvig Holberg (Theatre Arts).

RASMUS MONTANUS (*ca.* 1722) LUDVIG HOLBERG (Danish). Comedy. Rasmus Montanus returns from the university to his tiny village, full of pride in his command of Latin and his skill in metaphysical disputation. His pride suffers its first blow when he runs afoul of the village deacon, an illiterate but shrewd scalawag who makes his living by pretending a vast knowledge of Latin. Rasmus attempts a Latin disputation with the deacon; although the deacon cannot answer a single question, he fakes Latin with great aplomb. The villagers, unable to discriminate the true Latin from the false, applaud the deacon rather than Rasmus. Rasmus suffers further distress when he insists that the world is round, thereby offending his future father-in-law, who prefers the evidence of his senses that the earth is flat. Rasmus stubbornly refuses to soften his pronouncements and is about to lose the hand of his promised bride. He is rescued from his foolish pride by a wise lieutenant who tricks him into enlisting in the army by using Rasmus' own weapon of metaphysical logic. The play ends happily when Rasmus realizes that true knowledge should make a man more humble, not less. This play is a genuinely witty comment on the dangers of a purely "ivory-tower" education.

MEN (*8*): 4 are 20–40 (1 minor); 4 are 40–60. WOMEN (*3*): 1 is 20–40; 3 are 40–60. SETS: A village street before Rasmus' home; the humble living room of Rasmus' home. Sets need not be extensive or realistic. Arena production possible. COSTUMES: Peasant dress; student's gown; clerical gowns; army uniforms. The costumes may be of any period from the Middle Ages through the early 18th century. Elaborate period authenticity unnecessary. DIFFICULTIES: Requires good knowledge of Latin.

ROYALTY: Apply publisher. TEXT: Oscar James Campbell, Jr. and Frederic Schenck trans. in *Comedies by Holberg* (American-Scandinavian Foundation*).

Nineteenth and Twentieth Centuries

ANNA SOPHIE HEDVIG (1939) KJELD ABELL (Danish).
Problem play with allegorical overtones. Set in the years just
before World War II, the play serves as a sharp if indirect
reprimand of all those who were unwilling to act firmly against
evil forces coming to power. The middle-aged provincial
schoolteacher, Anna Sophie Hedvig, believes in action. Visiting her city cousin, she disrupts an important dinner party
with her story of how she killed the vicious teacher who was
about to be made headmistress at her school. Her cousin's
son John is the only one who defends her actions. The others,
especially the guest, Hoff, upon whom her cousin's husband
depends for business, take the conventional view that Anna's
act is unforgivable and that bold action against evil is not their
business. In the final symbolic scene, Anna is executed in sacrificial compliance with conventional attitudes.

MEN (*11*): 4 are 20–30 (2 minor); 7 are 40–60 (4 minor).
WOMEN (*10*): 3 in their teens (2 minor); 3 are 20–30 (minor);
4 are 40–60 (2 minor). SETS: Expensively furnished living
room in the middle 1930s; living room of the janitor's cheap
basement apartment at Anna's school; an open place. Lights
and sound figure importantly. COSTUMES: Fashionable mid-
1930s.
ROYALTY: Apply American-Scandinavian Foundation.*
TEXT: Hanna Astrup Larsen trans. in *Scandinavian Plays of
the Twentieth Century* (Princeton), Ser. II.

—— o ——

THE SWEDENHIELMS, OR THE NOBEL PRIZE (*Swedenhielms;* 1925) HJALMAR BERGMAN (Swedish). Comedy.
Rolf Swedenhielm, Sr., expansive and inventive father of the
household, and the tidy and practical Marta Boman, housekeeper, dominate the action with their respective concerns
with honor and cleanliness. The remarkable unity of the

235

charming and explosively diversified Swedenhielm family is
threatened by the discovery of several forged promissory notes
bearing the father's name. Wrongly suspecting his favorite son
of thus tarnishing his honor—newly brightened by the Nobel
Prize—Swedenhielm is disabused by his faithful housekeeper,
who confesses to having done the deed with good intentions.
Journalism and the theatre are among the many subjects satirized in the brilliant dialogue of the younger members of the
family: actress-daughter Julia; engineer-son Rolf, Jr.; aviation
lieutenant Bo; and his wealthy fiancée, Astrid—engaging and
articulate individualists all. The most solidly successful play of
a highly theatrical and witty author, second only to Strindberg
in national esteem.

MEN (5): 3 are 35–40; 2 are 60. WOMEN (3): 1 is 25, 1 is
35, 1 is 60. EXTRAS: 2 walk-ons. SET: A large, comfortable,
elegantly furnished drawing room with double doors to a dining room visible upstage. Suitable for arena. COSTUMES: Fashionable 1920s or contemporary; 3 changes: night clothes,
street dress, formal wear; Swedish lieutenant's uniform.

ROYALTY: Apply American-Scandinavian Foundation.*
TEXT: Henry Alexander and Llewellyn Jones trans. in *Scandinavian Plays of the Twentieth Century* (Princeton), Ser. III.

—— o ——

BEYOND HUMAN POWER (*Over aevne I;* 1895) BJORN-
STJERNE BJÖRNSON (Norwegian). Tragedy. Adolph Sang is
a sincere and highly successful faith healer who follows
Christ's dictates regardless of possible consequences to himself
and others. His wife, Clara, loves and admires her husband
deeply, but she does not share his unquestioning faith in the
healing miracles he has performed. She has spent her life trying to maintain the practical necessities of family life without
offending her husband's generous impulses. These efforts have
cost Clara her health. Adolph has been unable to heal her because she does not share his faith in miracles. However, she
admits to her sister that she might expend her last strength
and rise from her sickbed to demonstrate her love for her
husband. Adolph finally determines to pray for Clara's cure
in spite of her disbelief. A miracle occurs; a landslide which
should have destroyed Sang in his church veers to one side,
leaving him unscathed. When word of his miraculous escape
spreads, crowds gather in the churchyard to await Clara's cure.

Sensing that Sang's reputation is at stake, Clara rises and walks from her bedroom. But her effort of love is too great for her limited strength. She collapses and dies. Sang is suddenly struck with the essential selfishness of his desire to heal his wife miraculously and at the havoc this desire has wrought. Overcome with remorse, he falls dead by her side.

MEN (*10, plus optional extras*): 1 is 20–25; 9 are 40–60 (8 minor). WOMEN (*4*): 1 is 20–25; 3 are 40–60 (1 minor). SETS: Bedroom in a simple Norwegian cottage; living room of the same cottage. Neither set requires much detail. COSTUMES: Simple early 20th-century gowns for the women; clerical suits for 9 men; simple sport suit for one man.

ROYALTY: Apply publisher. TEXT: Lee M. Hollander trans. in *Chief Contemporary Dramatists* (Houghton Mifflin), Ser. I.

— o —

THE CONDEMNED (*Den dödsdömde;* 1949) STIG DAGERMAN (Swedish). A condemned man is proved innocent of his wife's death after spending four months in prison. Upon his release he is feted at a party at the "Rescued Men's Club" by a bizarre foursome who have all been rescued from death. He is taken into a small chamber by a beautiful prostitute whose favors he resists. Confusing her with his dead wife, he shoots her and is returned to prison. The condemned man is never really alive during the action of the play; he merely participates in a meaningless ritual. As he says at the end: "A condemned man dies when the sentence falls. A condemned man dies at once then because he has nothing more to hope for. To live is simply to hope."

MEN (*12*): 8 are 25–50; 1 is over 60; 3 are walk-ons. WOMEN (*2*): Both young; one must be beautiful and sensual. SETS: Prison anteroom; private dining room in a restaurant; a small chamber (can be an inset). Sets should be stark and fantastic. COSTUMES: Should suggest the character and mood of the play rather than period.

ROYALTY: Apply American-Scandinavian Foundation.* TEXT: Henry Alexander and Llewellyn Jones trans. in *Scandinavian Plays of the Twentieth Century* (Princeton), Ser. III.

— o —

BRAND (1866) HENRIK IBSEN (Norwegian). Feeling himself charged by God to lead men to salvation through total
commitment to the absolute, Brand struggles to destroy the
cowardice, hedonism, and irrationality rampant in his community. His unflinching idealism alienates him from mother
and community and costs him the lives of his wife and child.
As stern in his demands on himself as he is with others, he
undergoes great torment before choosing between his responsibilities as son, husband, and father and his avowed absolutism. In every instance, he accepts the call of the absolute.
Having sacrificed everything to his ideals, he at last stands
alone on the mountain from which he descended. Deserted and
beaten by his community, having sacrificed those he loved, in
his intense loneliness he suffers a terrifying doubt about the
value of his absolutism. Facing death from an avalanche, he
has just enough time to ask God whether his actions have
earned him salvation. Through the crashing snow and ice
which overwhelm him, the enigmatic answer comes—a voice
calls "He is the God of Love."

MEN (9, plus villagers. All men except Brand minor; some
doubling possible): 8 are 30–50; 1 is 8–12. WOMEN (5, plus
village women. All except Agnes minor; some doubling possible): 1 is 20–30; 3 are 40–60; 1 is 13–17. SETS: High in the
mountains above a Norwegian coastal village; a village by a
fjord; a farm above the fjord; outside Brand's house; inside
Brand's house; outside Brand's new church; on the highest
farm above the village. Realistic scenery unnecessary. Skillful
lighting essential to convey mood of the play. COSTUMES:
Anything suggesting dismal Norwegian peasant dress of the
mid-19th century. Clerical garb for Brand; some suggestion of
rank for town officials. DIFFICULTIES: A very strong Brand is
essential.

ROYALTY: Apply Miriam Howell, c/o Ashley-Steiner, Inc.,
579 Fifth Ave., N.Y., N.Y. TEXT: Michael Meyer trans.
(Doubleday).

—o—

PEER GYNT (1867) HENRIK IBSEN (Norwegian). Fantasy.
Peer Gynt is a rollicking, delightful rogue who wastes his life
in compromise and self-gratification. At the beginning of the
play he carries off a young bride from her wedding feast in
vengeance for another girl's slight. The other girl, Solveig,

follows him to the mountains and warns him that the village is
pursuing him. In the meantime, the villagers avenge themselves
on Peer's aged mother by stripping her of everything but her
bed. Peer deserts Solveig to escape his pursuers. He steals to
his dying mother's bedside and comforts her, as she dies, with
his fantastic stories. Then he flees Norway. Years later, we discover that Peer has become wealthy through slave-trading and
other nefarious dealings. But through his propensity for self-
delusion and pleasure-seeking, he has become involved with a
scheming dancing girl. She and his dishonest business associates swindle him out of all his wealth. Always a fantastic
braggart, Peer tells such tall tales that he lands in an insane
asylum and becomes its king. Finally, he escapes the asylum
and tries to return to Norway, where the faithful Solveig has
been waiting for him through the years. He nearly loses his
life in a shipwreck, but he is rescued by the prayers of Solveig.
Finally, disillusioned and wishing nothing more than to live as
a simple and honest man, he is reunited with Solveig. If Peer
has any chance of redemption, it is only because of Solveig's
faith in him.

MEN (*32, plus extras, much doubling possible*): 9 are 15–25;
4 are 25–35; 1 is 35–45; 4 are 45–55; 6 are 55–65; 8 are of
unspecified age, with 3 symbolic characters. WOMEN (*15, plus
extras, doubling possible*): 1 is 5–15; 7 are 15–25; 1 is 25–35;
3 are 35–45; 2 are 45–55; 1 is unspecified (only 2 are major).
Peer Gynt, Aslak and Solveig must grow from youth to old
age during the play. SETS: A mountain; Aase's hut; farm
courtyard; various parts of the Moroccan coast and desert,
with an Arabian tent specified in two scenes; a shipboard scene
and a coastline scene. COSTUMES: Norwegian peasant dress;
Arabian dress. DIFFICULTIES: Requires excellent lighting facil-
ities and swift changes of scenery.

ROYALTY: Apply publisher. TEXT: R. Farquharson Sharp
trans. (Dutton).

—o—

THE PILLARS OF SOCIETY (*Samfundets stötter;* 1877).
HENRIK IBSEN (Norwegian) Corruption, deceit, lies, and
stifling restrictions form the basis of society in a small Norwegian coast town. Behind the local shipyard owner, Consul
Bernick, the leading families of the town are marshaled in
provincial complacency. Step by step, Bernick's corruption is

revealed, and with it the rotten core of society. He had made his reputation by deserting the woman he loved, allowing a friend to take his blame not only in a scandalous affair with an actress, but also for a dishonest business venture. Enmeshed in deceit, Bernick attempts to dispose of this friend by sending him off in a rotten ship. Urged to recant by the woman he once loved and made aware that his own son is a stowaway aboard the same ship, he is shocked into recognition of the evil of his ways. Confessing everything in time, he is determined to make truth and freedom the pillars of society.

MEN (*10, plus extras*): 1 is 13; 3 are 30–40; 5 are 45–55; 1 is about 60. WOMEN (*9, plus extras*): 1 is about 20; 3 are 35–45; 2 are 20–30; 3 are 45–55. SET: The garden room of Consul Bernick's house. COSTUMES: Fashionable clothing, about 1875.

ROYALTY: Apply publisher. TEXT: Una Ellis-Fermor trans. in *Three Plays by Ibsen* (Penguin).

— o —

A DOLL'S HOUSE (*Et dukkehjem;* 1879) HENRIK IBSEN (Norwegian). Nora Helmer is childishly innocent, despite eight years of marriage and two children. She is protected from all responsibility and kept ignorant of even the most rudimentary knowledge of worldly affairs by her husband, Torvald, who feels that practical knowledge is unladylike. When her husband was ill and she needed money for medical expenses, she signed her dying father's name to a note. Her father died before he could put his legal signature on the document. Now, one of her husband's employees who had witnessed the forgery, desperate to keep his job, threatens to reveal her forgery to her husband unless she pleads for his job. Nora is convinced that her husband will understand that the forgery was an act of love and will forgive her. However, when Torvald learns of it, he upbraids her unmercifully. He relents as soon as he discovers that his employee has had a change of heart and will not expose Nora. But Nora is so shocked by her husband's attitude that she refuses to accept his forgiveness. She realizes that her husband has thought of her as a pretty, mindless toy for his amusement, not as a human being. She leaves Torvald and her children to seek some kind of life in which she can be more than a mere doll.

MEN (4): 3 are 35–45; 1 is 55–65 (minor). WOMEN (4): All 25–35 (2 minor). CHILDREN (3): 6–10, younger if practical. SET: Comfortable sitting room with a piano. COSTUMES: Fashionable clothing, about 1875. DIFFICULTIES: Requires an outstanding actress.

ROYALTY: Apply Brandt & Brandt.* TEXT: Eva Le Gallienne trans. in *Six Plays by Ibsen* (Random).

— o —

GHOSTS (*Gengangere;* 1881)   HENRIK IBSEN (Norwegian). Tragedy.   This play deals with Mrs. Alving's unsuccessful attempts to escape the consequences of the sterile Victorian tradition of her youth. She had married Captain Alving because he was socially acceptable. Later, she discovered him to be completely dissolute, but her Victorian sense of duty prevented her leaving him. After the birth of her son, she began actively to try to disentangle herself from the consequences of her marriage. She sent her son away so that he would not be corrupted by his father. After Captain Alving's death, she used his fortune to build an orphanage, thus hiding his true character forever and at the same time preventing her son from inheriting tainted money. When the play begins, Mrs. Alving believes that she has finally exorcised the ghosts of the past. Her son is about to return home for the dedication of the orphanage. However, as soon as Oswald arrives, ghosts begin to control the action. The son tries to carry on an affair with a housemaid who is actually his illegitimate half-sister. Then Oswald confesses to his mother that he is fatally ill of a social disease inherited from his father. Under the strain of learning about his father's degeneracy and the maid's true parentage, Oswald becomes ravingly insane and begs his mother to poison him. Rationally, Mrs. Alving knows that death is a merciful escape for him, but her feelings of motherhood keep her from administering the poison. As the final curtain falls, Mrs. Alving stands by her babbling son, unable to act.

MEN (3): 1 is 20–30; 1 is 45–55; 1 is about 60. WOMEN (2): 1 is 20–30; 1 is 45–50 and must be outstanding actress. SET: The conservatory of a large Norwegian country home. COSTUMES: Fashionable Victorian; clerical garb for 1 man.

ROYALTY: Apply Brandt & Brandt.* TEXT: Eva Le Gallienne trans. in *Six Plays by Henrik Ibsen* (Random).

— o —

AN ENEMY OF THE PEOPLE (*En folkefiende;* 1882)
HENRIK IBSEN (Norwegian). Dr. Stockmann is a scientist
totally inexperienced in the daily concerns of the world. He
has been a town hero, for he discovered that the local water
was particularly favorable for health baths and the town has
become a tourist center. However, he now learns that the
wastes from a tannery are polluting the baths. He proposes to
make his findings public and demands that the condition be
corrected, expecting that the community will be delighted with
his honesty. But the whole town turns against him for threatening its livelihood. Even those who recognize that his demands are just finally desert him because their businesses are
threatened by irate citizens. Stockmann makes a desperate
appeal in a public meeting, but the mob turns violently against
him. Unable either to understand the town's fear and anger or
to compromise his ideals, he finds himself completely isolated.
By the end of the play, his daughter has lost her fiancé and
the younger children have been driven from their school. But
Stockmann is not discouraged. Idealistically, he plans to start
his own school for the sidewalk urchins. As the play ends, he
confidently declares that "the strongest man in the world is the
man who stands alone." But his pronouncement has an ironic
ring, for he is surrounded and supported by his still-loving
family, without whose help he could not even dress or eat
properly.

MEN (*7*): 2 are 25–35; 3 are 45–55; 2 are 60–70. WOMEN
(*2*): 1 about 25; 1 about 45. BOYS (*2*): Both are 10–12.
EXTRAS: Townspeople, any age, both sexes. SETS: Stock-
mann's living room; a newspaper editor's office; a meeting hall;
Stockmann's study (may be set in the living room again).
COSTUMES: Fashionable clothes of the 1860s or 1870s
ROYALTY: Apply Brandt & Brandt.* TEXT: Eva Le Gal-
lienne trans. in *Six Plays by Ibsen* (Random).

—— O ——

THE WILD DUCK (*Vildan den;* 1884) HENRIK IBSEN
(Norwegian) Tragedy. Hjalmar Ekdal, a poor retoucher of
photographs, lives happily with his wife, Gina, and his daughter, Hedwig. He deludes himself that he is a master inventor
and spends his time dabbling in vague ideas while his wife
does the actual work in the family. He is supported in his delusion by Hedwig, who adores him and innocently accepts his

extravagant estimate of himself. Gregors Werle, the uncompromising idealist son of a wealthy local businessman, returns to town, rejects his father for his past lies, and turns to Hjalmar as a man capable of living the ideal life. A friend of the Ekdals, Dr. Relling, knows better. However, despite Relling's objections, Gregors tries to persuade Hjalmar to live by the whole truth. He tells Hjalmar that Hedwig is probably the daughter of old Werle, for whom Gina Ekdal worked at the time of her marriage. Instead of spurring Hjalmar to new conquests, the truth shatters his faith in his wife and daughter. Confused but still the staunch idealist, Gregors decides he must go farther in shattering Hjalmar's illusions. He tries to persuade the despondent Hedwig to kill her pet wild duck, which Hjalmar has taken as a symbol for all the exotic and rare things for which he yearns. Grief-stricken by her father's rejection of her, wishing to prove her love but confused about the kind of sacrifice Gregors demands of her, Hedwig shoots herself instead.

MEN (*9, plus extras*): 2 are 35–45; 4 are 45–55 (2 minor); 3 are 60–70 (1 minor). WOMEN (*3*): 1 is 14; 1 is 30–40; 1 is 45–55. SETS: The drawing room of a wealthy industrialist, *ca.* 1880; Hjalmar's photographic studio. COSTUMES: Middle- and upper-class clothing, 1880s.

ROYALTY: Apply publisher. TEXT: Una Ellis-Fermor trans. in *Three Plays by Ibsen* (Penguin).

— o —

ROSMERSHOLM (1886)   HENRIK IBSEN (Norwegian). Tragedy.   Johannes Rosmer, the master of Rosmersholm, has always stood for the respectable conservative tradition in the community. Recently, his half-mad wife Beata has committed suicide. The community is incensed because Beata's former companion, Rebekka West, has remained on at Rosmersholm with Rosmer. Rosmer is about to provoke the community further by announcing his alliance with the Liberal Party. He is prevented from making his announcement by an unscrupulous newspaper editor who threatens to publish a letter from Beata which intimates that Rosmer and Rebekka were having an affair before her suicide. The editor plans to have Rosmer write liberal articles under the guise of a conservative. Rosmer refuses to act so dishonestly, but he feels that he cannot compromise Rebekka by permitting the publication of the letter.

When Kroll, Rosmer's brother-in-law, learns that Rosmer has turned liberal, he, too, believes that Rebekka and Rosmer have been having clandestine relations. In a private conversation with Rebekka, he convinces her that Rosmer will never completely escape the conservative tradition, and that she, herself, has only a surface coat of liberalism. Convinced that Kroll is right, Rebekka confesses to Rosmer that she had insinuated the idea of suicide into Beata's disordered mind, partly from love for Rosmer and partly because she wanted him free to live a liberal life. Rosmer walks out on Rebekka. As she is about to leave Rosmersholm, he returns. He loves her, but he is tortured by the idea that Rebekka acted primarily out of a calculated desire to convert him to liberalism. He needs proof that she loves him as his wife did. To Rebekka, it seems as if Rosmer is asking that she, too, commit suicide. They both realize that the past and their own guilty passion will always prevent them from being happy. Believing death to be the only solution, they leap into the millrace together, as the unhappy Beata had done before them.

MEN (4): 3 are 40–50; 1 about 60. WOMEN (2): 1 is 31; 1 is 50–60. SETS: Sitting room at Rosmersholm, about 1870; Rosmer's study (this may also be set in the sitting room). COSTUMES: Fashionable 1870 clothing.

ROYALTY: Apply Brandt & Brandt.* TEXT: Eva Le Gallienne trans. in *Six Plays by Ibsen* (Random).

— o —

HEDDA GABLER (1890) HENRIK IBSEN (Norwegian). Tragedy. Hedda Gabler is a frustrated woman, capable only of destroying others. One of her amusements is practicing with a pair of dueling pistols which belonged to her aristocratic father. She marries a meek professor for security, not because she loves him. When she becomes pregnant, she refuses to admit her condition. Eventually, she tries to regain influence over Eilert Lovborg, a brilliant young scholar she had previously led to drink and destruction. Unable to find any satisfaction in her own life, she tries to find vicarious thrills by plotting the glorious suicide of Lovborg. Her plan succeeds, and Lovborg commits suicide with one of her dueling pistols, but Hedda discovers that his suicide was not glorious; he shot himself in the stomach, perhaps by accident. Furthermore, an unscrupulous judge finds the pistol and threatens to reveal its

true ownership unless Hedda consents to a clandestine affair
with him. Disappointed, frightened of scandal, and equally
frightened of an affair, she uses the other pistol to end her
own life.

MEN (*3*): All 35–45. WOMEN (*4*): 2 are 30–35; 2 about
60. SET: A handsome drawing room of the 1880s. COSTUMES:
Highly fashionable 1880s clothing.
ROYALTY: Apply Brandt and Brandt.* TEXT: Eva Le Gallienne trans. in *Six Plays by Ibsen* (Random).

—— o ——

THE MASTER BUILDER (*Bygmester Solness;* 1892) HEN-
RIK IBSEN (Norwegian). Tragedy. Halvard Solness, the protagonist, is an aging master builder who has long been the
leader in his field. Solness, however, is tormented by a sense
of guilt. He feels that his success has been achieved at the cost
of his wife's fulfillment as a mother. Solness' building business
was founded on insurance money from a fire which destroyed
his wife's family estate. As an indirect result of the fire, his
twin sons died, and with them seems to have died his wife's
will and joy in life. Solness feels doubly guilty because the
fire started in a defective chimney which he had failed to repair. He also feels guilty about his artistic achievement. Before
the fire, Solness had built magnificent church towers, but afterward he turned to building homes. He believes that the homes
are commercially "safe" substitutes for the less profitable but
more artistic churches. Desperate to recapture the artistic
integrity of his early years, he turns for inspiration to Hilda
Wangel, a young woman who had known him as a brilliant
church builder. Under her influence, he builds the highest
tower of his career atop the new home he has built for himself. According to tradition, he, as builder, must climb to the
top of the tower and crown it with a wreath. Although he
knows that height now makes him dangerously dizzy, at Hilda's
urging he determines to achieve this final symbolic act of
artistic rejuvenation. As he reaches the top of the tower, his
dizziness overwhelms him, and he falls to his death.

MEN (*4, plus extras*): 1 is 25–35; 2 are 50–60; 1 is about
70. WOMEN (*3, plus extras*): 1 about 22; 1 is 25–30; 1 is
45–55. SETS: Solness' workroom; the drawing room of his

home; the veranda of his home, scaffolding to the left. Cos-
TUMES: Fashionable clothing of the 1890s.

ROYALTY: Apply Brandt & Brandt.* TEXT: Eva Le Gallienne trans. in *Six Plays by Ibsen* (Random).

—— o ——

THE MAN WITHOUT A SOUL (*Mannen utan själ;* 1936)
PÄR LAGERKVIST (Swedish).   Seeking to escape arrest, "The
Man," who has committed a political murder, is befriended
by "The Woman," who bears his victim's child. His love for
this woman, although unrequited, changes him from a callous
political instrument "without a soul" to a self-questioning
seeker after justice and truth. Regretting his previous inhumanity as well as the death of his beloved and the infant,
he flees the cause in which he has lost faith and is executed
by his former comrades. The guilt-ridden protagonist "would
like so much to believe" as he disappears with head high into
the radiant light of the prison yard. Skeletal and terse dialogue,
reduction of character to essences, and "station" development
of the plot are appropriate to the allegorical style of this
modern morality play.

MEN (6): 1 is 25–35, requires an outstanding actor; 1 is
25–30; 3 are 40–60; 1 is 60–70 (minor). WOMEN (6): 1 is
25–35; 3 are 55–70; 2 are 20–40 (minor). EXTRAS: Guests and
others, men and women. SETS: A public barroom; a simply
furnished bedroom; room in a maternity hospital; outside the
gates of a cemetery; a prison cell. Sets should be minimal,
highly selective and suggestive. Suitable for arena. COSTUMES:
1930s or contemporary; uniforms for 2 policemen, an army
officer, a priest, a doctor, a nurse, a Salvation Army woman;
rags for beggar and flower-vendor.

ROYALTY: Apply American-Scandinavian Foundation.*
TEXT: Helge Kökeritz trans. in *Scandinavian Plays of the
Twentieth Century* (Princeton), Ser. I.

—— o ——

THE WORD (*Ordet;* 1932)   KAJ MUNK (Danish).   A re-
ligious "legend of today," the play deals with the struggle,
within one peasant family, between reason and pure faith. Old
Mikkel Borgen, head of the family, has long clung to the
Lutheran religion as a compromise between reason and faith.
His sons have gone in divergent directions. Young Mikkel, the

eldest, has substituted love of wife for religious belief. Johannes, the second son, is mad and utters only obscure prophecies. Anders, the youngest, is in danger of succumbing to a fundamentalist sect by marrying the daughter of the sect's preacher-tailor leader. The struggle reaches a climax when Inger, young Mikkel's wife, dies in childbirth. All the characters except Johannes, the mad son, display the inadequacies of their faiths by accepting Inger's death as a bitter and unchangeable fact. The shock of Inger's death, however, restores Johannes' sanity. Through his unswerving faith, he restores her to life, thus demonstrating to the other characters the power of uncompromising faith in the goodness of God. Munk's peasants are especially well characterized, in an unpatronizing way, as people with simple dignity. Much of the play's success comes from Munk's ability to deal primarily with the realistic rather than the purely ideological aspects of the conflict.

MEN (7): 4 are 20–40; 3 are 40–60. WOMEN (6): 3 are 20–40 (1 minor); 1 is 40–60; 2 children, 6–12. EXTRAS: Either sex, unspecified number. SETS: Living room in a comfortable peasant home; living room in a poor tailor shop. Neither set requires elaborate detail nor unusual furnishings. Arena production possible. COSTUMES: Simple peasant work clothes. DIFFICULTIES: The play contains several necessary references to Björnson's *Beyond Human Power* (see p. 236).
ROYALTY: Apply publisher. TEXT: R. P. Keigwin trans. in *Five Plays by Kaj Munk* (American-Scandinavian Foundation*).

— o —

THE GALLOWS MAN: A MIDWINTER STORY (*Galmannen: en midvintersaga;* 1922) RUNAR SCHILDT (Finnish). Tragedy. A highly dramatic, intense play dealing with the struggle of two people to surmount the essential materialism of the world in order to gain understanding and compassion from each other. A masterpiece of one-act playwriting, the story concerns Colonel Toll, who possesses a magic talisman—"the Gallows Man"—which has enabled him to achieve earthly power. As the play begins, Colonel Toll is aware of his approaching death. He is panic-stricken, for he must sell the Gallows Man before he dies lest his soul wander in eternal torment. However, each new owner must buy the talisman for less than the previous purchaser paid. Since the Colonel had paid only a grain of sand, he despairs of selling it. Driven by fear and a realization that his ill-bought power has gained him loneliness instead of love, he attempts to seduce his house-keeper, Maria, a proud, lonely woman of considerable in-tegrity, who at first resists his attempts, although she secretly loves him. However, when she learns about the Gallows Man she agrees to purchase it for the price of her chastity—a thing worth less than a grain of sand in the eyes of the world. The bargain is agreed upon and the Colonel gives her the talisman, first asking her to make her wish on it. But Maria asks for nothing. The Gallows Man disintegrates in her hands, de-stroyed by her unselfishness. The Colonel dies peacefully, hav-ing finally received some measure of love and compassion from another human being.

MAN: About 45; requires an outstanding actor. WOMAN: About 25; requires an outstanding actress. SETS: A bedroom-sitting room furnished with 1820–40 Scandinavian furniture. Set need not be realistic. Suitable for arena production. COS-TUMES: Scandanavian, *ca.* 1840; man requires a uniform. DIF-FICULTIES: A long one-act play.

ROYALTY: Apply American-Scandanavian Foundation.* TEXT: Henry Alexander trans. in *Scandinavian Plays of the Twentieth Century* (Princeton), Ser. I.

— o —

EYVIND OF THE HILLS (*Bjaerg-Ejvind ag hand hustru,* 1911) JOHANN SIGURJONSSON (Icelandic). Halla, a well-to-do widow, falls in love with her overseer, Kari. She learns through her brother-in-law, the bailiff Bjorn, that Kari is really an escaped thief for whom the law is eagerly searching. To gain time so that she and Kari can escape to the hills together, she promises that she will marry Bjorn. Although this plan fails, she nevertheless succeeds in escaping with her sweet-heart. They live a hard life, often on the point of starvation, and often on the point of being caught by pursuers. At first their love is enough to sustain them, but after she is forced to kill her two children to keep them out of the hands of pur-suers, Halla begins to lose faith in her relation with Kari. Finally, after innumerable hardships and once again on the verge of starvation, she can no longer stand the thought that she has suffered so much only to have lost every vestige of

Kari's love. As he steps out to collect faggots for their fire, she rushes blindly out into the storm to her death.

MEN (9, plus peasants and farm hands; doubling possible): 1 is 10–15 (minor); 3 are 20–30 (minor); 2 are 30–40; 3 are 40–50 (2 minor). WOMEN (2, plus peasant women): 1 is 30–40; 1 is 50–60 (minor). CHILD: Girl, age 3. SETS: The servant's hall of a well-to-do Icelandic farmhouse, mid-18th century; outdoors, a large sheepfold on one side and a large slope on the other; outdoors in the hills, a conical lava formation to the right and the wall of a stone hut to the left; a small hut in the hills. COSTUMES: 18th-century Icelandic peasant dress. Assorted dress for Halla, the bailiff, and the judge. Authenticity not necessary.

ROYALTY: Apply American-Scandinavian Foundation.* TEXT: Henninge Krohn Scharche trans. in *Chief Contemporary Dramatists* (Houghton Mifflin), Ser. III.

—o—

COMRADES (*Kamraterna;* 1886–88) AUGUST STRINDBERG (Swedish). Comedy. Axel and Bertha, both aspiring artists in Paris, have married with the understanding that they shall live together as comrades—absolute equals, with the husband having no more rights than the wife. Under this arrangement Axel becomes more and more submissive and effeminate, Bertha more masculine and assertive. Axel finally rebels, exposes Bertha as an incompetent artist, and walks out on her, saying that he can find his comrades at a bar; at home he wants a wife. The play is intended as a parody of Ibsen's *A Doll's House* (see p. 240). Some of the scenes verge on farce as Strindberg attacks the feminist movement and gibes at mannish women and effeminate men. But other scenes, in which Strindberg gives vent to his rancor, may strike a modern audience as too uncomfortable for laughter.

MEN (7): 6 are 20–40 (3 minor); 1 is 45–60. WOMEN (7): 2 are 18–20; 4 are 20–40 (1 minor); 1 is 45–60. SET: Artist's studio in Paris. Realistic. Arena production possible. COSTUMES: Parisian of the 1880s. 1 woman must be dressed in a very mannish way; 1 man in elegant evening clothes, including knee breeches; 1 man in Swedish Army uniform (the last 2 not absolutely essential).

ROYALTY: Apply publisher. TEXT: Arvid Paulson trans. in *Seven Plays by August Strindberg* (Bantam).

—— o ——

THE FATHER (*Fadren;* 1887) AUGUST STRINDBERG (Swedish). Tragedy. Fighting to control the upbringing of her child, Laura, destroys her husband, a cavalry captain, by instilling in his mind the suspicion that he is not father to the child, by goading him into a violent act, which gives credence to her accusations that he is insane, and by having his old trusted nurse slip a straitjacket on him, after which he suffers a stroke. Written before Freud described the Oedipus complex, the apparently unreasonable hatred that exists between husband and wife is given a Freudian explanation as Strindberg shows how love can turn to hate when the man seeking a mother-madonna finds in the sex act a mistress-whore. The conflict is presented with such searing intensity as to overwhelm all objections about the credibility of the action and the reality of the characters, who assume a larger-than-life stature as the play progresses.

MEN (*5*): 2 are 20–30 (both minor); 3 are 35–50. WOMEN (*2*): 1 is 30–45; 1 is 55–70. GIRL: About 14. SET: Living room of country house in Sweden. Set need not be realistic. Suitable for arena production. COSTUMES: Swedish, 1880s. Cavalry uniforms for captain and two soldiers. DIFFICULTIES: Requires a fine actor in the part of the captain, and a skillful actress for Laura.

ROYALTY: Apply publisher. TEXT: Arvid Paulson trans. in *Seven Plays by August Strindberg* (Bantam).

—— o ——

MISS JULIE (*Fröken Julie;* 1888) AUGUST STRINDBERG (Swedish). Tragedy. Miss Julie is the daughter of a weak-willed Swedish count and his strong, man-hating wife, who has taught her daughter to believe in the superiority of women and to hate men. The conflict between the teachings of her mother and her desire to have a normal relationship with a man is the basis for her tragedy, brought about by Jean, the count's valet. Jean dreams of bettering himself by rising above his class and sees Miss Julie as a symbol of the things he wants. When he seduces her he does so because she is that symbol. Gradually Miss Julie succumbs to Jean's appeal.

Afterward, when she realizes the dishonor involved and that the relationship could not be a satisfactory one, she exits to commit suicide. The characters are complex human beings drawn with sound psychological motivation.

MAN: 30. WOMEN (2): 1 is 25; 1 is 35. EXTRAS: Peasants to perform a song and dance, which can be done off stage. SET: The large kitchen of a Swedish manor house in the 1880s. COSTUMES: Fashionable 1880s; livery; Swedish peasant. DIFFICULTIES: The translation needs considerable textual work. The intensity of the play must be carefully built to avoid melodrama. (The play runs approximately 50 minutes.)

ROYALTY: Public domain. TEXT: Peter Watts trans. (Penguin).

—o—

TO DAMASCUS, PART I (*Till Damaskus, del I;* 1898) AUGUST STRINDBERG (Swedish). The first part of the *To Damascus* trilogy is complete in itself and is the most frequently performed part. Often considered the first true forerunner of expressionism, the play traces the spiritual journey of its hero, The Stranger. All that happens is seen through his eyes. At a critical juncture in his life, he runs off with another man's wife and is plagued by his conscience for this and other deeds, going back to his childhood. He sinks to his ultimate degradation in the most expressionistic scene of the play when the inmates of a monastery asylum, all of whom resemble people against whom he has sinned, pronounce a curse on him. The remaining scenes, reversing the order of the first scenes, bring The Stranger back to the beginning of his journey with some measure of peace restored to his soul. The symbolic texture of the play is extraordinarily rich. Foreshadowing *A Dream Play* in technique, *To Damascus* casts a unique spell because the audience, like the hero of the play, is unable to distinguish between the real and the unreal.

MEN (5, plus extras): 3 are 35–50; 1 is 40–54; 1 is 80. WOMEN (4, plus extras): 2 are 20–35; 2 are 40–60. SETS: Street corner in Paris; yard of a house; hotel room; seacoast; country road; ravine with a blacksmith shop; kitchen of a country house in Austria; rose room of the same house; refectory in an old monastery. Sets need not be realistic. Unit set called for. Not well suited for arena production. Cos-

TUMES: Fashionable Parisian, 1900; German walking dress. DIFFICULTIES: 2 fine actors are indispensable for the very demanding lead roles.

ROYALTY: Apply publisher. TEXT: Evert Sprinchorn trans. in *The Genius of the Scandinavian Theater* (Mentor).

— o —

THERE ARE CRIMES AND CRIMES (*Brott och brott;* 1898–99) AUGUST STRINDBERG (Swedish). Intoxicated by his success as a playwright and infatuated with Henriette, a sculptress, Maurice wishes that the child he fathered by his faithful mistress did not stand in the way of his happiness. The wish is father to the deed. The child dies. Maurice, seized by remorse, is pursued by the police and deserted by his friends and public. But it seems that the gods are only testing him and humbling him. The child is discovered to have died a natural death, and from his experience Maurice learns that all is vanity. The dark humor of some of the scenes may justify calling the play a comedy. The Parisian atmosphere, well-delineated secondary characters, and a subtle mixture of symbolism and realism add to the interest of the work. (Strindberg preferred the title *Intoxication.*)

MEN (*9; doubling of 1 possible*): 4 are 20–40; 2 are 40–60; 3 are 25–50 (minor). WOMEN (*3*): 2 are 20–35; 1 is 35–60. GIRL: 5. SETS: Montparnasse cemetery, Paris; a café; a country tavern; a restaurant in the Bois de Boulogne; the Luxembourg Gardens. Sets should probably have an impressionistic or poetic quality. Unit set possible. COSTUMES: Parisian, 1900. DIFFICULTIES: Maurice must be kept sympathetic.

ROYALTY: Apply publisher. TEXT: Arvid Paulson trans. in *Seven Plays by August Strindberg* (Bantam); Evert Sprinchorn trans. in *The Genius of the Scandinavian Theatre* (Mentor).

— o —

GUSTAV VASA (1899) AUGUST STRINDBERG (Swedish). History. The first three acts show King Gustav of Sweden, the father of his country, grown tyrannical and dispensing justice without mercy. In the fourth act, the king is humbled when everything he has built up seems about to be destroyed. His country is torn by rebellion, his friends desert him, and even his wife and son are alienated from him. But in the last act, Providence smiles again on the chastised and forlorn ruler as the peasants who fought for him at the beginning of his career return to offer their aid. The action takes place in the 16th century against a background of civil strife, emergent nationalism, and the Reformation. (Inspired partly by Shakespeare's *Henry IV* [*q.v.*], this is Strindberg's least characteristic play. The first two acts, in which the king does not appear but in which his presence and power are felt at every moment, are masterfully written. All of the characters, even the minor ones, are vividly drawn.)

MEN (*16, plus extras*): 5 are 17–35; 11 are 35–60. WOMEN (*6*): 2 are 17–25; 4 are 30–60. GIRLS (*1, plus extras*): 1 is 14. SETS: Interior of home in central Sweden; a guild office of the Hanseatic League; a tavern; the king's workroom; city square in Stockholm; the workroom of Master Olaf; the terrace of the palace in Stockholm. Sets need not be realistic. Unit set would be practical. Not well suited for arena. COSTUMES: Army, civilian, and court dress of 16th-century Sweden and Germany.

ROYALTY: Apply publisher. TEXT: Walter Johnson trans. in *The Vasa Trilogy* (University of Washington).

— o —

EASTER (*Påsk;* 1900) AUGUST STRINDBERG (Swedish). Eleanora, a 16-year-old girl of Christlike innocence, returns home from the insane asylum, and by her presence and example brings light into the troubled home of her mother and brother. The play is a religious idyll, subdued in tone, showing the need for faith and for resignation in the face of tribulation. Eleanora is the pivotal character, and the play succeeds only insofar as she is convincing. The action of the play is realistic, but the dialogue often verges on the poetic. The background music from Haydn's *Seven Last Words of Christ*, references to spring and resurrection, and a motif that stresses the need of suffering for others, makes the play into a parable, the three acts taking place on Holy Thursday, Good Friday, and Easter Eve.

MEN (*3*): 2 are 18–30; 1 is 50–70. WOMEN (*3*): 1 is 16; 1 is 20–30; 1 is 40–55. SET: A glass veranda converted into a living room. Need not be realistic. Arena productions have been given. COSTUMES: Ordinary 1900 dress. DIFFICULTIES: Eleanora is very difficult to cast. Translation needs textual work.

ROYALTY: Apply publisher. TEXT: Arvid Paulson trans. in *Seven Plays by August Strindberg* (Bantam).

—— o ——

CHARLES XII (*Karl XII;* 1901) AUGUST STRINDBERG (Swedish). History. Charles XII, King of Sweden from 1697 to 1718, won and lost an empire before he was thirty. For a while all of Europe trembled before this young "madman of the North." The play concentrates on the last three years of Charles' extraordinary career, telescoped into what seems a few months, from the time the king returns to his native country, virtually in ruins as a result of his wars, to the moment of his death in battle in Norway. (There is little action, only the sense of fate closing in on the king. There is no intrigue, no alignment of forces, nothing of the well-made play. Instead Strindberg proceeds indirectly, using counterpoint, parallelism, and symbols, and deploys around the central figure a wide array of characters who function somewhat as a Greek chorus. Musical in form and composition, expressionistic in its visual effects, *Charles XII* represents a new kind of history play and calls for the full utilization of the technical resources of the modern theatre.)

MEN (*25, plus some 13 nonspeaking parts*): 9 are 18–40 (4 minor); 15 are 30–60 (8 minor); 1 is a dwarf, 20–50. WOMEN (*3, plus 10 minor parts*): 2 are 18–30; 1 is 30–40. SETS: A burned town on the Swedish seacoast; a room in a professor's house in Lund; a town square; a garden in the town; the trenches and breastworks below the fortress at Fredrikshald, Norway. Sets probably should not be realistic. Unit set highly appropriate. Unsuitable for arena. COSTUMES: Swedish army uniforms and civilian dress of 1700. Historical accuracy called for. DIFFICULTIES: Requires brilliant staging and an actor of imposing presence.

ROYALTY: Apply publisher. TEXT: Walter Johnson trans. in *Strindberg's Queen Christina, Charles XII, Gustav III* (University of Washington).

—— o ——

A DREAM PLAY (*Ett drömspel;* 1901-2) AUGUST STRINDBERG (Swedish). The play presents, in the form of a dream, a panoramic view of life. The daughter of the god Indra comes down from the heavens to experience for herself the trials and tribulations of life on earth. Accompanying her on her downward journey, which reaches its nadir in marriage, are the officer, the lawyer, and the poet, obviously three aspects of the male dreamer. With and through them the daughter experiences the pangs of conscience, sees love turn to hate, and seeks in vain for a meaning to earthly suffering. At the end, when all the characters parade before her to burn their illusions in a purging fire, she ascends to heaven to present the complaints of mankind to her father. As in a dream, characters and scenes blend into one another; symbols, such as a growing castle surmounted by a huge chrysanthemum, have esoteric significance. (The dialogue often rises to heights of great beauty. Music and dance are called for in several of the scenes.)

MEN (*25; doubling possible*): 6 are 18–35 (3 minor); 6 are 30–50 (2 minor); 13 are 45–70 (3 minor). WOMEN (*13; doubling possible*): 9 are 18–35 (5 minor); 4 are 40–70 (2 minor). GIRL: Under 15. EXTRAS: Ballet dancers; grade-school children; supers for the crowd scenes. SETS: Castle exterior; officer's home; stage door; lawyer's office; church interior; sea grotto; lawyer's home; quarantine station on Foulstrand; resort on Fairhaven; schoolroom; Mediterranean coast (this scene can be cut). Unit set essential. Not suitable for arena. COSTUMES: Must be determined by the over-all style of the show. DIFFICULTIES: Design and direction demand great skill.

ROYALTY: Apply publisher. TEXT: Evert Sprinchorn trans. in *Strindberg: Selected Plays and Prose* (Rinehart).

— o —

THE GHOST SONATA (*Spöksonaten;* 1907) AUGUST STRINDBERG (Swedish). Universal guilt and spiritual vampirism are the two major concerns of this grotesquerie. Eighty-year-old Hummel, retired business director, insinuates himself into a fashionable home where live a colonel and his wife and daughter. At supper—a "ghost supper," for the diners are more dead than living—Hummel, in a macabre unmasking scene, strips his old rival the colonel of every vestige of respect. But the wife, formerly in love with Hummel, now a living mummy, exposes Hummel as a bloodsucker and leaves him to kill himself. Opposed to the vampire Hummel is the life-giving student, who has fallen in love with the colonel's daughter, really Hummel's. Even the student, however, is unable to protect the daughter against the corrosive forces of life, symbolized by a monstrous cook. The death screen is placed around the young girl, and the scene dissolves into the Island of the Dead. (An outline cannot suggest the rich theme of this play or the power it can exercise on an audience, even one that does not share in the least Strindberg's disgust with life.)

MEN (7, *plus extras*): 1 is 80; 4 are 45–70 (1 minor; 1 is 30–45; 1 is 20–30. WOMEN (8): 1 is 79; 3 are 45–65 (1 minor); 4 are 17–30 (1 minor). SETS: Façade of an elegant town house with the street in front; the round room in the house; the exotic hyacinth room in the house. Sets should probably be realistic. Everything must be made to seem as natural as possible. Questionable for arena production. COSTUMES: City dress, 1910.

ROYALTY: Elizabeth Sprigge trans., apply Willis Kingsley Wing;* Max Faber trans., apply International Copyright Bureau Ltd.;* Evert Sprinchorn trans., apply publisher. TEXT: Elizabeth Sprigge trans. in *Six Plays of Strindberg* (Doubleday); Max Faber trans. in *Miss Julie and Other Plays* (William Heinemann Ltd., 15–16 Queen St., Mayfair, London, W.1); Evert Sprinchorn trans. in *Strindberg: The Chamber Plays* (Dutton).

ITALIAN DRAMA

Eighteenth Century

THE SERVANT OF TWO MASTERS (*Il servitore de due Padroni; ca.* 1750) CARLO GOLDONI. Comedy. Truffaldino undertakes to serve two masters and thereby to collect pay from two sources. Unknown to him, one of his masters is a woman, Beatrice, masquerading as her own brother so that she may search for her lover, Florindo; the other master is the man for whom she is searching. The play's highly complicated plot grows out of Truffaldino's attempt to keep the secret of his dual employment. Set in the traditional framework of the improvised *commedia dell'arte*, the play employs many of the comic devices and techniques of its distinguished forebears.

MEN (*10; doubling possible*): 4 are 20–40; 4 are 40–60 (3 minor); 2 are 60–80. WOMEN (*3*): All 18–30. SETS: A room in Pantalone's house; a street by Brighella's inn; a street. Suited to unit set. COSTUMES: *Commedia* costumes with masks. Well suited to arena.

ROYALTY: Apply publisher. TEXT: Edward J. Dent trans. in *The Classic Theatre* (Doubleday), Vol. I.

—o—

THE MISTRESS OF THE INN (*La Locadiera;* 1753) CARLO GOLDONI. Comedy. Mirandolina, the mistress of an inn, is much sought after by the patrons of her establishment, in particular by two elderly gentlemen: a real member of the aristocracy and a parvenu count. In addition, she is loved by the pot boy at the inn. When a woman-hater arrives, Mirandolina decides to demonstrate to him the power of the varied charms of woman. Finally successful and faced with three suitors who would bring her out of her taproom and into the bright world of the drawing room, she decides to cast her lot with Fabrizio, the pot boy.

MEN (5): 3 are 20–40 (1 minor); 2 are 60–70. WOMAN: 20–35. SETS: A large room of an inn; the captain's room. Sets need not be realistic. Suited to arena production. COSTUMES: 18th century.

ROYALTY: Apply publisher. TEXT: Lady Gregory trans. in *The Classic Theatre* (Doubleday), Vol. I.

—— o ——

THE FAN (*Il ventaglio*; 1763) CARLO GOLDONI. Comedy. Sitting on her terrace in the village square, Signora Candida drops her fan. Evaristo, who is enamored of the young lady, attempts to retrieve the fan but breaks it in the process. In an attempt to replace the broken fan and to ingratiate himself with the girl, he purchases another fan from Susanna, the shopgirl. This purchase sets up a chain reaction among the principal characters, in the course of which the fan changes hands a number of times before it finally reaches the young lady for whom it was intended. The complications engendered with each exchange of the fan multiply the misunderstanding and misinterpretation until almost everyone in the village is drawn into the action.

MEN (*10*): 8 are 20–40 (minor); 2 are 40–60. WOMEN (*4*): 3 are 18–25; 1 is 40–60. SET: A village square with a number of houses and shops on its perimeter. Set need not be realistic. Arena production possible. COSTUMES: 18th century. DIFFICULTIES: Production difficult on a small stage.

ROYALTY: Apply Samuel French. TEXT: H. B. Fuller trans. (Samuel French).

Nineteenth and Twentieth Centuries

SUMMERTIME (*Il Paese delle Vacanze;* 1937) UGO BETTI. Comedy. Two young people, Francesca and Alberto, who have been childhood sweethearts and who are now about to go their separate ways, are unexpectedly thrown together at a summer picnic. Here they have an opportunity to see each other clearly once again, and they discover the real strength of the bond that links them. Although almost everyone seeks, for private reasons, to prevent the flourishing of their relationship, the two find that they are unalterably linked by a deep and abiding understanding, unknown and unknowable to those who strive to separate them.

MEN (6): 4 are 20–35 (3 minor); 2 are 45–50. WOMEN (5): 3 are 22–30 (1 minor); 2 are 45–50. SETS: Two small neighboring gardens; an alpine spot with an abandoned hut and a cliff edge; a room in a farmhouse. COSTUMES: Contemporary.

ROYALTY: Apply Madame Ninon Tallon-Karlweis.* TEXT: Henry Reed trans. in *Three Plays by Ugo Betti* (Grove).

— o —

THE QUEEN AND THE REBELS (*La Regina e gli Insorti;* 1949) UGO BETTI. When Argia, a prostitute, makes her way to a revolutionary stronghold in search of her lover, who is one of the soldiers in the revolutionary army, she is suspected of being the escaped queen for whom the army is searching. In a moment of kindness and pity, she allows the real queen, a groveling shell of a woman who has been posing as a peasant, to escape, thus involving herself in a conflict with Commissar Amos. Amos is determined not only to discover the identity of the queen but also to obtain from her the identity of the loyalist leaders. As the pressure exerted

261

upon her becomes stronger, Argia is moved, as if despite herself, to assume the full majesty of a queen.

MEN (7): 3 are 30–40; 4 are 40–60 (2 minor). WOMEN (3): All 30–40 (1 minor). EXTRAS: About 8 nonspeaking actors may be added. SET: A large hall in the public building of a small village. Need not be realistic. Suitable for arena. COSTUMES: Contemporary; some military.

ROYALTY: Apply Madame Ninon Tallon-Karlweis.* TEXT: Henry Reed trans. in *Three Plays by Ugo Betti* (Grove).

—— o ——

THE BURNT FLOWER BED (*L'Auola Bruciata;* 1951-52) UGO BETTI. Giovanni, a former political leader, has retired from the world to a mountain retreat where, with his wife, he broods over the death of his son, killed in an accident many years before. The political faction with which he had been allied comes to him with the purpose of using him in a ruse to provoke a war. Although he discovers that he would be shot the instant he appeared on the supposedly neutral plain, Giovanni resigns himself to the scheme even though the incident would result in war. The plan is blocked, however, when Rosa, a girl whose father had been used for a similar purpose many years before, sacrifices herself in his place in order to destroy his cynicism and restore meaning to his world.

MEN (5): All are 40–60 (1 minor). WOMEN (2): 1 is 18–25; 1 is 40–60. SET: The living room of Giovanni's home overlooking the mountains. Arena production possible. COSTUMES: Contemporary.

ROYALTY: Apply Madame Ninon Tallon-Karlweis.* TEXT: Henry Reed trans. in *Three Plays by Ugo Betti* (Grove).

—— o ——

LA GIOCONDA (1898) GABRIELE D'ANNUNZIO. Lucio Settala, an artist, finds himself torn between two conflicting forces: the deep love of his wife, Silvia, and the inspiring but dangerous relationship that has developed between him and his mistress and model, Gioconda. Silvia's efforts to reestablish a proper relationship with her husband are fruitless, and Lucio, choosing to pursue his art, abandons his wife and their child for the excitement offered him by Gioconda. Silvia is left broken in spirit, her "beautiful hands" crushed in a vain attempt to save Lucio's work from Gioconda.

MEN (*3*): 2 are 30–40; 1 is 60–70. WOMEN (*4*): 3 are 30–40; 1 is 18–25. CHILD: About 8. SETS: The elegant living room of Lucio's home; Lucio's studio; a simple room at the seashore. COSTUMES: Fashionable turn-of-the-century.

ROYALTY: Apply publisher. TEXT: Arthur Symons trans. in *Chief Contemporary Dramatists* (Houghton Mifflin), Ser. III.

—— o ——

BETWEEN TWO THIEVES (*Processeo a Gesu;* 1955) DIE-GO FABBRI. In an effort to discover the roots of racial preju-dice, a family group of German-Jewish players has traveled from town to town staging an improvised retrial of Jesus Christ. Each time they take their parts as judges, prosecutor, or counsels for the defense and attempt to investigate, from a contemporary view, whether or not Christ was guilty accord-ing to the prevailing Roman and Judaic Law. Tonight, after the interrogation of such witnesses as Caiaphas and Pilate, the trial takes another turn. The daughter of the head of the fam-ily, weary of seeking truth in the letter of the law, demands that the personality of Christ himself be explored. In a rear-rangement of the witnesses, Mary, Peter, John, Thomas, Judas, and Mary Magdalene testify. When the verdict is about to be given the session is interrupted by several members of the audience, among them a Catholic priest, an agnostic, a prosti-tute, and an anti-Semite, played by the former witnesses. The translator has tightened the dialogue of this well-constructed, unorthodox play, and has given it an improved ending, em-phasizing its message of tolerance and understanding.

MEN (*10, including doubling*): 6 are 20–40; 4 are 40–60. WOMEN (*4*): 3 are 20–30; 1 is 40–50. SET: The play may be performed on an empty stage or in a lecture hall. Suitable for arena production. COSTUMES: Modern street clothes; how-ever, occasionally garments are used to suggest a biblical character.

ROYALTY: $35–25, Samuel French. TEXT: Warner LeRoy trans. (Samuel French).

—— o ——

RIGHT YOU ARE IF YOU THINK YOU ARE (*Cosi e se vi pare;* 1917) LUIGI PIRANDELLO. Ponza, son-in-law to Signora Frola, refuses to allow the old woman to see his wife, whom the old lady insists is her daughter. He, on the other hand, insists that the Signora's daughter was his first wife, now deceased, and that the old woman is merely refusing to accept the fact of her daughter's death. Since the town records, which might have cleared up the issue, have been destroyed, it is impossible to determine the "truth" of either of the assertions. The actual uncertainty of the identities involved forms the central situation out of which the parable of the play—examining the problem of the necessity of illusion and the illusiveness of truth—grows.

MEN (*7*): 3 are 30–40; 3 are 40–50; 1 is 50–60. WOMEN (*7*): 1 is 19; 1 is 25–35; 2 are 40–50; 2 are 50–60; 1 is 60–70. EXTRAS: A few are needed. SETS: The fashionable parlor of Agazzi's house; the study in the same house. COSTUMES: Contemporary. DIFFICULTIES: Requires mature acting.

ROYALTY: Apply publisher. TEXT: Eric Bentley trans. (as *It Is So If You Think So*) in *Naked Masks* (Dutton).

—— o ——

SIX CHARACTERS IN SEARCH OF AN AUTHOR (*Sei personaggi in cerca d'autore;* 1921) LUIGI PIRANDELLO. Six characters from a play assume a life of their own and invade a theatre during a rehearsal of another play. The entire fabric of the theatre and its attempt to represent life breaks down as each of the characters strives for a kind of existence at once necessary to him and impossible for him to achieve. Each character, by virtue of his independence from his creator, is driven by his own motivations into actions never conceived of by his author. The play becomes a series of fragmentary scenes, alternatingly serious and comic, until motive and action are completely confounded.

MEN (*13; doubling possible*): 4 are 20–40; 9 are 40–60. WOMEN (*6*): 4 are 20–40; 2 are 40–60. BOY: 14 (no lines). GIRL: 4 (no lines). SETS: Minimal "rehearsal" scenery. Suited to arena staging. COSTUMES: Contemporary.

ROYALTY: Apply publisher. TEXT: Eric Bentley trans. in *Naked Masks* (Dutton).

—— o ——

HENRY IV (*Enrico IV;* 1922) LUIGI PIRANDELLO. The Marchioness Matilda Spina attempts to bring her friend, whom she believes mad, out of the delusion in which he imagines himself or pretends to be the Emperor Henry IV. She enters his elaborate fantasy of the eleventh-century monarchy accompanied by her daughter, who resembles the Marchioness as she was in her youth; the lover she has taken since Henry's madness; and an alienist who thinks he can restore Henry to sanity by giving him back his sense of time. This situation opens the way for an examination of madness and sanity, fantasy and reality.

MEN (*11*): 7 are 20–35 (2 minor, may be cut); 4 are 40–60 (1 minor). WOMEN (*2*): 1 is 45; 1 is 19 (they should resemble each other). SETS: A room decorated to look like an 11th-century throne room; a room adjoining the throne room. Sets need not be realistic. Arena production possible.

ROYALTY: Apply publisher. TEXT: Eric Bentley trans. in *Naked Masks* (Dutton).

— o —

NAKED (*Vestire gli ignudi;* 1922) LUIGI PIRANDELLO. Ersilia, a nurse, unsuccessfully attempts suicide and, believing she is dying, she embroiders for herself a romantic reason for her death: a blighted love affair. When, however, she recovers, she is approached by her former lover. She rejects him and admits the falsity of her imagined motive for death. This revelation leads the town to persecute her as an immoral influence. She finds herself stripped of the illusion with which she sought to clothe her barren and colorless life. The destruction of her illusion drives her to a second, successful, suicide attempt.

MEN (*4*): 3 are 25–35; 1 is 40–50. WOMEN (*2*): 1 is 20–25; 2 are 40–50. SET: The study of a suite of furnished rooms. COSTUMES: Contemporary; one black nurse's uniform.

ROYALTY: Apply publisher. TEXT: William Murray trans. (as *To Clothe the Naked;* Dutton).

— o —

EACH IN HIS OWN WAY (*Ciascuno a suo modo;* 1924) LUIGI PIRANDELLO. When La Vela, Delia Morello's lover, takes his own life, further doubt is cast upon her already doubtful reputation. Since La Vela's motive for committing suicide was an affair between Delia and Michele Rocca, his death provides a context for the examination of human motives and attitudes. An additional turn of the screw is applied when the whole play is seen to be a performance at which the principals involved in the stage action are present in the audience as spectators. These two aspects are revealed when we see the audience in the "lobby" between acts of the play within the play. The interaction of these two elements of reality ends in a complete breakdown of the "performance."

MEN (30): 5 are 25–35, (25 minor; cutting and doubling possible). WOMEN (10): 1 is 30–35; 1 is about 60, (8 minor; cutting and doubling possible). SETS: Sumptuous drawing room of the Palegari palace; lobby of the theatre where the "play" is being performed; a lounge and veranda in Savio's house. COSTUMES: Fashionable contemporary.

ROYALTY: Apply publisher. TEXT: Eric Bentley trans. in *Naked Masks* (Dutton).

—— o ——

AS YOU DESIRE ME (*Come tu mi vuoi;* 1930) LUIGI PIRANDELLO. An unknown woman appears. She is believed to have disappeared during the Austrian invasion and to have been the wife of Bruno Pieri. Although her resemblance to the missing woman is unmistakable, her identity is not established conclusively. She remains the Strange Lady, willing to be or to become whatever Bruno desires her to be. Bruno, however, cannot bring himself to accept her on this basis, and, as a consequence, she returns to her former tormented life.

MEN (11): 4 are 20–30 (minor); 5 are 40–50 (2 minor); 2 are 55–70. WOMEN (7): 1 is 18; 4 are 30–40 (1 has no lines); 1 is 40–50; 1 is 50–60. SETS: The magnificent living room of the Salter home; a luxurious room in the Villa Pieri. COSTUMES: Fashionable contemporary.

ROYALTY: Apply publisher. TEXT: Samuel Putnam trans. (Dutton, out of print).

GERMAN DRAMA

Eighteenth and Nineteenth Centuries

DANTON'S DEATH (*Dantons Tod;* 1835) GEORG BÜCH-
NER. Tragedy. Danton, idol of the masses, has fulfilled his
mission in carrying the French Revolution to its triumph, and
drifts now, a lonely man, into a life of pleasure. His opponent, the merciless dogmatist Robespierre, is also alone. The
Jacobins ridicule his ideals of virtuous abstinence but execute
his orders of death and terror. Robespierre acts, Danton pro-
crastinates. Once the infernal political machine is set in motion, not even Danton's exalted defense can save him from the
guillotine. In many flashing scenes the course of the fallen
giant's destiny is reflected, contrasted, and paralleled by the
action and reaction of the people, his friends, and his enemies.
Among the numerous sharply profiled characters, those of the
poet Camille Desmoulins, his childlike wife Lucile, and Robespierre's sinister aide Saint-Just are most impressive. The language ranges from aphoristic brevity to sweeping rhetoric,
from blatant ribaldry to lyrical tenderness.

MEN (*34; doubling possible*): 24 are 20–40 (14 minor); 10
are 40–60 (5 minor). WOMEN (*9*): 7 are 18–25 (4 minor);
2 are 40–60 (minor). EXTRAS: Numerous deputies; men and
women of the people; a few children. SETS: Paris during the
French Revolution; 32 location changes; spacious halls—the
Jacobins' Club, the National Convention, the Revolutionary
Tribunal; prison; several rooms; public squares and streets.
Not suitable for small or medium-size theatre. COSTUMES:
Jacobin attire of middle and lower classes in Paris, 1794. DIF-
FICULTIES: Requires a giant production. Dramatic unity un-
derneath a complex structure must be accentuated with
excellent coordination of the numerous crowd scenes.
    ROYALTY: Apply publishers. TEXTS: John Holmstrom trans.
in *The Modern Theatre* (Doubleday), Vol. V or Stephen

Spender and Goronwy Rees trans. in *From the Modern Repertoire* (Indiana), Ser. I.

—— o ——

LEONCE AND LENA (*Leonce und Lena;* 1836) GEORG BÜCHNER. Comedy. Imbecile King Peter of Popo plans to wed his son, Leonce, to Princess Lena of Peepee. Unwilling to be married to a lady unknown, the fastidious prince leaves the court with his companion, Valerio, an expert in idleness. Princess Lena is similarly disposed and flees, followed by her perturbed governess. Leonce and Lena meet in the woods and fall in love. The exuberant prince attempts to throw himself into the river but abstains when teased by Valerio about his "lieutenant's romanticism." In the meantime, King Peter and his fatuous councilors prepare for the royal wedding. As bride and groom cannot be found, a masked couple is married "in effigy"; they, of course, turn out to be Leonce and Lena. The king happily resigns in favor of his son, and Valerio appoints himself Minister of State. The meaning of this ironic comedy —disgust with a monotonous life is overcome by love—is hidden under a façade reminiscent of the *commedia dell'arte*. With his playfully ambiguous dialogue, Büchner successfully emulates the style of Shakespeare's sparkling and graceful clown scenes.

MEN (*9*): 1 is 18–25; 4 are 20–40 (2 minor); 4 are 40–60 (2 minor). WOMEN (*3*): 2 are 18–25 (1 must sing and dance); 1 is 40–60. EXTRAS: Ladies and gentlemen of the court; servants; peasants. SETS: Several interiors and exteriors in the absurd, topsy-turvy kingdom of Popo. Sets can be simplified to a minimum. Arena production appropriate. COSTUMES: Fanciful garments, influenced by *commedia dell'arte*, for the inhabitants of an imaginary kingdom. DIFFICULTIES: Only an unrealistic and delicate yet unaffected acting style can assure a successful production.

ROYALTY: Apply publisher. TEXT: Eric Bentley trans. in *From the Modern Repertoire* (Indiana), Ser. III.

—— o ——

WOYZECK (1836) GEORG BÜCHNER. The dramatist precedes his time by a wide margin in choosing a tragic and pitiful hero from the lowest class. Yet, more than a social accusation, this play is a mirror of human agony in existential loneliness. The fusilier, Woyzeck, serves as an orderly to the captain and as a guinea pig to the doctor. Marie, the mother of his child, is, like Woyzeck, a creature destined to suffer. Instinctively she turns away from her hapless, tortured companion, and betrays him with the drum-major, a vigorous and vain male animal. In jealous despair, Woyzeck kills Marie and then, after a brief plunge into the vortex of life at the inn, ends his life in the pond. The characters are sharply drawn; sometimes, as with the captain and the doctor, approaching caricature. In its strongly contrasted scenes, outcrying language, and revolt against bourgeois satiety, this play is a forerunner of expressionism. Transmitted only in fragmentary form, it lacks final polish but is impressive in its spontaneity.

MEN (*15; doubling possible*); 5 are 18–25 (3 minor); 6 are 20–40 (4 minor); 4 are 40–60. WOMEN (*4*): 3 are 18–25 (1 minor); 1 is 50–70. GIRLS (*3*): 6–10 (minor). EXTRAS: Horse; donkey; soldiers; children; ordinary people. SETS: 26 scenes in 15 different places; in and near Leipzig, 1834; various rooms, in front of and inside a fair booth; in the barracks; streets; open field; woodland near a pond. Locations can be suggested by stylized means. Arena production possible. COSTUMES: Clothes of German townspeople around 1830; several military and 2 policemen's uniforms. DIFFICULTIES: The main action, passing through a variety of brief scenes, must be strongly emphasized.

ROYALTY: $10, Samuel French. TEXT: Theodore Hoffman trans. in *The Modern Theatre* (Doubleday), Vol. I.

— o —

GOETZ VON BERLICHINGEN (1773) JOHAN WOLFGANG VON GOETHE. The pre-Reformation period in Germany, with its complex pattern of imperial warfare and private feuds, is captured in a wide historical panorama. Goetz, the Knight with the Iron Hand, defender of the oppressed, wages war against the bishop of Bamberg and later, at the head of the revolting peasants, against the emperor himself. Finally overpowered, he dies a prisoner, with the word *freedom* upon his lips. In a second plot, Goetz's former friend, Weislingen, is poisoned in mind and body by a seductive lady at the bishop's court. The stormy action is only loosely knit. Brief scenes in quick succession displays a cross section of life at the end of the Middle Ages. There is pure chivalry on the side of Goetz and his followers, sheer venality and vice at the bishop's court. The characters are lively and colorful. The fresh, sweeping élan of this play may compensate in a large degree for its dramaturgic deficiencies. Sir Walter Scott's translation, though full of blundering errors, is congenial in its romantic spirit.

MEN (*45; doubling possible*): 1 is 16–18; 30 are 20–40 (24 minor); 14 are 40–60 (9 minor). WOMEN (*11; doubling possible*): 4 are 18–25 (3 minor); 5 are 25–35 (2 minor); 2 are 40–60 (minor). BOYS (*2*): 6–8 (1 minor). EXTRAS: Courtiers; soldiers; peasants; gypsies. SETS: 54 location changes; late-medieval interiors; picturesque exteriors. Romantic style demands rich, varied scenery. Not suitable for arena production. Open-air performance recommended. COSTUMES: Early 16th-century German. DIFFICULTIES: The inherent demand for spectacle in this drama can be fulfilled only in a technically skillful and well-coordinated production.

ROYALTY: Public domain. TEXT: Sir Walter Scott trans. in *The Chief European Dramatists* (Houghton Mifflin).

—— O ——

EGMONT (1787) JOHAN WOLFGANG VON GOETHE. Tragedy. Count Egmont, leader of the Protestant revolt in the Netherlands against the Spanish, is here idealized and made the heroic exponent of freedom and justice. A tenuous plot binds the multitude of scenes: Egmont remains in Brussels in spite of all warnings, is taken prisoner by the Duke of Alba, and is executed. Every scene, every character points toward Egmont: he is popular with the burghers of Brussels; he is dear to his friend, the Duke of Orange; he is adored by his lovely warmhearted mistress, Clara; and even the zealously Catholic regent, Margaret of Parma, fears for him while fearing Orange. Goethe endows his hero with a captivating character of magical charm, insouciant and hopeful to the end, but politically imprudent and unrealistic. Egmont is indeed destined for the other, better world that appears to him in a vision of liberty as he dies, a free man. Beethoven's famous overture and background music have become an integral part of the play.

MEN (*15*): 1 is 18–20; 9 are 20–40 (1 requires powerful actor; 2 minor); 5 are 40–60 (3 minor). WOMEN (*3*): 1 is 18–25; 2 are 40–60. EXTRAS: Attendants; guards; burghers. SETS: Various streets and squares in Brussels, 1568; crossbow target-shooting area; palace interiors; Clara's house; prison. Arena production possible, though it would deprive the play of its spectacular picture-frame characteristics. COSTUMES: Austere attire of 16th-century Spanish aristocracy contrasted with colorful garments of Flemish people. DIFFICULTIES: The play calls for a lavish production, including, if possible, a live orchestra.

ROYALTY: Apply Samuel French. TEXT: Michael Hamburger trans. in *The Classic Theatre* (Doubleday), Vol. II.

—— o ——

FAUST, PART I (*Faust, Erster Teil;* 1808) JOHANN WOLFGANG VON GOETHE. Tragedy. In its entirety ranked among the highest achievements of the human spirit, *Faust* is an all-embracing dramatic poem of man in his relation to the cosmos. Built around the medieval legend of the man who sold his soul to the devil in exchange for magic power, Faust is ultimately saved as reward for his striving for fulfillment. This must always be borne in mind when viewing Part I as a relatively self-sufficient play. In the prologue in Heaven, God permits Mephistopheles to tempt the high-aspiring Dr. Faust. The first third of the play is dominated by the grandiose, philosophical monologues of the searching scholar Faust, who nearly despairs when he cannot face the spirits he has conjured. Then Mephistopheles, brilliantly witty and dangerously fascinating, captures the lead as he lures Faust to the vulgar drinking party in Auerbach's Cellar, and into Hell's Kitchen. The third part belongs to Margaret, innocent and pure, who, misled by her pandering neighbor Marthe, is seduced and deserted by Faust. Driven into child-murder and madness, her tragedy concludes Part I. Faust and Mephistopheles are on their way. (Compare the same theme in Marlowe's *Doctor Faustus;* see p. 64.)

MEN (*22; doubling possible*): 6 are 17–20 (5 minor); 2 are 20–25; 9 are 20–40 (2 minor); 5 are 40–60 (4 minor). WOMEN (*10; doubling possible*): 8 are 17–25 (6 minor); 1 is 30–40; 1 is 40–60. EXTRAS: Townspeople; witches; spirits. SETS: Heaven; study; rooms; tavern; cathedral; prison; several exteriors in a medieval German town; forest; plains; magic mountain. Sets need not be realistic. Arena production possible only if several scenic effects are sacrificed. COSTUMES: 16th-century German townspeople; witches and bewitched animals. DIFFICULTIES: Only a literary-minded audience will accept that the protagonist's destiny remains unresolved in Part I.

ROYALTY: Apply publishers. TEXT: C. F. MacIntyre trans. (New Directions) or Alice Raphael trans. (Holt).

—— o ——

JEST, SATIRE, IRONY, AND DEEPER SIGNIFICANCE (*Scherz, Satire, Ironie und tiefere Bedeutung;* 1822) CHRISTIAN DIETRICH GRABBE. The plot of this literary satire is quite inconsequential, but there is plenty of action for the grotesque, typified characters who speak in a sharp and witty tongue. There is the schnapps-thirsty schoolmaster, who cheats the peasants while discussing relativity. There is the asinine and cowardly poet Ratpoison. There are the three suitors of the beautiful damsel Liddy: the weak Wernthal, who sells her to the Devil; the brutal Mordax, who buys her from the Devil; and the absurdly ugly Mollfels, who wins her in the end. Then there is the Devil himself, freezing to death for lack of hell's temperatures, a puzzle to four shortsighted scientists. Last and least there is Grabbe, "dumb as a crowbar, insulting every other writer though he amounts to nothing himself." The play abounds in critical allusions, from Homer to Grabbe's contemporaries, many of them lost to our understanding. Yet the comedy seems strangely modern; most of all in its theme beneath the kaleidoscope of jest, satire, and irony—the paradox of man's existence.

MEN (*10; doubling possible*): 4 are 20–30 (1 minor); 10 are 30–50 (5 minor). WOMEN (*3*): 18–25 (1 minor). BOY 5–8. EXTRAS: Servants; 13 apprentice tailors. SETS: Various rooms; hill near a village; meadow; road in the village; bushy woods; inside a pavilion. The play can be given without scenery. Suitable for arena production. COSTUMES: Provincial 19th century; strong elements of caricature; 2 heavy fur coats. DIFFICULTIES: Slapstick must be carefully avoided. Several attempts on the German stage to replace the dated literary allusions have failed.

ROYALTY: Apply publisher. TEXT: Maurice Edwards trans. in *From the Modern Repertoire* (Indiana), Ser. II.

—— o ——

THE BEAVER COAT (*Der Biberpelz;* 1893) GERHART HAUPTMANN. Comedy. Set near Berlin at the end of the last century, this vigorous character and situation comedy is spiced with not altogether outdated social and political criticism. The heroine, the good old Mother Wolff, a brave washerwoman, steals at every opportunity—and there are plenty. She relies on the stupidity of the magistrate, Von Wehrhahn, an arrogant Prussian Junker who confuses the issues in his preoccupation with witchhunting. The boatman Wulkow wants a beaver coat. Kruger, a retired, rich carpenter, has got one, but not for long. Mother Wolff appropriates it in the spirit of righteous business enterprise. Kruger runs to the authorities, but Wehrhahn is busy suspecting the harmless Dr. Fleischer of subversive activities. Also, Kruger is a liberal; so, the theft inquiry leads to nothing. Very naturalistically, the play has no denouement. Wehrhahn compliments Frau Wolff on her honesty. She modestly protests. Wehrhahn is caricatured; the other characters are drawn from life.

MEN (*8*): 4 are 20–40; 4 are 40–60. WOMEN (*2*):Both 40. BOY: 8–10 (minor). GIRLS (*2*): 1 is 14; 1 is 16. SETS: Room in Mother Wolff's small, rustic house; Von Wehrhahn's office, decorated in the style of the Kaiser era. Naturalistic sets unnecessary. Suitable for arena production. COSTUMES: Semi-rustic, semiurban clothes of German upper and lower middle class in the 1880s. DIFFICULTIES: Some of the comic effect is derived from Prussian idiom, and is therefore lost in translation. Re-creation of the Prussian atmosphere must be achieved at all costs.

ROYALTY: Apply publisher. TEXT: H. Frenz and M. Waggoner trans. in *Gerhart Hauptmann, 3 Plays* (Holt).

—— o ——

HANNELE (*Hanneles Himmelfahrt;* 1894) GERHART HAUPT-MANN. Hannele has tried to drown herself. A woodcutter has dragged her out of the icy water, and Gottwald, a young schoolmaster, carries the adolescent girl to the almshouse. Hannele is an illegitimate child, an outcast. Her poor skinny body shows marks of brutal beating by her cruel stepfather. The doctor doubts that she will live. Attended by a sister of charity, the girl spends her last hours between waking and dreaming. The people of the almshouse are still there, but somehow transformed. Hannele's dead mother comes to call her. A droll little tailor brings her a bridal gown and glass slippers. Her drunken stepfather threatens her but is repulsed by a stranger, the Christ, who has the traits of Gottwald. Angels take her to heaven. In the almshouse the doctor bends over the dead child. Haupmann's compassionate picture of his young heroine is deeply moving. Reality and visionary dreams are mystically interwoven. Is all this only a sad illusion, or has Hannele been rewarded for her faith by the light of truth? The question remains.

MEN (*11*): 4 are 18–25 (1 minor); 4 are 25–40 (2 minor); 3 are 40–60. WOMEN (*8*): 3 are 25–40; 5 are 40–60 (4 minor). GIRL: Must appear to be about 14. EXTRAS: Schoolchildren; poor people. SET: Inside a village almshouse in winter. Very simple furniture. Naturalistic set must appear unreal in apparition sequences. Subtle lighting effects vital. Arena performance possible. COSTUMES: Provincial German around 1900; threadbare clothes for paupers; a deaconess' habit; angels' apparel as imagined by a child. DIFFICULTIES: This play requires very sensitive direction, contrasting and also blending the naturalistic and the romantic passages.

ROYALTY: Apply publisher. TEXT: H. Frenz and M. Waggoner trans. in *Gerhart Hauptmann, 3 Plays* (Holt).

—— o ——

THE SUNKEN BELL (*Die versunkene Glocke;* 1896) GERHART HAUPTMANN.   During the Middle Ages, elves and fauns are waging war against the spreading Christians. A faun rolls a new church bell into the lake. Heinrich, the founder, searches for his bell in vain and collapses exhausted in the mountains. He is found by Rautendelein, an elf maiden, who falls in love with him but cannot prevent the villagers from carrying the sick man back into the valley. Restored to ordinary life, Heinrich rejects his loving wife and wants to die. Rautendelein appears and leads him once again to the mountains. There he builds a temple for the worship of Nature. He ignores the warnings of the vicar and repels the villagers who attack him as a blasphemer. Then, from the bottom of the lake rises the sound of the sunken bell, struck by his drowned wife, and draws him down to earth. His will broken, unable to live in either world, he dies with Rautendelein's kiss upon his lips. Many symbolic allusions are woven into the fanciful, poetic fairy tale: the victory of neo-romanticism over naturalism;

the conflict between desire and duty; the tragedy of the artist; and the spiritual struggle of humanity.

MEN (6): 4 are 20–40 (1 requires outstanding actor, romantic hero); 2 are 40–60. WOMEN (3): 2 are 20–40 (1 minor); 1 is about 100. BOYS (2): 5–9. GIRLS (5): All are 16. EXTRAS: 6 dwarfs; villagers. SETS: Old well in a mountain glade; medieval room in Heinrich's house; glassworks in the mountains. Picturesque scenery with many supernatural light and sound effects. Horseshoe theatre production possible. COSTUMES: Clothes of medieval villagers; apparel of elves, fauns, and dwarfs. DIFFICULTIES: Symbolism seems somewhat contrived. In spite of the language loss in translation, the poetic atmosphere of the play must be re-created.

ROYALTY: Apply publisher. TEXT: Charles H. Meltzer adap. in *Seven Contemporary Plays* (Houghton Mifflin).

— o —

MARIA MAGDALENA (1844) FRIEDRICH HEBBEL. Tragedy. Clara, a young girl of the lower middle class, erroneously believing that the man she loves has left her forever, gives herself under pressure to an egotistical scoundrel, Leonard. Deserted by him, she commits suicide. Not Clara but her father, Master Anton, a man of rigid moral principles, stands in the center of this common-life tragedy. In her attempt to make her death appear an accident, Clara tries to preserve his reputation in the stern and selfish small-town community, and dies to save his honor, not her own. The powerful figure of Master Anton, unbroken and incapable of understanding when his world crumbles, is contrasted with his weak, obedient wife and their flippant son, Karl. Clara, however, in her dutiful acceptance of his standards, is very much her father's daughter. Like all the characters, Clara's two lovers are humanly convincing individuals within the frame of the period.

MEN (7): 1 is 18–25; 4 are 25–40 (2 minor); 2 are 50–60 (1 requires outstanding actor; 1 minor). WOMEN (3): 2 are 18–25 (1 minor); 1 is about 50. BOY: 8–12 (minor). SETS: A modest, clean room in Master Anton's house; Leonard's apartment. Sets can be very simple. Suitable for arena production. COSTUMES: Middle and lower-middle class German, first half of the 19th century; 2 red bailiff's coats. DIFFICULTIES: Play attacks concepts of morality which today are no longer upheld. Clara's suicide will raise little sympathy; Master Anton's attitude even less.

ROYALTY: Apply publisher. TEXT: Carl R. Mueller trans. (Chandler).

——o——

GYGES AND HIS RING (*Gyges und sein Ring;* 1856) FRIEDRICH HEBBEL. Tragedy. Kandaules, King of Lydia, has brought his beautiful queen Rhodope from faraway India, where women live in quiet seclusion. The king cannot be fully satisfied until he has proved that his hidden treasure is beyond compare. He persuades his young Greek favorite, Gyges, owner of a magic ring that renders its bearer invisible, to observe the queen secretly in her sleeping chamber. The youth, who only reluctantly agrees to the subterfuge, falls in love with the queen. Rhodope, deeply hurt when she divines how she was offended, demands of Gyges that he kill the king and take her for his wife, only to commit suicide after the wedding ceremony. In this blank-verse tragedy the center of the inner action is Kandaules, a man who has outgrown the spirit of his time and who, so Hebbel declares, "offers himself as a sacrifice when Rhodope is changed before his eyes from a thing into a person, in order to atone for the semiconsciously committed crime." (This is now generally considered Hebbel's masterpiece, not only because of its offering to psychoanalysis —the Kandaules Complex—but also for its classic beauty and its timeless exploration of individual rights.)

MEN (*4*): 1 is 20–25; 1 is 30–40; 2 are about 60 (1 minor). WOMEN (*3*): 2 are 17–21 (1 minor); 1 is 24. EXTRAS: Lydian people. SETS: Halls and Rhodope's chamber in Kandaules' palace; open space; the temple of Hestia. Greek mythological grandeur. Arena production feasible but not recommended since an intimate production would necessarily reduce the tragedy's required loftiness. COSTUMES: Princely mythological Greek. DIFFICULTIES: Much of the dramatic and poetic force of Hebbel's verse is lost in translation. Also, the contemporary Western attitude toward feminine modesty is so far removed from Hebbel's interpretation of Oriental mores that a modern audience will hardly accept Rhodope's suicide as the inevitable atonement—which may in addition distract the spectator from the play's far-reaching implications.

ROYALTY: Apply publisher. TEXT: L. H. Allen trans. in *Friedrich Hebbel, Three Plays* (Dutton, 1914, out of print).

— O —

THE BROKEN JUG (*Der zerbrochene Krug;* 1806) HEINRICH VON KLEIST. Comedy. Adam, the village judge, has entered the chamber of young Eve Rull at night and has been forced by Eve's fiancé, the peasant boy Ruprecht, to make a hurried exit. Next day, Frau Marthe Rull appears in court and accuses Ruprecht not only of having dishonored her daughter but also of having broken a precious jug. Adam is in trouble. This very day Councilor Walter has arrived on an inspection tour and will attend the trial. Only shrewdness can save the village judge now. He alternately puts the blame on Ruprecht and on another suitor of Eve; he invents reasons for adjourning the session; he blackmails Eve into silence; and, when all has failed, he involves the Devil himself as a possible suspect. Finally he takes to his heels. The honest and youthfully confident Eve, the robust and boisterous Ruprecht, the ambitious clerk Licht, the chatty, superstitious Frau Brigitte, and even the representative of higher justice, Councilor Walter—all have the healthy liveliness of le Veau's engraving which inspired Kleist to write the play. Adam is the Falstaff of the German theatre. Most memorable, next to his character, is that of the bickering, quarrelsome Frau Marthe Rull, who in the end decides to carry her case—along with the broken jug—to the supreme court.

MEN (6): 2 are 18–25; 4 are 40–60. WOMEN (5): 3 are 17–21 (2 minor); 2 are 40–60. SET: Courtroom in a small village in Holland. Suitable for arena production. COSTUMES: Provincial Dutch, 18th century. DIFFICULTIES: Kleist's sharp and spontaneous dialect is obscured in Krumpelmann's translation. Uncut, the play is barely long enough to be performed alone. The abridged prose version (by Katzin) will last approximately 70 minutes.

ROYALTY: Apply publishers. TEXT: John T. Krumpelmann trans. in *Poet Lore*, Vol. 45 (out of print); Winifred Katzin adap. in *Short Plays From Twelve Countries* (George H. Harrap & Co., Ltd., 36 Soho St. London, W 1).

— O —

PENTHESILEA (1808) HEINRICH VON KLEIST. The barbarous Amazons, following their primeval urge to seek their mates among their victims in battle, appear in the fields of Troy. Penthesilea, their queen, singles out Achilles as her only equal adversary. The Greek hero is likewise irresistibly driven toward her. When they meet on the battlefield, Achilles renders her unconscious with a forceful blow and, upon her awakening, pretends to be her prisoner. The spell of the enchantingly tender love scene that follows is broken when Penthesilea learns of her captivity. Achilles challenges her once more to fight, believing that his feigned defeat will restore her love; but the passionately raging queen pierces his breast with an arrow and, along with her hounds, rips the flesh off his limbs. When she realizes the monstrosity of her deed, she dies by an act of pure will. Several supporting characters, though clearly subordinated to the two central figures, are needed to relate the large portion of the action that takes place behind the scene. The anticlassical tragedy of naked, chaotic human nature combines ruthless psychological exposure with the evocation of a preclassical, Dionysiac Greece.

MEN (*15; doubling possible*): They are 20–40 (10 minor). WOMEN (*15; doubling possible*): 14 are 18–25 (10 minor); 1 is 40–60. EXTRAS: Greeks; Amazons. SETS: Several locations on the battlefields near Troy. Unrealistic mythological style. Esthetically and technically unsuitable for arena production. COSTUMES: Mythological Greek. DIFFICULTIES: Never has an actress wholly succceeded in the title role. "Half Grace, half Fury," the part demands a range from Juliet's lyrical tenderness to (and even beyond) the unchained elemental force of a Medea.

ROYALTY: Apply Samuel French. TEXT: Humphrey Trevelyan trans. in *The Classic Theatre* (Doubleday), Vol. II.

—— o ——

THE PRINCE OF HOMBURG (*Der Prinz Friedrich von Homburg;* 1811) HEINRICH VON KLEIST. Disobeying the Elector of Brandenburg's orders, the Prince of Homburg gains an overwhelming victory in battle but is condemned by a court-martial. Princess Natalia, his fiancée, and the whole officer corps intercede with the Elector—in vain. The prince is panic-stricken, and humbles himself to break the engagement with Natalia if only she will help him to save his skin. In the end, however, when the decision is put into his own hands, he attains the heroic height of self-conquest, and, by signing his own death sentence, obtains the Elector's pardon. The characters, in spite of taking sides in this struggle between law and individuality, are psychologically well-founded human beings. The prince, in particular, is strikingly modern. Among the representatives of martial honor, the outwardly stern but inwardly torn Elector, and Colonel Kottwitz, a warmhearted old fire eater, are effectively contrasted.

MEN (*16*): 4 are 20–25 (2 minor); 7 are 25–40 (4 minor): 5 are 40–60 (2 minor). WOMEN (*3*): 2 are 18–25 (1 minor); 1 is 30–50. EXTRAS: Ladies; gentlemen; officers; soldiers; pages. SETS: Brandenburg in 1675; halls and rooms in the electoral palace; the palace gardens; battlefields; peasant's rooms; prison. In recent years sets have been designed in expressionistic style. Arena production difficult. COSTUMES: Military apparel of the Prussian court in the 17th century. DIFFICULTIES: Overshadowing the theme of freedom and order, the play's militant Prussian spirit may antagonize the audience,

ROYALTY: Apply Curtis Brown.* TEXT: James Kirkup trans. in *The Classic Theatre* (Doubleday), Vol. II.

— o —

MINNA VON BARNHELM (1767) GOTTHOLD EPHRAIM LESSING. Comedy. At the end of the Seven Years' War, Von Tellheim, an honest and high-principled Prussian major, is unjustly discharged. Disgraced and impoverished, he considers himself unworthy of his fiancée, the Saxon heiress, Minna von Barnhelm. Minna, however, follows him to his refuge at a country inn, and wins him back by pretending to have lost her own fortune. Tellheim is finally exonerated and reinstated in his military position by order of King Frederick the Great. The characters are refreshingly unconventional, especially Minna and her lively maid Francisca, who leads Werner, Tellheim's robust sergeant-major, by the nose. The figure of the affected French adventurer Riccault de la Marlinière creates an effective contrast to Prussia's rugged soldiers. This play, which pays homage to womanly love, is considered by many the greatest classic of German comedy.

MEN (8): 6 are 20–40 (2 minor); 2 are 40–60. WOMEN (*3*): 2 are 18–25; 1 is 25–40. SETS: Hall in an inn; adjoining guest room. Appropriate for arena production. COSTUMES: Prussian ladies', gentlemen's, and servants' garb of the mid-18th century; 1 officer's and 3 soldiers' uniforms. DIFFICUL-TIES: Tellheim's belief in the code of honor of his time can hardly be shared by a modern audience. To preserve the balance of the play, every attempt must be made to retain the audience's sympathy for the unfortunate officer.

ROYALTY: Apply publisher. TEXT: William E. Steel trans. in *Laocoön and Other Writings* (Dutton).

—o—

NATHAN THE WISE (*Nathan der Weise;* 1779) GOTT-HOLD EPHRAIM LESSING. Borrowing from Boccaccio the tale of the three rings, Lessing ingeniously heightened its spiritual meaning and made it the heart of his play. Each of three brothers has inherited a precious ring from their father. One of these rings has the magic power to render its owner pleasing to God and men. But which is the right one? It will never be known so long as the brothers compete in good will and good deeds. Nathan the Jew tells this parable in answer to the Sultan's question about whether the Mohammedan, the Jewish, or the Christian religion is the true one. The plot is rather artificial, but this weakness is counteracted by the variety of rich and genuine characters. Cheerful passages alternate with serious ones and bring the play down to the level of real life. It is from this concrete, human plane that Nathan speaks with simple nobility to man and about man. With this play, his ideological testament, Lessing sought to show his countrymen, and the world, the way to religious and racial tolerance, generosity and peace.

MEN (*11*): 1 is 20–25; 6 are 25–40 (5 minor); 4 are 40–60 (1 requires outstanding actor). WOMEN (*3*): 1 is 16–20; 2 are 35–40. SETS: Palestine at the time of the Crusades; in and before Nathan's house; under palm trees; in the Sultan's palace; a cloister. Location can be hinted with modest means. Unit set appropriate. Suitable for arena production. COSTUMES: Colorful and rich Oriental garments; a knight-templar's apparel; a Christian patriarch's robe; a monk's habit. DIFFICUL-TIES: The great merits of the play will appear only if the plot —a typical 18th-century intrigue of mistaken identity—is de-emphasized in favor of the dialogue's impact of thought. It must be remembered that Nathan's part is strongly humorous; he never preaches.

ROYALTY: Apply publisher. TEXT: William E. Steel trans. in *Laocoön and Other Writings* (Dutton).

— o —

DON CARLOS (1787) FRIEDRICH SCHILLER. Tragedy. This play was originally planned as a royal-family tragedy: the love of the Spanish Infante Don Carlos for his young step-mother and his death by order of his father, Philip II. Later, Schiller raised it to the universal level, and made man's struggle for freedom of thought its theme. After a romantic beginning, interest shifts from the titular hero to the Marquis of Posa, who dies in his vain defense of religious tolerance. In the second half, however, Philip II gains more and more of the foreground. Though eighteenth-century historians depicted him as a monstrous tyrant, under Schiller's hand Philip's character attains tragic stature, very close to the modern historical view. Outstanding among a variety of plastically drawn characters are the passionate Princess Eboli, the tender young queen, the sinister Duke of Alba, and the majestic Grand Inquisitor. The idealistic spirit of this tragedy and its dramatic suspense makes it particularly attractive to youthful audiences.

MEN (*12*): 3 are 18–25; 2 are 25–40 (1 minor); 6 are 40–60 (3 minor); 1 is 60–80. WOMEN (*5*): 4 are 18–25 (2 minor); 1 is 40–60 (minor). BOY: 12–14. EXTRAS: Grandees; ladies; officers; soldiers; pages; 1 3-year-old child. SETS: Bright royal garden sites in Aranjuez, contrasted with austere halls and chambers in the Escorial. The partially romantic picture-frame character of this play makes it unsuitable for arena production. COSTUMES: Rich, severe apparel of the 16th-century Spanish court. DIFFICULTIES: Schiller's poetry loses much of its vigor in translation. The play also lacks structural unity.

ROYALTY: Apply Curtis Brown.* TEXT: James Kirkup trans. in *The Classic Theatre* (Doubleday), Vol. II.

— o —

WALLENSTEIN'S DEATH (*Wallensteins Tod;* 1799) FRIEDRICH SCHILLER. (In an essentially historical trilogy, Schiller unfolds the fateful career of Wallenstein, leader of the imperial forces in the Thirty Years' War. Though he does not appear in the prologue, *Wallenstein's Camp*, the protagonist's figure gains shape as an unseen power behind the wild, motley bands of his soldiery. In *The Piccolomini*, he is seen with his entourage, his friends, and his supposed friends. Gradually the complex traits of his character are uncovered; his dark, Caesarean ambition, his belief in the stars and in his star, and his reluctance to act. The third part, *Wallenstein's Death*, presentable as a separate play, brings the inevitable catastrophe.) Driven from treasonous dreams to treason itself, Wallenstein is finally deserted by his followers; only one remains, to become his murderer. Among a variety of soldierly types, Ottavio Piccolomini stands out as Wallenstein's opponent. The tender and tragic love story of Ottavio's son and Wallenstein's daughter is well integrated into the political intrigue. Wallenstein is justifiably considered the greatest character of German dramatic literature.

MEN (*21; doubling possible*): 6 are 18–25 (4 minor); 9 are 20–40 (4 minor); 6 are 40–60 (1 requires outstanding actor). WOMEN (*4*): 2 are 18–25 (1 minor); 2 are 40–50. EXTRAS: Soldiers; attendants. SETS: Several halls and rooms in the castles of Pilsen and Eger, Bohemia, 1634. Arena production possible. COSTUMES: 17th-century princely garments; officers' and soldiers' apparel and arms. DIFFICULTIES: Knowledge of the immensely interesting historical figure of Wallenstein and of the political events of his time will considerably increase the appreciation of this drama—knowledge that cannot be expected from an average audience outside Central Europe.

ROYALTY: Apply publisher. TEXT: Charles E. Passage trans. (Ungar).

—o—

MARY STUART (*Maria Stuart;* 1800) FRIEDRICH SCHILLER. Tragedy. The historic Mary, Queen of Scots, does not inspire much sympathy even though she was executed for reasons of state and not because of her crimes of twenty years before. Schiller changes all this. He shifts the issue from politics to the psychological realm of feminine rivalry. Mary is not a mere victim; she is actively, though indirectly, responsible for her doom. Moreover, the fervently Protestant poet endows her with great moral fortitude, as befits a tragic heroine. He also takes poetic license to make her a young, desirable woman of about 25, with Queen Elizabeth her elder by only a few years. In attracting Elizabeth's favorite, Leicester, Mary proves herself the stronger as a woman. As a queen, superior in spiritual nobility, she triumphs over her rival in their only personal encounter. This decides her fate. Mary's character is contrasted with that of Elizabeth, cold and cunning yet tragic in her solitude of final responsibility. The contrast is repeated in the male figures. Schiller opposes the weak and faltering Leicester with Mary's young admirer, Mortimer, and the hard, calculating statesman Burleigh with the warmhearted old counselor Shrewsbury. (This is Schiller's most popular play on the professional stage. See also Anderson's play, page 315.)

MEN (*14*): 3 are 18–25 (minor); 6 are 25–40 (3 minor); 5 are 40–60 (1 minor). WOMEN (*4*): 3 are 20–30 (1 minor); 1 is 40–60. EXTRAS: Lords; soldiers; attendants. SETS: Elizabethan era; hall and 2 chambers in the palace of Westminster; apartment in the castle of Fotheringay; outside the castle. Sets need not be elaborate. Arena production possible. COSTUMES: Resplendant robes for Queen Elizabeth and her court; tastefully modest clothes for Mary and her suite. DIFFICULTIES: Since Schiller's sonorous language cannot be faithfully rendered in English, an appropriate style must be found for the tragedy's subdued pathos—this is not a romantic melodrama.

ROYALTY: Apply Peters & Ramsay, 14 Goodwins Court, London WC 2. TEXT: Stephen Spender trans. (Faber and Faber*).

— o —

WILLIAM TELL (*Wilhelm Tell;* 1804) FRIEDRICH SCHILLER. The hero of this drama of the Swiss people, represented by many individuals whose revolt against local and personal injustice unites them into a nation fighting for freedom. A people, pure and natural in the Rousseauian sense, succeeds in ridding itself of the oppressive forces from without. Three circles of action are closely interwoven: the peasants from three Swiss cantons who live up to the Rutli-Sermon, the legendary Swiss declaration of independence; a young man and a girl of noble birth who are united in their love of their country; and the strong and simple-hearted William Tell, set apart from the others in his self-reliance, who kills the cruel Austrian governor Gessler in defense of the smallest unit within the nation, the family. Beyond the richness of the vast historical pageant and the dramatic impact of its many episodic scenes, it is most of all the poet's enthusiastic plea for liberty that explains this drama's popular appeal.

MEN (*35; doubling possible*): 30 are 20–40 (14 minor); 5 are 40–60. WOMEN (*7*): 1 is 18–25; 6 are 20–40 (3 minor). BOYS: (*4*): 2 are 6–8; 2 are 14–16. EXTRAS: Soldiers; peasants; artisans; monks; women; children. SETS: Inside and in front of medieval Swiss peasant houses; public squares; several rocky forest sites and lake shores. Sets should have acting space on different levels. Amount of scenery and players make this drama unsuitable for arena. Amphitheatre performances possible. COSTUMES: Early 14th century; clothes of peasants, soldiers, monks, and noblemen; crossbows and other medieval arms. DIFFICULTIES: A very large stage, excellently equipped for quick changes and complicated scenery, is absolutely necessary.

ROYALTY: Apply publisher. TEXT: Sir Theodore Martin trans. in *The World Drama* (Appleton), Vol. II.

—o—

SPRING'S AWAKENING (*Frühlings Erwachen;* 1892) FRANK WEDEKIND. Tragedy. A play about children in their intoxicated enchantment, aimless fear, and lonely suffering on the threshold of the mysterious spring of life. Choked by a hypocritical bourgeois morality, some of them succumb. Melchior, Moritz, and their schoolmates are groping for knowledge about sex. Wendla, like the girls in her class, receives from her mother only an elusive, nonsensical answer. Melchior and Wendla fall in love and find each other in the final embrace. Wendla becomes pregnant but still does not understand. Her mother arranges an abortion, and the girl dies. Distracted by his confused feelings, Moritz fails to graduate. He commits suicide. The funeral is grotesque: father and teachers are unanimous in their contempt for the dead boy. Melchior, put into a reformatory, escapes and seeks Wendla's grave. The phantom of Moritz tries to draw him into the realm of death, but a muffled man—life itself—interferes. From the awakening of spring the way leads into the hard reality of adult life.

MEN (*14*): All are 30–50 (8 minor). WOMEN (*3*): 1 is 20–25; 2 are 35–40. BOYS: (*7*): All are about 14 (5 minor). GIRLS: (*4*): All are about 14 (2 minor). SETS: Middle-class German; 19 location changes; teacher's room, living rooms, bedrooms, streets, park, woods, a cemetery. Sets should be simple and stylized. Arena production possible. COSTUMES: Stuffy, constraining clothes of teachers, parents, and high school pupils in Germany at the end of the last century. DIFFICULTIES: Wedekind's telegraphic, pre-expressionistic language requires a corresponding acting style. This must be achieved, not only in the bitingly sarcastic portraiture of the adult world but also in the delicate and poetic scenes of adolescent love. Because of the fundamental change in society's attitude toward sex education, Wedekind's parents and teachers appear today almost absurd, but the appeal of the children's inner tragedy remains.

ROYALTY: $25–20, Samuel French. TEXT: Eric Bentley trans. in *The Modern Theatre* (Doubleday), Vol. VI.

— o —

EARTH-SPIRIT (*Erdgeist;* 1895) FRANK WEDEKIND. The playwright accuses society of hypocritically subduing man's natural instincts. Only those beings beyond the control of a limited bourgeois world will escape suppression and destroy society in turn. In the prologue a barker presents his main circus attraction, Lulu, "the true, savage, beautiful animal," a snake. Lulu's origin is unknown. Her first lover is Editor-in-Chief Dr. Schön; her first husband old Dr. Goll. At the sight of his wife in the arms of Schwarz, a painter, Dr. Goll dies of a stroke. Schwarz becomes Lulu's next husband and victim: unable to share her life of depravity, he cuts his throat. Whoever crosses her path is drawn into the vortex of her sensuous attraction. Lulu's third husband, Dr. Schön, surprises her in a risqué situation with a horde of lovers and admirers—among them a circus athlete, Rodrigo; a schoolboy, Hugenberg, the Lesbian Countess Geschwitz; and Dr. Schön's own son, Alwa. Dr. Schön hands Lulu a revolver and demands that she end her life; but Lulu shoots him instead. Her further destiny is depicted in the sequel play, *Pandora's Box* (see p. 289).

MEN (*10*): 5 are 20–30 (3 minor); 2 are 30–40; 3 are 40–60. WOMEN (*3*): 2 are 18–25 (1 minor); 1 is 35–40. BOY: 15. SETS: Entrance of a circus tent; painter's studio; elegant drawing room; theatre dressing room; hall with staircase and gallery. Time (about 1900) and place (Munich) not absolutely essential. Sets should correspond to the style of Wedekind's language—crass, often bordering the grotesque. Emphasizing the demonstrative nature of the play, the author raises an imaginary barrier between stage and spectators. Arena production not recommended. COSTUMES: Elegant early 20th century or contemporary; costumes of a snake, an animal tamer, and a Pierrot. DIFFICULTIES: Shifting abruptly from the ridiculous to the tragic, Wedekind uses his characters to hammer his anti-bourgeois doctrine into the audience. They must paradoxically combine the unnatural quality of marionettes with a tremendously forceful vitality.

ROYALTY: Apply publisher. TEXT: Frances Fawcett and Stephen Spender trans. in *Five Tragedies of Sex* (Theatre Arts).

—— o ——

THE MARQUIS OF KEITH (*Der Marquis von Keith;* 1900) FRANK WEDEKIND. "The most splendid business," according to the Marquis of Keith, "is morality." This is why the marquis, an imposter, can only succeed in the existing social and moral set-up. The protagonist, a distorted version of Nietzsche's Superman, is an unscrupulous schemer endowed with the ruthlessness and the fascination of an untamed beast. He gulls some reputable industrialists into financing a fantastic project, the Fairyland Palace, to display the talents of beautiful Countess Werdenfels as a Wagnerian singer and salvage his finances. When his mistress, Molly, a poor little wretch with old-fashioned moral standards, drowns herself, Keith's false play is exposed. He briefly considers suicide, then decides to continue his way on the "roller coaster of life." The philistine industrialists, still better businessmen than Keith, take over his fraudulent enterprise. Wedekind directs his biting criticism mainly against the bourgeoisie, represented by a gallery of sharply contrasted types, whose hypocritical social order provokes the emergence of the impostor. Ernst Scholz, Keith's friend and counterpart, is a dedicated moralist who voluntarily retires into a lunatic asylum when he finds life and his ideals incompatible.

MEN (*12*): 4 are 20–30 (2 minor); 3 are 30–40 (2 minor); 5 are 40–60 (2 minor). WOMEN (*8*): 5 are 20–30 (2 minor); 3 are 35–50 (minor). BOYS: (*2*): 1 is 13 (minor); 1 is 15. EXTRAS: People from the street (can be cut). SETS: Spectacular settings in expressionistic style. The marquis' study; garden room; boudoir. Production in horseshoe theatre possible. COSTUMES: Fashionable German of about 1900. DIFFICULTIES: A forerunner of expressionism, Wedekind conveys the message of his tragicomic extravaganza in tense, epigrammatic phrasings that must be rendered in a forceful, antinaturalistic style. ROYALTY: Apply publisher. TEXT: Beatrice Gottlieb trans. in *From the Modern Repertoire* (Indiana), Ser. II.

—— o ——

PANDORA'S BOX (*Die Büchse der Pandora;* 1902) FRANK WEDEKIND.   Lulu, the magnificent corruptress of *Earth-Spirit*, had destroyed her lovers with the innocence of an animal. At the beginning of *Pandora's Box* she is serving a prison term for having killed Dr. Schön. Saved by the devotion of the Lesbian Countess Geschwitz, who unhesitatingly takes her place in the prison infirmary, Lulu moves with the depraved gang of her admirers to Paris, where she assumes a leading role in the demimonde. As the incarnation of sex, she exercises a ruinous power over men, but with the gradual loss of her physical attractions she becomes their victim instead. Threatened by the blackmailer Casti-Piani, who intends to sell her to a bordello, she flees to London. A streetwalker of the lowest kind, exploited by her pimps—Dr. Schön's miserable son Alwa and her parasitical pseudo-father Schigolch—she is finally disemboweled by Jack the Ripper. Countess Geschwitz, the only creature capable of love, since in her abnormality she does not fully belong to mankind, is also killed. *Earth-Spirit* (see p. 287) and Pandora's Box have proved adaptable for performance together in a single evening.

MEN (*11*): 2 are 20–30 (1 minor); 6 are 30–40 (2 minor); 3 are 40–60 (2 minor). WOMEN (*5*): 3 are 18–25 (2 minor); 2 are about 40 (1 minor). BOYS (*2*): 15. GIRL: 12. SETS: Hall with staircase and gallery; Lulu's salon; room in a dingy attic. Nonrealistic sets should symbolically accentuate the change from luxury to wretchedness. Wedekind's deliberate juxtaposition of performers and spectators cannot be carried out in arena production. COSTUMES: Early 20th century or contemporary; demimonde elegance at the beginning, slum poverty at the end. DIFFICULTIES: Even more than in *Earth-Spirit*, Wedekind eschews naturalism. He disregards dramatic motivation and makes the characters deliver his message in brief, sententious phrases, often as monologues, addressing the audience rather than each other.

ROYALTY: Apply publisher. TEXT: Frances Fawcett and Stephen Spender trans. in *Five Tragedies of Sex* (Theatre Arts).

Twentieth Century

THE MAN OUTSIDE (*Draussen vor der Tür;* 1946) WOLF-
GANG BORCHERT.   Several years after World War II, Corporal
Beckmann returns to a ruined Germany from a prisoner-of-
war camp in Russia. Lame and grotesque, he is rejected by
his wife (who has a lover), by his former commanding officer, by a cabaret producer with whom he seeks a job, and—
seemingly—by all of society. Burdened by a heavy guilt that
he feels because he was the only survivor of a fatal patrol
he had led at Stalingrad, Beckmann realizes that no one else
will share in the responsibility, that no one at all feels himself
to be a murderer in a generation filled with senseless killing.
The play opens with Beckmann's attempt at suicide, but even
the Elbe throws him back, refusing his death. Throughout the
play the path of the corporal is haunted by an unknown figure
who optimistically advocates life in the face of the contemporary agony. At last Beckmann can only turn to the audience
and cry out for answers to the torturing questions of existence
today. Cast in the mold of a "dream play," *The Man Outside*
recalls the expressionist style of both Georg Kaiser and Ernst
Toller and evokes the grim world drawn and painted by
George Grosz.

MEN (*10*): 6 are 20–40; 2 are about 50; 1 is ancient; 1 is
ageless. WOMEN (*5*): 3 are 22; 2 are 45–50. SETS: Locales
range from the bottom of the Elbe to interiors ranging from
poor to well-to-do. An expressionistic approach is most appropriate, with the use of a bare stage and projections presenting
the best solution for the rapid change of scenes. COSTUMES:
Middle class and shabby in the years following World War II;
1 colonel's and 2 enlisted men's uniforms from German
Army of this period. DIFFICULTIES: The dialogue is extremely
repetitive and would require, on the part of the director, a
keen musical sense of language.

ROYALTY: Apply publisher. TEXT: David Porter trans. in *The Man Outside* (New Directions).

— o —

IN THE JUNGLE OF THE CITIES (*Im Dickicht der Städte;* 1923) BERTOLT BRECHT. One of a series of Brecht's early experiments, this play directly reflects his preoccupation with sports (which went so far as to inspire him to write a poem to be read before the films of the Dempsey-Tunney fight). Where stage directions usually appear are these words: "Watch now the inexplicable wrestling match between two men and witness the fall of a family uprooted from the prairies into the jungle of the big city. Don't worry your brains over the motives of this fight but make yourself share in the human stakes. Judge without prejudice the fighting form of the contenders and keep your eyes fixed on the outcome." This succinct advice also outlines the play. For no apparent reason a Malayan lumber dealer and George Garga, member of an uprooted family, pledge themselves to destroy each other. At the end of the play the Garga family is atomized, the lumber dealer is dead of natural causes after barely escaping a lynch mob set on him by George, and George himself is leaving Chicago and his friends for New York. As he leaves he speaks one of the many messages of the play: "To be alone is a good thing. The chaos is spent. It was the best time." The plot sequence which tells this story is simple and direct, but few motivations are apparent, and as a result the purpose of the play can be understood in almost as many ways as there are presuppositions in viewers.

MEN (*12*): 1 old Oriental; 1 old Caucasian; others of unspecified age. WOMEN (*5*): Only the mother need be old. EXTRAS: 2 musicians and a lynch mob. The latter can be 1 or 2 faces plus sound effects. SETS: Play in 11 episodes of which 8 are different locales, but all that is needed for any of the scenes is a distinctive prop or setpiece. COSTUMES: Modern poor for all except the Malayan, who needs a Chinese robe. DIFFICULTIES: Mostly interpretive. If the play is approached not as a drama which offers no solution but rather the description of a quandary, many of the puzzling aspects disappear.

ROYALTY: Apply Bertha Case, 485 Lexington Ave., N.Y.,

N.Y. TEXT: Gerhard Nellhaus trans. in *Theatre Arts Magazine*, August 1961 issue.

—— o ——

GALILEO (1937) BERTOLT BRECHT. Galileo Galilei teaches his pupils that they must believe the evidence of their senses rather than the conclusions of tradition, for it is his belief that "Truth is the daughter of Time, not of Authority." The Dutch invention of the telescope allows him to test the hypothesis that the Earth is but one of many worlds and that the Sun does not revolve about this planet. Galileo's discoveries of a new cosmic geography shake the foundation of all authority. The Inquisition summons him to Rome. His heresy has already ruined his daughter's marriage prospects. Galileo fears physical pain, so when he is confronted with the instruments of torture, he quickly recants. His pupils desert him because he did not prove a hero. Galileo remains a prisoner of the Inquisition until his death. However, he is allowed to live in his home, be waited upon by his spinster daughter, and indulge his love of comfort and food. Galileo continues his writing and manages to have his great work smuggled out of Italy. Prudence, rather than valor, forwards the cause of science.

MEN (*54*): 9 are 7–20 (1 young man should resemble the actor who will play the part as a grown man; 8 minor and can double in various roles); 21 are 20–40 (17 minor; doubling possible); 24 are 40–60 (18 minor; doubling possible). WOMEN (*12*): 4 are 15–20 (all minor; can serve in crowd scenes); 5 are 20–40 (4 minor; can double in other scenes); 3 are 40–60 (2 minor; can be used in crowd scenes). SETS: 14 scenes, ranging from the modest study of Galileo to a chamber in the Vatican; from a street or market place to a palace of the Medici. The sets should not be realistic but should suggest through platforms, projections, curtains, and decorative and symbolic items the feeling of Renaissance Italy in the early 17th century. Real properties, easily manipulated, are necessary to the telling of the story. COSTUMES: 17th-century peasants; street singers; scholars; variety of ladies, officials, and monks; cardinals and pope (authentic papal attire requires several layers of vestments). DIFFICULTIES: Acting style must avoid sentimentality. Heightened theatrics will only vulgarize and destroy this natural drama.

Scene 9, in the marketplace, is difficult in its demands on the ensemble.

ROYALTY: Apply publishers. TEXT: Charles Laughton trans. in *From the Modern Repertoire* (Indiana), Ser. II. Music by Hans Eisler in Eisler's *Lieder und Kantaten*, VEB Breitkopf und Härtel, Leipzig.

— o —

THE GOOD WOMAN OF SETZUAN (*Der gute Mensch von Setzuan;* 1938–40) BERTOLT BRECHT. Three gods come down from heaven in search of a truly good person and discover Shen Te, the prostitute, to be the only one worthy of being called virtuous. They reward her with gold, which she uses to buy a tobacco shop. Immediately she becomes the victim of parasites, because in her goodness she cannot refuse help to the less fortunate. In order to survive she impersonates an imaginery evil cousin, Shui Ta, whose harshness in business matters keeps Shen Te solvent. Thus the play is a parable of man's enforced dual nature; his desire to be good is thwarted by his need to keep alive. Brecht achieves many fine comic effects in picturing man's pretensions to morality subverted by his instinct for survival. Two scenes conceived on a broad scale are Shen Te's wedding, which collapses when the groom rejects the bride because she lacks the necessary capital, and Shui Ta's trial for the murder of his other self. The action is paced by dream interludes which show the gods gradually falling victim to the troubles and despair that assail mankind. A number of songs expounding the ironic theme are introduced with fine comic and theatrical effect.

MEN (*21*): 3 are 5–10; 1 is 15; 11 are 20–40 (4 minor; doubling possible; 3 must sing); 6 are 40–60 (4 must sing). WOMEN (*10*): 1 is around 6 (minor, can be cut); 1 is around 15 (must sing); 5 are 20–40 (1 must sing); 3 are 40–60. SETS: Gates of Setzuan; Shen Te's tobacco shop (also converted to an office); the municipal park; Wong's den in the sewer pipe; a city square; a private dining room in a cheap restaurant; Shui Ta's tobacco factory; a courtroom. The settings should employ certain realistic elements such as doors, windows, counters. Unit set with changeable panels, slide projections, etc., is a solution to problem of multiple setting. COSTUMES: Traditional Chinese; modern Western garb; a dinner jacket; 3 judges' robes; 1 policeman's uniform. DIFFI-

CULTIES: A substructure of realism in each of the characters to avoid gross caricature; the characters should be played as Western, with only a suggestion of the Oriental in movement, speech, and make-up; emphasis on some of the harsher and more ironic effects in the play; songs should be sung with precision.

ROYALTY: Apply Samuel French. TEXT: Eric Bentley and Maja Apelman trans. in *Parables for the Theatre* (Grove); music by Paul Dessau (Samuel French).

—— o ——

MOTHER COURAGE (*Mutter Courage und ihre Kinder;* 1939) BERTOLT BRECHT. Mother Courage is an itinerant merchant who lives off the troops of both sides during the Thirty Years' War. She uses all her shrewdness and tenacity to keep her family intact and to retain her wagon of goods, the symbol as well as the means of their survival. In a world that often uses the virtues for base purposes, Mother Courage at last loses her entire family, each member a victim of his own heroic actions. But by her own hard realism, unsentimental and often ignoble, Mother Courage survives the misfortunes of senseless war and continues to pull her wagon across the battlefields—unaware of a central truth: that she, because she lives off war, is partly responsible for the death of her family. Epic in the actual as well as the technical sense in which Brecht uses this term, his play is a biting commentary on man's tragicomic struggle to survive.

MEN (*19*): 12 are 20–40 (7 minor, 3 must sing; doubling possible); 7 are 40–60 (2 minor; 1 must sing; doubling possible). WOMEN (*5*): 2 are 15–40 (1 must convey everything through pantomime alone, 1 must sing); 3 are 40–60 (2 minor, 1 must sing). Minor characters can serve as background crowds. SETS: Highway with a town in the background; tent of the Swedish commander; the outside of an officer's tent; a war-ruined village; the inside of a canteen tent; highway; camp in front of a ruined parsonage; highway near a farmhouse; an empty stage. Certain items must be realistic, such as the wagon and a rooftop, which must serve as acting areas. A turntable for setting the wagon in motion is desirable but not absolutely necessary. COSTUMES: 17th-century peasant and soldier garb would be appropriate, but historical accuracy is not essential; a standard nonidentifiable dress or uniform for most characters, with a suggestion of period through hats and other accessories. DIFFICULTIES: A harsh, ironic style of acting and singing is required.

ROYALTY: Apply Samuel French. TEXT: Eric Bentley trans. in *The Modern Theatre* (Doubleday), Vol. II; music by Paul Dessau or Darius Milhaud (Samuel French).

— o —

THE CAUCASIAN CHALK CIRCLE (*Der kaukasische Kreidekreis;* 1944–45) BERTOLT BRECHT. During a civil war the deposed governor's son is rescued by one of the palace maids and carried beyond the mountains for protection, at great risk and embarrassment to the unmarried girl. It proves to be a deed of kindness filled with danger for the doer, for, as the chorus sings, "Terrible is the temptation of Goodness." The civil war, through a fluke, makes a powerful judge of a drunken rascal who proceeds to turn justice upside down. In the course of events, the new judge is asked to decide on the custody of the governor's son; should he and the estates be awarded to the governor's widow and the actual mother, who abandoned her child in her haste to pack her dresses, or to the adopted mother, a lowly servant girl who has loved the child and shielded him from all danger? The judge renders his decision somewhat in the manner of Solomon, but from a different point of view. There are many scenes of vivid and colorful action, humor, and character: the overrunning of the palace; the chase through the mountains; the combination wedding-and-funeral feast; and the series of trials presided over by the rascally judge. The role of the judge, Azdak, is one of the richest in modern dramatic literature. Compare plot of the Chinese play, *The Chalk Circle*, p. 421.

MEN (*48*): 31 are 20–40 (22 minor); 17 are 40–60 (13 minor, 2 must sing). Many of the minor roles and several of the more important roles can be doubled. WOMEN (*18*): 12 are 20–40 (7 minor, 1 must sing); 6 are 40–60 (minor); doubling is possible. BOYS (*3*): 5–10 (minor). GIRL: About 10. SETS: Exterior of governor's palace; interiors of cottages; abyss in the mountains; Lavrenti's farm kitchen; a workroom on farm; peasant's bedchamber and adjacent room; the court of justice; a tavern. The sets are not realistic, but certain props are needed for the proper effect. Unit set appropriate. An Oriental approach to setting would also be appropriate.

COSTUMES: Peasant; servants; nobility; professional and soldier dress of an Oriental land in late Middle Ages. DIFFICULTIES: The many scenes of this sprawling structure must move rapidly, in cinematic fashion. Sentimentality must be avoided in acting a play rich with feeling and humor. There are many opportunities to use the devices of "Epic Theatre"—Chinese conventions, signboards and projections, direct address to the audience, and so on—but quaintness and self-consciousness in their use should be avoided.

ROYALTY: Apply publisher. TEXT: Eric Bentley and Maja Apelman trans. in *Parables for the Theatre* (Grove). Musical score by Paul Dessau in *Lieder und Gesänge*, Henschel-Verlag, Berlin.

— o —

FROM MORN TO MIDNIGHT (*Von Morgens bis Mitternachts;* 1916) GEORG KAISER. A soft look of appeal from a beautiful foreign woman jars the cashier loose from the routine and lethargy of his existence. He embezzles 60,000 marks from the bank, abandons his family, and begins a mad odyssey in search of the thrills that money can buy. This nonentity of the modern industrial commercial world makes a desperate bid for life, and finds that his money brings only corruption and his own betrayal. Much of the play's effectiveness comes from the nightmarish intensity and speed of its seven scenes. Identities are often deliberately vague and the characters abstract and masked.

MEN (*21*): 10 are 20–40 (7 minor); 10 are 40–60 (9 minor): 1 is 15 (minor). WOMEN (*15*): 2 are 10–20 (minor); 12 are 20–40 (10 minor); 1 is 60 (minor). Doubling necessary and desirable. EXTRAS (*10–15*): Men and women for crowd effect (possible doubling of actors playing speaking roles). SETS: Interior of a small bank; the writing room of a hotel; a snow-covered field; the parlor of the cashier's house; the steward's stand at the cycle races; a private dining room at a fashionable restaurant; a Salvation Army hall. Settings should be suggestive and symbolic rather than realistic. Unit set perhaps desirable. Projections might solve the problem of numerous settings. COSTUMES: Contemporary or 1920s, some stylish, others very ordinary; police and Salvation Army uniforms needed; some evening suits and party dresses; masks for the party girls. Realism of costume should be sacrificed to abstraction. DIFFICULTIES: The characters must serve the theme and act according to certain arbitrary moves made by the author. Often the characters speak in a rapid, staccato manner and act in an anguished, nightmarish fashion that could be easily overdone.

ROYALTY: Apply Theatre Guild.* TEXT: Ashley Dukes trans. in *Chief Contemporary Dramatists* (Houghton Mifflin), Ser. III.

—— o ——

THE CORAL (*Die Koralle;* 1917) GEORG KAISER. (The first play of a trilogy that includes the two parts of *Gas.*) The billionaire has amassed his wealth in order to escape the terror of his impoverished past. His hope for the future lies in the son and the daughter who despise wealth and reject their father because his riches come from the misery of the poor. Thus rejected, the billionaire tries to confiscate the happy past that belongs to his secretary who is his exact double. Only a coral fob on the secretary's watch chain distinguishes servant from master. The billionaire murders the secretary, assumes his identity by means of the coral, and is executed as the murderer of himself. He dies, content in his new self, for he has escaped to a truly happy past. A play of guilt and expiation and of the eternal war between father and son, master and servant. The characters, as in many expressionist plays, are nameless and often represent abstract characteristics. Their speech is, to a large extent, rapid and staccato and the action nightmarish in quality.

MEN (*14, doubling possible*): 7 are 20–40 (6 minor); 7 are 40–60 (2 minor). WOMEN (*4*): 3 are 20–40 (2 minor); 1 is around 50 (minor). GIRL: About 10 (minor). SETS: The billionaire's office; the deck of his yacht; his workroom; the judges' interrogation room; a small yard in the prison. Sets should be expressionistic, in keeping with the abstract nature of the characters and the nightmarish feeling of the action. COSTUMES: Of the 1920s, ranging from middle class to fashionable; some should define such professions as judge, ship's captain, priest, guards. DIFFICULTIES: The staccato speech of expressionistic drama; motivation is often sacrificed to theme, making characterization arbitrary and filled with sudden changes.

Royalty: Apply publisher. Text: Winifred Katzin trans. in *Twenty-Five Modern Plays* (Harper).

—o—

GAS, PART I (*Gas, Erster Teil;* 1918) Georg Kaiser. (The second play of a trilogy; takes place a generation after the period of *The Coral.*) The billionaire's son, in pursuit of his ideal that all men will share in his wealth, heads a cooperative gas-manufacturing industry. A great explosion destroys the plant and thousands of workers. The billionaire's son, out of love for mankind, refuses to rebuild the factory, although the workers clamor for its restoration. He preaches the end of industrialism and a return to the soil where men can live out their lives in peace and freedom. Industrialism, he says, will annihilate humanity. But the workers follow the engineer, who preaches the benefits of the industrial world. Then the government intervenes and forces the rebuilding of the factory because gas will be needed to manufacture munitions for the coming war. The billionaire's son prays for the deliverance of mankind from the darkness of its ways.

Men (*15; doubling possible*): 7 are 20–40 (4 minor); 8 are 40–60 (6 minor). Women (*4*): 3 are 18–40 (2 minor); 1 is 60 (minor). Extras: Chorus of soldiers, workmen, and workwomen, number depending on the producer's resources. Sets: The office of the billionaire's son; an oval room belonging to the billionaire's son; a great circular hall of concrete with a domed ceiling; a ruined wall of brick. The settings should be expressionistic. Costumes: Contemporary, ranging from the severe dress of factory workers to rich uniforms and fancy dress; preferably exaggerated and stylized to conform to the abstract nature of the characters. Difficulties: The staccato language of the expressionists, together with a forced poetic prose when the play becomes visionary and prophetic. There is also the technical problem of staging an explosion so that the buildings in the background disintegrate (perhaps with the use of motion picture) while the foreground shakes with the impact.

Royalty: Apply publishers. Text: Hermann Scheffauer trans. in *Twenty-Five Modern Plays* (Harper) or in *Milestones of Thought* (Ungar).

—o—

GAS, PART II (*Gas, Zweiter Teil;* 1920) GEORG KAISER.
(The concluding play of a trilogy; takes place a generation
after *Gas, Part I.*) The great war between the figures in blue
and the figures in yellow is at a stalemate. The billionaire
worker, grandson of the billionaire's son, urges a general
strike and declares mankind's freedom. Gas production is
stopped, but the enemy figures in yellow overrun the country
and force the resumption of gas production. The chief engineer, symbolizing the destructive power of industry and war,
produces a death gas and urges a new war against the yellows.
The billionaire worker tries to prevent this mad surrender to
savage destruction, but seeing the futility of pleading with
mankind for its own good, he himself hurls the bomb. The
world is destroyed. The anonymous figures in blue and figures
in yellow operating control panels with varicolored lights as
well as the great explosion at the end afford opportunities for
startling stage effects.

MEN (*19*): 1 is 18–20; 2 are 20–40; 2 are 40–60; 14 are of
no specified age (number can be cut to 7 if blues and yellows
double). EXTRAS: A chorus of workers, men and women,
range of ages 20–60; the number in the chorus can vary according to the producer's resources. SET: All 3 acts take place
in a concrete hall topped by a marble dome. The setting must
have mobility. It need not be realistic, and it must allow for
flexibility of lighting effects in the expressionistic mode. COS-
TUMES: Stylized uniforms for the anonymous figures and
workers. Shaved heads. DIFFICULTIES: Mob scenes call for
shouting and moving in unison. The dialogue is, to a large
extent, in a poetic prose which is often stiff and turgid. There
is the customary staccato of the expressionistic style. The set
must change from the concrete wall to a pile of concrete
slabs resembling gravestones during the great explosion of the
last act.

ROYALTY: Apply publisher. TEXT: Winifred Katzin trans.
in *Twenty-Five Modern Plays* (Harper).

— o —

THE RAFT OF THE MEDUSA (*Das Floss der Medusa;*
1943) GEORG KAISER. During World War II a liner, taking children from bombed English cities to Canada, is sunk by
a German submarine. Some children escape death in a lifeboat. Allan and Ann are the natural leaders among the ten- to

twelve-year-old boys and girls. There is also a smaller child, a mute and motionless redheaded boy whom they call Foxy. Allan loves Ann. On the second day, when they are still not saved, Ann makes a terrible discovery—they number thirteen. Ever since the Last Supper it has brought disaster when thirteen eat together. Allan uses all his authority and makes the children eat. But Ann knows they will not be saved until one of them dies. Who? Foxy does not row, he is not good for anything. Allan claims killing Foxy would be a sin. Ann, however, is able to prove that Christians do kill when there is a just cause. Allan builds a primitive tent in the boat to protect Foxy. On the sixth day Ann consents to marry Allan. While the marriage is consummated in the tent, the other children dispose of Foxy. The next morning they are rescued by a seaplane—all but Allen, who ". . . refuses to return into this accursed life. He loathes it. He has grown and has said No."

Boys (7): 1 is 5–8 (no lines); 6 are 10–12. Girls (6): All are 10–12. Set: A lifeboat on the open sea. Important light and sound effects (storm, fog). Arena production possible. (The children are taken into the seaplane by means of a rope ladder.) Costumes: Children's clothes, 1940. Difficulties: Though Kaiser's language is no longer expressionistic, the children's talk is not natural. They are grown-ups in their behavior and thinking and serve the author as instruments to demonstrate his views about the "hypocritical morality" of Western civilization. Plays less than 2 hours.

Royalty: Apply translators. Text: H. F. Garten and Elizabeth Sprigge trans., 10 Priory Mansions, Drayton Gardens, London, SW 10, or Ulrich Weisstein trans. in *First Stage*, Vol. I, No. 2, 1962 (Purdue University, Lafayette, Ind.).

—— o ——

THE SNOB (*Der Snob;* 1912) Karl Sternheim. Comedy. Christian Maske is a bourgeois, determined to rise in the world. Already having established his brilliance in the world of finance, he uses his genius to effect his marriage into the nobility. After divesting himself of a mistress who has helped his business career and temporarily shelving his parents until it is convenient to "present" them, Christian, in a moment of inspired improvisation, invents a noble ancestor for himself and assures his position in society. Among the more hilarious scenes is the meeting between Christian's clownish father and his future father-in-law, the count—the true aristocrat and the former peasant are immediate friends. Unusual in the modern theatre, *The Snob* is a chilling and exacting comedy in the tradition of Ben Jonson and Molière.

MEN (*4*): 2 are 20–40 (1 minor, 1 requires a brilliant sense of satiric style); 2 are 40–60 (both require high style). WOMEN (*4*): 3 are 20–40 (1 minor); 1 is 60. SETS: Christian Maske's furnished room; the drawing room in his newer quarters; the drawing room of a hotel suite. The sets can be realistic but should be greatly exaggerated in style; they could move to expressionism. COSTUMES: Middle-class and fashionable German dress of the period just before World War I; maid's and butler's uniforms. DIFFICULTIES: This play requires a most exacting comic style of playing, but it can be rewardingly funny when properly acted.

ROYALTY: $15, Samuel French. TEXT: Eric Bentley trans. in *From the Modern Repertoire* (Indiana), Ser. I.

—o—

MAN AND THE MASSES (*Masse-Mensch;* 1919) ERNST TOLLER. The Woman, an idealist, deserts her class to join the workers whom she urges to strike against the state, protesting war and industrial exploitation. The spirit of mass frenzy, symbolized by the Nameless One, takes over and the revolution is triggered. Before the state finally suppresses the revolt there is senseless butchery on both sides. The Woman is executed after refusing help from both factions, which offer compromise on the one hand and murder on the other. Among the more effective scenes are the second, fourth, and sixth "dream pictures" which expound the theme in near-balletic fashion. But the straight scenes are likewise rendered in a nonrealistic mode, less fantastic only in comparison with the dream scenes.

MEN (*3*): All 40. WOMAN: 40. EXTRAS (*25–30*): 15–20 men doubling in numerous parts of various ages; 10 women doubling as workers and prisoners. The minor parts make up a chorus. The production requires quick changes of disguise, but for the crowd scenes darkness can shroud the actors and make costume change unnecessary. SETS: 7 scenes depicting the back room of a workmen's tavern; a room of the stock exchange; a great meeting hall; a courtyard; the meeting hall;

an open space; a prison cell. Both the relatively real scenes and the dream scenes should be rendered symbolically, with more fantasy given to the dreams. The entire production can be done on a bare stage, broken by various levels, with place defined by props, projections, and lighting effects. COSTUMES: Contemporary, ranging from workers' dress to bankers' clothes and including special garb for prisoners, a priest, and some sentinels. Masks could be used effectively in the dream pictures. DIFFICULTIES: The movement and gestures in the dream sequences must help to set these scenes apart by means of a dancelike or stylized quality; the speech in these scenes is staccato and must be precise in timing. Characterization throughout is abstract and subservient to the theme. The dialogue in verse generally tends to be abstract and turgid, actors must always strive for the plain sense in order to avoid sinking in verbal effects. Both movement and speech in the crowd scenes must be minutely plotted.

ROYALTY: Apply Theatre Guild.* TEXT: Louis Untermeyer trans. in *Contemporary Drama* (Scribner's) or in *Seven Plays by Toller* (Liveright).

— o —

GOAT SONG (*Bocksgesang;* 1926) FRANZ WERFEL. Tragedy.   At the close of the eighteenth century, in a Slavic land beyond the Danube, some wealthy landowners are briefly overrun by insurgent peasants and a frenzied army of the dispossessed. The revolt is led by Juvan, a student of unknown origin. The passions of the mob, however, are really sparked by the deformed and beastlike son of the wealthy Stevan Milic, who has hidden the creature since his birth. After the troops have quelled the revolt, Stevan views the ruins of his lands and the loss of his son with relief, considering himself freed at last of hate, possessions, and the dreadful secret of his monstrous offspring. Much of the play's power stems from the mystery of the changeling who is always present but never seen, a symbol of the animal passion and religious fervor attached to Dionysus. The rationalist physician explains him away as an evolutionary freak and a symbol of superstition and dark fears; the rebels hail the monster as their spiritual leader; and Stanja, betrothed to the beast's normal brother, becomes the actual bride of "Dionysus" and the mother of his child. The events of the play reveal the tragic consequences of the Dionysiac principle of passion, both in its acceptance and its denial.

MEN (*22*): 8 are 20–40; 14 are 40–60; doubling possible in many roles. WOMEN (*6*): 2 are 18–40; 4 are 40–60. EXTRAS: 10–15 for crowds of peasants, gypsies, and soldiers (minor roles can double as crowd). SETS: The farm kitchen of a wealthy landowner; the council room of the elders; the garden of a decayed inn; the interior of a wooden Greek Orthodox village church; the exterior ruins of the landowner's farm. The settings will contribute more to the production if they are designed in a symbolic style; unit set may prove most practical as well as most appropriate to the mood of the play. COSTUMES: Late 18th-century Slavic peasants, wealthy landowners, vagabonds, Greek Orthodox priests, soldiers in Turkish uniforms (Janissary); the physician and the American in Western European clothes; the Jew in the clothes of a peddler of the period. DIFFICULTIES: Act IV requires careful staging of a mob possessed of religious frenzy.

ROYALTY: Apply Theatre Guild.* TEXT: Ruth Langner trans. (Doubleday, 1921, out of print).

— o —

JACOBOWSKY AND THE COLONEL (*Jacobowsky und der Oberst; ca.* 1944) FRANZ WERFEL. Comedy. While France crumbles before the German invasion of 1940, an aristocratic Polish colonel and a Jewish refugee, complete opposites in every respect, form a partnership to enable them to escape the Nazis and bring secret documents safely to England. The proud, courageous, and stubborn colonel learns from Jacobowsky what it is to be a refugee. Jacobowsky, a professional in the art of survival, also manages to teach his pupil something of pity and humor. The colonel's fiancée, Marianne, and his orderly, Szabuniewicz, help with the tutoring during a comic but suspenseful odyssey from Paris to the coast and rescue. The journey is set against the tragic background of the fall of France, with a number of vignettes depicting the heroism and humor as well as the treachery and stupidity that mark the behavior of humanity under fire.

MEN (*26; doubling possible*): 1 is 10; 11 are 17–40; 14 are 40–60; only 3 of the men are major. WOMEN (*7*): 4 are 18–40; 3 are 40–60; only 1 of the women is major. SETS:

The subterranean laundry of a small Parisian hotel; the square
outside the hotel with Paris in the background; a lonely country road running by a villa; a clearing in the wood; a waterfront café; a stone landing near the water. Selective realism
required, though a certain amount of distortion or suggestion
will be effective. COSTUMES: European 1940, mainly middle-
class civilian; one Tyrol tourist suit; uniforms for a Polish
colonel and his orderly, a Gestapo agent, a German lieutenant, two German soldiers, a French commissaire of police, a
gendarme, a sergeant of police. DIFFICULTIES: Performances
can easily move to caricature if not done with sympathy; 3
scenes require a motorcar which must be driven on and off
the stage.

ROYALTY: $50–25, Dramatists Play Service. TEXT: S. N.
Behrman adap. (Dramatists Play Service), or Gustave O.
Arlt trans. (Viking).

—o—

THE CAPTAIN OF KÖPENICK (*Der Hauptmann von
Köpenick;* 1931) CARL ZUCKMAYER. Comedy. Wilhelm
Voigt, victim of bureaucratic indifference, learns one important lesson in his years in and out of prison: that to be dressed
in the proper uniform equals power and position in a society
that fawns upon the military caste. Denied a permit to work
or even to live, the ex-convict resorts at last to a daring masquerade as an army captain in an effort to force bootlicking
officials to give him the necessary papers for rescue from his
stateless limbo. His daring *coup* becomes a national joke.
Certain scenes in the play dramatize the declining fortunes of
the captain's uniform as it passes from officer to officer, finally
coming to rest in the old-clothes shop where Voigt makes his
inspired purchase. Zuckmayer calls his play "a modern fairy
tale" which he based on actual fact. His satire is sharp but not
bitter. Wilhelm Voigt, like his real-life model, is not filled
with hate, for he is able to see his oppressors as ludicrous and
human. Central to the theme of the play are these words from
the Brothers Grimm that Voigt recites one day at the bedside
of a dying girl: "Come with me! One can always find something better than Death."

MEN (*140*): 5 are 15–20 (4 minor); 78 are 20–40 (most
minor); 57 are 40–60 (most minor). WOMEN (*32*): 3 are
15–20 (1 minor); 17 are 20–40 (15 minor); 12 are 40–60
(10 minor). BOYS (*2*): 4–5 (minor). GIRL: 4–5 (minor).

Doubling is possible, but the cast will still be of considerable size. SETS: 21 scenes requiring clearly defined locales. These must of necessity be rendered through suggestion, although some real properties are needed (tailor's dummies, period furniture, portraits of Kaiser Wilhelm II, roll-top desks, old-style typewriters, and so on). The scenes are the interior of a flophouse, various offices, restaurants, shops, and homes. A unit set might provide helpful solutions to the problem of keeping the play in motion. COSTUMES: Pre-World War I German, ranging from disreputable to fashionable, and including a great variety of army and police uniforms of various ranks. The main uniform will be needed in at least duplicate since it must pass through more than one condition, from new and elegant to worn but respectable. DIFFICULTIES: Aside from the hazards of a large cast and many settings, there is the danger of making the satire too ill-tempered and of portraying the Prussian official with too much caricature. The people are real, sincere, and quite unaware that they are ludicrous. They should approach the exaggerated and the grotesque in the same way as do the cartoons of George Grosz.

ROYALTY: Apply publisher. TEXT: David Portman trans. (Geoffrey Bles Ltd., 16 W. Central St., London, WC 1; 1932; out of print).

—— o ——

THE DEVIL'S GENERAL (*Des Teufels General;* 1946) CARL ZUCKMAYER.   Though the author went into voluntary exile shortly after the Nazis rose to power, his drama of the Hitler regime is unequaled in its authenticity. Inspired by the fate of General Udet, a famous flier in World War I who had accepted a position in Hitler's Luftwaffe and had died under mysterious circumstances, Zuckmayer makes his hero fall because he has sworn loyalty to the forces of evil. General Harras is a hard-living, hard-drinking daredevil, popular with his soldiers, with women, with everybody except the members of the Nazi Party. His provocative jokes leave no doubt of his inner opposition to the Third Reich; yet he serves it as Chief of Aircraft Production. Called upon to investigate sabotage that has recently caused the explosion of many German bombers in mid-air, he discovers his chief engineer, Oderbruch, to be the instigator. Harras could save his skin by denouncing the resistance fighter to the Gestapo. But Oderbruch is his friend. Furthermore, Harras realizes his guilt as a mercenary of the Devil. In a final bravura gesture, he mounts one of the deficient planes and crashes to his death. The robust, lively figure of the protagonist is surrounded by a multitude of compellingly drawn characters.

MEN (*20*): 6 are 20–30 (4 minor); 6 are 30–40 (2 minor); 8 are 40–50 (1 must be a powerful actor, 4 minor). WOMEN (*5*): 3 are 18–45; 2 are 40 (1 minor). SETS: Reserved party room in Berlin's most exclusive restaurant; the general's flat; engineering office at the Luftwaffe airport. Realistic sets and a large stage recommended; this and the important function of doors and windows render arena production impractical. COSTUMES: Fashionable German during World War II; uniforms of 8 officers; 1 soldier of the Luftwaffe; 1 officer of the SS. DIFFICULTIES: The play is very long and requires cuts, particularly of passages and allusions that might not be understandable to a non-German audience.

ROYALTY: Apply Marie Rodell and Joan Daves, Inc.* TEXT: Ingrid and William Gilbert trans. in *Masters of Modern Drama* (Random).

AMERICAN DRAMA

Eighteenth and Nineteenth Centuries

THE STREETS OF NEW YORK (also called *The Poor of New York;* 1857) DION BOUCICAULT. Melodrama. Gideon Bloodgood recoups his losses in the Panic of 1837 by appropriating the savings of a dead sea-captain, Fairweather, leaving the captain's widow and children to starve. The Panic of 1857 finds them in dreadful circumstances and Bloodgood wealthy. His clerk, Badger, knows his secret, however, and after trying blackmail, redeems himself by revealing all to the suffering unfortunates. Fairweather's daughter is united with her love, Livingston, and the deserving poor inherit Bloodgood's wealth. The piece is highly theatrical, full of sudden turns and highly dubious coincidences. There is a spectacular fire scene typical of plays of the period. The situations, while overdrawn, create a vivid social picture, and the play suffers less from dated material than is usually the case with nineteenth-century melodrama.

MEN (*17; doubling possible*): 12 are 20–40 (8 minor); 2 are 30–50; 3 are 40–60. WOMEN (*7*): 5 are 18–35 (3 minor); 2 are 40–60. SETS: Private office of a New York banking house; the park near Tammany Hall; exterior of Bloodgood's bank; sumptuous room in Bloodgood's home; Union Square in winter; vestibule of the Academy of Music; 2 dismal adjoining attic rooms; a neat garden in Brooklyn Heights overlooking the city; the exterior of a tenement house (which burns during the scene); the drawing room of Bloodgood's mansion. COSTUMES: Fashionable and threadbare examples of the Crinoline period; several policemen's costumes. DIFFICULTIES: Reliance upon coincidence, partially for plot advancement, partially for effect, is heavy even for melodrama. Fire scene and some spectacle scenes demand considerable technical ingenuity.

ROYALTY: Public domain. TEXT: Samuel French.

UNDER THE GASLIGHT (1867) AUGUSTIN DALY. Melodrama. Laura, a poor waif brought up by the wealthy Courtlands, flees in fear and shame when her past is made known
to society. She is pursued by her former suitor, Ray Trafford,
and by Byke, an unscrupulous wretch whom Laura believes to
be her father. After a number of spectacular and hair-raising
adventures, it is revealed that Laura is truly the Courtlands'
daughter, and Byke is forced to flee the country. The scattered
plot is largely held together by Snorky, a one-armed Civil War
veteran somewhat in the tradition of the comic servant. Several scenes demonstrate Daly's love of spectacle, the most
famous of which is the classic railway scene, in which Byke
ties Snorky in the path of an oncoming train.

MEN (*17; doubling and cutting possible*): 6 are 20–30 (4
minor); 5 are 30–50 (3 minor); 5 are 20–50 (minor, 1 is
Negro). WOMEN (7): 5 are 18–30 (2 minor; 2 are 40–60 (1
minor). BOY: 10–15 (minor). SETS: Fashionable parlor at the
Courtland home; gentlemen's cloak room at Delmonico's; Blue
Room at Delmonico's; interior of a dismal basement; the Tombs
police court; exterior of the court; foot of Pier 30 near Jersey
City (scene calls for a practical rowboat); an elegant residence;
woods near Shrewsbury station; the railroad station at Shrewsbury road (scene calls for tracks and a practical train); a
fashionable boudoir at the Courtlands'. Stylized settings almost
essential. COSTUMES: Fashionable 1860s dress; threadbare
clothes; uniforms for Snorky, policemen, porters, railway
worker. DIFFICULTIES: Large cast, many settings. Requires
some cutting.

ROYALTY: Public domain. TEXT: Samuel French.

—— o ——

SECRET SERVICE (1896) WILLIAM GILLETTE. Melodrama. The Federal Army is threatening Richmond. The
two Dumont brothers, members of the Secret Service, are
detailed to seize control of the telegraph office in order to
send false orders to the commander of the Confederate Army,
thus enabling the Union forces to capture Richmond. Disguising himself as a wounded Confederate cavalry officer, one of
the brothers succeeds in making his way into the city, where
he makes love to the commanding general's daughter as a
means of obtaining access to the telegraph office. But he falls
genuinely in love with her; conscience-stricken by his duplicity

he rejects the opportunity to telegraph the false message. His identity is discovered and he is about to be shot when a last-minute reprieve saves him.

MEN (*21, plus extras*): 1 is 16; 14 are 16–25; 2 are 20–25; 1 is 25–30; 1 is 35–40; 2 are 40–50. WOMEN (*5*): 2 are 16–22; 3 are 45–50. SETS: General Varney's drawing room and War Department telegraph office. The office paraphernalia must be credible since essential plot business depends upon it. COSTUMES: Civil War period; military uniforms for both Confederate and Union characters.

ROYALTY: Public domain. TEXT: Samuel French, or *Representative American Plays* (Appleton).

— o —

FASHION (1845) ANNA CORA MOWATT. Comedy. Mr. Tiffany's success as a merchant leads his wife to assume all the affectations of high society and to fill her home with would-be esthetes and presumed European nobility. Trueman, an honest upstate farmer, comes to visit his old friend and decries the changes that have taken place in the Tiffany home. With the aid of Gertrude, the family governess, he helps the Tiffanys shake off their baneful companions and return to a more simple life. An amusing variety of characters satirize life in New York society. The gloomy Fogg, the affected Twinkle, and the Uriah-Heeplike Snobson are entertaining burlesques. Count Jolimaitre, a French fop provides a contrast to the plain but honest Yankee heroes, Colonel Howard and Farmer Trueman. Much of the well-knit plot concerns the exposure of the count.

MEN (*8*): 6 are 20–40 (1 is Negro; a few extras may be needed for a ball scene); 2 are 40–60. WOMEN (*5*): 3 are 18–25; 2 are 35–45. SETS: A splendid drawing room in Tiffany's home; a room at Tiffany's counting house; interior of a lush conservatory; Mrs. Tiffany's parlor; the housekeeper's room; a fashionable ballroom. COSTUMES: Fashionable Crinoline period; American army uniform; servant's livery; maid costume.

ROYALTY: Public domain. TEXT: Samuel French.

— o —

UNCLE TOM'S CABIN (1852) HARRIET BEECHER STOWE (dramatized by George L. Aiken). Melodrama. The trials of the pre-Civil War Negro are illustrated by the misfortunes of the much-abused but saintly Uncle Tom, by Eliza and George who flee to Canada with their child, and by a host of other figures. Characterization is varied but not profound; sympathetic spokesmen for both North and South are included. The adaptation from a novel shows in the play's great number of brief scenes, some of which exist primarily for spectacle (e.g., Eliza crossing the ice, Eva ascending into heaven). This episodic approach prevents the more extremely drawn characters, good and bad, from becoming irritating, but the more sentimental passages may still prove difficult for a modern audience to accept seriously.

MEN (21): 18 are 20–40 (5 Negro, 5 minor); 3 are 40–60. WOMEN (6): 3 are 18–25 (all Negro); 2 are 25–35 (1 Negro); 1 is 40–60. BOY: 5–10 (Negro). GIRLS: (2): 8–10 (1 Negro). SETS: Plain chamber at the Haley plantation; dining room of the great house; snowy landscape with Uncle Tom's cabin; room in a riverside tavern; the Ohio River, filled with floating ice; handsome parlor at St. Claire's; St. Claire's garden; a chamber at St. Claire's; a rocky pass in the hills; the bank of a lake, a corridor at St. Claire's; a street in New Orleans; an auction mart; the garden of Miss Ophelia's home in Vermont; a rude chamber on Legree's plantation; a room in Miss Ophelia's home; a roofless shed on Legree's plantation; celestial scene with clouds and sunlight. COSTUMES: Fashionable pre-Civil War period; assorted threadbare clothes; a Quaker costume. DIFFICULTIES: Cutting necessary.

ROYALTY: Public domain. TEXT: Samuel French.

—— o ——

THE CONTRAST (1787) ROYALL TYLER. Comedy. Dimple has returned from the Continent with a good supply of debts, affectations, and scorn for all things American. Taking Chesterfield as his guide, he plans to break off his contracted match with Maria, marry the rich Letitia, and take Charlotte as his mistress. His plans are foiled, largely through the prowess of the superlatively noble Colonel Manly, Charlotte's brother and a soldier under Washington. Manly and Maria receive the blessing of Maria's father, Vanrough, and all ends happily. Comic gossip scenes between Letitia and Charlotte strongly recall Richard Brinsley Sheridan; broader humor is provided by the goodhearted bumbling of Jonathan. Manly's ingenuous Yankee servant, the first of his type in drama. Comic capital, too, is made by contrasting the affectations of Dimple and his servant Jessamy. Unintentional humor is provoked by Manly's relentless virtuousness.

MEN (5): 4 are 20–40 (2 masters, 2 servants): 1 is 40–60. WOMEN (4): All are 18–25. SETS: A room at Charlotte's apartment; a room at Vanrough's house; Dimple's room (all these should be rather fashionable—Dimple's the most so, Vanrough's the least); the Mall. Sets should be fairly realistic. If stylized, should suggest period settings. COSTUMES: Fashionable late 18th century Northern dress; livery; Revolutionary War uniform; servants' costumes.

ROYALTY: Public domain. TEXT: In *Representative American Plays* (Appleton).

Twentieth Century

THE AMERICAN DREAM (1960) EDWARD ALBEE. A long one-act play which the author names as an examination of the American scene, an attack on the substitution of artificial for real values in our society, a condemnation of complacency, cruelty, emasculation, and vacuity; it is a stand against the fiction that everything in this slipping land of ours is "peachy-keen." Mommy is both insipid and tyrannical; Daddy is impotent, bored, and boring. They coexist in a sterile apartment that reflects the benefits of modern civilization. Alas, as Daddy complains, nobody comes to fix the fixtures. Mommy still suffers from the shock of having been cheated into buying the wrong hat. She is also exasperated by Grandma, who shrewdly thwarts any attempt to put her away in a nursing home. The militant old girl has apparently saved her spirit from a long-past era. A lady caller, Mrs. Barker, chairman of the Women's Club, does not really know why she has come but adapts herself remarkably well: whether it is a matter of crossing her legs, smoking a cigarette, or taking off her dress, she does not mind if she does. The urban idyll is completed by the arrival of a young man whose exterior attributes—a tee shirt, blue jeans, and muscles—are familiar from television and motion pictures. He is cool and indifferent, unable to feel, to strive, to love. All he has to offer are his looks and a certain sexual capacity; yet, he seems to meet the requirements of American dreaming.

MEN (2): 1 is 18–25; 1 is 40–50. WOMEN (3): 2 are 35–50; 1 is 60–80. SET: A contemporary living room, prosperous but ugly. Suitable for arena production. COSTUMES: Contemporary American middle class. DIFFICULTIES: Symbolism must be handled with care.

ROYALTY: $25, Dramatists Play Service. TEXT: Coward-McCann.

ELIZABETH THE QUEEN (1930) MAXWELL ANDERSON.
Tragedy. Essex loves Elizabeth I, but also wants to share the
throne with the much older Queen. Elizabeth loves Essex, but
she will yield her throne to no one, and often fears that Essex
loves only the throne. Rival politicians trick them into a misunderstanding. Essex takes Elizabeth prisoner, but releases her
when she promises to share the throne. She immediately orders
his arrest and execution for treason. As the execution approaches, Elizabeth waits in the Tower for Essex to send the
ring by which she had promised to forgive him any crime. At
last she sends for him and demands the ring; he refuses because he knows that he would strive for power again and that
this would hurt England. Essex goes to his death and Elizabeth
crumples on her throne. Penelope is the only other woman's
role of consequence—a bright lady-in-waiting also in love
with Essex. The many rewarding male roles include the colorful Sir Walter Raleigh, a Fool, Richard Burbage, Francis
Bacon, Lord Burghley and cunning Sir Robert Cecil, who has
some fascinating scenes of double-dealing. This drama might
be called over-romantic today, but is still an excellent play for
university and community theatres.

MEN (*23, plus guards; doubling possible*): 4 are 20–30
(minor); 8 are 30–50 (minor); 3 are 35–40; 3 are 40–45; 3
are 65–70; 1 is 80. WOMEN (*5, plus maids-in-waiting*): 3 are
16–20 (minor); 1 is 18–25; 1 is 68. SETS: A hallway in White-
hall; the Queen's Study; the Council Chamber; a tent in Ireland; the Queen's apartment in the Tower. See Halstead's
Stage Management for the Amateur Theatre (Crofts, 1937,
out of print) for the plan of a semi-unit setting that could be
used. Arena production possible. COSTUMES: Elizabethan
court dress; suits of silver armor; changes needed for about
half the cast. DIFFICULTIES: Dialogue needs to be beautifully
spoken with romantic fervor. Elizabeth needs a bravura performance; most of the men need strong maturity. The Burbage
scene in the last act is extremely difficult, demanding exceptionally fine comedy playing by actors who appear for about
3 minutes.
ROYALTY: $25, Samuel French. TEXT: Samuel French.

— o —

MARY OF SCOTLAND (1933) MAXWELL ANDERSON.
Tragedy. Catholic Queen Mary returns to Protestant Scot-

land when the death of her husband, Francis II, King of
France, blocks the plan to combine the kingdoms of France
and Scotland. Mary falls in love with Lord Bothwell, a Scottish noble. Many Catholics consider Mary the rightful queen
of England; Elizabeth I therefore fears her and dreads the
popular support Mary might raise if she married the forceful
Bothwell. Elizabeth and her minister Burleigh trick Mary into
marrying the weak Lord Darnley because he also has a strong
claim to the English throne; they trick her into other similar
ill-advised actions and then plant forged evidence that Mary
and Bothwell have murdered Darnley. Between these plots
and opposition by John Knox, Mary is driven into exile in
England. Elizabeth gives her "sanctuary" in prison, and the
pseudo-historic final scene is a confrontation of Mary and
Elizabeth in which Mary scores verbally but loses the political
battle. (See also Schiller's play on the same theme; page 284.)

MEN (*25, plus extras; some doubling possible*): 1 is 15;
2 are 20; 1 is 20–25; 2 are 25; 2 are 25–30; 2 are 30; 8 are
30–40; 6 are 45–50; 1 is unspecified age. WOMEN (*6*): 1 is
20; 3 are 18–22; 1 is 25–30; 1 is 30. SETS: A foggy pier;
Queen Elizabeth's study (can be on a small wagon); Great
Hall of Holyroodhouse; courtyard of another castle; a room
in Carlisle Castle used as a prison. COSTUMES: Elizabethan
court dress; changes for Mary and a few others. DIFFICUL-
TIES: Dialogue needs to be beautifully spoken with a romantic
fervor. The play requires strong, mature men, and 2 excellent
women.

ROYALTY: $25, Samuel French. TEXT: Samuel French.

—— O ——

WINTERSET (1935) MAXWELL ANDERSON. Tragedy. A
play of social injustice, revenge, and renunciation, set in the
New York slums in a dilapidated tenement close to the towering Manhattan Bridge; written chiefly in verse. Mio, the son
of a radical named Romagna who was executed for murder,
is consumed with the desire to clear his father's name. On the
track of Garth, the one witness who could exonerate his
father, Mio meets Miriamne, Garth's sister. They fall deeply
in love. The girl and her father, the philosophical rabbi Esdras,
want to protect Garth, who is closely watched by the real
killer, gangster Trick Estrella. An old and demented man,
Judge Gaunt, who sentenced Romagna to death, also finds his

way to Esdras' living quarters. Obsessed by the memory of the trial he tries to justify his decision. Mio could force Garth to testify, but Miriamne has caused him to lose the taste for revenge. In the end the lovers defy death together and are killed by Estrella's gunmen. Several minor characters, representing the very poor, form a counterpoint of squalor and frustration which is transcended by the poetic impact of the love story.

MEN (*14*): 2 are 17; 3 are 20–30 (2 minor); 5 are 30–40 (3 minor); 4 are 40–60 (2 minor). WOMEN (*4*): 1 must appear 15; 2 are 18–25; 1 is 40–60. EXTRAS: 2 gunmen, tramps, street urchins. SETS: A river bank under a bridgehead; a cellar apartment. Arena production possible. COSTUMES: Contemporary American apparel of the inhabitants of big city slums; 2 policemen's uniforms and oilskins. DIFFICULTIES: Staging a verse treatment of a violent theme of our times requires a fine sense of style, setting this modern tragedy apart from both the gangster thriller and the sentimental melodrama.

ROYALTY: $25, Dramatists Play Service. TEXT: Dramatists Play Service.

—— o ——

ANNE OF THE THOUSAND DAYS (1948) MAXWELL ANDERSON. Anne Boleyn, wife and victim of Henry VIII, is a prisoner in the Tower, awaiting her execution. She thinks back to the time the king first came to claim her, of the years she lived as his mistress, and of the thousand days she was his queen. Henry, at the same time, is about to sign the death warrant. He, too, thinks back. The crucial episodes that decided her fate and changed the course of history are shown in flashback: her resistance to Henry's advances, his break with Rome, the court intrigues, his disappointment at the birth of a girl, their quarrels, and her trial. Anne, in Anderson's interpretation, has the force and grandeur needed to be heroine of his ambitious, resounding verse drama. Fiery and passionate, she chooses death rather than exile to save the succession of her daughter, Elizabeth. Henry is a full-blooded animal, ruthless as a child in his pursuit of pleasure, yet attractive for all his brutality. The worldly Cardinal Wolsey, the cunning Duke of Norfolk, the sinister Thomas Cromwell, Anne's compromising parents, the martyr Sir Thomas More, and other supporting characters contribute to this vivid chronicle of a tempestuous period in the history of England.

MEN (*21, some can be cut*): 10 are 20–30 (7 minor); 8 are 30–60 (1 requires a powerful actor, 5 minor); 3 are 50–70 (1 minor). WOMEN (*6*): 4 are 20–25 (3 minor); 1 is 20–30 (requires an outstanding actress); 1 is 40–50. SETS: Various exteriors and interiors in England, 1526–36. Stylized scenery. Strong emphasis on lighting, which effects the many location changes and sets the mood. Arena production possible. COSTUMES: Sumptuous, early 16th century. DIFFICULTIES: Unusual in this sense among modern plays, this drama of uncontrolled passions requires a style of flamboyant, theatrical grandeur.

ROYALTY: $50–25, Dramatists Play Service. TEXT: Dramatists Play Service; music by Lehman Engel (Dramatists Play Service).

— o —

BERKELEY SQUARE (1929) JOHN BALDERSTON. Comedy. Peter Standish, a young American living in Berkeley Square, London, finds a diary of an ancestor bearing his name. He moves back in time to 1784 to become this ancestor, who came to this same house to court and marry Kate Pettigrew. Retaining his modern viewpoint, Peter lives an eighteenth-century life. Sir Joshua Reynolds paints his portrait; he is the toast of London society because of his wit and clairvoyance. He falls in love with Kate's sister Helen, who, like Peter, does not seem to belong to her time. Peter realizes he cannot bridge the centuries and bids Helen goodby, taking as a remembrance the Crux Ansata, an Egyptian symbol of life and eternity. He returns to the present, breaks his engagement, and remains alone in Berkeley Square, living with his memories.

MEN (*7*): 2 are 20–30 (1 requires an outstanding actor); 1 is 30–40 (minor); 2 are 40–50 (minor); 2 are elderly (minor). WOMEN (*8*): 5 are 20–30 (1 minor); 1 is 50–60 (minor); 1 is elderly; 1 any age. SET: Morning room of Queen Anne period, in 1784 and 1928 (or today). The same set is used for both periods with changes of curtains, paintings, and few pieces of furniture. Arena productions have been given. COSTUMES: 4 (2 male and 2 female) are modern; all others fashionable London dress of 1784.

ROYALTY: $25, Samuel French. TEXT: Samuel French.

— o —

HERE COME THE CLOWNS (1938) PHILIP BARRY. The back room of Ma Speedy's Café des Artistes is reserved for the players and for the personnel from the vaudeville theatre next door. The theatre is called the *Globe;* its artists represent "the world in miniature—the variety show par excellence." The routine of these shabby, mediocre people is shaken when a malevolent illusionist, Max Pabst, who has the double-edged gift of making men reveal the truth, stages a special performance. Under his influence a dwarf relives his tragic separation from his son who grew up to normal height; a young dancer who is repulsed by small creatures admits that he does not dare to marry because he is a foundling; and a ventriloquist uses his dummy for accusing his wife of Lesbianism. The central character is Dan Clancy, a former stagehand, deserted by his wife, homeless, jobless, in quest of God to find an answer for his suffering. He believes he has found Him in Mr. Concannon, the mysterious, absent owner of the *Globe.* At last Concannon appears, but it is only the Mephistophelean illusionist impersonating him. Fatally wounded by a bullet destined for Pabst, Clancy recognizes God in the free will of man.

MEN (*10*): 1 is 20–25; 5 are 30–40 (2 minor); 4 are 40–60 (1 is a dwarf, 1 minor). WOMEN (*3*): 1 is 18–22; 2 are 25–30. SET: Back room of Ma Speedy's Café des Artistes in an American city during Prohibition; the room has a small stage used by the characters to reveal themselves in performance. Arena production possible. COSTUMES: Street clothes of vaudeville actors in the '20s; a ventriloquist's dummy. DIFFICULTIES: An acting style of selective realism, blending the human and the symbolic quality of the characters, must be found.

ROYALTY: $50, Samuel French. TEXT: Samuel French.

— o —

BIOGRAPHY (1932) S. N. BEHRMAN. Comedy. Marion Froude, a portrait artist renowned for the celebrity of her subjects and the nature of her relations with them, alarms her politically ambitious childhood sweetheart, Bunny Nolan, when she agrees to publish a serialized account of her colorful life. With the aid of his prospective father-in-law and fellow conservative, Orrin Kinnicott, Bunny secures the dismissal of Richard Kurt, the youthful editor who had first conceived the project. A rabid proletarian, Kurt now begins to view Marion's biography as a weapon against the established social order he abhors and determines to finance publication of the work himself. Before he can do so, Marion, saddened by the furor her book has caused, destroys what she has written and in so doing destroys the love Kurt has meanwhile come to feel for her. Through Marion, Behrman affirms his allegiance to the comic virtues of detachment and tolerance, while offering partial endorsement of Kurt's passion for involvement in the troubles of the times.

MEN (5): 2 are 25–30 (1 must be strikingly handsome); 3 are 40–55. WOMEN (3): 2 are 35–40 (1 must be a first-rate performer; 1 minor); 1 is 25–30. SET: Marion's studio-apartment, a cavernous room furnished in a random assortment of styles. COSTUMES: Fashionable 1930s; updating possible. DIFFICULTIES: The material is slightly dated.

ROYALTY: $35, Samuel French. TEXT: Samuel French.

—— o ——

END OF SUMMER (1936) S. N. BEHRMAN. Comedy. Leonie Frothingham, captivatingly irresponsible oil million-airess, narrowly escapes financial exploitation by Dr. Kenneth Rice, an ambitious psychiatrist. Leonie's strong-willed daughter, Paula, exposes Rice through feigned responsiveness to the attentions he directs her way behind Leonie's back. Behrman uses this slight intrigue as a framework for a conflict of attitudes toward the social ills of the depression years. Among the points of view expressed are those of the gracious but ineffectual aristocracy (Leonie), febrile young radicals bent upon wholesale social reconstruction (Will Dexter and Dennis McCarthy), and amoral opportunists preying upon the widespread sense of despair and futility for ruthless self-aggrandizement (Dr. Rice). Though there is little action in the conventional sense, the characters are richly differentiated and the dialogue is witty and urbane.

MEN (7): 2 are 20–25; 5 are 40–60. WOMEN (3): 1 is 20; 1 a youthful 40; 1 is 60, representing 3 generations of the same family. SET: Interior of a summer cottage on the Maine coast. COSTUMES: Fashionable 1930s; an elegant wedding gown of the 1890s.

ROYALTY: $35–25, Dramatists Play Service. TEXT: Random.

— o —

NO TIME FOR COMEDY (1939)   S. N. BEHRMAN. Comedy.   Amanda Smith encourages comic dramatist Gaylord Esterbrook, with whom she is romantically involved, to apply his talent to materials more relevant to current international problems. Under her influence he writes a serious play but, finding it "thin and petulant" he resolves to go to Spain, taking Amanda along, in search of genuine identification with the important conflicts of the day. In this project he is opposed by his wife Linda, who argues that the gaiety and understanding his plays contain can serve a useful, necessary function. When he persists with his longing for participation in the contemporary clash of ideologies, Linda turns for comfort to Philo, Amanda's serenely detached husband. Eventually, Philo's contempt for Gaylord shows Linda where her true affections lie, and she saves her marriage by persuading Gaylord to write a comedy about the very situation in which they have been entangled—one through which the disturbances and agonies of the times will be refracted. The play reflects Behrman's misgivings about the efficacy of the comic spirit in times of peril.

MEN (4): 2 are 30–40; 2 are 40–50 (1 minor). WOMEN (3): 25–35 (1 is a working-class Negro). SETS: A living room of a well-appointed New York apartment; luxuriously furnished upstairs living room of a New York town house. COSTUMES: Fashionable 1930s.

ROYALTY: $35, Samuel French. TEXT: Samuel French.

— o —

JOHN BROWN'S BODY (1928)   STEPHEN VINCENT BENÉT.   A concert reading adaptation for the stage of Benét's long narrative poem about the American Civil War, in which the slavery question and abolitionist John Brown's raid on Harper's Ferry serve as an epic theme to portray dramatically many aspects of life in the troubled 1860s. Events and effects of the war are seen mainly through the eyes of Jack Ellyat, the Connecticut intellectual, and Clay Wingate, the dashing Southern romanticist. Their families, backgrounds, battle experiences, romances are treated with poignant verity: Ellyat with Melora Vilas, lovely "nider" girl of the wilderness, and Wingate with the troubled Southern belle, Sally Dupré. Many individual scenes are particularly moving, especially Lincoln's anguished soliloquy in the White House, Ellyat's experience at the Battle of Gettysburg, the birth of Melora's child, the proud Southern aristocrat Mary Lou Wingate defying a foraging Northern soldier, and the exchange of prisoners. An *a capella* speaking and singing chorus gives depth to Benét's battle songs and love songs.

MEN (2): 1 is 20–35; 1 is 50–60; both read several parts. (Since this is a dramatic reading, and not a play in the strict sense, the ages of the men may vary, provided they are able to capture vocally the approximate ages of Benét's characters.) WOMAN: 20–35 (age may vary); she reads several parts. CHORUS (16): 4 soprano, 4 alto, 4 tenor, 4 bass; 2 must be able to do ballroom dancing; all must speak as well as sing. SET: Simple property pieces only: a long wooden bench; seats for the chorus on a raised platform; 3 wooden chairs for the principals; gray or black curtains should enclose the stage. Some lighting effects should be used to suggest variations in mood, time, and locale. Realistic scenery inappropriate; space staging is advisable. Well suited to arena. COSTUMES: Dark suits or dinner jackets for chorus men; chorus women may wear full-length costumes of simple uniform design; principal men should wear dinner jackets and the principal woman a full-length evening dress in classical style. DIFFICULTIES: Most of the problems lie in vocal interpretation. The narrative poetry is long in certain speeches, requiring great vocal sustaining power by the actors involved. Many of the lines are chanted or sung by the chorus, in answer to lines spoken by the principals, necessitating precise timing and smoothness of transition. 3 highly capable and versatile oral interpreters are required, since all 3 must read several characters of varying ages as well as narrate. Chorus members must be able to sing, recite in unison or singly, and make certain sound effects.

ROYALTY: $40–25, music $10, Dramatists Play Service. TEXT: Dramatists Play Service (Yale acting version).

—o—

THE GRASS HARP (1952) TRUMAN CAPOTE. Dolly Talbo, a kindhearted elderly spinster, lives in the house of her rich, dominating sister Verena in a small Southern town. When Verena, with the assistance of the shady Dr. Morris Ritz, tries to exploit commercially Dolly's secret gypsy cure for dropsy, the little woman takes refuge in a forest tree house in the company of her adolescent nephew, Collin, and Catherine Creek, a vigorous, outspoken Negress. There they are joined by a kindred spirit, old Judge Charlie Cool, who proposes to Dolly while they listen to the tales of the wind in the rustling grass. The townspeople are deeply shocked and organize an armed posse to force the rebels out of their arboreal retreat. Dolly, however, returns to reality of her own free will when Verena, now a lonely, broken woman, confesses that she needs her. Maude, Collin's wistful high school girl friend; Miss Baby Love Dallas, a traveling cosmetics saleswoman; and other characters (among them the minister and his wife, the barber, the baker's wife, the postmaster, the sheriff, and the choirmistress) complete a diversified, picturesque cast.

MEN (9): 4 are 25–40 (3 minor); 5 are 40–65 (2 minor). WOMEN (7): 1 is 30–40; 6 are 40–55. BOY: 16. GIRL: 16. SETS: Southern traditional-style dining room; a tree house in the forest. Poetic stylization. Use of scrims recommended. The solidly built tree must support seven persons. Arena production can be given only if many scenic effects are sacrificed. COSTUMES: Fanciful, strangely outmoded clothes, any time in the 20th century. DIFFICULTIES: The staging of this fantasy play requires a deft, delicate touch and poetic imagination.

ROYALTY: $50–25, Dramatists Play Service. TEXT: Dramatists Play Service; music by Virgil Thomson, c/o L. Arnold Weisberger, 509 Madison Ave., N.Y., N.Y.

— o —

HARVEY (1944) MARY CHASE. Comedy. Elwood P. Dowd is a middle-aged bachelor who likes company and liquor, which is how he met Harvey. One day, leaving Charlie's Place after a couple of drinks, Elwood saw Harvey leaning against a lamppost. They started to talk and have since become inseparable. Elwood does not mind that Harvey is a six-foot-tall rabbit and that other people usually fail to see him. But Veta, Elwood's widowed sister, does mind. A woman of social obligations, determined to marry off her daughter Myrtle Mae, she cannot tolerate an oversized bunny among her respectable guests. Elwood will have to be committed to a sanitarium for wacky alcoholics. So she takes him to Chumley's Rest. Unfortunately, once Veta starts talking of Harvey, she gets locked up herself. In the end, Elwood is permitted to keep his rabbit companion, who manages to appear to Dr. Chumley himself —at Charlie's Place, naturally. Elwood is an affable, ingratiating fellow who lives up to the author's counsel that we should not take ourselves too seriously. Veta, actually very funny in her confusion, is closer in spirit to her brother than she would admit. The supporting cast—an elderly socialite lady, a judge, and the staff of Chumley's Rest—are all drawn into comic situations because of the imagined rabbit. Or perhaps Harvey is real.

MEN (6): 3 are 20–30 (1 minor); 3 are 40–60. WOMEN (6): 3 are 20–25 (1 minor); 2 are 40–50; 1 is 60–70. SETS: Library of the old Dowd family mansion; main office at Chumley's Rest. Realistic sets form an effective contrast to the fantasy action. Arena production possible. COSTUMES: Contemporary upper class; medical whites. DIFFICULTIES: Director and actors must refrain from overstressing the comic elements in order to preserve the gentle fantasy mood. Doors and such mysteriously open and close.

ROYALTY: $50–25, Dramatists Play Service. TEXT: Dramatists Play Service.

— o —

FAMILY PORTRAIT (1939) LENORE COFFEE and WILLIAM JOYCE COWEN. Christ's words about the prophet who is not without honor except in his own country and among his own kin (Mark VI: 4–6), constitute the theme of the play. The creation and interrelation of many of its characters are based upon the literal interpretation of the preceding lines (Mark VI: 3) referring to Jesus' brothers and sisters. Christ does not appear, but the impact of his life and death is reflected by the varied reactions of his close relatives. His brothers resent the loss of a good carpenter when he leaves their shop forever. Learning of his successes, they try to exploit his fame and share his glory but fall back into disbelief when he fails as a preacher in Nazareth. In the end they carry the memory of his crucifixion as a burden of shame. Only Mary, the central character, never loses faith in her oldest son. With tenderness, simplicity, and maternal dignity she holds the family together in good times and bad. Her portrait is the play's main asset. Apart from the numerous family members several characters appear in some theatrically effective episodes. Among them are a fervent disciple who pledges to die for his master—Judas Iscariot; a Roman who offers to the carpenters an order for more than a hundred crosses; and a merchant from Damascus who comes to arrange the marriage of his son to Mary's granddaughter.

MEN (*16; doubling possible*): 3 are 16–18 (2 minor); 6 are 20–30 (3 minor); 7 are 40–60 (4 minor). WOMEN (*12; doubling possible*): 1 is 15–18 (minor); 3 are 20–30; 7 are 40–50 (1 requires an outstanding actress, 3 minor). BOY: About 6. EXTRAS: Peasants, fishermen. SETS: Courtyard of a carpenter's house; wine shop; street; room of the Last Supper. Very simple; not historically authentic. Arena production possible. COSTUMES: The authors call for peasant clothing of Central Europe.

ROYALTY: $25, Samuel French. TEXT: Samuel French.

— o —

THE GREEN PASTURES (1929) MARC CONNELLY. The Negro children in a Louisiana Sunday School ask many questions about the Old Testament. The gentle old preacher does not have all the answers; in some cases he tells them, "de Lawd expects us to figger out a few things for ourselves." Then follows the dramatization of the well-known biblical tales as visioned in the childlike, untutored, yet richly imaginative and humbly pious mind of the primitive Southern Negro. Heaven is a happy playground, with a delicious fish fry going on eternally. The Lord is a white-haired Negro patriarch in a black frock coat, calm and benevolent, but firm when necessary. He does not feel himself above mingling with the people He created, particularly when they get into trouble—which happens all too often. There is the fatal mistake of Adam and Eve, Cain's fratricide, and Noah's narrow escape from the Flood. The Lord selects Moses to lead Israel's Children out of Egypt and into the Holy Land. When they betray Him in Babylon and fall back into sin, He almost abandons them. But man in his suffering is convinced of His infinite mercy. And the Lord will suffer, too. This unique modern mystery play has the emotional power, the unsophisticated humor, and the tender beauty of the spirituals which introduce each scene.

MEN (*39, reducible through doubling to about 20*): 20 are 20–40 (11 minor); 19 are 40–60 (8 minor). WOMEN (*15; doubling possible*): 5 are 18–25 (2 minor); 10 are 35–60 (6 minor). BOYS (*4*): 3 are 5–8; 1 is 12–14. GIRL: 5–8. EXTRAS: Schoolchildren; townspeople; angels; officials and soldiers at Pharaoh's court; patrons of a night club in Babylon. The entire cast is Negro. SETS: Sunday School; Heavenly Fish Fry; Garden of Eden; outside the Garden; roadside; the Lord's private office; Noah's house; the Ark; mouth of a cave; Pharaoh's throne room; Babylonian cabaret; in front of the temple at Jerusalem. The scenery should render with modest means the colorful image of the biblical places as conceived by an uneducated Negro. The Lord's office, for instance, should look like that of a Negro lawyer in a Louisiana town; the Babylonian cabaret like a New Orleans night club. Arena production possible. COSTUMES: Fanciful mixture of contemporary dress and conventional attributes of biblical figures, such as crowns, plumes, swords, and angels' wings. DIFFICULTIES: This unusual naïve approach to the sublime must contain all the subtle qualities and profound reverence of the Negro spiritual.

ROYALTY: $25, Dramatists Play Service. TEXT: Dramatists Play Service; music, apply Dramatists Play Service.

— o —

BILLY BUDD (1950)   LOUIS O. COXE and ROBERT CHAPMAN.   The men of *HMS Indomitable* find the brutal behavior of the master-at-arms, John Claggart, almost unbearable. Held back from retaliating only by strict discipline and the knowledge of swift and harsh punishment, they grumble and fight among themselves. Everything becomes peaceful, however, when the new recruit, Billy Budd, comes aboard. His sincere goodness and innocence favorably affect everyone but Claggart, who revels in the control his authority gives him over the men and in the bitterness of their hatred for his consciously evil treatment of them. He is angered because they turn from hating him to loving Billy. Managing to find petty excuses to put Billy on report, he hopes to arouse the boy to violent rebellion against his authority; he actually hopes to cause the boy's death. But Billy is too good himself to believe that anyone can be as evil as Claggart. This further enrages Claggart, and he falsely reports Billy as the leader of a mutiny. The captain, Edward Vere, forces Claggart to confront Billy with the charge. The lad is so taken aback by the charge that he is overcome by a fit of stuttering, and, momentarily beside himself, strikes Claggart, who dies from the blow. Captain Vere and his fellow officers feel that Claggart deserved what he got and that Billy deserves freedom, but with anguish they realize that the military law under which they function demands Billy's life. Without understanding Captain Vere's troubled explanation of the reasons why he must be executed, Billy takes the captain's decision on faith. As he climbs up the lines to the noose, he shouts "God Bless Captain Vere," thus quelling the mutiny which is about to start in his defense.

MEN (*24*): 1 is 15–20 (minor); 2 are 20–30; 18 are 30–40 (mostly minor); 2 are 40–50; 1 is 50–60. SETS: All the action takes place aboard *HMS Indomitable* at sea in 1798. Scenes above and below decks, some in the captain's cabin, some on main and quarter decks. COSTUMES: British sailor uniforms of the period. DIFFICULTIES: The play requires skillful handling of language. Vere especially must be played by a capable actor.

ROYALTY: $50–25, Dramatists Play Service. TEXT: Dramatists Play Service.

—— O ——

HIM (1927) E. E. CUMMINGS. Perhaps the best description of the plot of this surrealistic play is in *him*'s description of himself as "the sort of a man who is writing a play about a man who is writing a sort of a play." Both as a person and playwright *him* struggles with the question of reality. He is no more certain of his own identity, even when mirrored, than he is certain of the identity of the world in which he moves. Nor is he certain of the reality of the love of his girl friend, *me*. At her request, he conjures numerous scenes from the play written by the other *him*, the man in the mirror. These include such varying subjects as an enactment of the ballad of "Frankie and Johnnie"; a Fascist outburst led by Mussolini, dressed as Caesar and surrounded by homosexuals; and a Paris café where ladies order men from the menu instead of food. Several of these scenes are as bewilderingly comic as they are extraneous; *him*'s struggle to define reality remains unresolved at the end of the play, although he is able to declare, "Time is the because with which some dolls are stuffed." The play affords the opportunity for experimental staging, integrated dance and music, and strikingly theatricalized scenic effects.

MEN (*approximately 20 with doubling*): *him* is 20–30; the Doctor, 30–50 (must play 9 other roles); a "multitude of shapes," "black figures," "2 centurions." WOMEN (*10–15 with doubling*): *me* is 20–30, all others play small roles as weirds, whores, and freaks. SETS: Various rooms, drops, and spatial arrangements; may be elaborate or bare stage. COSTUMES: Approximately 70, elaborate or simple as required. DIFFICULTIES: Diffuse and overlong, the director must direct the focus and cut throughout the script; the play is also already peculiarly dated.

ROYALTY: Apply Brandt & Brandt.* TEXT: In *From the Modern Repertoire* (Indiana), Ser. II.

— o —

ETHAN FROME (1936) OWEN and DONALD DAVIS. Tragedy. This dramatization of the novel by Edith Wharton tells of the tragedy of Ethan Frome, a rugged farmer in northern New England tied to a nagging, self-pitying, hypochondriac wife, Zeena. To their poor house comes Mattie Silver, an even poorer cousin, as a hired girl. She is young and willing and Ethan likes her at once, although nothing she does pleases Zeena. Slowly Ethan and Mattie fall in love, and as Zeena realizes this she insists on hiring another girl and getting rid of Mattie. As Ethan, torn between love and duty, drives Mattie to the station, they declare their love for each other, and in a last desperate attempt to win a sort of freedom, they go down the sled run aiming for a big elm tree and certain death. From the prologue we know that disfigurement and not death is Ethan's fate. In the epilogue we discover that Mattie has become an incurable, whining, imbecilic invalid waited on by Zeena. Their sense of duty binds these people together at last in a terrible, tragic trap.

MEN (*11*): 7 speaking roles, others in the dance scene. Ethan is 28 during most of the play, 48 during prologue and epilogue; 1 is young; others can be any age. WOMEN (*8*): Zeena is 25–30, Mattie is 20 (both age during play); 2 are 25–40 (minor); 4 for dance scene. SETS: The farmyard; outside the church; the crest of the hill (must suggest the top of the sled run); the farm kitchen; bedroom. The play shifts from outdoors to indoors within the acts. COSTUMES: Country-

style winter garb and house clothes of the 1920s. DIFFICUL-
TIES: New England dialect essential.

ROYALTY: $25, Dramatists Play Service. TEXT: Dramatists
Play Service.

— o —

REQUIEM FOR A NUN (1951) WILLIAM FAULKNER.
Nancy Mannigoe, a colored servant in the house of Gowan
and Temple Stevens, is on trial for having killed their baby.
The former prostitute accepts the death verdict with humility.
She has not revealed her motives, not even to her defense
attorney, Gavin Stevens, an uncle of Gowan. Gavin pursues
Temple relentlessly, convinced that she can and must give an
explanation. On the eve of Nancy's execution, he forces Temple to appeal to the governor of the state. Her story leads to
the time when, as a college girl—Temple Drake, the heroine of
Faulkner's novel *Sanctuary*—she ran away with Gowan, be-
came involved in a murder and was made an all-too-willing
captive in a brothel. Beneath the surface respectability of her
marriage to the guilt-ridden reformed playboy she still yearned
for her sordid past. When she decided to return to the gutter
and to take her baby along as a hostage for blackmailing her
husband, Nancy smothered the infant. Gavin knew in advance that Temple could not save Nancy from the gallows; yet
he urged her to seek atonement through the torture of her
confession. Temple cannot conceive redemption; Nancy, childlike, is convinced of having found it.

MEN (6): 2 are 20–30 (1 minor); 4 are 40–50 (2 minor).
WOMEN (2): 1 is 25; 1 is 30 (Negro). EXTRAS: Court officers;
members of the jury (can be cut). SETS: Courtroom; the
Stevens' living room; the governor's office; inside the jail. The
author recommends unit set with platforms on different levels.
Arena production possible. COSTUMES: Fashionable contemporary American.

ROYALTY: $50–25, Samuel French. TEXT: Samuel French.

— o —

THE KING AND THE DUKE (1939) FRANCIS FERGUS-
SON. The author calls this a "melodramatic farce from
Huckleberry Finn." Around an episode from Mark Twain's
novel the playwright has woven a folk-dance comedy drama.
The people of the town of Piperville act as a sort of merry

Greek chorus, country-dancing through their entrances and exits and talking by means of the words of familiar songs. We see Huck and Jim trapped into helping the rascally King and Duke impersonate the brothers of the deceased Peter Wilks of Piperville. The "noble" pair hope thus to get hold of the Wilks estate, which rightfully belongs to the three nieces. They convince the townspeople of their identity, but before they can abscond with the money, the real brothers arrive from England. Huck, meanwhile, half in love with niece Mary Jane, has hidden the cash part of the inheritance in the dead man's coffin. The King and Duke are run out of town, and Huck and Jim continue down the river on their raft, leaving all well behind them. With some aspects of a minstrel show, some of a dance-drama, some of a musical, this play is well above the usual stage treatment of Twain's material and is colorful, amusing, and original.

MEN (*11; 4 to 6 for dances*): 4 older men are important; 3, young to old, have lines; 2 enter near end. Also young Huck and Negro Jim. WOMEN (*6; 4 to 6 for dances*): Young Mary Jane, older widow have main roles; also 2 other young, 2 older. The townspeople should be of varying ages; a few children desirable. SETS: Painted backdrop of the River; painted act curtain of Piperville. Otherwise, furniture, props, and lighting are used to establish locale. COSTUMES: Summer, mid-19th century.

ROYALTY: Apply publisher. TEXT: In *From the Modern Repertoire* (Indiana), Ser. II.

—— o ——

THE HEIRESS (1947) RUTH and AUGUSTUS GOETZ. Catherine Sloper is quite inadequate as mistress of the beautiful house on Washington Square. Her father, a wealthy doctor, cannot forget that his adored wife died in giving birth to her and despises her because she lacks her mother's charm. Driven to pathetic uneasiness by her father's sardonic remarks, yearning for love and attention, the plain and no-longer-very-young girl thrusts herself into the arms of Morris Townsend, a suave young fortune-hunter. On the night of her planned elopement Catherine waits in vain for her suitor, who in the meantime has learned that such a step would lead to her disinheritance. Some time later Dr. Sloper dies, leaving all his possessions to his daughter. With the help of Catherine's matchmaking aunt,

Mrs. Penniman, Townsend once more obtains access into her house. Again he proposes a sudden marriage and again she consents. But at night, when he comes to fetch her, he finds the door locked. Based on Henry James' novel *Washington Square*.

MEN (*3*): 2 are 25–30 (1 minor); 1 is 50–60. WOMEN (*6*): 2 are 18–25 (minor); 1 is 28; 1 is 30–35; 2 are 50–60 (1 minor). SET: Front parlor of Dr. Sloper's house on Washington Square, 1850. Rich, tasteful furniture. Staircase desirable. Suitable for arena production. COSTUMES: Fashionable mid-19th century.

ROYALTY: $50–25, Dramatists Play Service. TEXT: Dramatists Play Service.

—— o ——

THE DIARY OF ANNE FRANK (1955) FRANCES GOODRICH and ALBERT HACKETT. Hiding from the Gestapo for two years in a narrow Amsterdam attic during World War II, Anne Frank, a 13-year-old Jewish girl, wrote a diary which in the stage adaptation retains much of its freshness, simplicity, and lucid awareness of the human condition. In the dingy shelter offered to them by Dutch friends, eight people are cramped into a forced intimacy and interdependence: the Franks with their two teen-age daughters; the Van Daans with their boy; and Mr. Dussel, an elderly bachelor. Their struggle to survive together, their anguish and their petty quarrels, great hopes and little joys are re-created on the stage in nine scenes, bridged by Anne's narration of brief passages from the diary. The quite ordinary behavior of these innocently condemned people gains dramatic tension by implication. The characters are vividly alive—above all Anne, the spirited, imaginative little girl, quick-tempered and sometimes terribly capricious, who is awakening to become a tender, lovely women. Her indomitable straightforwardness and open-eyed affirmation of human existence makes the play, as it did the diary, a tribute to the beauties of life rather than a testimony of man's injustice and cruelty.

MEN (*4*): 1 is 30–40 (minor); 3 are 40–60. WOMEN (*4*): 2 are 18–22 (1 minor); 2 are 40–50. BOY: 15–17. GIRL: 13–15. SET: Attic of a warehouse in Amsterdam, subdivided into 1 relatively large and 3 small living areas. Scenery need not be realistic, yet the simple furniture and household articles must be. Arena production has been given. COSTUMES: Street and house clothes, 1942. DIFFICULTY: Avoiding sentimentality.

ROYALTY: $50–25, Dramatists Play Service. TEXT: Dramatists Play Service.

—— o ——

IN ABRAHAM'S BOSOM (1926) PAUL GREEN. Unlike his colored fellow workers, who have learned how to avoid trouble, Abe McCranie has set his mind on giving his people a basic education that will enable them to rise from the bondage of low labor in the North Carolina turpentine belt. The son of a white man, he tries to emulate his oppressor's cool, calculating attitude but cannot control his flaring, passionate nature. Unable to ignore provocation, he is repeatedly crushed by the whites and jeered at by the blacks. Shortly after he is given a school, the parents withdraw their children when he is accused of having whipped a pupil. Goldie, his wife, can offer him love and loyalty but not understanding; Muh Mack, his nagging, superstitious aunt, preaches subservient piety; and Douglass, his son, becomes a tramp. In the end the incensed Abe kills his abusive white half-brother and dies from the bullets of an avenging mob.

MEN (8): 4 are 16–24; 2 are 20–40; 2 are 40–60. WOMEN (3): 1 is 18; 1 is 20–40; 1 is 50–70. BOY: 10. All characters except Colonel McCranie (40–60) and his son (20–40) are Negro. There is a time lapse of 21 years between the 1st and the last scene of the play. EXTRAS: A white lynching party. SETS: The turpentine woods of North Carolina; Abe's cabin; schoolroom; another room; a road. Scenery can be very simple. Arena production possible. COSTUMES: Rural Southern, latter part of the 19th century and first part of the 20th.

ROYALTY: $25, Samuel French. TEXT: Samuel French.

—— o ——

THE HOUSE OF CONNELLY (1931) PAUL GREEN. The cracked walls of the colonial mansion and the neglected fields of the plantation reflect the decay of a family that once ranked among the South's proudest and most powerful. Will Connelly, the young head of the house, lacks the energy to stem the tide until he falls in love with the unspoiled, aggressive Patsy Drake, daughter of a poor-white tenant farmer who provokes him to shed his pride, tear himself away from a choking tradition, and make his family face the truth. His uncle, a lecherous, garrulous old colonel, commits suicide; his invalid mother dies of a broken heart; his sisters, two dried-up old maids, leave home forever; but the barren land will become strong and fertile again. As a chorus, two huge, sybil-like Negresses mock, giggle, and prance about in earthly vitality, prophesying doom for the moribund and symbolizing the eternal renewal of life. The characters are drawn with Chekhovian suggestiveness, creating an atmosphere of fatalism, sympathy, and understanding.

MEN (5): 1 is 25–35; 3 are 45–55 (2, both Negro, minor); 1 is 65–70. WOMEN (8): 1 is 18 (Negro); 2 are 20–25; 2 are 40; 3 are 60–70 (2 Negro). EXTRA: Tenant farmers; children. SETS: Field of the Connelly plantation; dining room in Connelly Hall; ruined garden of Connelly Hall. Scenery, although it must establish an atmosphere of disintegration, need not be realistic. Arena production possible. COSTUMES: Apparel of impoverished Southern planters and tenants in the early 20th century.

ROYALTY: $25, Samuel French. TEXT: Samuel French.

— o —

JOHNNY JOHNSON (1936) PAUL GREEN. An honest, truth-loving fellow volunteers to be a soldier in the war that was to have ended all wars. Johnny is shown at the dedication of a peace monument as President Wilson proclaims war; with his romantic fiancée, Minnie Belle, who is enraptured by the glories of martial heroism; in the recruiting office; addressing the Statue of Liberty; on the front, contracting a private peace with a young German soldier; in the hospital; at the Allied Supreme Command dosing the generals with laughing gas and thus temporarily succeeding in calling off the war; in a lunatic asylum where he is discovered suffering from that rare but dangerous delusion, the St. Francis complex; and finally selling toys at a street corner—not very successfully, since he does not carry tin soldiers. According to the author, the first act is conceived as a comedy, the second as a tragedy, and the third as a satire; the elements of these three forms intermingle from the start. Green communicates his shattering antiwar message in a succession of expressionistic sketches, pervaded by weird songs, ballads, marches, and hymns by Kurt Weill.

MEN (*about 47; doubling possible*): 27 are 20–40 (23 minor); 19 are 40–60 (14 minor); 1 is 70. WOMEN (6): 3 are 18–25 (2 minor); 3 are 30–50 (2 minor). BOYS: (3): 1 is 10–12; 1 is 12–14; 1 is 16–17. EXTRAS: Villagers; soldiers; hospital personnel. SETS: 14 locations in America and France during World War I and some time later. Expressionistic scenery, permitting quick changes. Arena production possible. COSTUMES: Clothes of American small-town people, World War I period; uniforms of American, British, French, and German officers and soldiers and of the multinational Allied Supreme Command; medical whites; apparel of inmates of a lunatic asylum. Costumes need not be authentic. DIFFICUL-TIES: Singing required of many characters.

ROYALTY: $50, Samuel French. TEXT: Samuel French; music by Kurt Weill, apply Samuel French.

— o —

THE CHILDREN'S HOUR (1934) LILLIAN HELLMAN. Two young women, Karen Wright and Martha Dobie, have set up a private boarding school. Their prospects for a happy and secure future are shattered when one of their pupils, Mary, a spoiled and mischievous problem child, runs away to her grandmother, Mrs. Tilford, a pillar of local society, and—to prevent being sent back—accuses her teachers of an abnormal sexual relationship. Though Mary has only a vague notion of what she is talking about, she convinces the shocked old lady and cunningly counters exposure in a cross-examination by blackmailing another girl into corroborating her story. Once started, the rumor gains momentum. When Martha's exasperat-ingly foolish aunt, Mrs. Mortar, fails to appear as an exonerat-ing witness, the teachers lose their libel suit. The school is wrecked; Karen breaks her engagement to a reluctantly loyal young doctor; Martha, accusing herself of hitherto suppressed unnatural feelings, commits suicide. Too late the broken Mrs. Tilford attempts to undo her wrong. The author underlines the play's broader implications by stating that "this is really not a play about lesbianism, but about a lie. The bigger the lie the better, as always."

MAN: 30–35. WOMEN (5): 2 are 28; 2 are 40–50 (1

minor); 1 is 60–70. Boy: 10–14 (minor). Girls: (9): 12–14
(5 minor). Sets: Living room of the Wright-Dobie School;
Mrs. Tilford's living room. Except for the furniture, scenery
can almost be dispensed with. Suitable for arena. Costumes:
Contemporary American, upper-middle class. Difficulties:
Since the hypocritical little culprit, Mary, is captivating, her
absence in Act III may be felt a loss unless the director emphasizes that the central characters are Karen, Martha and
Mrs. Tilford, victims and executioner.

Royalty: $35–25, Dramatists Play Service. Text: Drama-
tists Play Service.

—— o ——

THE LITTLE FOXES (1939)   Lillian Hellman.   Oscar
and Benjamin Hubbard join forces with their sister, Regina
Giddens, to raise money to establish a cotton mill in their
small Southern town. Birdie Hubbard, Oscar's gentle and
sensitive wife, does not approve of the Hubbard greed and
urges Alexandra, Regina's daughter, to escape the avaricious
plotting of the family. Regina's husband, Horace, president of
the local bank, is under treatment for a heart ailment in a
Baltimore hospital. After letters to Horace fail to bring the
necessary money, Regina sends Alexandra to bring her father
home. Weakened by the trip, Horace refuses the money his
wife wishes. Benjamin and Oscar steal securities belonging to
Horace and cut Regina out of her share of the scheme. When
Horace tells his wife the stolen securities will be her share of
his will, she becomes enraged. The realization of Regina's
true character causes Horace to suffer a heart attack; Regina
refuses to give him the necessary medicine, and Horace dies.
Regina confronts Oscar and Benjamin with the theft of the
securities, demanding seventy-five per cent of the business in
return for not prosecuting them. In the final scene Alexandra
bids her mother farewell, unable to bear any longer the greed
and selfishness of the family.

Men (6): 5 are 40–50 (3 require good character actors, 1
Negro servant); 1 is 20. Women (4): 1 is 17 (ingénue); 3
are 40–45 (strong leading lady, 1 good character actress, 1
Negro servant). Set: A fashionable living room in a small
Southern town at the turn of the century. Set should be fairly
realistic. Suitable for arena. Costumes: Fashionable early
1900s. Change of costume necessary for 3 women.

ROYALTY: $25, Dramatists Play Service. TEXT: Dramatists
Play Service.

—o—

ANOTHER PART OF THE FOREST (1946) LILLIAN
HELLMAN. The Hubbard family is depicted here 20 years
earlier than in *The Little Foxes*. Marcus Hubbard dominates
his conniving son, Benjamin, and his weaker son, Oscar, with
the tyranny that has made him a rich and powerful man. He
has reduced his sensitive and religious wife, Lavinia, to a mental patient. Only his beautiful daughter Regina, whom he
worships, can control Marcus, which she does for her own
selfish purposes. She wishes to marry John Bagtry, whose sister Birdie has appealed to Benjamin for a loan which would
salvage the family's plantation. He arranges the loan at a substantial profit to himself. When Regina discovers the money
would enable John to leave town, she stops the transaction.
Oscar brings the local prostitute to a Hubbard party where she
creates a scene when Benjamin purposely gets her drunk.
Marcus orders both sons to leave home. Benjamin learns from
his mother that his father's fortune was made dishonestly and
blackmails Marcus into giving him control of the family funds.
Now he becomes the new tyrant of the house, ordering Oscar
to marry Birdie and Regina to give up John. Although she
hates him, Regina turns her attentions to Benjamin to further
her own desires. Just as he has destroyed others, Marcus is a
broken and lonely man at the end of the play, victim of his
own greed.

MEN (8): 6 are 30–36 (1 requires an outstanding actor; 1
is a Negro servant; 2 minor); 2 are 63–65 (1 minor). WOMEN
(5): 3 are 20; 1 is 30 (Negro servant); 1 is 58 (requires a
good character actress). SETS: Exterior of a Southern Greek-
revival portico of an 1850 mansion; living room of the
mansion. Sets should be fairly realistic. Suitable for arena.
COSTUMES: Fashionable summer dress of 1880. The 3 women
have more than 1 costume change.
ROYALTY: $50–25, Dramatists Play Service. TEXT: Dra-
matists Play Service.

—o—

THE AUTUMN GARDEN (1951) LILLIAN HELLMAN.
A Chekhovian treatment of a group of guests in a Southern

heartbreak house: Colonel Griggs and his wife, Rose, who cannot cope with his repeated demands for a divorce; three generations of the Ellis family, including the seventy-year-old matriarch, Mary, controller of the family purse; her widowed daughter, Carrie; Carrie's son, Frederick, who has consented to a loveless engagement with a young German refugee; and Crossman, a long-time ineffectual admirer of Constance, the owner of the house. All of these guests suffer a common malaise, the disenchantment of knowing that their lives might have been otherwise. Returning after forty years to the scene of his youth, Nick, an artist, plays nursemaid to them all, not in order to help them so much as to fulfill his own needs. He is accompanied by his disillusioned wife, Nina, who reveals he has not been able to finish a painting during the last five years of their nomadic life. The realization that "at any given moment, you're only the sum of your life up to then" comes as the guests discover they are unable to transplant themselves to a different life.

MEN (5): 1 is 25; 1 is a young Negro butler; 2 are 40–50; 1 is 50–60. WOMEN (7): 4 are 40–50; 1 is 17; 1 is 20–40 (minor); 1 is 70. SET: Sitting room and porch of a large Southern house "inherited from another day." Arena productions have been given. COSTUMES: Modern (1949) summer dress. DIFFICULTIES: Two characters must be able to deliver several speeches in flawless German; another must speak French and German. Middle-aged characters must be believable.

ROYALTY: $50–25, Dramatists Play Service. TEXT: Dramatists Play Service.

—o—

THEY KNEW WHAT THEY WANTED (1924) SIDNEY HOWARD. Tony, a kindly 60-year-old Italian winegrower, has courted a young San Francisco waitress, Amy, by mail. Afraid to disclose his age, he has sent her instead of his own photograph that of his young, husky foreman, Joe. When Amy is to arrive, Tony fortifies himself with liquor and drives to the station, but breaks both legs in an accident. In her resentment at having been deceived but unwilling to return to the wretched life she has led, Amy gives herself to Joe the night of her wedding to the crippled Tony. In the following months she comes to love her naïve, good-natured husband.

When Tony learns of his wife's pregnancy, he overcomes his
first impulses of rage and finds it easy to forgive his beloved
Amy her only misstep and to take the child as his own. The
somewhat commonplace plot is enlivened by the vigorous
characterization of straightforward people in their longings,
passions, frustrations, and joys.

MEN (*8*): 4 are 20–30 (2 minor); 3 are 30–50 (2 minor);
1 is about 60. WOMEN (*3*): 1 is 22; 2 are 30–40 (minor).
BOY: About 9. GIRL: 6–9. EXTRAS: Guests at a wedding party.
SET: Main room in the house of an Italian winegrower in
Napa Valley, California. Scenery should be colorful and atmospheric but not necessarily realistic. Arena production possible. COSTUMES: Western rural clothes. DIFFICULTIES: The
creation of a genuine Italian-American background is important. Italian phrases are freely used by most of the characters.
Tony has to play the whole of Act II from a bed.
ROYALTY: Apply Samuel French. TEXT: Samuel French.

—— o ——

THE SILVER CORD (1926) SIDNEY HOWARD. Mrs.
Phelps, a wealthy widow, has poured all the love she could
not release in her unhappy marriage onto her now-grown
sons, David and Robert. David has studied in Europe and,
out of his mother's protective reach, has married Christine, a
biologist. Robert is engaged to Hester, a charming, sensitive
girl. Consumed by her exalted mother-love, Mrs. Phelps desperately tries to keep her adored sons for herself. With subtle
insinuations and lies she persuades Robert to break off his engagement, she nearly succeeds in wrecking David's marriage.
But after a great showdown scene in which Christine tears off
her mother-in-law's mask of the devoted, self-sacrificing Victorian mother and reveals her as "a self-centered, self-pitying,
son-devouring tigress, with unmentionable proclivities suppressed on the side," David leaves the house with his wife.
Robert remains kneeling at the feet of his mother, who finds
relief in quotations from the Bible concerning that love that
suffereth long and is kind. Though Howard denied the influence of Freudian theories, he could not prevent his play from
being interpreted as a demonstration of the then-sensational
Oedipus complex.

MEN (*2*): Both are 24–30. WOMEN (*4*): 1 is 18–22; 1 is

25–30; 1 is 50–60; 1 is 20–60 (minor, no lines). SETS: Living room of Mrs. Phelps's house in an eastern American city; David's bedroom. Arena production possible. COSTUMES: Fashionable, early 1920s. DIFFICULTIES: The character of the mother requires an exceptional actress.

ROYALTY: $25, Samuel French. TEXT: Samuel French.

— o —

YELLOW JACK (1934) SIDNEY HOWARD. Based on Paul de Kruif's *The Microbe Hunters* and written in collaboration with him, the play gives the case history of a remarkable adventure in science—man's fight against yellow fever. The gradual progress of research is shown retrogressively, beginning in a London laboratory in 1929, when science is on the verge of conquering the disease, then tracing the development back to the experiments in South Africa in 1927 and the tracking down of the death-carrying mosquito by Walter Reed and his associates in Cuba in 1900. In spite of interference, red tape, and scientific skepticism, the members of Reed's Army Medical Commission carry on with inexhaustible patience and tenacious curiosity, not only risking and sacrificing their own lives but also taking chances with that of an unsuspecting outsider. The fanatic struggle of the scientists is contrasted with the life of the bored, homesick soldiers of the American occupation force in Cuba, represented by the four men who eventually volunteer to serve as human guinea pigs. A document of human grandeur in the form of a suspenseful scientific mystery play.

MEN (*27; doubling possible*): 14 are 18–30 (7 minor); 7 are 30–40 (4 minor); 6 are 40–60 (3 minor). WOMAN: 35. EXTRAS: Doctors; scientists; soldiers. VOICES AND SOUNDS: A male quartet, singing tunes of 1900; tom-tom; bugle calls. SETS: Laboratories; tents; hospital ward; and several nondescript locations. Little scenery necessary, but needs complicated lighting effects. Unit set highly recommended. Not suitable for arena; simultaneous performance on three locations with a large cast is essential. COSTUMES: Medical whites; uniform of British RAF major; summer uniforms of 7 officers and about 12 soldiers of the U.S. Army, 1900. DIFFICULTIES: The numerous transitions require swift and smooth artistic and technical direction.

ROYALTY: $25, Dramatists Play Service. TEXT: Dramatists

Play Service or in *Three Plays About the Medical Profession* (Washington Square).

—— o ——

LUTE SONG (1946) SIDNEY HOWARD and WILL IRWIN. The Chinese classic *Pi-Pa-Ki*, from which this play is derived, is more than 500 years old. It tells of a brilliant young scholar, Tsai-Yong, who obeys his father's order to seek fortune and fame at the Court of the Son of Heaven, though he would prefer to stay with his beloved young wife, Tchao-ou-Niang. Upon arrival in the capital of the Middle Kingdom, he is forced by imperial command to marry the beautiful Princess Nieou-Chi, daughter of the wicked imperial Preceptor, and is held a virtual prisoner. Tchao-ou-Niang, unshakable in her faith, waits in vain. She dutifully serves her husband's parents until they die in a famine, then sacrifices her beautiful hair to pay for the funeral. Then, clad as a mendicant nun, she sets out in quest for Tsai-Yong who, when they finally meet, does not recognize her. But the princess discovers the truth and in noble resignation reunites the loving couple. The simple tale is set against a magnificent background of Oriental pageantry. (As a straight play *Lute Song* much surpasses the musical version in authenticity and gentle poetic beauty.)

MEN (*19; doubling possible*): 8 are 20–40 (7 minor); 11 are 40–60 (8 minor). WOMEN (*7*): 3 are 18–25; 4 are 50–60 (3 minor). EXTRAS: Property men; guards; attendants; students; merchants; servants; coolies; beggars; children. SETS: Numerous locations in China, 15th century or earlier. Interiors are represented on a raised platform, exteriors on the stage proper. Change of scenery, indicated by different hangings, is carried out by property men in full view of the audience. Production in a large arena theatre is conceivable. COSTUMES: Colorful medieval Chinese, ranging from sumptuous princely robes to beggar's rags. DIFFICULTIES: The acting style must combine unaffectedness with formality; the traditions and conventions of a very remote culture must be unobtrusively integrated.

ROYALTY: Apply publisher. TEXT: Dramatic Publishing.

—— o ——

COME BACK, LITTLE SHEBA (1950) WILLIAM INGE. Little Sheba was a puppy, so cute that she should have stayed young forever—and one day she was gone. Lola still dreams of her and hopes she will return. Twenty years ago, Lola was a pretty, romantic girl. Mentally she has not matured since the day when Doc had to marry her in a hurry, give up his medical studies, and become a chiropractor. Their child died. Now she is a sloppy and garrulous housewife, Doc a reformed drunk. In her urge for attention, Lola tries to break the monotony of her daily routine by involving anyone she can in a one-sided conversation—the postman, the milkman, or the busy woman next door; and she encourages the goings-on between Marie, the comely art student who boards with them, and Turc, a collegiate track star. Doc treats Marie with nostalgic affection. He resents Turc and one morning, when he catches Turc slipping out of Marie's room, all his long-suppressed frustrations break loose. He gets drunk, threatens Lola with a hatchet, and is finally carried off to the alcoholic ward by two dedicated friends from the AA. A week later he returns to resume a dreary life at the side of his pathetically inadequate wife.

MEN (8): 3 are 19–24 (1 minor); 1 is 25–30 (minor); 1 is 25–30 (minor); 3 are 40 (2 minor); 1 is 50 (minor). WOMEN (3): 1 is 18–19; 2 are 40 (1 minor). SET: Living room and kitchen in an old house in a run-down neighborhood of a Midwestern city. Both rooms must be visible at the same time. Arena production has been given. COSTUMES: Middle-class everyday clothes, present.

ROYALTY: $50, Baker's or Samuel French. TEXT: Samuel French.

— o —

PICNIC (1953) WILLIAM INGE. The scene is a drab, sun-drenched back yard, shared by the all-female inhabitants of two modest houses in a small Midwestern town. Mrs. Owens, a widow who has been married to the wrong man, has the usual problems in bringing up her daughters. Madge, the older girl, is the local beauty queen, engaged to the son of the richest man in town, but tired of being considered merely a lovely ornament. Her 16-year-old sister, Millie, has all the brains and an engaging personality, but she is plain and she knows it. A frustrated, unmarried schoolteacher, Miss Sidney, boards with them. When their neighbor, good old Mrs. Potts, admits boastful, muscle-conscious young vagabond Hal Carter into her house, the women and girls respond in their different ways to his physical appeal. Within a day, Hal changes the course of their lives. He lures Millie out of her tomboy reclusion and almost breaks her heart; he stimulates Miss Sidney into a humiliating but eventually successful fight for the hand of a reluctant bachelor; he seduces Madge. The dance scene, in which Hal and Madge, urged by the pulsating rhythm, are drawn into each other's arms, has a primeval force. The next day Hal leaves, the police on his heels, and takes Madge along. Mrs. Owens desperately watches her daughter repeat the mistake of her own youth.

MEN (*3*): 2 are 20–30; 1 is 40–50. WOMEN (*6*): 1 is 18; 4 are 40–50; 1 is 60. BOY: 16. GIRL: 16. SET: Back yard and porches of two neighboring houses in a small town in Kansas. Arena production has been given. COSTUMES: Contemporary everyday clothes of Midwestern small-town people.

ROYALTY: $50–25, Dramatists Play Service. TEXT: Dramatists Play Service.

— o —

THE TOWER BEYOND TRAGEDY (1925) ROBINSON JEFFERS. Tragedy. Based in part on sections of Aeschylus' *Oresteia* (see pp. 16–18), this play retells the circumstances surrounding the curse-ridden deaths of Agamemnon, Aegisthus, Clytemnestra, and Cassandra. As in Aeschylus' work, the legend is still the curse on the House of Atreus, but Jeffers altered some details. King Agamemnon has been away, fighting the Trojan War. In his absence, Queen Clytemnestra has taken as paramour the younger Aegisthus; together they have plotted Agamemnon's murder. Now returning from victory over the Trojans, Agamemnon enters triumphantly, bringing with him as mistress the prophetess Cassandra. Clytemnestra leads Agamemnon into the palace and murders him. Afterward she defends her action to the king's angry followers and, aided by Aegisthus, placates them despite Cassandra's accusations, howled out madly by her in the hollow voice of the dead king. Eight years pass. Agamemnon's children, Electra and Orestes, arrive to avenge his murder. Orestes slays Clytemnestra and, half-crazed at his matricide, also kills Cassandra at Electra's bidding. Orestes refuses to rule Mycenae, spurns Electra's incestuous love, and leaves Mycenae forever.

MEN (*10; doubling possible*): 2 are 18–25 (1 requires an outstanding actor, 1 minor); 2 are 20–35 (minor); 2 are 30–45; 3 are 40–60 (minor); 1 is Chorus (age may vary, preferably old). WOMEN (*5*): 1 is 18–25 (requires an outstanding actress); 2 are 20–35 (1 must be tall and an outstanding actress, 1 has no lines); 2 are 35–50 (1 must be short and an outstanding actress). EXTRAS: Several spearmen attendant on Agamemnon, Aegisthus, Clytemnestra, and Orestes; slaves; retinue of Aegisthus (all male); waiting-women; citizens (male and female). SET: An area in front of Agamemnon's palace at Mycenae; a large door atop the royal porch, pillars, stone steps, and a ramp up to it. Either traditional formal staging or modern proscenium permanent setting appropriate. Unit set advisable. Arena staging possible but extremely difficult. COSTUMES: 5th-century B.C. Grecian; rich royal attire for certain major characters; much military dress and accessories; some common, tattered clothing for slaves, attendants, and citizens. DIFFICULTIES: Play is in verse. Cassandra is especially difficult to play, particularly in one scene where she must take on the voice of the dead king.

ROYALTY: $25, Samuel French. TEXT: In *Roan Stallion and Other Poems* (Random; out of print).

— o —

MEDEA (1946) ROBINSON JEFFERS. Tragedy. Freely adapted from Euripides' *Medea* (see p. 26), this play tells substantially the same tragic story. Medea, the barbarian princess who killed her own father and brother to help her Argonaut-hero lover Jason in his quest for the Golden Fleece, has married Jason and borne him two sons. Jason, approaching middle age, has tired of her love. Politically ambitious, he forsakes his foreign wife Medea to marry the daughter of Creon, ruler of Corinth, thereby ensuring his own succession to the throne. Creon banishes Medea and her children because he fears her hatred of his family. Although apprehensive of her reputed occult power, he grants her request to remain one day more. Aegeus, the visiting king of Athens, promises her sanctuary when she agrees to cure his sterility with her magic. The extra day allows Medea time to work her jealous revenge on both Jason and Creon: by means of a poisoned cloak and coronet, she murders the princess and Creon, and then slaughters her own young children.

MEN (*5, plus extras*): 1 is 18–25 (minor); 1 is 40–50; 2
are 50–60; 1 is 60–80 (minor); attendants to Creon, Jason,
Aegeus (ages and number may vary; no lines; doubling possible). WOMEN (*7*): 1 is 18–25 (chorus); 1 is 20–35 (chorus);
2 are 30–45 (1 requires a superlative actress; other is chorus);
1 is 60–80; 2 are unspecified ages (no lines). BOYS: (*2*): 1 is
6–8; 1 is 9–11 (minor; 1 has no lines on stage, both speak
briefly off stage). SET: An area in front of Medea's house in
Corinth; large door; stone pillars, steps. Traditional formal
staging or modern proscenium permanent setting appropriate.
Unit set advisable. Arena staging possible. COSTUMES: 5th-
century B.C. Grecian; royal dress for rulers of Corinth and
Athens; common apparel suggested for chorus and others;
some armor and military accessories for attendants. DIFFI-
CULTY: Medea is an extraordinarily demanding role.

ROYALTY: $50, Baker's or Samuel French. TEXT: Samuel
French.

—o—

THE CRETAN WOMAN (1951) ROBINSON JEFFERS. Trag-
edy. Euripides' *Hippolytus* (see p. 27) is the source for this
adaptation of the classic tragic triangle of the king, Theseus,
his second wife Phaedra, and his son, Hippolytus. Phaedra is
much younger than the aged Theseus and, unknown either to
father or son, has fallen madly in love with Hippolytus. In the
king's absence she declares her love to Hippolytus who scorns
love, is scandalized and repulses her. Frustrated, injured, and
revengeful, Phaedra lies to the returning Theseus, telling him
that Hippolytus has raped her. Theseus summons Hippolytus
and kills him. Then Phaedra tells the truth, she berates Theseus
for his stupidity and reveals her hatred for him. She challenges
Theseus to kill him too; when he ignores her, Phaedra enters
the house and hangs herself. Agonized with remorse, Theseus
hurls himself onto the body of his dead son.

MEN (*8*): 2 are 18–25 (1 must be tall); 3 are 20–35
(minor, 1 has no lines); 1 is 40–60 (minor); 2 are 70–80.
WOMEN (*6*): 1 is 18–25 (minor); 2 are 25–35 (1 must be an
outstanding actress, 1 is chorus and must be able to play the
zither); 2 are 35–50 (1 is chorus); 1 is 50–70 (chorus). SET:
An area before the house of Theseus at Troezen; large door;
a stone altar of Aphrodite. Traditional formal staging or modern proscenium setting appropriate. Unit set practical. Arena

staging possible. COSTUMES: 5th-century B.C. Grecian; classical royalty suggested in dress of the major characters; element of fantasy proper in costuming of the goddess; tattered rustic clothes appropriate for women of the chorus; military armor and accessories for attendants to Theseus. DIFFICULTIES: Play is in sometimes awkward verse; some technical problems (especially lighting) in 2 scenes where a goddess must appear and disappear on stage.

ROYALTY: $25, Samuel French. TEXT: Samuel French.

— o —

BORN YESTERDAY (1946) GARSON KANIN. Comedy. A senator, according to Harry Brock, is a poor devil who earns about two hundred bucks a week. This does not apply to Senator Hedges, who is on Harry's payroll ($80,000). Harry has come to Washington to buy himself some legislation that will enable him to pocket all the scrap iron still lying around on the battlefields of World War II; Harry is a junk magnate, a gross and violent bully who is sometimes boorishly charming and at other times childishly naïve in his ruthless pursuit of profit. His staff consists of his cousin, Eddie Brock, employed as his servant, and of Ed Devery, a once-promising lawyer who has become a legal mercenary. And he has also brought along his mistress, Billie Dawn, an ex-chorine who behaves as if she had been born yesterday. After her disastrous deportment on meeting Senator and Mrs. Hedges, Harry gets the equally disastrous idea that she needs some tutoring in mind and manners and hires for this purpose Paul Verrall, a young, serious-minded reporter from the *New Republic*. Paul and Billie naturally fall in love. Paul not only succeeds in educating her but also awakens her social conscience, and together they put a stop to Harry's antisocial activities.

MEN (5): 2 are 25–35 (1 minor); 2 are 45; 1 is 60–65. WOMEN (3): 2 are 25–35 (1 minor); 1 is 50–60. EXTRAS: Assistant Manager; barber; manicurist; bootblack; waiter; 2 bellhops. SET: Large, luxurious suite in the best hotel in Washington, D.C. Arena production possible. COSTUMES: Very fashionable, post-World War II.

ROYALTY: $50–25, Dramatists Play Service. TEXT: Dramatists Play Service.

— o —

ONCE IN A LIFETIME (1930)   GEORGE S. KAUFMAN and
MOSS HART. Comedy.   Hollywood is panic-stricken; the invention of the talkies has thrown the industry into chaos. This
is the great chance for a third-rate vaudeville trio consisting of
May, an attractive but somewhat vulgar girl; Jerry, an enterprising young man who is not stupid; and George, who is.
With the help of gossip columnist Helen Hobart, they set up a
school of voice culture at the famous Glogauer Studios.
Caught up in a whirl of insanities peculiar to the Capital of
the Eighth Art, May and Jerry gain the favor of the great
Herman Glogauer himself and then are suddenly fired. Not
so George, whose muddled utterances establish him as a
genius in the eyes of the film magnate. Given dictatorial
powers, George proves himself as a movie director. He uses
the wrong script and forgets to have the lights turned on, but
his success is so colossal that Glogauer entrusts him with the
fortune of the entire Studio. George orders it torn down—
probably another stroke of genius. The turbulent action involves the entire film industry, represented by such types as
Kammerling, a movie director with a German accent; Miss
Leighton, a confused and confusing secretary; Mrs. Walker, a
stage mama; her daughter Susan, destined to become the
Mary Pickford of the talkies; and a glamorous array of Hollywood beauties and cuties. Last but not least there is Mr. Vail,
a successful writer, who receives a fabulous salary, sits for
three months in the waiting room, and then goes to pieces.

MEN (*24; doubling possible*): 14 are 20–30 (10 minor);
10 are 30–50 (7 minor). WOMEN (*14; doubling possible*):
11 are 18–25 (8 minor); 3 are 30–50 (1 minor). EXTRAS:
Hotel guests; policemen; bridesmaids; studio employees and
crew. SETS: Furnished apartment in New York; corner of a
Pullman car; Gold Room of the Stilton Hotel, Hollywood;
reception room of the Glogauer Studios; on the set. Hollywood settings combine opulence with unparalleled bad taste.
Not suitable for arena. COSTUMES: Fashionable Hollywood in
the late 1920s; lavish apparel for wedding scene in movie
super-production. Costumes are to match scenery in complete
phoniness.

ROYALTY: $50, Samuel French. TEXT: Samuel French.

— o —

YOU CAN'T TAKE IT WITH YOU (1936)   GEORGE S. KAUFMAN and MOSS HART. Comedy.   How to enjoy life with just enough money to take it easy; how to select hobbies; how to evade the income tax—all demonstrated by the Vanderhof-Sycamores who live in a sphere of heartwarming fun. Amiable, philosophical Grandpa Vanderhof collects stamps and live snakes. His daughter Penny is a painter turned playwright because a guest forgot a typewriter. Her husband Paul fabricates dangerous fireworks in the cellar with Mr. De Pinna, who came to deliver ice eight years ago and was invited to stay. Essie, Paul and Penny's daughter, is devoted to toe dancing and candy-making, while Ed, her husband, is torn between the xylophone and the printing press. The second daughter, Alice, a Sycamore in spirit though not in extravagance, provides the conflict when she and Tony Kirby fall in love. Mr. Kirby senior, a business tycoon plagued by indigestion, and his socialite spouse, are as unfulfilled and frustrated as millionaires can possibly be. The painful meeting of the two families is aggravated by the consecutive intervention of a wrestling Russian, an inebriated actress, and a raid squad from the FBI. Since this is a comedy, Mr. Kirby can eventually be converted and thus guarantee a happy ending.

MEN (*12*): 7 are 20–40 (1 is Negro, 3 minor); 4 are 40–60; 1 is 75. WOMEN (*7*): 4 are 20–35 (1 is Negro); 3 are 50. SET: Large living room containing, among other delights, a printing press, a xylophone, and a snake bowl. Fulminous firework explosions take place. Arena production possible if stairs leading to cellar and to second floor can be installed. COSTUMES: Slightly extravagant middle-class American, 1936 or present.

ROYALTY: $25, Dramatists Play Service. TEXT: Dramatists Play Service.

—o—

THE SHOW–OFF (1923)   GEORGE KELLY. Comedy.   A fast-talking braggart, Aubrey Piper, marries Amy Fisher over her parents' objections. Amy's mother is a sharp-spoken woman who dislikes Aubrey because he brags and lies—especially concerning his finances. Yet, she and others are to some extent fascinated by his egoism and nerve. Mrs. Fisher's predictions of Aubrey's actual finances were correct, and he and Amy have to move in with her. Aubrey is not dismayed and continues to brag. He tells people it is his house and that he lets his mother-in-law live with him. In the last scene, he has been fined for driving a borrowed car without a license and hitting a policeman. Mrs. Fisher discovers the lies he has been telling. At this low pitch of fortune, Amy's brother Joe reveals the sale of his invention for double the sum he had expected. It turns out that Aubrey had gone to the purchasers to inform them that, as head of the family, he wouldn't allow Joe to sell unless they doubled the price. They did. Aubrey becomes the hero of the hour. Mrs. Fisher is very funny, and comedy arises from the contrast of her inane and pedestrian remarks with Aubrey's high-pressure dialogue.

MEN (6): 2 are 20–30; 1 is 30–35; 3 are 40–60. WOMEN (3): 1 is 50–60; 1 is 20–25; 1 is 25–30. SET. Realistic living room in a middle-class American home. Suitable for arena. COSTUMES: Early 1920s. DIFFICULTIES: The part of Aubrey is very difficult because his character is nearly obnoxious yet the audience must like him. Some of the language is dated.

ROYALTY: $50, Samuel French. TEXT: Samuel French.

— o —

DETECTIVE STORY (1949) SIDNEY KINGSLEY. Starkly naturalistic in concept and execution, this story of Detective James McLeod and his obsession with preserving the letter of the law at all costs, provides tense action and tragic impact of near-classic proportions. In the dingy squad room and office of a New York precinct police station, McLeod and his fellow detectives deal with a typical assortment of routine cases brought before them in a single day. Two are particularly significant: a young man who has stolen for the first time and a professional abortionist accused of performing an illegal operation. McLeod, unable to compromise his own misdirected principles of justice, tries to have the boy convicted and administers a beating to the abortionist. But when the man's lawyer, to protect his client, forces McLeod's wife into confessing her own use of the abortionist at one time, McLeod's world crashes down about him. The wife he has worshiped, his one true happiness in an otherwise routine existence, is no better to McLeod than the criminals he detests. At the climax, McLeod is shot by a prisoner attempting escape and killed—but not before he recognizes his errors, forgives his wife, frees the young man, and prays divine pardon for his own misdeeds.

MEN (*25; doubling possible*): 8 are 25–35 (4 minor); 2 are 27; 5 are 35–40 (1 is lead, requires outstanding actor; 2 minor; 1 has no lines); 5 are 40–50 (1 minor); 3 are 50–55 (2 minor); 2 are 60–70 (minor, 1 has no lines); several non-speaking extras may be added. WOMEN (*9; doubling possible*): 4 are 25–35 (2 minor); 1 is 27; 1 is 30–35; 1 is 35–45 (minor); 2 are 60–80 (minor). SET: Detective squad room and police lieutenant's office of a New York precinct police station, the 2 separated by a door and an invisible wall. Set should be severely naturalistic, closely approximating reality. Arena production possible but difficult. COSTUMES: Modern dress, late 1940s or early 1950s; a few patrolmen's uniforms; a person wears formal evening attire in 1 scene. DIFFICULTIES: Staging is extremely complex.

ROYALTY: $50–25, Dramatists Play Service. TEXT: Dramatists Play Service.

— o —

DARKNESS AT NOON (1950) SIDNEY KINGSLEY. Based on Arthur Koestler's novel, this play strikes boldly at the hollow tenets of dialectical materialism which destroy the human soul. Soviet Commissar N. S. Rubashov, who has had considerable power in the Party, is jailed at the play's beginning for having opposed the Party line through "counter-revolutionary tactics." For the next six weeks he is put through a series of tormenting experiences and memories, some occasioned by sadistic military police placed over him in the stark prison, the rest brought on by his own thoughts and silent recall of the events in his past life which have led to his imprisonment. His torment and frustration is dramatically heightened by considerable pathos and intense self-examination. In the end, rather than compromise himself by signing his captors' trumped-up confession, Rubashov goes stolidly to his execution with the ironic realization that he has helped establish the Communist rule which even now betrays his own ideals.

MEN (*26; doubling possible*): 12 are 25–35 (11 minor, 2 have no lines); 2 are 35–50 (minor); 7 are 40–60 (minor, 6 have no lines; 1 is 45–50 (minor); 2 are 50–55 (1 requires an outstanding actor); 1 is 55–65; 1 is 65–75; also soldiers, sailors, and jurors. WOMEN (3): 2 are 18–25 (minor; 1 has no lines); 1 is 20–35. SET: The corridor of an ancient Russian prison, buried deep underground; a thick, iron portcullis set into a high Byzantine arch; a steep flight of stone steps curving up; a tier of cells; a cell with an iron bed and straw mattress. Scrim walls dissolve to reveal the separate tiered cells and to define at least 7 other locales in flashback memory and dream sequences. Multiroom unit set employing theatrical naturalism is appropriate. Not suited to arena. COSTUMES: 20th-century modern (late 1930s); tattered prisoners' clothing and Russian military uniforms; assorted stark peasant garb; merchant sailors' dress; etc. DIFFICULTIES: The action of the play oscillates between the Russian prison and Rubashov's memories and thoughts. Scrim walls and complex lighting and sound effects are required to project convincingly the recurring visual and audial illusions.

ROYALTY: $50, Samuel French. TEXT: Samuel French.

— o —

THE FIRST LEGION (1934) EMMET LAVERY. Father Fulton and Father Rawleigh, two Jesuits, have begun to doubt their vocation when the sudden healing of the paralyzed Father Sierra restores their faith. Dr. Morell, the atheistic house physician, declares that the cure cannot be accounted for by science. The Rector, Father Duquesne, sees in it a divine sanction for the canonization of the founder of the House of St. Gregory, who had appeared to Father Sierra in a vision. A brilliant former lawyer, Father Mark Ahern, is to plead the cause in Rome. But Father Ahern cannot believe in this miracle. His doubts are confirmed when the doctor admits, under the seal of the confessional, that driven by sensationalism he had concealed what could easily be explained by medicine. In the meantime, the House is invaded by pilgrims who believe it another Lourdes. Unable to bear the weight of his secret any longer, Father Ahern is about to leave the Order when a crippled boy of unshakable faith takes the first few steps in his life. This time it is indeed a miracle. Well-constructed plot, sharply contrasted characterization in the all-male cast, and the simple presentation of the universal problem of human conscience have—particularly in Europe—made this play appealing to audiences of all faiths.

MEN (*10*): 4 are 30–40; 4 are 40–60; 2 are 60–70. BOY: 10–12. EXTRAS: Novices (can be cut). CHOIR: All male (recording possible but not recommended). SETS: Community room in the House of St. Gregory; 2 cell-like rooms; a confessional. The playwright recommends modified Gothic style. Sets need not be realistic. Suitable for arena. COSTUMES: Jesuit's cassocks; contemporary civilian clothes of a parish priest (Monsignor), the doctor, and the boy.

ROYALTY: $25, Samuel French. TEXT: Samuel French; music, apply Samuel French.

— o —

ROGER BLOOMER (1923) JOHN HOWARD LAWSON. This expressionistic play is an indictment of the American dream of success in the same way as are the works of such writers as Sinclair Lewis and Sherwood Anderson. Roger is the only son of a prosperous Iowa couple who want him to go to Yale and make a success of his life. He rebels, and with the help of a shopgirl, Louise, escapes from his family to New York. There he gradually becomes more and more disillusioned and destitute. Louise is killed under odd circumstances, and Roger is at first suspected and then released, with the result that he develops a new understanding of life. In and around the narrative sections of the skeleton plot are woven dream sequences, stream-of-consciousness musings, and dance interpretations. The climax is a giant montage, half-nightmare, half-vision, in which Roger at last finds his way of life.

MEN (*18*): 2 are 18–20; 1 is 40; 2 are 50–60; 13 are of varying ages (minor). Doubling possible. WOMEN (*10*): 3 past middle age and 1 young have the major parts. Of the other 6, 2 are young, 2 somewhat older, 2 are ancient. SETS: Author suggests "division of the stage into sections" with articles of furniture and portable settings, and painted drops "conveying impression" of many scenes. Visual aspect important. COSTUMES: Approximately 1920s. Final scene requires impressionistic dance costumes. DIFFICULTIES: Expressionistic style presents problems of both design and direction, particularly in the closing allegorical dance scene; complicated play to produce.

ROYALTY: Apply publisher. TEXT: In *Drama and Theatre* (Holt).

— o —

THE MEMBER OF THE WEDDING (1949) CARSON
McCULLERS. A touching character sketch of a girl in that
lonely state of hopes and fears when she first ceases to be a
child. Frankie, an awkward, hot-tempered, and highly imaginative ugly duckling of twelve, feels that the world should
take notice of her. She longs for companionship; she must
have a *we*. Her mother is dead, her father pays little attention
to her, and the older girls refuse to elect her to their club.
Most of her time she has to spend with Berenice Sadie Brown,
the good-natured cook, and with her little cousin, John Henry,
a nice, well-mannered busybody of seven. That cannot be all
life has to offer. In her frustration she decides to accompany
her brother Jarvis and his bride on their honeymoon. She is
heartbroken when they leave without her. Three months later,
Frankie has become Frances and the freckled thirteen-year-
old football husky next door appears to be a Greek god.
Adapting her novel for the stage, Mrs. McCullers did not
attempt to follow the established pattern of dramatic construction. "It is an inward play," she writes, "and the conflicts
are inward conflicts. The antagonist is not personified, but is
the human condition of life."

MEN (*4*): 2 are 20–25 (1 is a Negro); 2 are 40–60 (1 is a
Negro). WOMEN (*4*): 1 is 18–24; 1 is 25–35 (minor); 1 is 40
(requires a strong, mature Negro actress); 1 is about 90
(minor, Negress; can be cut). BOYS (*2*): 1 is 7 (a very important part); 1 is 13 (minor). GIRLS (*4*): 1 is 12 (she must
be a sensitive, outstanding very young-appearing actress); 3 are
13–15 (minor). SET: Kitchen and back yard in a small town
in Georgia. Set need not be realistic. Suitable for arena production. COSTUMES: Southern provincial.

ROYALTY: $50–25, Dramatists Play Service. TEXT: In
Famous American Plays of the 1940's (Dell).

—— o ——

JEANNE D'ARC (1906) PERCY MACKAYE. Tragedy. The
source of this play is the familiar Joan of Arc story, but with
more concentration on the childhood and successful campaigns
of the heroine and less on the trial than most other playwrights
have given. Another difference in approach is in the treatment
of the voices and visions; each vision is played out for the
audience but is neither seen nor heard by cast members other
than Jeanne. The script is written in a rhythmic prose. (See

also Shaw's play on the same theme; page 140.)

MEN (*35*): 17 appear in more than 1 act. Age requirements from very old to very young. Acting ability is not so important as in other plays because of the epic or oratorio style of the script. WOMEN (*7*): Only 2 appear in more than 2 acts; other 5 are young. Also calls for St. Michael, St. Margaret, and St. Catherine; "Ladies of Lorraine," who are fairies in the opening scene; and extras. COSTUMES: 15th-century peasant and court dress, with the heavenly spirits costumed in Victorian lyric style. SETS: 6 sets called for, but a current production would almost certainly substitute some abstract treatment, which the style of the play will permit. DIFFICULTIES: Some reworking of dated material probably necessary.

ROYALTY: Apply publisher. TEXT: Macmillan, 1928; out of print.

—o—

THE SCARECROW (1910) PERCY MACKAYE. A "tragedy of the ludicrous." The story is the familiar one of love making a human being out of a witch, but it is handled in an unusual manner. The Devil, in a "Yankee improvisation," joins a Massachusetts woman blacksmith in making a scarecrow into which life is breathed by means of a continually smoking pipe. The figure, introduced into the community as Lord Ravensbane, is coached to ensnare Rachel Merton, niece of the oppressive and self-righteous Justice Merton. In so doing, Lord Ravensbane falls in love with Rachel and nobly turns against his creators. He destroys himself by breaking his pipe when he learns that he is only an animated scarecrow. When he does this, the Mirror of Truth, which shows men as they really are, suddenly reflects him as a true man. The plot introduces a group of interesting characters and an atmosphere in which the work of the urbane Devil, the punishment of the hollowly righteous Merton, and the skill of the European dandy in dazzling the naïve "best people of Massachusetts" are all effective and exciting.

MEN (*10*): 4 about 50; others from young and attractive Lord Ravensbane to ageless Dickon, the Yankee Devil. WOMEN (*6*): 2 are mature or older; 1 offers an actress wide scope; the 3 young roles are not difficult. SETS: Justice Merton's parlor; blacksmith shop, which requires many props and some trick effects, notably the changing of the wrought-iron scare-crow into a man and the Mirror of Truth. COSTUMES: Early American provincial, except Lord Ravensbane, who dresses as a European dandy; 1 uniform required.

ROYALTY: $25, Samuel French. TEXT: Samuel French.

—o—

J.B. (1956) ARCHIBALD MACLEISH. A modern version of the Biblical story of Job set in a worn, tattered circus which symbolizes the world. Two ex-actors, Zuss and Nickles, now circus vendors, enter and, prompted by a distant voice, play the parts of God and Satan in the struggle for Job's soul. J.B., the modern counterpart of Job, is a successful businessman. As in the biblical story, everything is taken from him—his children are killed, his fortune is lost in an atomic disaster, and his wife, advising him to curse God and die, leaves him. He asks God for a reason and demands to know his guilt. Three comforters arrive, a psychiatrist, a Marxist, and a dogmatic clergyman. They fail to help Job, and he again demands an answer from God. Biblical lines are quoted by the distant voice, and he seems to repent his query. Then, as he is restored by God, he sees the answer—that mortals can never know God's reasons, but that they are given love as a comfort. (See also *The Tragedy of Job*, page 445.)

MEN (9): 1 is an off stage voice; 3 are 20–30 (2 assume several small roles); 5 are 35–50. WOMEN (7): 2 are 20–30 (minor); 5 are 30–50. BOYS (4): 8–13 (minor). GIRLS (3): 6–12 (minor). SETS: A circus tent with a ring and a platform symbolizing heaven. Arena production possible. COSTUMES: Contemporary soldier uniforms; evening clothes; maid outfits; masks for God and Satan; threadbare clothing.

ROYALTY: $50, Samuel French. TEXT: Samuel French.

—o—

CHILDREN OF DARKNESS (1929) EDWIN JUSTUS MAYER. Mr. Snap, the jailer, welcomes young Cartwright, a poet, to his lodgings adjoining Newgate Prison, 1725. Here prisoners are given special privileges by Snap (who robs them at every turn) and are waited upon by Laetitia, his buxom daughter. A debtor, the philosophic Count La Ruse, rich only in language and wit ("If naught else damns you, Madam, your choice of adjectives will"), has become Laetitia's lover. She is as determined to keep him her prisoner as he is determined to be free one day to see his illegitimate son. He enters into a scheme to obtain money from Jonathan Wild, the highwayman of Henry Fielding fame, on the pretense of buying a reprieve for Wild. Once the Count has the money, Wild is taken away and executed. La Ruse, now in a position to pay his debts, encounters a newly arrived prisoner, the venomous Lord Wainwright, a poisoner who has murdered his wife and son because he realized La Ruse was the boy's father. La Ruse, impressed by Cartwright's poetic talent and pure spirit, comes to look upon him as a son. He gives the money to Cartwright, urging him to seek his destiny. When the boy is gone, La Ruse commits suicide, leaving Laetitia who is pregnant by him for the detestable Wainwright. One of the unsung comedies of the American theatre.

MEN (9): 1 is 20–30; 1 is 35–40; 1 is 35–50; 2 are 40–50; 1 is 45; 1 is 50–60; 2 (the bailiffs) may be any age. WOMEN: (1): 29. SET: A room in a house adjoining Newgate Prison, 1725. Arena productions have been given. COSTUMES: Mid-18th century (see Hogarth's engravings for *The Rake's Progress*); only one nobleman's costume need be elaborate. DIFFICULTIES: The cynical wit as well as the savage and sardonic humor of the characters require exceptional and sophisticated actors in every role.

ROYALTY: $25–20, Samuel French. TEXT: Samuel French.

— O —

ALL MY SONS (1947) ARTHUR MILLER. During World War II the shipment of defective cylinder heads has caused the death of more than twenty combat fliers. Joe Keller, manufacturer of airplane parts, has been exonerated but his partner is still serving a prison term. Keller has two sons: Larry, a pilot declared missing for more than three years, and Chris, who has just returned from combat. Chris and Ann Deever, Larry's former fiancée and daughter of Keller's partner, intend to marry in spite of the resistance of Chris' mother, Kate Keller, who refuses to believe that Larry is dead. It is gradually revealed that her attitude is based upon her knowledge of her husband's guilt. Keller's negligence has sent many young men to death, but she will not concede that Larry could have been among them. Chris desperately tries to believe in his father's innocence until he can no longer lie to himself. In a dramatic climax he forces his father to confess. The idealistic son can find no excuse for his father's facile business ethics. Joe first promises to give himself up, then commits suicide. Several supporting actors contribute to the atmosphere of life in the back yard of a typical American home—in this case a home shattered because its owner has subordinated his responsibilities toward society to his own financial welfare.

MEN (5): 3 are 30–35; 1 is 40; 1 is 55–60. WOMEN (4): 2 are 24–28; 1 is 40; 1 is 50–55. BOY: 8. SET: Back yard of the Keller home in the outskirts of an American town. Realistic scenery recommended. Arena production possible. COSTUMES: Middle-class American, shortly after World War II.
ROYALTY: $35–25, Dramatists Play Service. TEXT: *Famous American Plays of the 1940's* (Dell).

—o—

DEATH OF A SALESMAN (1949) ARTHUR MILLER. Willy Loman, a traveling salesman, always believed that back-slapping and perseverance were the keys to success in business as well as in life. At sixty-three he has reached a dead end. The long drives on the road make him dizzy. He talks to himself and has hallucinations in which past and present are intermingled. Episodes of long ago gain a new meaning in their relation to the present. Loman is seen pampering his boys, Biff and Happy; he is convinced Biff will conquer the world as easily as he does the football field. Willy Loman appears to himself the perfect American, the ideal father and husband—an image shattered for Biff when the boy comes upon his father in a hotel with a woman. Willy's older brother, Ben, who had led a life of adventure instead of only dreaming about it and then died many years ago, comes to call him again and again. The tired salesman pulls himself together. He asks his young, indifferent boss for an in-town job but is fired instead. Biff forces him to realize that they are both failures. Willy Loman is through. His insurance is all paid up; if he dies in an accident he will be worth more than he is alive. He goes to the garage and starts the car. Loman, the successful go-getter, was a fake; Loman, the beaten, pitiful human being, attains stature through the devotion of his wife, Linda, who loves him for what he is and who foresees the catastrophe but can do nothing to prevent it.

MEN (*8*): 5 are 25–35; 3 are 55–65 (1 requires outstanding actor). WOMEN (*5*): 3 are 18–25; 1 is 30–40; 1 is 50–60. SET: Unit setting of Loman's house; its room, kitchen, cellar, and back yard. The same scenery, transformed by lighting, also serves for various locations in Boston and New York City. Transparent walls. Complex lighting, including projection. Arena production possible. COSTUMES: Middle-class American, present time and mid-1930s. DIFFICULTIES: The numerous transitions from the present to the past require subtle direction and disciplined, experienced acting.

ROYALTY: $50–25, Dramatists Play Service. TEXT: Viking; music by Alex North (Dramatists Play Service).

—— o ——

THE CRUCIBLE (1952) ARTHUR MILLER. In dramatizing the Salem witch hunts at the end of the seventeenth century, Miller explores the roots of intolerance and mass hysteria. A few girls, fettered by a rigid Puritan moral code, seek an outlet in secret dances at night in the woods. Discovered, they manage to elude punishment by declaring themselves victims of the Devil and by ecstatically accusing several harmless women of witchcraft. The whole community is caught in a frenzy. Envy, greed, and superstition rule. The Devil's supposed human assistants are blamed for every mishap, be it the miscarriage of a woman or the death of a pig. Deputy-Governor Danforth, a monster of dogmatism, meticulously executes the verdict of mob madness. The central plot concerns John Proctor, a forthright farmer, his wife Elizabeth, and Abigail, the ringleader of the girls. Abigail had once seduced Proctor and now tries to eliminate Elizabeth by declaring her a witch. Attempting to clear his wife, Proctor implicates himself. He refuses to save his neck with a false confession and is led to the gallows. Though the characters sometimes seem to lack human substance, they are effectively profiled and clash in grippingly dramatic scenes. In his concern for historical accuracy and a universal comment, Miller does not emphasize contemporary parallels.

MEN (*10*): 5 are 25–40 (2 minor); 3 are 40–60; 2 are 70–85. WOMEN (*5*): 1 is 25–35; 3 are 40–60 (1 is Negro, 1 is minor); 1 is 70–75. GIRLS (*5*): 1 is 10; 4 are 16–17. SETS: Bedroom; common room; wood; vestry room; prison cell. Heavy, rude furniture. The author recommends the use of

drapes for backdrop and side curtains. Suitable for arena. Cos-
TUMES: Severe New England Puritan, 1692.

ROYALTY: $50–25, Dramatists Play Service. TEXT: Bantam.

— o —

A VIEW FROM THE BRIDGE (1955) ARTHUR MILLER.
Eddie Carbone, a longshoreman of Italian descent, lives on
the Brooklyn waterfront with his wife, Beatrice, and his orphaned niece, Catherine. He treats the 18-year-old girl like
a child and loves her, so he thinks, like a daughter. When two
of his wife's cousins, still poorer than he, are smuggled in from
Sicily to work illegally on the docks, he gives them shelter in
his home. Marco, the older Sicilian, is quiet, sturdy, and a
hard worker. His strikingly handsome brother, Rodolpho, is
easygoing, always ready for a joke and a song. When Catherine and Rodolpho fall in love and want to marry, Eddie refuses to let the girl go. Driven near insanity by his repressed
desire for his ward, he accuses Rodolpho of homosexuality
and of wanting to marry only in order to obtain the American
citizenship. When Eddie fails to convince the girl, he reports
the Sicilians to the immigration authorities. Before being de-
ported, Marco kills Eddie. All this is told in flashbacks by an
elderly, compassionate lawyer who serves as chorus and, in
the end, draws a parallel between the brutal deeds on the
stage and the violent myths of antiquity.

MEN (9): 7 are 20–35 (1 must sing bel canto, 5 minor);
1 is 40; 1 is 50–60. WOMEN (2): 1 is 18; 1 is 40. EXTRAS:
Longshoremen; neighbors. SET: The Carbone apartment and
its environment on the Brooklyn waterfront. Skeletal unit
setting providing simultaneous acting space for the slightly
elevated apartment, the street at stage level, and the lawyer's
office forestage. Columns recall Greek and roman antiquity.
Arena production possible. COSTUMES: Contemporary lower-
class American.

ROYALTY: $50–25, Dramatists Play Service. TEXT: Drama-
tists Play Service or Bantam.

— o —

AWAKE AND SING (1935) CLIFFORD ODETS. A Jewish
family, the Bergers, live in an apartment in the Bronx, struggling to survive during the Depression. The young son, Ralph,
is pulled in three directions. He loves a girl and would like

to marry her. His grandfather, who plays Caruso records and reads revolutionary material, urges him to revolt, to try to do something to stop the unhappiness in the world, rather than marry and forget it. His mother violently opposes his marriage because the girl is poor. The mother wants him to accept the world as it is and help with the struggle to make ends meet. In the end he accepts the grandfather's philosophy and decides to awake and sing. The family is sympathetically drawn. In addition to the mother, the grandfather, and Ralph, there are Ralph's sister, a proud, beautiful girl forced into an unhappy marriage in order to have a father for her expected child; Uncle Morty, a wealthy, shallow businessman; and Ralph's father, a touching failure.

MEN (7): 3 are 20–30 (1 limps); 4 are 45–65 (1 minor and has a German accent). WOMEN (3): 2 are 20–30; 1 is 45–55. SET: An apartment in the Bronx; should be realistic. COSTUMES: 1930 clothing which should reflect the struggle for money. DIFFICULTIES: Bronx Jewish dialect.

ROYALTY: $50, Dramatists Play Service. TEXT: Random.

—— o ——

GOLDEN BOY (1937) CLIFFORD ODETS. Joe Bonaparte, a young boy of Italian descent, is torn between playing the violin, which gives him fulfillment and a feeling of humanity, or making money as a prize fighter. He falls in love with Lorna Moon, his manager's mistress, who returns his love but won't leave Tom, the manager, because he needs her. Joe becomes a champion, but kills another fighter when he knocks him out. He realizes then that he has won a hollow victory, and that he had turned his back on the happiness he would have known as a musician. It is too late to return to music—his hands are ruined. He and Lorna go off together to find a city "where poverty is no shame, and a man is glad to be himself." In the last scene, Joe's father, an old-fashioned Italian who wants Joe to be a musician, and the men from the fight game are arguing over Joe's future when word comes that Joe and Lorna have been killed in an automobile accident.

MEN (16): 9 are 20–30 (3 minor; 1 is Negro; 1 Jewish accent; 1 Italian accent); 7 are 40–60 (3 minor; 1 Italian accent). WOMEN (2): 25–30. BOY: 12–16 (minor). SETS: Possible to use partial settings or set pieces. A cheap office;

the Bonaparte home; a park bench; a gymnasium; a gym dressing room. COSTUMES: Lower-middle class, 1930; some outfits for fighters.

ROYALTY: $25, Dramatists Play Service. TEXT: Dramatists Play Service.

— o —

THE COUNTRY GIRL (1949) CLIFFORD ODETS. Frank Elgin, an alcoholic has-been actor, is offered a chance to make a comeback when Bernie, a dynamic young director, offers him a role. Frank is afraid to admit his weaknesses or fight his own battles, so he lets his wife Georgie fight for him. He compensates for his failures by lying about Georgie and blaming her for his problems. Bernie believes him and is hostile to Georgie. The truth is revealed when Frank goes on a binge and is found drunk in his dressing room. With the help of Georgie and Bernie, he makes a success in the play and gains self-respect by learning to stand up for himself and discovering that it is no crime to admit failure or weakness. The backstage atmosphere is theatrically effective, established by the settings and such characters as a young playwright, a cynical producer, and a naïve ingenue. Style and language are powerful and realistic.

MEN (6): 3 are 25–30; 3 are 45–55 (1 minor). WOMEN (2): 1 is 30–40; 1 is 18–23. SETS: Realistic, may be fragmentary: bare stage; cheap furnished rooms; Boston theatre dressing room; New York theatre dressing room. COSTUMES: Modern.

ROYALTY: $50–25, Dramatists Play Service. TEXT: Dramatists Play Service.

— o —

BEYOND THE HORIZON (1918) EUGENE O'NEILL. Robert Mayo, a sensitive youth, has long dreamed of leaving the family farm for adventure in far-off lands. On the eve of his departure he confesses his love to Ruth, the girl the family assumed Robert's brother, Andrew, would marry. Robert marries Ruth while his brother, unable to remain near the couple, goes to sea against his father's wishes. Robert, unsuited mentally and physically for farming, is a failure; Andrew achieves success at sea. Ruth realizes it is Andrew she really loves and hopes to tell him so when he returns following his father's death. Before she is able to do so, however, Andrew goes back to sea after telling Ruth that he realizes he never loved her. Ruth and Robert's child dies and the farm deteriorates. When Andrew returns from his second voyage, he finds his brother impoverished and dying, longing for the freedom he never found. Ruth watches, too broken to comfort Robert or hope for a life with Andrew.

MEN (6): 3 are 58–65 (2 minor); 2 are 23–37; 1 is 30–35 (minor). WOMEN (3): 2 are 48–55; 1 is 20. GIRL: 3. SETS: A field with a highway in spring; interior of a farmhouse living room; top of a hill on a farm in summer; field of a farm in late autumn. Suitable for arena production. COSTUMES: Modern dress and farm clothes.

ROYALTY: $35–25, Dramatists Play Service. TEXT: Dramatists Play Service.

—— o ——

ANNA CHRISTIE (1920) EUGENE O'NEILL. Chris Christopherson, the tough hard-drinking old captain of a coal barge, blames all his failures upon "dat ole davil, sea." To protect his daughter Anna from his sordid environment, he sent her as a child of five to a farm in the West. Now, 15 years later, Anna returns. It is obvious to everybody except her father that she has become a cynical prostitute. Chris manages to get rid of Marthy, a good-natured, worn-out woman who had shared his cabin for years, and leads his daughter triumphantly to his barge. Anna is strangely purified by the sea and by the fog that seems to blot out her past. She falls in love with Mat Burke, a husky Irish stoker, who impetuously wants to make her his wife. When Chris refuses to give his daughter to a sailor, Anna defiantly reveals the truth about herself. The outraged, desperate men go ashore and get drunk. Anna cannot bring herself to leave the boat, still hoping that Mat might return. He does, and together they face the future. Their fate is undetermined ". . . all of them at the end have a vague foreboding that, although they have had their moment, the decision still rests with the sea which has achieved the conquest of Anna."

MEN (8): 5 are 20–30 (4 minor); 3 are 40–50 (2 minor). WOMEN (2): 1 is about 20; 1 is 40–50. EXTRAS: 3 sailors. SETS: Saloon on the waterfront; stern of a coal barge; cabin of the barge. Sets need not be realistic. Arena production possible. COSTUMES: Apparel of people on the waterfront around 1910. The play can easily be adapted to take place in the present.

ROYALTY: $35–25, Dramatists Play Service. TEXT: Dramatists Play Service.

—— o ——

THE EMPEROR JONES (1920) EUGENE O'NEILL. Practicing tricks learned from the whites, the Negro former Pullman-car porter and escaped convict Brutus Jones has made himself emperor of an island in the West Indies, "as yet not self-determined by White Marines," and has exploited his primitive and superstitious subjects. One day his "palace" is deserted. Jones knows that his time is up. From the hills comes the faint, steady thump of a tom-tom. Jones is not afraid. As he explains to the only remaining person, the low-caste British trader Smithers, he has made his plans. This very night he will cross the forest and sail to a country where his gold is deposited. The action of the six following monodramatic scenes occurs in the mind of the hero. The persistent beat of the tom-tom accelerates at the rate of his growing psycho-biological fear as he faces the ghosts of his own past and that of his forefathers: the "Little Formless Fears," the man he has killed, a chain gang, a slave auction, the galleys, and a Congo witch doctor. Crazedly seeking his way, Jones staggers in a circle through the forest and returns to its edge where the avengers are waiting.

MEN (3): 2 are 30–45 (1 requires a powerful Negro actor, the other must be able to speak Cockney); 1 is 50–70 (Negro, minor). WOMAN: 60–80 (Negress, minor). EXTRAS: The "Little Formless Fears" ("about the size of a creeping child"); Negro convicts; prison guard; planters, auctioneer; slaves; Congo witch doctor. SETS: Bare room in the Emperor's primitive palace; the edge of the forest. Expressionistic style. Arena production possible. COSTUMES: Worn-out white riding suit; the Emperor's pompous uniform; a Pullman-car porter's uniform; a prison guard's uniform; apparel of Southern planters around 1850; a crocodile's head; rags and loin cloths. DIFFICULTIES: Rhythmic coordination of the pantomime action is essential for creating an atmosphere of intense growing fear. Plays less than 2 hours.

ROYALTY: $35–25, Dramatists Play Service. TEXT: Appleton.

—— o ——

THE HAIRY APE (1922) EUGENE O'NEILL. Yank Smith, stoker on an ocean liner, takes pride in his great strength and sense of belonging. Mildred Douglas, a passenger, comes to the stokehole. Revolted by his primitive appearance, she calls him a "filthy beast" and faints. Yank's sense of security is shattered; the rest of the play traces his attempts to justify his place in a society which turns its back on him. He is scorned in turn by a church crowd on Fifth Avenue, his cellmates in jail, the I.W.W., and the police. In the last scene he finds himself in front of the gorilla cage at the zoo. After a poignant monologue he steps into the cage to assert his kinship with the ape, but is rejected again as the gorilla crushes him to death.

MEN (*12 or more*): Total will vary with number of stokers used; all 20–40 (1 Cockney; 1 Irish; several assorted dialects). WOMEN (*5*): 4 are 20–30 (3 minor); 1 is 40–60. SETS: The forecastle; the deck; the stokehole; Fifth Avenue; a jail cell; the I.W.W. office and street outside; the monkey house at the zoo. Sets should not be realistic. Unit arrangement, revolving stage, or set pieces could be effective. Arena not recommended. COSTUMES: Early 1920s or contemporary. Several uniforms required; gorilla suit. DIFFICULTIES: Staging of the last scene presents a problem, although it can be done with shadows projected onto the stage.
ROYALTY: $35–25, Dramatists Play Service. TEXT: Random.

—— o ——

DESIRE UNDER THE ELMS (1924) EUGENE O'NEILL. Tragedy. Ephraim Cabot is a stern, tyrannical old man, hard as the stony ground of his New England homestead. Many years ago he married and buried two wives. His three sons hate him. Simeon and Peter join the California gold rush. Eben, the youngest son, stays. Blaming his mother's death on his father, he considers himself the rightful heir of the house under the brooding elms and will not yield when Cabot takes young, sensuous Abbie Putnam as his third wife. In the ensuing struggle for possession of the farm, Abbie seduces Eben so she can bear a child that Cabot would believe to be his own and thus secure her inheritance to the property, but the two young people are caught in the vortex of an all-consuming passion. To prove her unrestrained love for Eben, Abbie smothers the child. Repelled, Eben first reports her to the sheriff, then returns to her side and claims his share in her crime. With the conscious, almost exalted acceptance of their doom, these two tormented creatures acquire the basic grandeur of human beings, inspiring terror and pity in the Aristotelian sense.

MEN (8): 2 are 20–30 (1 minor; he must play the fiddle); 4 are 30–40 (2 minor); 2 are 70–80 (1 minor). WOMEN (2): 1 is 18–25 (minor); 1 is 35. EXTRAS: Farm people. SET: In and immediately outside the Cabot farmhouse, 1850. Unit setting emphatically recommended since part of the action takes place simultaneously outside the house and in some of its rooms. "Two enormous elms are on each side of the house. They appear to protect and at the same time to subdue. There is a sinister maternity in their aspect. . . ." Suitable for arena. COSTUMES: Apparel of New England farm people, 1850. DIFFICULTIES: New England dialect.

ROYALTY: $35–25; Dramatists Play Service. TEXT: New American Library.

— o —

THE GREAT GOD BROWN (1925) EUGENE O'NEILL. O'Neill experimented with the use of masks in this play to dramatize the lack of understanding in human relationships. Outwardly, Dion Anthony is gay, creative, and sensual as a young Pan. This is the Dion his wife Margaret knows and loves, the Dion of the Mask. When the mask is removed, Dion appears haunted, filled with deep sadness, a portrait of the spiritual and lonely artist. When Margaret glimpses him unmasked, she is frightened and fails to understand him. The prostitute, Cybel, understands the unmasked Dion: she believes that life itself is not sacred—only the *you* inside is. Dion's best friend, William Brown, hopes to acquire Dion's power for love, and in protecting him also seeks to possess him. Dion wills himself to Brown and dies. Brown assumes Dion's mask and identity and takes his place in the family, gaining Margaret's love, which he has desired since childhood. But fully to become Dion he must kill Brown, the Brown beneath Dion's mask. Calling her "Earth Mother," Brown dies in the arms of Cybel. Asked the name of the body, Cybel replies, "Man!" Margaret, surrounded by her sons, finds solace in her belief that love does not die and Dion lives under her heart.

MEN (9): 3 are 18 (minor); 2 are 25–35 (must be outstanding actors); 2 are 20–30 (minor); 2 are 50–60 (minor). WOMEN (5): 1 is 25–35; 2 are 20–30 (1 minor); 2 are 45–50 (minor). SETS: The pier of the Casino; sitting room of Margaret Anthony's apartment; Billy Brown's office; Cybel's parlor; drafting room of Brown's office; library of Brown's home. Unit set possible; play may also be produced with simple tables and benches or entirely with lights. COSTUMES: Moderate modern dress of middle class. The masks, essential to the success of the production, require special consideration.

ROYALTY: $35–25, Dramatists Play Service. TEXT: In *Nine Plays by Eugene O'Neill* (Random).

— o —

MARCO MILLIONS (1925) EUGENE O'NEILL. Unable to find a hundred wise men who could prove the value of Christianity to Kublai Khan, the ruler of the East, the "sardonically resigned" Pope sends a 15-year-old boy, Marco Polo, instead. In Cathay, Marco invents the cannon, introduces paper money, breaks the heart of little Princess Kukachin, and returns 15 years later to Venice, a millionaire, where he marries a former sweetheart, Donata, now a fat, bovine lady. Marco's development into a hard-boiled businessman is depicted in three, mainly satirical travel scenes, presenting the civilizations of Persia, India, and Mongolia. The generous spirit of Oriental culture is personified in Kublai Khan, its wisdom in the sage Chu-Yim, and its tender beauty in Kukachin. The scenes set in the East are poetically powerful and end in tragedy—the old Kublai Khan weeping at the coffin of his "Little Flower." In the Epilogue, Marco Polo appears among the applauding theatre audience. Only for a moment disturbed by what he has seen on the stage, he leaves, a complacent man of property.

MEN (*32; can be reduced by doubling to about 18*): 1 is 18–20 (requires an outstanding actor who appears to be 15 at the beginning of the play, and 33 at the end); 6 are 20–30 (4 minor); 20 are 30–50 (15 minor); 5 are 50–70 (2 minor). WOMEN (5): 1 is 17–25; 4 are about 30 (minor). GIRL: 12.

EXTRAS: Ladies and gentlemen of Venice; soldiers; musicians; servants; people of Persia, India, Mongolia, Cathay; courtiers; nobles; ladies; wives; warriors of Kublai's court; musicians; dancers; chorus of mourners. SETS: 12 locations in Italy, Syria, Persia, India, Mongolia, and the Empire of Cathay toward the close of the 13th century; resplendent Western and Eastern palaces; outside of Donata's home on a canal in Venice; a sacred tree in Persia; the royal wharf in Zayton; deck of Princess Kukachin's junk. This play calls for fanciful and elaborate scenery. Many of the visual effects cannot be achieved in an arena production. Unit set has been successfully used. COSTUMES: Various ranks and classes of Occidental and Oriental civilization in the 13th century. Costumes should be rich and colorful. DIFFICULTIES: The always contrasting, never blending, satirical and poetic elements must be subtly balanced in order to facilitate a swift change of mood. Plays for 3-4 hours.

ROYALTY: $35–25, Dramatists Play Service. TEXT: In *Nine Plays by Eugene O'Neill* (Random).

—— o ——

STRANGE INTERLUDE (1928) EUGENE O'NEILL. Nina Leeds hates her father and leaves home because he has prevented her from marrying her fiancé, killed near the end of the war. She returns home after her father dies, marries Sam Evans and becomes pregnant. When she learns of a streak of insanity in her husband's family she destroys her unborn child. Nina then makes a bargain with Dr. Darrell and gives birth to his child. She watches her son grow up and marry. After Sam dies she marries Charlie Marsden, an old admirer who has become a father image for her.

MEN (5): First appear in the play as follows: Marsden 35; Leeds 55; Darrell 27; Evans 25; Gordon 11 (then 21). Most men age variously during the 25 years that elapse. WOMEN (3): Nina ages from 20–45; Madeline is 19; Mrs. Evans is 45. SETS: A library; dining room; sitting room; another sitting room; the afterdeck of a motor cruiser; a terrace. Realistic settings probably most effective. Arena production possible. COSTUMES: Upper-middle class American, 1918–1943. DIFFICULTIES: O'Neill uses asides and soliloquies to reveal his characters' thoughts, and employs these devices as frequently as traditional dialogue. Playing time is about 4 hours.

ROYALTY: $35–25, Dramatists Play Service. TEXT: In *Three Plays* (Knopf).

—— o ——

MOURNING BECOMES ELECTRA (1931) EUGENE O'NEILL. Tragedy. O'Neill achieved with this trilogy "a modern psychological approximation of the Greek sense of fate . . . , which an intelligent audience of today, possessed of no belief in gods or supernatural retribution, could accept and be moved by." Retaining the structure of Aeschylus' tragedy (*q.v.*), he parallels the fall of the House of Atreus with that of a proud New England family, the House of Mannon. Townspeople gathered in front of the Mannon house form "a chorus of types representing the human background to the Mannon tragedy."

In the first play, *Homecoming*, they watch Christine Mannon and her daughter Lavinia with awe and suspicion, and try to solve the mystery behind the cold, forbidding façade of the house and its inhabitants. General Ezra Mannon is expected to return soon from the Civil War. In his absence, his wife has begun a love affair with sea captain Adam Brant, a member of a "disgraced" branch of the Mannon family. Lavinia hates her mother. Is it that she cannot bear to see her adored father betrayed, or is it, as Christine asserts, that the girl wants her mother's place as the wife of Ezra, as the mistress of Adam Brant, and as the mother of her beloved brother Orin? The general returns and is poisoned by Christine and her lover. But Lavinia knows.

The second part, *The Hunted*, comprises Lavinia's revenge. Orin comes home from an army hospital. He loves his mother intensely. Christine and Lavinia struggle for the domination of the weak young man. Lavinia wins. Orin kills Brant and drives his mother into suicide.

The third play, *The Haunted*, ends with the disintegration of the House of Mannon. Seeking to forget, Orin and Lavinia have traveled to exotic lands. A striking change has come over them. Orin resembles his father, while Lavinia has become sensuous and feminine like her mother. She wants to begin a new, uncomplicated life as the wife of a young neighbor, Peter Niles. Orin becomes engaged to Peter's sister, Hazel, but he is still "possessed by hate and death." In death alone can he join his mother. After Orin's suicide, Lavinia desperately tries to escape from her surroundings. But then she realizes she cannot marry Peter; the dead are too strong. Lavinia becomes her former self again. Not in death but in a long life of mourning will she expiate the curse upon her family. She returns into the house.

MEN (*13; doubling possible*): 2 are 20–25; 5 are 45–50 (3 minor); 6 are 60–75 (5 minor). WOMEN (*7*): 2 are 18–24 (1 requires outstanding actress); 2 are 35–45 (1 minor); 3 are 45–50 (minor). SETS: Grecian temple portico of the Mannon house, New England; Ezra's study, bedroom, and sitting room in the house; the stern of Brant's clipper ship. Sets should convey an atmosphere of imposing ugliness and decaying grandeur. Arena production, though technically possible, not recommended; there is a vast barrier between the House of Mannon and the rest of the world. COSTUMES: New England upper class at the time of the Civil War; 1 general's and 2 officers' uniforms of the Union Army; clothes of townsfolk. DIFFICULTIES: Even with considerable cutting, the complete trilogy has a playing time of more than 5 hours. Nevertheless, for the sake of its unity it should be performed in 1 evening— possibly with a dinner interval. The strong relationship among the Mannons, their physical and mental resemblance, requires a subtly formalized acting style.

ROYALTY: $75, Dramatists Play Service. TEXT: In *Three Plays* (Knopf).

— o —

AH, WILDERNESS! (1933) EUGENE O'NEILL. Comedy. The Millers, a typical middle-class American small-town family lead a pleasant and harmonious life. If there are complications, they can be resolved. Nat Miller, the head of the household, is a good-humored man, a loving husband, and a tolerant, understanding father. Essie, his loyal wife, has the gift for creating a happy home. Lily Miller, the maiden aunt; Sid Davis, the uncle who drinks too much; and four children complete the family portrait. Such plot as there is concerns Richard Miller, 16, whose love poems to Muriel McComber, his high school lady-love, provoke the wrath of her severe father. Misunderstood by the world, Richard seeks vice and depravity in the arms of a "college-tart." Though he succeeds only in getting very sick, his family is gravely alarmed. The next day, Richard is straightened out by his father about the facts of life, and, since he is also reconciled with Muriel, life could not be more beautiful. Nat and Essie watch with nostalgic affection the awakening of spring in Richard, but autumn, it seems, has its beauty, too.

MEN (7): 2 are 19 (1 minor); 2 are 25–40 (minor); 3 are 40–60. WOMEN (4): 2 are about 20 (1 minor); 2 are 40–50. BOYS (2): 1 is 11; 1 is 16. GIRLS (2): Both are 15. SETS: Sitting room of the Millers' modest home in a large small-town in Connecticut; dining room; back room of the bar in a small hotel; a strip of beach along the harbor. Arena production possible. COSTUMES: Middle-class American, early 20th century.

ROYALTY: $50, Samuel French. TEXT: Samuel French.

—— o ——

LONG DAY'S JOURNEY INTO NIGHT (1940) EUGENE O'NEILL. The past haunts the tragic Tyrone family. James Tyrone, a highly successful matinee idol well past his prime but still active, prefers to buy worthless land rather than spend his money for proper doctors to attend his family. His wife, Mary, nervous and ill, still reflects the innocence she possessed as a convent girl in spite of the loss of a child and long confinement in a hospital. Their older son, Jamie, who unsuccessfully followed his father into the theatre, is cynical and dissipated. Edmund, twenty-three, has returned from the sea with what the family fears is consumption; he is sensitive and studious and the idol of his mother even though it was his birth that caused a quack doctor summoned by Tyrone first to administer the drugs to which Mary has since been addicted. While she has promised not to take them again, Jamie believes Edmund's illness has so unnerved her that she is taking them secretly. As the day passes, his suspicion proves to be correct. Edmund learns he must go to a sanatorium. Jamie and Tyrone, drinking heavily, begin to evoke old sorrows. Jamie foresees that in destroying himself he may also destroy Edmund. Mary, lost in her memories, appears carrying her wedding gown in her arms, still attempting to find the past.

MEN (3): James is 65; Jamie is 33; Edmund is 23. All must be outstanding actors. WOMEN (2): Mary is 54 (requires a mature and experienced actress); Cathleen, the maid, is 20–30. SET: The plain and almost ugly living room of the Tyrone summer house, Connecticut, 1912, with a suggestion of a front porch as well as large front hallway. COSTUMES: Average summer dress, 1912. DIFFICULTIES: The 4 acts are long and not easily sustained unless performed by actors of unusual ability. An early curtain is necessary. Under no circumstances should this play be cut.

ROYALTY: Apply Richard J. Madden Play Co., 522 Fifth Ave., N.Y., N.Y. TEXT: Yale.

— o —

THE TEAHOUSE OF THE AUGUST MOON (1952)   JOHN PATRICK. Comedy. Purdy, pompous army colonel, sends Captain Fisby, a former college professor, to an Okinawan village to help make it self-supporting and to introduce democracy. Upon arriving, Fisby finds it is easier to accept the native customs than to try to follow Purdy's idea of "making the natives learn democracy even if he has to shoot everyone." He builds a teahouse instead of a pentagon-shaped schoolhouse and allows a geisha girl to instruct the ladies of the village in her art. The village becomes self-supporting through the sale of a native brandy. The satire in the play is directed at the army and at rigid American ideas of success, morality, and democracy. The play is narrated by a roguish native interpreter, Sakini. Various native types add color and humor. There is some use of dialogue in Okinawan, and a few dialects.

MEN (*18, 11 minor*): 9 are 25–40 (1 is a fat, professional wrestler); 8 are 40–60; 1 is 70–80. WOMEN (*8*): 2 are 25–30 (1 is required to do a dance); 5 are 30–50; 1 is 50–60. CHILDREN (*3*): 4–10 (either sex, no lines). SETS: 4 panels of split bamboo, in back of the house curtain, which raise and lower independently to reveal Col. Purdy's office; Captain Fisby's quarters (with a bundle-laden jeep and a goat); Tobiki village; office in Tobiki; a teahouse which is partially assembled in view of the audience. Not suitable for arena. COSTUMES: Threadbare Oriental clothing; kimonos; geisha-girl dress; white suits; army uniforms of the 1940s. DIFFICULTIES: The narrator carries much of the show; a strong actor is needed. The settings are elaborate and require a large stage since some of them are used simultaneously.

ROYALTY: $50–25, music, $5, Dramatists Play Service. TEXT: Dramatists Play Service.

— o —

ACCENT ON YOUTH (1934) SAMSON RAPHAELSON. Comedy. Steven Gaye, a successful playwright approaching old age, has attempted on various occasions to retire, travel, find real love, and start living life instead of writing about it. He was always stopped by an idea for a new play. Regardless of what happens to him, he can't help looking at life from the viewpoint of a playwright, manipulating it, and filing scenes for future reference. He has written a play about a romance between an old man and a young girl, and a parallel situation develops between him and his secretary. She leaves him for a younger man, but returns after a taste of life with an accent on youth. At the end of the play, somewhat older, Steven concludes that youth is not everything, and starts work on another play with the help of the girl. The play derives much of its humor from witticisms about the theatre, and from some very funny sight gags, comic entrances, and exits. The cast includes several actors and actresses and a very theatre-wise butler. The style is sophisticated, and the dialogue is fast-moving and witty.

MEN (6): 3 are 25–30 (all 3 look athletic); 3 are 45–60. WOMEN (3): 2 are 25; 1 is 50. SET: The study of an expensive New York duplex apartment, includes a bar and a piano, should be realistic. Excellent for arena. COSTUMES: The play was written in the 1930s, but could be costumed in modern dress; livery for a butler and fashionable evening cothes for men and women. DIFFICULTIES: The actors need a good sense of style to sustain the urbane dialogue. .

ROYALTY: $35, Samuel French. TEXT: Samuel French.

— o —

THE ADDING MACHINE (1923) ELMER RICE. This expressionistic play evokes a ghastly vision of mechanized civilization, stocked with shabby, commonplace little creatures. Mr. Zero is a nonentity. An office clerk adding up figures for twenty-five years, he is to be replaced by an adding machine. Desperate rather than rebellious, he kills the Boss and is tried and executed. After his death, Zero reaches the Elysian Fields, an idyllic country site, unbounded by the prison walls of human conventions. Mr. Zero has no use for unlimited freedom; he eschews the "unrespectable" place. A celestial repair shop for worn-out souls is more to his liking. There he is permitted to work on an adding machine for what he expects to be eter-

nity. But no! Allured by an illusory blonde called Hope, he is
led back to earth where his slave nature will find fulfillment in
operating a hyper-super adding machine with his big toe. The
characters are types, not individuals. In the first scene the
overawed little man remains silent while Mrs. Zero pours out
her reflections upon the movies and matrimony. At the office,
Zero and Miss Devore, a woman clerk, speak out their thoughts
while adding up figures. He thinks of sexual conquest and a
pay raise; she, of sexual surrender and suicide. The trial consists of Zero's incoherent stream-of-consciousness soliloquy to
a petrified jury. In his afterlife, Zero meets Shrdlu, who had
killed his sweet mother and is perplexed to find himself in
Heaven instead of Hell. Most impressive is the third scene, in
which the Zeros entertain the Twos, Threes, Fours, Fives, and
Sixes at a party starting with gossip and off-color jokes and
culminating in the exalted praise of Liberty and the unanimous
condemnation of foreigners, Catholics, Negroes, and Jews.

MEN (*14*): 3 are 20–30 (minor); 11 are 35–50 (7 minor).
WOMEN (*3*): 1 is 20–30 (minor); 2 are 35–50. SETS: Bedroom; office; living room; place of justice; graveyard; pleasant
place; another office. Scenery is to represent a distorted picture
of the world as it appears to Mr. Zero. Many scenic and lighting effects. Unit setting as well as arena production conceivable. COSTUMES: Stylized apparel of average city types in the
20th century. DIFFICULTIES: If the comic aspects are even
slightly overstressed, the audience will miss the central impact of the play.

ROYALTY: $50, Samuel French. TEXT: Samuel French.

—— o ——

STREET SCENE (1929) ELMER RICE. The heat and humidity of an oppressive New York summer evening have
driven the inhabitants of the huge, dilapidated tenement to
their windows or into the street. There they sit or lean and
comment upon the heat, the humidity, and other worn-out
topics. Conglomerated by circumstance, these Swedes, Irish,
Italians, Germans, and Jews, with their diverse social and
cultural backgrounds and their different moral and political
opinions, are a natural cross section of urban lower-class society. The happenings are commonplace, and so are the people.
There is the helpless white-collar clerk whose fragile wife is
expecting her first baby, the radical reformer, the good-natured

music teacher, the young deserted mother who faces eviction, the elderly spinster who has sacrificed her life for her ailing mother, the schoolteacher, the iceman, the policemen, the drunkards, the gossiping housewives, the shopgirls, the children—no one has been left out. Then tragedy strikes: a brutal stagehand finds his wife in the arms of the collector for the milk company and kills them. This is an exciting day for the people in the tenement. But life goes on, and soon another couple moves into the vacant apartment. Though it is mainly prejudice that keeps these people from total depersonalization in the metropolitan crucible, there is still hope: a young man and a girl seem to have the potential inner strength to resist their environment.

MEN (*27; doubling possible*): 6 are 20–30 (2 minor); 11 are 30–40 (7 minor); 7 are 40–50 (4 minor); 3 are 60 (2 minor). WOMEN (*15; doubling possible*): 6 are 18–25 (4 minor); 5 are 25–40 (2 minor); 4 are 40–55 (1 minor). BOYS (*3*): 2 are 10–12; 1 is 14–16. GIRLS (*2*): 1 is 8–10; 1 is 12–14. EXTRAS: Passers-by. SET: Realistic exterior of a walk-up brownstone house in a mean quarter of New York. Several practical windows at the 1st and the 2nd floor. Arena production not possible. COSTUMES: Everyday clothes of middle- and lower-class New Yorkers, 1928; 3 policemen's uniforms.

ROYALTY: $50, Samuel French. TEXT: In *Famous American Plays of the 1920's* (Dell).

— o —

COUNSELLOR–AT–LAW (1931) ELMER RICE. George Simon, once a penniless Jewish boy in the gutters of the East Side, is now one of New York's most prominent attorneys and the husband of a society beauty. At the height of his career he is suddenly confronted with the threat of disbarment when one of his anti-Semitic colleagues discovers a flaw in his professional record: five years before he had used a rigged alibi to save a man from life imprisonment. In a desperate counterattack, Simon succeeds in forcing his blue-blooded opponent to retract his accusations. Deserted by his wife, who has left for Europe with an admirer of her own social background, he attempts to take his life. Regina, his loyal, efficient, and attractive secretary, prevents him from committing suicide and sets his mind back on the pursuit of his profession. Brilliant revelation of a diversity of city types in their characteristic behavior. The publicity-happy murderess, the Harvard law graduate, the old Jewish mother, the ostentatiously Gentile stepchildren, the inflamed Communist, the lazy office boy, the reformed criminal, and the amorous girl on the switchboard—all are captivating, frequently amusing, and amazingly familiar characters who appear and reappear in a vivid panorama of office life and lend to the play an intense atmospheric quality.

MEN (*15; doubling possible*): 5 are 20–30 (3 minor); 10 are 30–50 (5 minor). WOMEN (*9*): 2 are 18–25; 5 are 28–40 (2 minor); 2 are 60. BOYS (*3*): 2 are 10–12; 1 is 14–15. GIRL: 8–10. SETS: Elegant law office suite in mid-Manhattan; 9 scenes alternating between the reception room and Simon's private office. Genuine office equipment is important. Arena production possible if realistic staging of attempted suicide through skyscraper window can be accomplished. COSTUMES: Street clothes of all classes of city people, early 1930s or present.

ROYALTY: $50, Samuel French. TEXT: Samuel French.

——o——

DARK OF THE MOON (1945)   HOWARD RICHARDSON and WILLIAM BERNEY.   A dramatization of "The Ballad of Barbara Allen" in which a witch boy, John, tries to become human in order to marry Barbara Allen. He does, but she is unfaithful to him and he becomes a witch again. The play takes place in a backwoods area of the Smoky Mountains and depicts the superstition and ignorance of the people. There is a revival scene in which Preacher Haggler and the members of the community convince Barbara she must leave John, and a few scenes of humor in which the people's viewpoints on morality and religion are satirized. Occasionally folk songs, such as "Down in the Valley," are sung to the accompaniment of a guitar or an accordian. John's memories of the pleasant life of a witch are demonstrated by a dance he does with two female witches who are trying to get him to come back. The dialogue is a backwoods American dialect.

MEN (*12*): 4 are 20–30 (1 must dance); 8 are 40–60 (4 minor, several sing or play instruments). WOMEN (*12*): 6 are 18–25 (1 must sing, 2 dance); 6 are 35–55. BOY: 15, sings and plays guitar. SETS: Need not be realistic: a mountain ridge; town square; cabin interior; cabin exterior; clearing in the woods; church interior. Suitable for arena. COSTUMES: Backwoods farm clothes; a revivalist preacher; 3 witches.

ROYALTY: $50, Brownstein and Basel, 25 W. 45th Street, New York, New York. TEXT: Theatre Arts (music is published with play).

— o —

GREEN GROW THE LILACS (1930) LYNN RIGGS. A play in six scenes which tells a simple folk tale about Curly, a cowhand, and his courtship of Laurie, a pretty, spoiled young girl. It takes place in Oklahoma in 1900. The play is interspersed with traditional folk songs such as "Green Grow the Lilacs," which is played on a guitar and sung by Curly. Laurie's Aunt Eller voices her philosophy that young folks, women in particular, have many problems in this world and that the only thing to do is to be hearty and stand it. The beauty and fullness of life are expressed by Curly and Laurie and are effectively contrasted by the ominous presence of the dirty hired hand, Jeeter Fry. The atmosphere of the Oklahoma Territory is established through scenes of traditional activities such as a party, a square dance, and a shivaree, in which a group of men tease Curly and Laurie by dragging them out to a haystack on their wedding night. In this scene, Jeeter appears and sets fire to the haystack and is killed in a knife fight with Curly. The dialogue is written in an Oklahoma dialect.

MEN (10): 7 are 20–30 (5 minor; 1 plays a fiddle, 1 plays a banjo, 1 plays a guitar); 3 are 30–50. WOMEN (4): 2 are 18–25 (both sing); 2 are 40–60 (1 sings). EXTRAS: Crowd of farmers, cowboys, and girls of varying ages. SETS: 8 scene changes, 5 sets: farmhouse front room; bedroom; smokehouse interior; farmhouse exterior; a hayfield which catches on fire. Realistic settings. Probably not suited for arena. COSTUMES: Farm clothing of the early 1900s.

ROYALTY: $50, Samuel French. TEXT: Samuel French.

— o —

MY HEART'S IN THE HIGHLANDS (1939) WILLIAM SAROYAN. A hungry poet lives with his Armenian mother and his nine-year-old but ageless son, Johnny, in Fresno, California. The boy spends most of his time trying to make contact with birds, train whistles, bicycle riders with ice cream cones, and the world as seen when standing on his head, until one day MacGregor, an old man who plays the trumpet and claims to be an actor, arrives upon the scene. MacGregor's heart, however, is in the Highlands, he says. When MacGregor plays sweet, sad songs upon his trumpet, the little people of Fresno gather around and bring food. In the end, the father's poems are returned by the *Atlantic Monthly*, the old man dies quoting *King Lear*, and father, grandmother, and Johnny leave for parts unknown. Poetic in nature, simple in style, the play is sweetly poignant and never without an aura of love and naïve charm. Imaginatively staged and sensitively acted, it serves as the basis for a special but very moving theatrical experience.

MEN (*13*): 8 are 20–40; 1 is 50–60. Old man must be able to play or to fake the playing of a trumpet. WOMEN (*2*): 1 is 20–25; 1 is 50–55 (should speak Armenian or similar language). BOYS (*4*): 1 is 9; 3 are 13–17. GIRL: 9. EXTRAS: May be doubled; all ages. SETS: Stylized, suggested house exterior; interior; grocery store. Arena staging possible. COSTUMES: Threadbare, approximately 1914; 2 guard uniforms. DIFFICULTIES: Needs an excellent boy actor; trumpet playing is difficult to fake effectively; script has difficult stage directions (for example, a dog who walks about loose on cue); fantasy elements difficult.

ROYALTY: $25, Samuel French. TEXT: Samuel French.

— o —

THE TIME OF YOUR LIFE (1939) WILLIAM SAROYAN. Comedy. Nick's waterfront saloon in San Francisco houses a charming collection of bizarre barflies, including Joe, who is exploring the possibilities of living a life which does not hurt anyone. His simple errand boy, Tom, falls in love with Kitty, a young streetwalker who is as gentle as her dreams of a better life. Through the actions of the habitués of the bar, particularly those of a rustic pioneer has-been called Kit Carson, a threat to the security of the young lovers is averted, and Joe finally leaves on a note of wistful happiness. This is an enchantingly whimsical comedy bordering on the cartoon with a concern for ordinary people and simple values of life.

MEN (*18*): 1 is 13–16 (must sing tenor); 14 are 20–40; 3 are character roles. Requires at least 3 very good actors; minor

roles are on stage almost constantly; 1 dancer who can im-
provise jazz movement; 1 pianist; 1 harmonica player. WOMEN
(7): 6 are 20–40; 1 elderly woman (Nick's mother) can be
cut. SETS: Waterfront saloon; Kitty's bedroom. Degree of
realism required is relative (for example, Kitty's room can be
played in a suggested setting or in an area within the saloon
setting). Arena production possible. Requires some space and
careful attention to placement of set props (bar, piano, inset
stage, pinball machine, juke box, and at least 3 sets of table
and chairs). COSTUMES: Seedy 1919; 1 set of male and female
formal clothes; 3 policemen's uniforms; cowboy buckskins
and boots. DIFFICULTIES: Casting problems of dancer who
must have some comic style, and pianist, who should be a thin
Negro boy.

ROYALTY: $35, Samuel French. TEXT: Samuel French.

——o——

THE BEAUTIFUL PEOPLE (1941) WILLIAM SAROYAN.
Comedy. A boy of fifteen describes himself as a punk and
writes books consisting of one word (*Tree*); his docile sister,
Agnes, pretends to accept her brother's pretense that the mice
in the house spell out her name in flowers on her birthday; and
a devil-may-care father, full of philosophy and love for all
humanity, has been living by cashing in the old-age pension
checks of a dead stranger. The play's talk centers about inti-
mations of cosmic disturbance, money, religion, and art; it
comes to the conclusion that the only thing of any real consequence is love. As in other plays of Saroyan's, the language is
beguilingly simple, and the atmosphere of innocence which
borders upon some sort of blessed insanity is sustained with
only the slightest sense of strain.

MEN (7): 1 is 15 (major role); 2 are 19–20 (1 must play
the cornet); 3 are 30–60. WOMEN (2): 1 is 17; 1 is a "little
old lady." SET: Living room; front porch; yard of an old
house in the Sunset District of San Francisco. Suitable for
arena. Decor need not be realistic. COSTUMES: Summer dress;
Catholic priest's suit. DIFFICULTIES: Requires even more sense
of gentle whimsey than do the earlier Saroyan plays. The
young boy requires an extremely sympathetic actor who can
sustain the play in many scenes. Perhaps the greatest difficulty
lies in establishing and maintaining proper level of fantasy

amid the commonplace surroundings the script indicates.
ROYALTY: $25, Samuel French. TEXT: Samuel French.

—— o ——

THE GENTLE PEOPLE (1939) IRWIN SHAW. This play
depicts the revolt of the downtrodden and persecuted and the
overthrow of a tyrant. The oppressed are two kindly old men,
Jonah Goodman and Philip Anagnos, who fish in the eve-
nings from a small boat moored off Steeplechase Pier at Coney
Island. The tyrant, Harold Goff, is a small-time mobster who
tries to extort five dollars a week from the two men for "protection." Driven to extremity by Goff's brutality, the two men
contrive to take justice into their own hands and kill their oppressor. They succeed, just barely managing to avoid detection. A subplot concerns the plan of Jonah's daughter to elope
with Goff. Although the author calls the play "a fairy tale with
a moral," the characters and the milieu are too realistically
drawn to be accepted on the level of fantasy, making the fishermen's extralegal act seem somewhat more immoral than
amoral. Both the play and its heroes nevertheless have a defi-
nite charm and poignancy.

MEN (*10; 2 can be cut*): 5 are 25–35 (2 minor); 5 are
50–60 (2 minor, 1 must be very fat). WOMEN (*3*): 1 is
20–25; 1 is 40–45; 1 is 50–55. SETS: A small motorboat
moored off Steeplechase Pier, Coney Island; the living room of
the Goodman home, clean but threadbare; a night court; steam
room of a Russian bath. The scene changes several times
within each act, which makes arena production impractical.
Settings should be selectively realistic, but simple enough to
permit quick changes. Every other scene is a pier scene which
can be played shallow in front of a drop. COSTUMES: Modern; some threadbare; 1 New York policeman's uniform.
ROYALTY: $25, Dramatists Play Service. TEXT: Dramatists
Play Service.

—— o ——

THE PETRIFIED FOREST (1935) ROBERT E. SHERWOOD.
Alan Squier is a penniless, disillusioned young writer, an aimless hitchhiker with little hope to give his life a meaning. He
finds a cause worth dying for at the Black Mesa Bar-B-Q, a
lonely outpost in the Arizona desert. Gabby Maple, the fresh,
innocent daughter of the dull, self-important owner of the

place, is determined to escape her small oppressive world and follow her French mother who had returned to her homeland many years ago. In her longing for fulfillment she offers herself to Alan, who refuses; she is on the verge of giving in to her local admirer, Boze, a primitive ex-football hero, when the Bar-B-Q is occupied by a gang of fleeing desperadoes. Alan, who lacks the vitality to live but is just strong enough to die gallantly, arranges that his life insurance will be paid to the girl and then makes Duke Mantee, the famous killer, shoot him. Gramp Maple, who loves to talk of the long-past pioneer days; a stuffy banker and his frustrated wife; a pompous commander of the American Legion; and a radical telegraph lineman lend color to the suspenseful action. Yet there is a message, well integrated into the melodrama: nature, physically overcome by man, hits back by destroying man's individual spirit. The pioneer is gone; and even Mantee, individualism turned to anarchy, is obsolete. The only hope lies in Gabby's aspirations, in the renewal of the spirit. But Alan, the sophisticated, sensitive intellectual, will be buried in the Petrified Forest, the meaning of which he had expounded: "Platonism—patriotism—Christianity—romance—the economics of Adam Smith—they're all so many dead stumps in the desert."

MEN (*16; doubling possible*): 6 are 20–30 (3 minor); 4 are 30–40 (2 minor); 5 are 40–50 (3 minor); 1 is 60–70. WOMEN (*3*): 1 is 17–21; 1 is 35; 1 is 40–50 (minor). EXTRAS: 2 deputy sheriffs. SET: Gas-station lunch room in the Arizona desert. Suitable for arena production. COSTUMES: Western and traveling clothes, 1934 or present; elegant apparel of society couple; one chauffeur's uniform; three American Legion uniforms; several guns and submachine guns.

ROYALTY: $25, Dramatists Play Service. TEXT: Dramatists Play Service.

—o—

IDIOT'S DELIGHT (1936) ROBERT E. SHERWOOD. Elements of satire, farce, and tragedy in a prophetic vision of the outbreak of World War II. An odd assortment of travelers is detained in an Italian mountain-resort hotel near the borders of Switzerland and Austria when the frontiers are closed because of an imminent war. Among the hotel guests are Harry Van, an American song-and-dance man and manager of six dancing girls, a French armaments manufacturer with his

Russian mistress Irene, who tells romantic tales of her mysterious past, a young British couple on their honeymoon, a voluble French revolutionist, and an apparently enlightened German scientist. When the war breaks out the Europeans succumb to extreme nationalism—except the munitions magnate, who impartially serves the opposing forces with the means for mutual destruction. The smallness and banality of people in their futile effort to escape the impending disaster is revealed in several episodes. Only Harry Van and Irene, in whom he recognizes a former vaudeville player he once and forever loved, face together the inevitable slaughter, drinking champagne and singing together "Onward, Christian Soldiers," while outside the bombs begin to fall.

MEN (*17; doubling possible*): 10 are 20–35 (6 minor); 7 are 40–50 (4 minor). WOMEN (*10*): 7 are 18–25 (6 must participate in a song-and-dance act); 3 are 30–40 (2 minor). EXTRAS: A small dance orchestra. SET: Cocktail lounge of an Italian mountain-resort hotel, ultramodernistic in terms of 1936. Pyrotechnics must give illusion of a disastrous bombardment. Production in a fairly spacious arena theatre possible. COSTUMES: Fashionable middle 1930s; 6 Italian officer's uniforms; 6 showgirl's costumes.

ROYALTY: $25, Dramatists Play Service. TEXT: In *Famous American Plays of the 1930's* (Dell).

— o —

YES IS FOR A VERY YOUNG MAN (1945) GERTRUDE STEIN. The play contrasts the unthinking, self-centered acceptance of the *status quo* represented by a shallow young wife, Denise, with the struggle for improved conditions and the desire to grow represented by her young brother-in-law, Ferdinand. An American spinster, Constance, with whom Ferdinand is infatuated, represents passive resistance to unfavorable conditions. Denise accepts the puppet regime in France under German occupation and moans only for lost material luxuries and the prewar happiness with her husband Henry—who, though he appears to be unemployed, is secretly working with the underground resistance movement. Ferdinand rejects the shallow thinking of his sister-in-law, leaves the motherly protectiveness of Constance, and joins his brother in the active fight against the enemy. When the occupation of France ends, Henry, Constance, and, of course, Denise, are most satisfied with the idea of returning to the prewar *status quo*. Ferdinand alone realizes that it is more important to finish a war on all fronts.

MEN (*4*): 1 is 18–20; 2 are 25–30 (1 minor); 1 is 45–55. WOMEN (*4*): 1 is 20–22; 1 is 30–35; 2 are 40–50 (minor). SETS: The garden outside Denise's chateau; a park adjoining Constance's house; a village railroad station; Constance's salon. Sets can be selectively realistic. Arena staging possible. COSTUMES: Rural French during World War II; 1 German soldier's uniform. DIFFICULTIES: Much variety of vocal emphasis and throwing away of lines will be needed to deal with Gertrude Stein's often-repetitive prose. The dialogue *sounds* surprisingly more true-to-life than would appear from reading it on the printed page.

ROYALTY: Apply publisher. TEXT: In *Last Operas and Plays* (Holt).

— o —

OF MICE AND MEN (1937) JOHN STEINBECK. George and Lennie are a strange team of migratory farm laborers who stick together although they have nothing in common but their dream of a piece of land of their own. Lennie is a feeble-minded giant, happy when permitted to stroke the soft, furry back of a mouse or a puppy, disconsolate when his heavy hand has crushed it. He is totally dependent on the intelligent, good-natured George, who always pulls him out of trouble. Recently they have been forced to flee because Lennie had frightened a girl when trying to fondle her silken dress. At their new job they come close to buying a couple of acres when Candy, an old cripple, offers to pitch in his savings. Soon they will have enough money, if only Lennie can keep away from the Boss' mean, belligerent son, Curley, and from Curley's pretty, coquettish wife. It cannot be. Curley's wife provokes Lennie into stroking her hair, then screams in a sudden panic, and Lennie, attempting to quiet her, breaks her neck. When Curley and his men set out after Lennie, George kills his friend to prevent him from being lynched. The characters are compellingly realistic; yet, in spite of the brutal environment, there is a subdued tenderness in the longing of these tough, primitive farmhands for settling down on their own land—a dream never to be fulfilled because of a defective social structure and even more because of the cruelty of life itself.

MEN (*9*): 5 are 20–40; 4 are 40–65 (1 is a Negro). WOMAN: 18–25. An old, decrepit dog is used in an important scene. SETS: Bank of the Salinas River, California; the bunkhouse; a lean-to; a barn. Sets should evoke the rough, close-to-nature atmosphere of farm labor. Arena production possible. COSTUMES: Western farm clothes.

ROYALTY: $25, Dramatists Play Service. TEXT: Bantam.

— o —

THE MALE ANIMAL (1940) JAMES THURBER and ELLIOTT NUGENT. Comedy. Admirably pointed high comedy, wit, and satire are combined cleverly with pure and simple farce to accentuate a basic theme having serious domestic and academic overtones. Midwestern university English professor Tommy Turner (Thurber's typically quiet, inoffensive little man) is married to his college sweetheart, Ellen. When her ex-beau arrives for the annual Homecoming football game, the battle of the sexes begins. Further complicating things is a trustee-faculty controversy over Tommy's academic freedom to read the allegedly anarchistic Vanzetti letter to his English class. His dismissal imminent, Tommy rejects Ellen's attempt to dissuade him, literally forces her to run off with the ex-beau, then garners enough courage to win her back through fisticuffs. Impressed with this new side of her male animal, Ellen is won over completely when Tommy refuses to deny publicly that he will read the letter, thereby standing firmly on his principle of academic freedom. Thurber's hand is evident, not only in his comic evolution of the ageless domestic War between Men and Women, but also in his statement of the equally ageless plea for independence of thought.

MEN (*8*): 3 are 20–23 (1 minor); 1 is 20–35 (minor); 1 is 33 (lead); 2 are 34–38; 1 is 65–70. WOMEN (*5*): 1 is 19; 1 is 20–35 (minor; Negro dialect); 1 is 29–30; 1 is 38–40 (minor); 1 is 55–65 (minor). SET: Living room in the pleasant but inexpensive house of Professor Thomas Turner, in a Midwestern university town in the 1940s. Set is realistic. Arena production possible. COSTUMES: Conventional 1940s; some emphasis on collegiate fashions; 1 male bandleader's uniform.

ROYALTY: $50, Samuel French. TEXT: Samuel French.

— o —

THE DAMASK CHEEK (1942) JOHN VAN DRUTEN and
LLOYD MORRIS. Comedy. The Randalls, New York socialites
at the beginning of the century, are visited by a cousin from
England, Rhoda Meldrum. Rhoda has a winning personality
and plenty of money, but she is rather plain and over thirty.
Mrs. Randall, a domineering matriarch, though skeptical about
her niece's marriage prospects, feels obliged to find her a respectable husband. But the young lady has her own ideas. She
is secretly in love with her amiable, fun-loving cousin, Jimmy
Randall, who, alas, treats her as a friend and confidante only.
Furthermore, he is engaged to a somewhat flashy actress, Calla
Longstreth. Only when Rhoda is "compromised" by taking a
carriage ride at night through Central Park with Neil Harding,
a renowned Don Juan, does Jimmy realize how much he cares
for her. The actress is paid off and the suitable partners can
be united in marriage. Daphne, Jimmy's teen-age sister, provides a touching note with her desperate declaration of love
to the dashing Neil Harding; young Michael Randall has an
amusing scene in which he excitedly describes a shocking
Broadway hit; and Miss Palmer, an elderly manicurist, helps
create the atmosphere of New York in the good old days with
its rigid conventions, gracious manners, and old-fashioned
charm.

MEN (2): Both are 30–35. WOMEN (5): 1 is 20–25; 1 is
20–40 (minor); 1 is 30–35; 2 are 50–55. BOY: 16. GIRL: 17.
SET: Living room in Mrs. Randall's house in the East 60s,
New York City, 1909. Scenery should genuinely render the
period. Suitable for arena. COSTUMES: Fashionable day clothes
and evening dress, 1909.
ROYALTY: $35, Samuel French. TEXT: Samuel French.

— o —

I REMEMBER MAMA (1944) JOHN VAN DRUTEN. An
adaptation of Kathryn Forbes's series of sketches titled *Mama's
Bank Account* that depict the life of a Norwegian-American
family in San Francisco in a sequence of everyday episodes.
They are held together by Mama, the pivotal character of the
play as well as of the family, a woman of wonderful good
sense and unending devotion. The stories are told in retrospect
by Katrin, the oldest daughter, who also participates in the
action when her reminiscences come to life. Mama, wife of a
modest carpenter and mother of four children, always finds a

way to solve her many problems. Papa is benevolent and hard-working; the children, three girls and a boy, are lively and natural. The "head of the family" is ferocious Uncle Chris, who drinks, lives with a "woman," and hides his generosity behind a grim façade. There are also three aunts, two of them rather nasty, the third a touchingly timid old maid who finds belated romance with the bashful Mr. Thorkelson, an under-taker. Several characters, among them an elderly British actor and a celebrated lady writer, are drawn into Mama's refresh-ingly bright and healthy world.

MEN (8): 1 is 18 (he must appear to be 15 at the beginning of the play); 2 are 18–25 (minor); 1 is 30–45 (minor); 3 are 45–55; 1 is 60–70. WOMEN (12): 3 are 17 (1 must look 13 at the beginning, 2 minor); 1 is 18–22 (her age ranges from 14 in the play to 22 as narrator); 2 are 25–40 (minor); 6 are 40–55 (2 minor). BOY: 8. GIRL: 8. EXTRAS: Scrubwoman; nurses; doctors; hotel guests. A live cat. SETS: Kitchen room and several other locations in and near San Francisco. Multiple set, preferably with 3 acting areas on different stage levels. Traveler curtain in front of the center stage is recommended. Sets need not be realistic and can be simplified to a minimum. Complicated lighting effects. COSTUMES: Modest lower-middle-class American, 1910.

ROYALTY: $35–25, Dramatists Play Service. TEXT: In *Three Dramas of American Family Life* (Washington Square).

—— o ——

ALL THE KING'S MEN (1959)   ROBERT PENN WARREN. The story relates the rise of Willie Stark (a character based on ex-Governor Huey Long of Louisiana) from an idealistic hick to governor of the state. Although Willie Stark's politics are corrupt, not all is evil; a hospital for the people is built. Stark is the strongest and most interesting figure of the play, but much of the action concerns a young newspaperman who works for him. The play is nonrealistic and makes free use of time and space. The framework is a ceremony to dedicate the hospital to Stark's son. A professor makes the opening speech and comments on the action throughout the play, which oc-curs in a series of flashback scenes.

MEN (14): 3 are 45–55; 10 are 30–45; 1 is 19–23 (some doubling possible). WOMEN (4): 2 are 25–35; 2 are 40–50.

SET: Open stage with blocks, possibly a framework suggesting the hospital at the back. Emphasis on lighting. Arena staging possible. DIFFICULTIES: A peak of excitement is reached in Stark's speech to a crowd at the end of Act I, and the following scenes may not top it.

ROYALTY: $35–25, Dramatists Play Service. TEXT: Dramatists Play Service.

— o —

OUR TOWN (1938) THORNTON WILDER. Life, death, and the hereafter as experienced by the people of Grover's Corners, New Hampshire, about the turn of the century. The story is told in episodic fashion by a "stage manager" narrator, and centers around Dr. Gibbs's son George and newspaper editor Mr. Webb's daughter Emily. These two are seen going to high school together, falling in love over sodas at the corner drugstore, being married, suffering tragedy as Emily dies giving birth to her second child, and in a poignant third-act scene, united briefly at the graveside after Emily has discovered how painful a return to living can be, when one walks among those by whom the beauties of life are taken for granted. We also meet many of the other people of the village, learning of their lives and dreams as they are set off against a background of social, philosophical, and religious tradition. The play is delightful yet profound; humorous, picturesque, and pathetic.

MEN (17): Range from 50–60 to several teen-age or younger boys. Maturity is particularly valuable in 3 major roles—Stage Manager, Mr. Webb, and Dr. Gibbs. WOMEN (7): Range from 50–60 to teen-age. Two character women for Mrs. Gibbs and Mrs. Webb. EXTRAS: As available, for church choir, group at graveside, and assorted characters in Act. I. SET: Bare stage with chairs, tables, and stepladders comprising the major set props. No scenery. Good flexible area lighting desirable. Good for arena production. COSTUMES: 1901–1913 New England.

ROYALTY: $25, Baker's or Samuel French. TEXT: Baker's or Samuel French.

— o —

THE SKIN OF OUR TEETH (1942) THORNTON WILDER. Comedy. The Antrobus family represents mankind, both now and in the Stone Age; Mr. Antrobus, dressed in modern clothes, rolls in the wheel he has just invented and plays with the baby dinosaur they keep as a pet. Later, Antrobus judges a beauty contest at Atlantic City and almost has a love affair with one of the beauties, who played the maid in the first act. There are scenic tricks of a corresponding nature. But the mood rapidly grows serious when the Antrobuses try to teach their children the accumulated knowledge of the world as the Ice Age descends upon them, and when he fights against the fascistic spirit which develops in his son in a postwar period. This Pulitzer Prize play is enormously rich in its amusing and serious comments upon modern life. The play abounds in deliberate anachronisms, obvious theatricalism, and rapid alternations of mood.

MEN (*25; doubling possible*): 1 is 12; 2 are 20–25; 9 are 30–35; 3 are 40–45; 6 are 50–55; 2 are 60; 1 ages from 15 to 29. WOMEN (*11; doubling possible*): 3 are 20–25; 1 is 30; 1 is 35–40; 1 is 50; 4 are 60–70; 1 ages from 13 to 26. SETS: A projection screen for slides; a living room of which parts are flown during the action; a speaker's platform; a section of the boardwalk at Atlantic City; the Antrobus living room with walls tipped helter-skelter but later pulled back in order. COSTUMES: Modern, with some eccentric variations; prehistoric-animal costumes. DIFFICULTIES: Some unusual properties. Scenic effects tricky, though not very difficult. A great many technical cues, requiring rehearsal time.

ROYALTY: $50–25, Samuel French. TEXT: Samuel French.

— o —

THE MATCHMAKER (1954) THORNTON WILDER. Comedy. Mrs. Levi pretends that she is promoting the marriage of Horace Vandergelder, a hot-tempered middle-aged widower of Yonkers, to a young milliner, Mrs. Molloy, but Mrs. Levi intends to marry him herself. Two of the clerks in Vandergelder's store steal a holiday in New York. They duck into Mrs. Molloy's millinery shop to avoid meeting Vandergelder and then have to hide under a table and in a cupboard when he enters the shop. After he leaves, the young men flirt with Mrs. Molloy and one of her assistants. All these characters then have supper in the same restaurant, with only a screen between them. In addition, Vandergelder's daughter, Ermengarde, and the suiter whom Vandergelder despises, come to the same restaurant for a stolen supper party before Ermengarde starts her visit to an aunt. Farcical confusions are inevitable. Similar confusions continue at the home of the aunt before all are paired off happily. This is a broad farce with much horseplay, direct address to the audience, and eccentric characterizations, written with a fine sense of style. The same script, except for a few alterations, was published in 1939 as *The Merchant of Yonkers*, based on an 1842 farce in German by Johann Nestroy.

MEN (9): 1 is 18; 2 are 25; 2 are 35; 2 are 45; 1 is 55; 1 is 60. WOMEN (7): 2 are 20–25; 1 is 30; 1 is 50; 3 are 60–70. SETS: Vandergelder's living room with a trapdoor down to his store; Mrs. Molloy's millinery shop; the Harmonica Gardens Restaurant; Miss Van Huysen's living room. The style of the play permits this to be very "painty" scenery, and probably would permit wing and drop scenery if this were thought desirable. COSTUMES: Bourgeois 1880s (some adjustment possible). Only Mrs. Levi needs a change, but several women need coats. DIFFICULTIES: Accuracy of timing and comedy pointing are needed to project the humor fully.

ROYALTY: $50–25, Samuel French. TEXT: Samuel French.

——— o ———

THE GLASS MENAGERIE (1945)   TENNESSEE WILLIAMS. Tom Wingfield, alternating in the roles of narrator and participant of the "memory play," evokes the home in St. Louis which he left years ago: the drab reality of the little flat in a dark alley; his monotonous job in a warehouse from which he escapes by writing poetry; his mother, a former Southern belle who tried to govern her two grown children by the constantly recalled standards of her girlhood; his sister Laura, a shy, slightly crippled girl who found refuge in the imaginary kingdom of her glass animal collection; and Jim, a friend from the warehouse whom Mother, determined to find a "gentleman caller" for her daughter, had forced Tom to invite, and who for a moment falls under the spell of Laura's dream world. Tom, too, flees from his mother and sister, but he cannot banish the thought of their fragile, helpless existence. (All the parts are rewarding, in particular that of the fussy, anxious mother, infuriating and pitiful in her futile meddling with the lives of her children. The play has the delicate twilight atmosphere of time remembered, "truth in the pleasant disguise of an illusion.")

MEN (*2*): Both 20–30. WOMEN (*2*): 1 is 20–30; 1 is 40–60. SET: The Wingfield apartment and its fire-escape entrance. Transparent walls, separating the living room downstage from the upstage dining room. Dim, nonrealistic scenery and lighting. The projection of images and titles, intended to give an additional dimension of memory associations, was not used in the Broadway production. Arena production possible. COSTUMES: Middle-class American, early 1930s; 1 ballroom dress of 1910. DIFFICULTIES: This play calls for subtle blending of psychological realism and lingering pathos in order to produce the required iridescent mood of reminiscence.

ROYALTY: $50–25, Dramatists Service. TEXT: In *Six Great Modern Plays* (Dell); music by Paul Bowles, Dramatists Play Service.

—— o ——

YOU TOUCHED ME! (1945) TENNESSEE WILLIAMS and DONALD WINDHAM. Suggested by D. H. Lawrence's short story. The Rockley household in rural wartime England is dominated by Emmie Rockley, a spinster possessed of "feverish drive" and "aggressive sterility," who attempts to shape the life of her young niece Matilda in her own image. Matilda's father, a former sea captain, in succumbing to the rule of his sister, regains memories of his adventurous past through alcohol. In a drunken escapade the captain interrupts the local minister's proposal of a clandestine marriage to Emmie. The return of Hadrian, whom the captain had reared from boyhood in spite of Emmie's admonishments, further thwarts the spinster's plans. Hadrian, now an officer in the Royal Canadian Air Force, openly declares his love for Matilda and his determination to take her away with him. As Emmie attempts to prevent this, the captain wholeheartedly helps further the romance, in which he sees the salvation of his daughter from a wasted and lonely life. It is finally Matilda herself who overcomes her shyness to accept and return Hadrian's love. The young couple leave for a new life as the old captain rejoices.

MEN (*4*): 2 are 20–30 (1 minor); 1 is 40–50; 1 is 60–70 (requires an outstanding character actor). WOMEN (*3*): 1 is 20; 1 is 20–30; 1 is 40–50. SET: A cross section of an English living room and a bedroom furnished as a sea captain's cabin. Set should have a "dreamy, aqueous effect." Arena production possible. COSTUMES: Modern English dress; 1 Royal Canadian Air Force Lieutenant's uniform.

ROYALTY: $50, Samuel French. TEXT: Samuel French.

— o —

A STREETCAR NAMED DESIRE (1947) TENNESSEE WILLIAMS. The sisters DuBois are the last members of an impoverished Southern plantation family. Stella has married Stanley Kowalski, a brutish laborer. Though she lives as his slave while he plays poker with his swearing and sweating friends, she has found happiness in their intense sexual relationship. Into their squalid, heat-oppressed tenement in New Orleans comes Stella's sister Blanche, who claims to have taken leave of absence from her job as a schoolteacher but who was in reality run out of town as a prostitute. She gives herself the airs of the refined, gracious lady from the South, and tries to entice Mitch, Stanley's good-humored and somewhat civilized friend. When Stanley exposes her past and ruins her frail chances of marriage, she escapes into a psychotic world. Eventually, she has to be taken away to an asylum. The action is brutally naturalistic, the characters stripped raw in psychoanalytical vivisection; yet there are poetic overtones in Blanche's spiritual yearning for gentleness and "the kindness of strangers."

MEN (7): 1 is 17–20 (minor); 4 are 25–35 (2 minor); 2 are 40–60 (minor). WOMEN (6): 3 are 25–35; 3 are 35–50 (minor). EXTRAS: People on the street. SET: 2-room apartment in the French Quarter of New Orleans. Both rooms are visible at the same time. Complex lighting, sometimes revealing through the screen walls the street beyond. Arena production possible. COSTUMES: Contemporary lower class in New Orleans; Blanche's gowns of slightly faded elegance. DIFFICULTIES: Sensationalism must be avoided.

ROYALTY: $50–25, Dramatists Play Service. TEXT: New American Library.

— o —

SUMMER AND SMOKE (1948) TENNESSEE WILLIAMS. On one side of a small park in Glorious Hill, Mississippi, in 1916, lives Alma, the nervous and puritanical daughter of a minister and his demented wife. On the other side lives Dr. John, whose "demoniac unrest" has labeled him the wildest man in town. When John comes home from medical school. Alma urges him to abandon his dissipated behavior and to reflect the dignity of the medical profession. John attends one meeting of Alma's so-called intellectuals but leaves quickly to seek the company of Rosa Gonzales. When John takes Alma to Moon Lake Casino and suggests they hire a private room, she runs away. John's father suddenly returns to find Rosa and her drunken father living in his house, and is wounded in the ensuing argument. Alma confesses she summoned the older doctor in an effort to make John redeem himself. John, pointing to an anatomy chart, shows Alma there is no such thing as a soul. As winter comes, John takes over his father's work and distinguishes himself, while Alma becomes ill and remains secluded. Finally, when she goes to John to offer herself to him, he reveals that he has come to share her belief that there is more in a human being than can be seen on an anatomy chart. Nellie, one of Alma's former piano pupils, tells her that she and John are engaged. In the park Alma suggests to a young traveling salesman that they visit the Casino.

MEN (8): 5 are 20–30; 2 are 45–60; 1 is 60–70. WOMEN (6): 1 is 18–20; 3 are 20–30; 2 are 45–60. If the prologue is used, John and Alma must be enacted by 2 10-year-olds who perform the entire scene by themselves. SETS: Cross section of the living room of the rectory; park with a statue of a stone angel; doctor's office. Also, the arbor at the Casino must be suggested. Sets should not be realistic. Numerous arena productions have been given. COSTUMES: Small-town dress of 1916.

ROYALTY: $50–25, music $5, Dramatists Play Service. TEXT: Dramatists Play Service.

— o —

THE ROPE DANCERS (1959) MORTON WISHENGRAD. Margaret Hyland feels guilt because of the sensual love she felt for her husband. Her child, Lizzie, was born with six fingers on her left hand. Margaret believes that this was God's punishment for her husband's drunkenness and her lust. She has left her husband, and keeps Lizzie at home all the time. She attempts to hide what she considers the physical evidence of her guilt by making Lizzie wear a mitten, and adopts a cold, nonsensual attitude toward everyone. She and Lizzie move frequently to avoid the truant officer, and as the play begins, the husband, James, has just located them. A truant officer and a policeman appear, and Lizzie has hysterics. The doctor who is called calms her and later operates to remove the sixth finger. In the final scene, Margaret comes to understand herself and what her guilt has done to Lizzie. Lizzie dies, and the doctor conjectures that years of deformity and guilt cannot be cut away. With her new understanding, Margaret is able to express love without shame, and she and James are reunited.

MEN (5): All are 30–50. WOMEN (2): 30–40. GIRLS (2): 10–12. SET: A 2-room flat in a New York tenement. Unit set appropriate. The play is realistic. Arena staging possible. Hyland supposedly makes his initial entrance from a fire escape through a window. COSTUMES: Lower class early 1900s; policeman's uniform. DIFFICULTIES: Irish and Yiddish accents needed.

ROYALTY: $50–25, Samuel French. TEXT: Samuel French.

— o —

MANNERHOUSE (1925) THOMAS WOLFE. The prologue is set in the Colonial period. Ramsay, a stern, unrelenting Virginian, surveys the wretched Negro slaves who are to build his house. With ease he suppresses a revolt and disdainfully accepts the submission of its leader, a former African king. A minister sermonizes to the uncomprehending native upon the divine order of master and slave by quoting from the Bible. The play takes place at the outset and after the end of the Civil War. Eugene, concealing his sensitivity behind a mask of Byronic disdain, reluctantly follows his father, the grand, authoritative General Ramsay, into the war. When they return, the old seignorial order has been destroyed by the industrial poor-whites. The general is compelled to sell his ancestral estate to Porter, a vulgar but extremely successful member of the rising class. The general dies. Years later, Eugene, now an aimless vagabond, returns and is employed by Porter to remodel the house. Realizing the evanescence of aristocratic splendor, yet unable to accept the new materialistic approach, he tears down a pillar and is buried under the collapsing structure of the house. This highly symbolic play aims far beyond its historical and regional setting as, in its fierce burlesquing of old romanticism, it defends the thing it attacks, and expresses passionate belief in all myth, in the necessity of defending and living not for the truth—but for divine falsehood.

MEN (*14; doubling possible*): 1 is 16–18; 4 are 20–30 (2 minor, 1 Negro); 4 are 25–40 (minor, 2 Negro); 3 are 40–55; 2 are 55–60 (1 Negro). WOMEN (*2*): 1 is 20–25; 1 is about 50. EXTRAS: Guests; soldiers; slaves. SETS: On a hillside; General Ramsay's study. Unit set recommended, showing the column erected in the prologue later to be a part of the house. Symbolic stylization. Several technical effects, among them the collapse of the house, make the play unsuitable for arena production. COSTUMES: Clothes of Colonial pioneers, 1 ministerial garb, rags worn by slaves; attire of Southern gentry before and after the Civil War; Confederate Army uniforms.

ROYALTY: Apply Edward C. Aswell, Administrator C.T.A. (of the Estate of Thomas Wolfe), 330 W. 42 St., N.Y., N.Y. TEXT: Harper.

—— o ——

EXCURSION (1937) VICTOR WOLFSON. Comedy. The story of the farewell cruise of the *SS Happiness*, an old ferry which runs from Harlem to Coney Island. On this final trip the captain, Obadiah Rich, is joined by his brother Jonathan and a cross section of humanity. The *Happiness* makes Coney Island uneventfully, but Obadiah hates to contemplate the return trip, when all the passengers will return to the disillusionments of real life. He decides to sail the old ferryboat to a secret island near Trinidad. Just off Sandy Hook, the ferry had been found by a Coast Guard cutter which was alerted when the *Happiness* did not return to her pier. Reluctantly the captain sails back to Harlem, but the crew and passengers are new people because of the hope they experienced during their short adventure. All are ready to return to their old life with new enthusiasm. As a final touch, the owner of the *Happiness* decides to let her sail for one more year. The plot of this play is second in importance to the characterization and message.

MEN (*7*): 2 are 45–55; 2 are 25–40 (dialect comic parts); remainder can be any age from juvenile to middle-aged. WOMEN (*9*): 2 dialect parts; 2 are 40–50; others need only be matched in age to their respective spouses. BOY: 5–10. GIRL: 5–10. SETS: Captain's cabin; deck of the *Happiness*.

Must be able to shift quickly. (6 alternations of the 2 scenes.)
COSTUMES: Modern street dress; 2 uniforms.

ROYALTY: $25, Dramatists Play Service. TEXT: Dramatists
Play Service.

—o—

THE *CAINE* MUTINY COURT MARTIAL (1953) HER-
MAN WOUK. Wouk adapted a portion of his best-selling
novel into a tight, self-contained courtroom play. Lieutenant
Maryk, executive officer of the USS *Caine*, is tried for mutiny
in time of war. He is accused of having forcefully relieved his
superior officer, Lieutenant Commander Queeg, from his command during a typhoon in the Pacific. The defense counsel,
Lieutenant Greenwald, who accepted his assignment only reluctantly, displays at the beginning an apparent lack of spirit,
but proceeds step by step to expose Queeg's mental incom-
petence. Each of the witnesses called by the judge advocate,
Lieutenant Commander Challee, has an effective scene of his
own. There is Lieutenant Keefer, a recreant intellectual; Lieutenant Keith, a loyal but unconvincing young officer; Captain
Southard, a navigation expert; Dr. Lundeen and Dr. Bird, two
omniscient psychiatrists; and Urban, an inarticulate sailor who
was too afraid to see anything at all. The star witness is Queeg,
manly, correct, and seemingly self-assured at his first interrogation, but disintegrating into a pitiful, confused wreck when
recalled by the defense. In an epilogue at the celebration
party for Maryk's acquittal, Greenwald, conscience-ridden
and drunk, deplores that he had to break Queeg, a once-
meritorious career officer, and denounces Keefer as the demoralizing instigator of the mutiny.

MEN (*13*): 11 are 20–40 (2 minor); 2 are 40–60. EXTRAS:
6 members of the court; officers at Maryk's celebration party.
SETS: Functional military courtroom; banquet room. No
scenery is required except for a judge's bench and a few chairs
and tables. Suitable for arena production. COSTUMES: Navy
"blues"; officers' uniforms; a flier's uniform.

ROYALTY: $50, Baker's or Samuel French. TEXT: Samuel
French.

RUSSIAN DRAMA

HE WHO GETS SLAPPED (*To, Kto poluchaet poshchet-schini;* 1915) LEONID ANDREYEV. The story of a man who flees the hypocrisy of upper-class society to frankly bear the slaps and buffets of his fellow man in the world of the circus, *He Who Gets Slapped* is a pessimistic indictment of life in this world as contrasted to man's potential for happiness. In this extremely theatrical and almost hysterical work, *He*, a mysterious gentleman, becomes a clown who is slapped again and again in the circus of Briquet and his wife Zinida. He becomes Baron Regnard's rival for Consuela, the bareback rider. Finally, to claim her, he poisons her and plans to join her in death. The Baron, however, kills himself before *He* has had an opportunity to do so and the eternally beaten and frustrated clown concludes the play by destroying himself so the Baron will not reach his beloved before him.

MEN (*13*): 5 are 25–30; 4 are 30–35; 2 are 40–45; 2 are 50–55. Tilly and Polly, musical clowns, must be able to play some sort of small wind instrument. WOMEN (*7*): 6 are 20–25; 1 is 33. EXTRAS: Clowns, aerialists, etc., of Papa Briquet's Circus. SETS: A dressing tent or dressing room just outside the circus ring. The setting can be highly stylized. COSTUMES: Circus garb and street dress of any period.

ROYALTY: $25–20, Samuel French. TEXT: Gregory Zilboorg trans. (Samuel French).

—— O ——

THE SEA GULL (*Chaika;* 1895) ANTON CHEKHOV. Among the people gathered at the Sorin estate, only two are sure of themselves—Madame Trepleff, the self-centered middle-aged actress, and her lover Trigorin, the popular, pleasure-seeking writer. Konstantine, Madame Trepleff's son, wants to be a fine writer, to create new forms, and to marry Nina, the young daughter of a nearby landowner. He is frustrated in every aim.

His writings are naïve, vague, and filled with confusing symbols; Nina, awed by Trigorin's fame and her own ingenuous desire to be a great actress, runs off as Trigorin's new mistress. Everyone else is also frustrated in some important way. Sorin, Madame Trepleff's brother, now old and sick, had always wanted to marry and to be a writer. Masha, the daughter of Sorin's steward, had wanted to marry Konstantine but instead married the poor schoolteacher Medvedenko. Medvedenko cannot get Masha to accept her responsibilities as mother and wife, and he is constantly upset by his near poverty. Confronted by his mother's unconcern, the sham of her art and Trigorin's, the frustrations around him, and finally by Nina's second rejection of him after she has been deserted by Trigorin, Konstantine commits suicide.

MEN (7): 1 in his 20s; 2 are 35–45; 4 are 50–65 (1 minor). WOMEN (7): 1 in her late teens; 3 are 20–30 (2 minor); 3 are 40–60 (1 minor; a man could be cast). SETS: A section of the park on Sorin's estate with a small stage; a croquet lawn; the dining room in Sorin's house; one of Sorin's drawing rooms which has been turned into a study. COSTUMES: Late 19th century fashionable dress. Reasonable period authenticity is important.

ROYALTY: $25, Samuel French. TEXT: Stark Young trans. (Samuel French).

— o —

UNCLE VANYA (*Diadia Vania;* 1899) ANTON CHEKHOV. Ever since the arrival of old Serebriakoff and his young wife Elena, everything has been disorder on the Serebriakoff estate. Uncle Vanya, the brother of Serebriakoff's first wife, has lost his formerly intense desire to manage the estate. He is disillusioned by the retired professor's dull, egotistical, nagging ways and confused by his own unreturned love for Elena. Sonia, Serebriakoff's daughter by his first wife, tries to continue running the estate; but her strength is inadequate. What little strength she possesses is also drained by her deep love for the local doctor, Astroff, who is himself so frustrated by life that he cannot return her love. Unable to understand the unselfish ways of Uncle Vanya, Sonia, Astroff, Serebriakoff, and Elena lead useless, disorderly lives while drawing on the attention and energies of the others. A crisis is reached when Serebriakoff discusses his plan to sell the estate, an act which would leave Vanya, Sonia, and Vanya's mother destitute. The crisis is averted when Elena, who has remained faithful to Serebriakoff despite her unhappiness with his pettiness, persuades him to leave. She is afraid of the passion Astroff is beginning to arouse in her. With the departure of the Serebriakoffs, matters return to their former states. Astroff once more becomes interested in healing the sick and in reclaiming the land, and Uncle Vanya and Sonia begin with renewed determination to manage the estate and to bear their suffering.

MEN (5): 1 is 30–40; 3 are 40–50 (1 minor); 1 is 60–70. WOMEN (4): 2 are 20–30; 2 are 60–70. SETS: A garden (part of the house and its terrace can be seen); dining room in Serebriakoff's house; living room in the same house; a bedroom, also used as the estate office. COSTUMES: Late 19th century. Reasonable period authenticity is important. DIFFICULTIES: Comments on *The Cherry Orchard* (see p. 400), are applicable.

ROYALTY: $25, Samuel French. TEXT: Stark Young trans. (Samuel French).

— o —

THE THREE SISTERS (*Tri sestri;* 1901) ANTON CHEKHOV. A year after the death of their father, who had commanded the local army post, Olga, Masha, and Irina Prozoroff find their lives purposeless and lonely. Each tries to find some substitute for the gaiety and hope she had formerly felt. Olga tries to find satisfaction in teaching, although she dreams of a home and family. Unhappy in her marriage to a pedantic schoolmaster, Masha stumbles into a hopeless affair with a married colonel. Irina seeks to find purpose through the "dignity of work" in the local telegraph office. As the play progresses, all three become increasingly aware that their efforts are futile. Their sense of futility is greatly increased by their brother's marriage to Natasha, a coarse peasant woman. She gradually encroaches on the family home until the sisters are robbed of even the solace of a private refuge from the realities of their situation. They dream of starting a new life in Moscow, but they are too burdened by the practicalities of life to make the move. They finally admit the hopelessness of their substitute pursuits when the army post is withdrawn from the town. Despite their past failures, they resolve to seek again some sense of purpose and hope in life.

MEN (*9*): 5 are 20–35; 3 are 40–55; 1 is 60–70. WOMEN
(*5*): 4 are 20–35; 1 is 60–70. SETS: The drawing room of the
Prozoroff home (dining room seen to one side); the bedroom
of Olga and Irina; the garden behind the Prozoroff house.
COSTUMES: Women wear 1890 gowns, fashionable but not
expensive. Men wear Russian Army uniforms and business
suits. Reasonable period authenticity is important. DIFFICUL-
TIES: Comments on *The Cherry Orchard* (see below) are
applicable.

ROYALTY: $25, Samuel French. TEXT: Stark Young trans.
(Samuel French).

—— o ——

THE CHERRY ORCHARD (*Vishnevii sad;* 1903) ANTON
CHEKHOV. The play explores the attempts of the Ranevskayas
to maintain their aristocratic values in an increasingly bourgeois
world. The Ranevskaya finances are so precarious that part of
the family estate, a large cherry orchard, must be sold in order
to maintain the remainder of the estate. But although each
member of the family realizes the necessity of raising money,
no one can bear to sell the orchard—the orchard symbolizes
in a different way to each person the happiness of a lost past.
To Madame Ranevskaya, the orchard symbolizes a time when
she was young, innocent, and secure with a husband and son.
To Gayeff, her brother, it symbolizes the time when he could
be a carefree gentleman farmer, concerned primarily with
billiards instead of banking. To Lopahin, the freed serf, it
represents a time when love and loyalty were more important
than material success. Throughout the play, the characters
collide comically; although each can see the impracticality and
blindness of the others, he is unaware of his own folly. And
although they all struggle heroically to face the new Russian
world, each retreats into fantastic daydreams whenever his
own private dream is threatened. Inevitably, the entire estate is
sold. The Ranevskayas set out for new lives in which, it is
clear, they will continue to live graciously and ridiculously in
an outmoded manner.

MEN (*10*): 3 are 20–30; 6 are 40–60; 1 is 87. WOMEN
(*5*): 1 is 17; 3 are 20–35; 1 is 40–60. SETS: The nursery of
the Ranevskaya home; a field on the estate; the drawing room
of the Ranevskaya home. Late 19th century. COSTUMES: Early
20th century, daytime and formal wear. Reasonable period

authenticity is important. DIFFICULTIES: The apparently rambling speeches must reveal the real motivations which gave rise to them, achieving a blend of pathos and warm comedy.

ROYALTY: $25, Samuel French. TEXT: Stark Young trans. (Samuel French).

—— o ——

THE INSPECTOR–GENERAL (*Revizor;* 1836) NIKOLAI GOGOL. A satire on the duplicity and greed of humanity. The citizens of a provincial town abounding with civic graft and bribe-taking discover (through the unscrupulous post-master, who intercepts a letter) that a government inspector is to visit the town. In sudden terror the civic officials mistake a young, out-of-pocket clerk and his disreputable manservant, who are staying in the local hostelry, for the government inspector and his valet. They confront him with this and he, Klestakhov, being an opportunist, accepts their blandishments, bribes, protestations of honesty, and the proffered affections of the mayor's daughter. Finally, he escapes with his loot; and, while the townsmen are busily recriminating one another, the true inspector arrives, and they are frozen in a tableau of terror as the final curtain drops.

MEN (*approximately 20*): 1 is 23; others 50–60; most should be character actors or antic types; a number of roles are very minor; 10 superb character portraits. WOMEN (6): 1 is 18–20; 1 is 40–45. SETS: The parlor of the town governor; a wretched hotel room. Suitable for arena production. COSTUMES: Contemporary 1830s; some fashionable, most provincial.

ROYALTY: Apply publishers. TEXT: David Magarshack trans. in *The Storm and Other Russian Plays* (Hill and Wang), or F. D. Reeve trans. in *An Anthology of Russian Plays* (Random), Vol. I.

—— o ——

THE LOWER DEPTHS (*Na dne;* 1902) MAXIM GORKI. A group of outcasts—the beaten, the unscrupulous, the dying —are crowded into the one-room cellar of Kostilyoff, the landlord, like lost souls in the depths of hell: Kleshtch, a proud but poor locksmith; his wife, Anna, whom he constantly beats even though she is dying; the Baron, a decadent noble-man who keeps himself alive by pimping for Nastya, the prostitute; the Actor, a has-been who irritates everyone with drunken descriptions of his imaginary triumphs; Pepel, a thief who has been carrying on a liaison with Vassilisa, the landlord's wife, but who is now making passes at Natasha, her sister; and Satine, a gambler who is the only realist in the sorry lot. Luka, a pilgrim, comes among them and offers pity and understanding. He helps Anna die in peace; he interrupts a fight between Pepel and Kostilyoff; he convinces the Actor that some town has a free hospital for alcoholics. Then Luka disappears as suddenly as he arrived. Satine, Nastya, and the Baron argue about the old pilgrim's distortion of the truth, Satine deciding that he lied—out of sheer pity. Meanwhile, other lodgers enter; the brawling begins anew. There is a shout and the Baron announces that the Actor has hanged himself.

MEN (*12, plus extras*): 1 is 20; 2 are 25–35; 5 are 40; 3 are 45–55; 1 is 60; distinctive physical types. WOMEN (*5, plus extras*): 3 are 20–25; 2 are 30–40. SET: Basement room in a state of disrepair and a cleared area behind it connected by a stairway. COSTUMES: Rags, but carefully chosen to indicate both what character is and what he *thinks* he is. DIFFICULTIES: Extremely naturalistic detail.

ROYALTY: Apply publisher. TEXT: David Magarschack trans. in *The Storm and Other Russian Plays* (Hill and Wang).

—— o ——

THE SMUG CITIZENS (*Meshchane;* 1902) MAXIM GORKI. Bezsemenov, a petty, self-complacement bourgeois, considers himself a highly respectable patriarch. His despotism has intimidated his wife, Akulina, into servile submission, and has led his weakly resisting children, Tanya and Peter, into frustrated misery. Only Nil, Bezsemenov's foster son, a vigorous, primitive railroad worker, opposes the tyrant successfully when refusing a profitable match in favor of marrying Polya, a poor girl of his own choice. Tanya, secretly in love with Nil, takes poison but fails to kill herself. Peter, an idealistic dreamer who has been suspended by the university, declares he will marry a young widow who shares his liberal-radical ideas. Teterev, a drunken, philosophical choir-singer who boards with the Bezsemenovs, predicts that Peter will probably return and, in due time, will become as greedy, cruel, and self-assured as his father. The play is a somewhat Chekhovian portrayal of an unchangeable, stagnant society. Much of its spirit is expressed by Tanya: "Life is not tragic. It's dull and dreary and monotonous. Life is just a big, muddy river—and one gets so bored with it one doesn't even care enough to wonder why it flows."

MEN (7): 3 are 24–28; 4 are 40–60 (1 minor). WOMEN (10): 4 are 24–26; 6 are about 50 (1 minor). SET: Living room in the house of Bezsemenov. Stuffy atmosphere. Typical Russian objects such as icons and samovar. Suitable for arena production. COSTUMES: Middle-class Russian at the turn of the century. DIFFICULTIES: The main asset of this play must be found in its minute observation, richness of nuance and intense atmosphere.

ROYALTY: $25–20, Samuel French. TEXT: Miriam Goldina adap. as *The Courageous One* (Samuel French).

—— o ——

EGOR BULYCHOV AND THE OTHERS (*Egor Bulychov i drugie;* 1931) MAXIM GORKI. Egor Bulychov, a *nouveau riche* whose ruthless energy conquered him a place among the Russian bourgeoisie, is stricken by cancer. Near death, he deplores the emptiness of his life. He has remained an outsider in a world of corrupt merchants and pompous churchmen, a stranger to his well-born wife and to the children she has raised after her fashion. Only Shura, his illegitimate daughter, loves and understands him. In the chaotic days of 1917, when war is succeeded by revolution, Bulychov realizes that the marching masses in the streets have come to bury him and his kind. The play is the first of a trilogy covering the period from the collapse of the Tsarist Empire to the establishment of the Soviets. Superior to its sequels, it is accepted in the Russia of today as a classic of social realism and is frequently performed. However, at its Moscow premiere in 1931 Gorki was reprimanded by the critics for assigning a secondary role to the representative of the working class, for permitting the audience to sympathize with Bulychov—a rich man—and for portraying him as an atheist instead of demonstrating the conspiracy of Church and capitalism.

MEN (13): 4 are 20–30 (2 minor); 9 are 40–60 (6 minor). WOMEN (9): 5 are 18–25 (1 minor); 4 are 40–60 (1 minor). SET: Living room in Bulychov's house. Heavy, cumbersome furniture. Suitable for arena production. COSTUMES: Middle-

class Russian, 1917; a policeman's uniform; habits for two
nuns and a priest.

ROYALTY: Apply Maxim Lieber, 489 Fifth Ave., N.Y.,
N.Y. or A. M. Heath & Co., 188 Picadilly, London, W 1.
TEXT: Alexander Bakshy trans. in *Lower Depths and Other
Plays by Maxim Gorky* (Yale) or Gibson-Cowan adap. in
The Last Plays of Maxim Gorki (Lawrence and Wishart Ltd.,
81 Chancery Lane, London WC 2; out of print).

—o—

THE BEDBUG (*Klop;* 1928) VLADIMIR MAYAKOVSKY. Comedy. The first act of this "extravaganza in nine scenes" shows
the Russia of 1928 and its representative philistine hero, Ivan
Prisypkin. Accidentally frozen into a block of ice, then discovered and resurrected in the hygienic and soulless paradise of
1978, Ivan is a lonely curiosity with but one companion in
exile—a bedbug which has been frozen and defrosted with
him. Both are incarcerated and displayed in the zoological
gardens as the historic *bedbugus normalis* and *bourgeoisius
vulgaris*, "different in size, but identical in essence." Widely
performed in post-Stalin Russia, this devastating satire of
Communist excesses suggests some of the Aristophanic vitality
and social concern of the author.

MEN (*12, plus extras*): 4 are 20–30; 2 are 30–40; 2 are
40–50; 2 are 50–60; 1 is 60–70; 1 is unspecified age. WOMEN
(*4, plus extras*): 2 are 20–30; 1 is 40–50; 1 ages 50 years during play. SETS: First 4 scenes realistic modern (market place,
workers' hotel, banquet room, outside banquet room); last 5
scenes 50 years in future (voting station, operating room, a
plaza, hospital room, zoological gardens). Originally produced
in constructivist style; demands quick changes and simple
treatment. COSTUMES: Modern Russian peasants, workers,
bourgeois (formal wear), firemen and futuristic doctors, students, reporters, officials, children.

ROYALTY: $50–25, apply publisher. TEXT: Max Hayward
and George Reavey trans. in *The Bedbug and Selected Poetry*
(Meridian).

—o—

THE STORM (*Groza;* 1860) ALEXANDER NICOLAYEVICH
OSTROVSKY. A young wife, Katherine, saddled with a milk-sop husband and an incredibly nagging mother-in-law, con-

tracts what she considers to be an adulterous liaison with a young gentleman. Discovered, Katherine is dogged with an almost pathological guilt and as a result of her minor dalliance she destroys herself. A superb example of what the literary historian Prince Mirsky called the "ethnological drama of Russia," which demonstrates the real qualities, the soul, the essence of Russian life in the author's time. Because of the unique Russian character of Ostrovsky's work, his dramatic reputation has been largely limited to his own country.

MEN (6, *plus extras; doubling possible*): 1 is 20; 3 are 25–30; 1 is 50; 1 is 55–60. WOMEN (6, *plus extras; doubling possible*): 1 is 20–25; 2 are 25–30; 2 are 50–60; 1 is 70; some of the extras have lines. SETS: A park; a room in the woman's house, the gates to her garden; an arcade by the riverbank. They should be realistic. COSTUMES: 1860 Russian.

ROYALTY: Apply publishers. TEXT: David Magarshack trans. in *The Storm and Other Russian Plays* (Hill and Wang) or F. D. Reeve trans. in *An Anthology of Russian Plays* (Random), Vol. I.

—o—

THE DIARY OF A SCOUNDREL, OR ENOUGH STUPIDITY IN EVERY WISE MAN (*Na vsiakovo mudretsa dovolno prostoti;* 1868) ALEXANDER NICOLAYEVICH OSTROVSKY. Comedy. A young scoundrel, Glumov, flatters, bribes, stoops to anything in order to gain his own advancement. He talks outrageously behind the backs of his so-called friends and gossips incessantly. Privately he writes down in his diary just what he thinks about all of those with whom he comes in contact. When his diary is stolen from him, the young detractor is faced suddenly with the horrible embarrassment of having his diary read aloud in the presence of the very people about whom it is written. He brazens it out, and with his own unique brand of clever rascality turns the whole thing to his advantage. This play is very similar in many respects to *The Inspector-General* (see p. 401), though it lacks the heavy overtones of the other and occasions less difficulty in production.

MEN (8): 4 are 25–35; 4 are 60–65. WOMEN (7): 1 is 20–25; 4 are 40–50; 2 are elderly. SETS: Apartment interior; a conservatory; drawing room of a country house. COSTUMES:

1860s; fashionable or pretentious dress, depending upon nature of characters; 1 Hussar military uniform.

ROYALTY: Apply International Copyright Bureau Ltd.*
TEXT: Rodney Ackland trans. in *The Modern Theatre* (Doubleday), Vol. II.

—— o ——

EASY MONEY (*Beshenyia den'gi;* 1870)   ALEXANDER NICOLAYEVICH OSTROVSKY.   The money that beautiful, pampered Lydia Cheboksarova and her frivolous mother spent for a life of luxury and leisure came and went easily because they had not earned it themselves. Threatened with financial ruin, the young lady decides to save herself by contracting a profitable marriage; but, unable to get a cavalier who "can squander a fortune with inimitable grace," she stoops to Savva Vassilkov, a disgracefully provincial businessman. Shortly after their wedding, when her robust, resolute husband refuses to pay for her extravagances, Lydia leaves him and returns to her degenerate aristocratic circle. But her unreliable admirers have only a little "easy money" and are not solvent themselves. Savva consents to take her back on the condition that she regain his trust by serving an indefinite term as his housekeeper in the provinces. Lydia, resigned but not converted, complies. Though the author intended this play to be a Russian version of *The Taming of the Shrew*, he retained little of the plot and still less of the spirit of Shakespeare's comedy. The play's main merits lie in vivid rendition of local color and in lucid demonstration of the effects of social conventions upon human behavior and thinking.

MEN (5): 4 are 20–40 (1 minor); 1 is about 60. WOMEN (2): 1 is about 24; 1 is about 50. EXTRAS: Servants, park strollers. SETS: Park and café; richly furnished apartment; modest room; elegant boudoir. Realistic scenery (used in recent Russian productions) may intensify atmosphere. Arena production possible. COSTUMES: Fashionable Russian during the second half of the 19th century.

ROYALTY: Apply publisher: TEXT: David Magarshack trans. in *From the Modern Repertoire* (Indiana), Ser. II.

—— o ——

BORIS GODUNOV (1825)   ALEXANDER PUSHKIN. Tragedy. Boris Godunov, the power-hungry son-in-law of Ivan the

Terrible, is responsible for the murder of the Tsar's young son, Dimitry. Years later, after Boris has ascended the throne, a young runaway monk, Grigory Otrepev, takes advantage of the rumors that surround the slaying of the boy and declares himself the miraculously saved Tsarevich. Cunningly exploiting Boris' enemies who in turn intend to use him as an instrument for weakening the Tsarist Empire, the false Dimitry flees to Poland and returns with an army. Boris, a usurper himself, sees in the impostor's success the revenging hand of fate. Before Dimitry reaches the walls of Moscow, Boris dies, a victim of his guilt. In dramatizing this turbulent period of Russian history, Pushkin avowedly emulated the structure of Shakespeare's chronicle plays and revealed himself a master in the handling of crowd scenes. The episodes that show the development of the pretender from a scheming adventurer to a cold-blooded politician are rich with physical action, but psychologically inferior to the scenes that expose the gradual self-destruction of the Tsar's mind.

MEN (*about 28; doubling possible*): 12 are 20–40 (11 minor); 14 are 40–60 (10 minor); 2 are 60–80. WOMEN (*4*): 2 are 18–24 (1 minor); 2 are 30–40 (minor). BOYS (*2*): 1 is 10–12; 1 is 14–16. GIRL: 15–17. EXTRAS: Boyars, ladies, officers, soldiers, servants, people. SETS: Interiors of several palaces, a monastery, a tavern, and a tent; exteriors: public squares, a garden, and open spaces. Sets must be spacious but need not be realistic. Arena production not practical. COSTUMES: Apparel of ruling classes and people in Russia at the turn of the 16th century. Rich, colorful costumes desirable.

ROYALTY: Apply publisher. TEXT: F. D. Reeve trans. in *An Anthology of Russian Plays* (Knopf), Vol. I.

—— o ——

THE POWER OF DARKNESS (*Vlast tmi;* 1887) LEO TOLSTOY. Nikita, a handsome farm laborer whose greed, lechery, and drunkenness lead him to accept an unprincipled code of behavior, experiences a series of circumstances which lead to murder, adultery, and infanticide. There is a tragic inevitability to Nikita's fall into foulness as he is egged on by his mother, Matryona, one of the most completely evil personages in the history of drama. Against her efforts, the father of the boy struggles nobly to save him from his own passions. Ultimately, Nikita is saved in a sort of eleventh-hour conversion; he confesses and in the typical manner of Russian mysticism achieves the regeneration of repentance and goes off to accept his punishment.

MEN (*11*): 1 is 25; 2 are 20–30 (minor); 4 are 35–40 (minor); 2 are 40–45 (minor); 2 are 50. WOMEN (*8*): 1 is 16; 1 is 22; 2 are 30–35; 3 are 40 (minor); 2 are 50. GIRLS: (*3*): 1 is 10; 2 are 12–15 (minor). EXTRAS: Peasant men, women and children. SETS: A simple dirt-floor Russian peasant's house (used in three scenes); the street outside; the yard; the threshing floor of the barn. Multiple setting possible. COSTUMES: 1880's period; Russian peasant, both well and poorly dressed.

ROYALTY: Apply publishers. TEXT: David Magarshack trans. in *The Storm and Other Russian Plays* (Hill and Wang) or F. D. Reeve trans. in *An Anthology of Russian Plays* (Knopf), Vol. I.

—— o ——

A MONTH IN THE COUNTRY (*Mesiats v derevne;* 1850) IVAN SERGEVICH TURGENEV. A masterful sketch of the psychological development of a married woman, bored with her husband and the stuffiness of provincial life. Natalya Petrovna becomes jealous of the love between her ward, Vera, and Vera's tutor and falls victim of a "delicate despair" brought about by her inability to capture his love herself. *A Month in the Country* deals in the minutiae of life and through its long five acts there is little overt action. This is a play of small meaningful actions and psychological exploration. The play retains a freshness that permits successful staging today.

MEN (*7*): 1 is 21; others range from 30–48. WOMEN (*5*): 1 is 29; 1 is 17; others range from 20–58. BOY: 10. Requisites are sincerity, natural elegance, and humor. SETS: Two rooms with French furniture and a garden of a Russian country estate. COSTUMES: Fashionable French dress of the 1840s.

ROYALTY: Apply A. P. Watt and Sons, Hastings House, Norfolk St., London WC 2, or Samuel French. TEXT: Constance Garnett trans. in *Turgenev* (Hill and Wang), or Emlyn Williams adap. (Samuel French).

IRISH DRAMA

THE HOSTAGE (1958) BRENDAN BEHAN. Comedy. The play takes place in a seedy Dublin hostel where some raffish characters contribute to a series of rowdy actions. The slight plot concerns a young English soldier who is held hostage by the Republicans in reprisal for an Irishman sentenced to death in Belfast. When the latter is executed, the I.R.A. threaten to kill their prisoner, but their intentions are complicated by the fact that they now like him. The play gives full vent to the animal spirits of the characters in some undisciplined scenes, alive with bumptious humor in which nothing is sacred and no holds are barred (ebullient theatricalism).

MEN (8): 4 are 20–30; 4 are 30–50. WOMEN (5): 1 is about 20; 2 are 25–35; 2 are 35–50. EXTRAS: Assorted colorful characters in a Dublin brothel: sailors; whores; policemen; etc. SET: Disreputable Dublin lodging house. COSTUMES: Modern dress; some uniforms needed for soldiers, sailors, and policemen. DIFFICULTIES: Demands an exuberant, earthy performance with mixture of speech, song, and dance.

ROYALTY: Apply Samuel French. TEXT: Grove or Samuel French.

—— o ——

SHADOW AND SUBSTANCE (1937) PAUL VINCENT CARROLL. Canon Skerritt is a man of taste and discernment, but something of a martinet in office. He regards his curates as barbarians, his niece as a ninny, and the schoolmaster as a troublemaker. Only for the simple serving girl, Brigid, does the canon have trust and affection. When she tells him she sees the suffering St. Brigid in visions, he tells her it is not possible and orders her to cease such foolish dreaming. A furor is raised regarding a book criticizing the church, and the canon takes matters into his own hands, dismissing the schoolmaster, whom he has discovered to be the author. Both of these authoritarian actions backfire when Brigid rushes out to prevent a violence she has foreseen and is struck down by a rock thrown by the mob at the schoolmaster. She dies and the proud canon is left a broken man. The narrowness of several of the local citizens is comically drawn.

MEN (6): 4 are 20–40; 2 are 40–60 (1 requires an outstanding actor). WOMEN (4): 2 are 18–22; 2 are 40–60. SET: Beautifully furnished living room of the priest's house in a small Irish town. Preferably realistic, might be simplified or treated symbolically. Suitable for arena. COSTUMES: Rural Irish, 1930s or contemporary; clerical garb for the canon and 2 curates. DIFFICULTIES: Dialect required of most of the characters.

ROYALTY: $35–25, Dramatists Play Service. TEXT: Dramatists Play Service.

— o —

THE SHADOW OF A GUNMAN (1923)   SEAN O'CASEY. Donal Davoren, a struggling poet who has come to stay with his friend Seumas Shields, is mistaken by other residents of a Dublin tenement for a gunman on the run. He encourages the misconception because he enjoys the admiration of pretty Minnie Powell. The young men discover a bag of bombs has been left in their room by a real member of the underground, and they panic when the Auxiliary Guard raid the tenement. Minnie bravely takes it on herself to save them, and, caught with the evidence, she is killed in the ensuing melee. Short (two acts) and the first of O'Casey's plays to be produced, it anticipates his more famous realistic plays with a background of Irish rebellion and synthesis of the comedy and tragedy of life.

MEN (8): 5 are 20–40 (2 minor); 3 are 40–60. WOMEN (3): 1 is 18–25; 2 are 40–50. SET: Room in a Dublin tenement, should be realistic. Arena production possible. COSTUMES: Common Irish, 1920; uniforms for the Auxiliary Guard. DIFFICULTIES: Authentic dialect necessary.

ROYALTY: $25, Samuel French. TEXT: In *Three Plays* (St. Martin's).

— o —

JUNO AND THE PAYCOCK (1924) SEAN O'CASEY.
The Boyle family lives in a Dublin tenement at "the time of
the Troubles." "Captain" Jack (the Paycock) avoids work
and spends his time idling with his crony Joxer, while his wife,
Juno, supports the family. Fortune seems to come their way
when Boyle is left a legacy, but it proves an illusion. The
money is not forthcoming; the daughter Mary, expecting a
child, is abandoned by her lover; and the war-crippled son
Johnny, revealed as an informer, is killed by his comrades.
While Boyle rails on about the "terrible state of chassis" the
world is in, Juno, in her suffering, reveals her strength and
fortitude.

MEN (*13, some doubling possible*): 6 are 20–30 (1 has
crippled arm, 3 minor); 4 are 30–40 (minor); 3 are 40–60
(2 must be outstanding character comedians). WOMEN (*6*):
1 is 18–25 (some singing); 2 are 25–40 (minor); 3 are 40–60
(2 must sing, 1 must be outstanding, mature actress). SET:
Living room of a tenement house, probably realistic. Some
furniture changes during play. Arena production possible.
COSTUMES: Shabby, 1920s. DIFFICULTIES: Irish lilt must be
expertly handled.

ROYALTY: $25, Samuel French. TEXT: In *Three Plays* (St.
Martin's).

—— o ——

THE PLOUGH AND THE STARS (1926) SEAN O'CASEY.
The residents of a Dublin tenement are seen before and during
the uprising of Easter Week, 1916. Jack Clitheroe, a brick-
layer, goes off to do his duty as a Commandant of the Irish
Citizen Army despite the remonstrances of his wife Nora. The
other tenants proclaim their loyalty to the Plough and the
Stars (the banner of Irish independence) with fervor, renounc-
ing Bessie Burgess, whose son and sympathies are with the
crown. However, when violence breaks out their chief concerns
seem to be to plunder and to save their own necks. The un-
romantic realities of such an uprising are made abundantly
clear. Clitheroe dies for Ireland; Bessie, trying to protect Jack's
wife, who has lost her mind, is also killed. Mollser, a consump-
tive child, is an indirect casualty of the conflict. Despite the
seriousness of the theme, comedy is inextricably woven into
some of the characterizations.

MEN (*10*): 1 is a voice and shadow only; 6 are 20–30; 2 are 40–50; 1 is 60–70. WOMEN (*5*): 3 are 20–25; 2 are 40–50 (must be excellent actresses). GIRL: 10–15. SETS: Living room of a flat in a Dublin tenement; public house; street outside the tenement; attic room in the tenement. Sets should be realistic but might be simplified. COSTUMES: Irish, around 1916, including 3 uniforms of the Irish Citizens Army and 2 of the Wiltshires. DIFFICULTIES: Requires a number of strong actors; Irish dialect.

ROYALTY: $25, Samuel French. TEXT: In *Three Plays* (St. Martin's).

— o —

THE SILVER TASSIE (1927) SEAN O'CASEY. The story of Harry Heegan, athletic hero and winner of the Silver Tassie, who loses the use of his legs during World War I. Forsaken by his girl and his friends, embittered and useless, he becomes an unwanted reminder of the war. "The Lord hath given and man hath taken away." His case is paralleled by that of Teddy Foran, who loses his sight. As usual, O'Casey provides a comic contrast to the tragic situation he has built. The play is a powerful indictment of war and includes an expressionistic second act (the others are semirealistic) chanted by an almost completely separate cast of soldiers. (It was over this play that O'Casey broke with the Abbey Theatre, refusing to temper its bitterness or expressionism.)

MEN (*18*): 12 are soldiers in Act II only (most should have some musical ability); 2 are 20–25 (1 should sing); 2 are 30–40 (1 must sing); 2 are 50–65. WOMEN (*5*): 2 are 18–25; 2 are 30–40 (1 minor); 1 is 50–60. SETS: Main room in Heegan's house; the front in France; hospital ward; clubroom of the Avondale Football Club. Sets can be simplified. Since Act II needs to be somewhat expressionistic, the others should probably tend in that direction. COSTUMES: World War I era, including a dozen British uniforms; 1 doctor; 1 nurse; 1 Sister of the Ward. DIFFICULTIES: Act II must convey an impression of the boredom and horror of war through its chanting (music is appended), and also must be reconciled in style with the other acts. Dialect is chiefly apparent among the older characters.

ROYALTY: Apply publisher. TEXT: In *O'Casey: Selected Plays* (Braziller).

——o——

PURPLE DUST (1940) SEAN O'CASEY. This "wayward comedy" chronicles the misadventures of two English antiquaries, Cyril Poges and his nephew Basil, when they attempt to renovate and inhabit an old Tudor mansion in the Irish countryside. With them are their Irish mistresses, Souhaun and Avril, who are soon distracted by the virile, romantic figure of O'Killigain, the foreman in charge of the reconstruction. The latter points out the folly of trying to live in the past, but the English gentry obstinately refuse to listen. The Irish workmen take advantage of their vanity and ineptitude and the mansion crumbles about them. Avril and Souhaun, however, have seen the light and flee with O'Killigain and another of the workmen before the river rises to drown the castle and the illusions of the squires. Farce is combined with symbolism and poetry as it becomes maddeningly apparent that this type of English mind will never understand the Irish.

MEN (*11, doubling of 2 or 3 possible*): 6 are 20–35 (1 must sing well); 5 are 45–65. WOMEN (*3*): 2 are 20–26; 1 is 33 (all must sing a bit). There is also "the stylized head of a cow." SET: "A wide, deep, gloomy room that was once part of the assembly or living room of an Elizabethan mansion." Certain parts of the set must come or be taken apart during the action, one bit of which calls for a workman to stick his head down through the ceiling. COSTUMES: Fashionable English; Irish workmen; priest; postmaster. DIFFICULTIES: Besides the crumbling sets and props, some compromise will be necessary with the final stage direction: ". . . the green waters tumble into the room through the entrance from the hall."

ROYALTY: Apply publisher. TEXT: In *Collected Plays* (St. Martin's), Vol. III.

——o——

COCK-A-DOODLE-DANDY (1948) SEAN O'CASEY. Comedy. Earthy Irish reactionaries have a hard time coping with the creatures of joyous fantasy in this symbolic comedy, which strikes vigorously at Irish penury, bigotry, and intolerance. Old Michael Marthraun, who has three pretty women in his house (daughter, Loreleen; second wife, Lorna; and a servant,

Marion), is fearful of the supernatural evil he believes to be present in the temptation of women and in connection with a handsome black rooster that roams the neighborhood. He, his crony, Sailor Mahan and their friends are in a constant superstitious torment until Bishop Domineer attempts to exorcise the evil spirits by Latin imprecations, the burning of books, and the repression of women's charms. In the process a man is killed. Loreleen is driven away for tempting Mahan, and Lorna, Marion and Marian's boyfriend, Robin Adair, follow. The spirits are indeed gone, but joy has left with them.

MEN (*16*): 5 are 20–30 (1 must play accordian and sing; 3 minor); 8 are 40–60 (3 minor); 1 is 65; 1 is "very, very old"; 1 is a handsome, dancing rooster. WOMEN (*4*): 3 are 18–25; 1 is 25–35. SET: Front garden outside an Irish house; colorful, unrealistic. Arena staging not possible, but horseshoe practicable. COSTUMES: Modern Irish; mixed rough and fanciful, including a uniform, various ceremonial robes, and a cock's plumage. DIFFICULTIES: A number of trick technical effects, such as disappearances, collapsing chairs, and the like are required. Dialect essential.

ROYALTY: Apply publisher. TEXT: In *The Modern Theatre* (Doubleday), Vol. V.

— o —

THE FAR-OFF HILLS (1931) LENNOX ROBINSON. Comedy. The household of blind Patrick Clancy is run by his eldest daughter, Marian, who has sacrificed for the present her ambition to enter a convent. She disapproves of her father's friends and regulates the lives of her younger sisters. They hope to escape her tyranny and are delighted at the success of their scheme to marry their father to an old friend. Marian, however, feels it is her duty to stay with her sisters until their education is completed. She comes to realize that she likes to manage things too well to belong in a convent, and after frightening off Harold, a long-time suitor, by threatening him with marriage, she is swept off her feet by ambitious young Pierce, who promises her a chance to help "run the town" with his new business enterprises. Harold is amusing and so is the maid, Ellen, who changes fiancés regularly because "the far-off hills" look greener.

MEN (*5*): 1 is 20–30; 1 is 30–40; 3 are 40–60 (1 is blind).

WOMEN (5): 2 are 16–17; 1 is 22; 2 are 30–40. SETS: "Comfortable, unpretentious" dining room; the girls' bedroom. Sets should probably be realistic (bedroom can be an insert). Arena production possible. COSTUMES: Middle-class. DIFFICULTIES: Authentic Irish accents.

ROYALTY: $25, Samuel French. TEXT: Samuel French.

— o —

THE WELL OF THE SAINTS (1905) JOHN MILLINGTON SYNGE. Martin and Mary Doul, though they are blind and weatherbeaten beggars, live happily together, both believing Mary to be a great beauty, as they have been told by well-meaning friends. A wandering saint miraculously disabuses them of this illusion, giving them sight. Both Martin and Mary are embittered when they see the truth of each other, themselves, and the world, and they go their separate ways. Martin finds everyday work hard, and he is scorned when he woos fair Molly Byrne. The miraculous cure proves temporary and when their sight fades Martin and Mary again find consolation in each other. When the saint insists on repeating the cure, Martin dashes the holy water from his hand, preferring to live a life of illusion, free from the tormenting sights of the world.

MEN (4, plus extras): 4 are 40–50. WOMEN (3, plus extras): 2 are 18–25; 1 is 40–50. SETS: Roadside with the ruined doorway of a church; village roadside with a forge. Settings need not be realistic. Arena production possible. COSTUMES: Threadbare Irish peasant. DIFFICULTIES: Rich Irish dialect is required.

ROYALTY: $25, Samuel French. TEXT: In Complete Plays (Knopf).

— o —

PLAYBOY OF THE WESTERN WORLD (1907) JOHN MILLINGTON SYNGE. Comedy. Christy Mahan, a shy youth taken in as potboy at a county Mayo pub, becomes a local wonder when he reveals that he has slain his terror of a father and fled. The daughter of the publican, Pegeen Mike, and the Widow Quinn vie for the affections of so brave a lad. Reveling in his changed status, Christy wonders why he was so foolish as "not to kill my father in the years gone by." He triumphs in local sports and wins the spirited Pegeen away from her terrified fiancé. Old Mahan shows up, however, battered but alive, seeking his son, and the cheers (including Pegeen's) turn to jeers. With his new-found assurance Christy turns the tables, tames his father, and walks out on Pegeen Mike to be the "Playboy of the Western World." A comedy springing from the heart of a peasant people, but soaring high in the lyricism of its language.

MEN (*6, plus extra peasants*): 2 are 18–25; 2 are 30–40; 2 are 50–60. WOMEN (*5*): 4 are 18–25; 1 is 30. SET: Country public house. Set should probably be realistic, though a more fanciful romantic style may be considered. Arena production possible although provision must be made for observing action out a large window. COSTUMES: Irish peasant, early 20th century; 1 jockey uniform. DIFFICULTIES: The play is extremely lyrical and authentic Irish lilt is necessary.

ROYALTY: $25–20, Samuel French. TEXT: In *Complete Plays* (Knopf).

— o —

DEIRDRE OF THE SORROWS (1910)   JOHN MILLINGTON SYNGE. Tragedy.   It has been foretold that the beautiful Deirdre will bring destruction to Ireland. Unwillingly betrothed to aging Conchubor, High King of Ulster, Deirdre flees with the young Naisi and his brothers. They have spent seven happy years in exile when Conchubor sends his friend Fergus with offers of amnesty. Despite warnings and forebodings, Naisi and Deirdre return to Ireland. Better a sharp end to something brave and glorious, she reasons, than to let it wither with age and regrets. Conchubor betrays and kills Naisi and his brothers to possess Deirdre. Outraged by this treachery, Fergus rises in revolt against the king. Deirdre fulfills the prophecy by taking her own life.

MEN (*8*): 6 are 20–35 (2 minor); 2 are 40–60. WOMEN (*3*): 1 is 20–30 (requires an outstanding and beautiful actress); 2 are 50–60. SETS: Lavarcham's house; wood outside a tent; inside a tent. Sets probably should not be realistic. COSTUMES: Roughly 10th century: long tunics and surcoats for the women; short tunics, leggings, and short mantles for the men; several hooded, full-length traveling cloaks.

ROYALTY: Apply Samuel French. TEXT: In *Complete Plays* (Knopf).

ASIAN DRAMA

Chinese

THE CHALK CIRCLE (*Hoei lan kia;* 13th or 14th century)
ANONYMOUS. Haitang is lifted from a squalid life of prosti-
tution to become the legal second wife of the childless Ma
Chun Shing. Haitang fulfills Ma Chun Shing's deepest wish by
bearing him a son, and the first wife is insanely jealous. She
schemes with her lover, Ch'ao, to poison the husband, cast out
Haitang, and take the boy child herself as a security against
disinheritance. She accuses Haitang, in court, of adultery and
murder and claims that she herself is the true mother. Haitang
is tortured into a false confession and condemned. She is
dragged on a painful journey through the snow to a second
court to receive final sentence. Her guards have been bribed
to kill her, but are prevented by the timely intervention of her
brother. The second judge is upright, and sets out to discover
the truth by a test as classic as Solomon's. The child is set
inside a chalk circle, from which only the true mother will be
able to lead him out. The first wife twice snatches the boy
from the circle, but Haitang sits patiently by; her love forbids
that she should maim the child by tearing at him. The judge
recognizes the sincerity of her love and pronounces her the
mother. Her persecutors are condemned to public execution.
A poignant parable of the suffering of innocence and the triumph of patience and love over malevolence and injustice.
Compare with Brecht's *Causasian Chalk Circle* (see p. 295).

MEN (*18, doubling possible*): 2 are elderly; the balance
range from youth to adulthood. WOMEN (6): 1 is elderly.
BOY: 5 (few lines). SETS: The play is intended for a presentational style of production on a traditional Chinese stage. There
is no scenery, although 5 different locales are indicated. Simple
properties are used to suggest 2 courtrooms, 2 domestic interiors, a snowy mountain pass, and a wine shop. COSTUMES:
Chinese, 13th or 14th century: court officials; middle-class

citizenry. DIFFICULTIES: Establishing a sign language of conventional gestures to suggest such activities as taking a trip.

ROYALTY: Apply publisher. TEXT: Ethel Van der Veer trans. in *World Drama* (Dover), Vol. I.

——o——

LADY PRECIOUS STREAM (*Wang pao ch'mau;* medieval) ANONYMOUS. A traditional folk play on the theme of the willful father and his three daughters. The two elder sisters are evil and proud and married to arrogant and ambitious generals. The youngest, Lady Precious Stream, is modest and good, and goes against her father's will to choose a simple man of the people for her husband. Hsieh is no more than a gardener, but he moves the heavy stone that the brothers-in-law are powerless to budge, and he writes the poem they lack the talent to compose. Lady Precious Stream leaves her father's house to dwell beside her husband in a cave. Hsieh joins a military expedition to the Western Regions, and enjoins his wife to wait for him. He is absent eighteen years. Word comes that he is dead. But his lady staunchly remains in her cave, refusing her family's attempts to win her back and marry her to another. In the meantime, Hsieh has become King of the Western Regions, outwitting his brother-in-law, Wei, who tried to kill him. The Princess of the West would marry him, but Hsieh flees back to China to find his true wife—still faithful though in rags. There is a joyful reunion; Wei is punished; and happiness comes at last to the loyal Lady Precious Stream.

MEN (*27; doubling possible*): 1 becomes 60 during the course of the action; the rest vary from youth to adulthood; 4 are silent. WOMEN (*13; doubling possible*): 5 major roles, 8 minor. SET: The play is intended for a presentational style of production on a traditional Chinese stage. There is no scenery. Simple but colorful properties (many made of cloth and bamboo) are used to suggest pavilions, palaces, snowstorms, mountain passes, horses, and chariots. These are manipulated by two "invisible" property men. COSTUMES: Ancient Chinese; courtiers, soldiers, peasants. DIFFICULTIES: Establishing a sign language of conventional gestures to suggest such activities as taking a trip or riding a horse.

ROYALTY: Apply Samuel French. TEXT: S. I. Hsiung adap. (Samuel French).

Indian

SHAKUNTALA (*Sakoontalá, ca.* 5th century A.D.) KALI-
DASA. This leisurely and legendary royal romance in seven
acts, depicts the courtship, marriage, untimely separation, and
ultimate reunion of the historical King Dushyanta and his
mystic bride Shakuntala, daughter of a Divine Sage and a
wood nymph. The scenes of courtship in the sacred grove are
vibrant, sensuous, and ecstatic; exotic and suggestive flower
imagery is interwoven with insect and animal symbolism to
create an earthly paradise where the divine is mated with the
human in a union at once sacred and illicit. The King Chari-
oteer moves through the drama in a panoply of earthly splendor, flying over the stage in pursuit of an imaginary antelope
in Act I, descending from the sky in Act VII, fresh from leading India's army against a rebellious race of giants. The cast
is numerous and varied, comprising figures as diverse as
Brahman hermits, a silent chorus of Yavana warrior women
(bows in hand), a court jester, a fisherman, and trees that
speak.

MEN (*22; doubling possible*): 2 are old sages; the balance
are between late youth and adulthood. WOMEN (*14; doubling
possible*): 2 of the women are old, the rest young. BOY: 5–6.
EXTRAS: A silent chorus of Yavana warrior women; officers;
hermits; members of the king's retinue; a chorus of speaking
trees. SETS: A neutral unit set with movable props (*e.g.,*
throne, chariot) would be sufficient, or a setting which simultaneously represents several places. The play is presentational
in style. 8 of the 9 suggested locales are exterior; 1 is a room
in the palace. Machines for the descent of the nymph and the
king from the sky are desirable but not mandatory. COSTUMES:
Indian, 5th-century A.D.: royalty; courtiers; monks, officials;
common people; nymphs.

ROYALTY: Apply publisher. TEXT: Sir Monier-Williams trans. in *World Drama* (Dover), Vol. I.

—— o ——

THE LITTLE CLAY CART (*Mṛcchakaṭika; ca.* 4th century A.D.) KING SHUDRAKA. A middle-class play of romantic passion with a picaresque atmosphere of bazaars and gambling casinos, peopled with merchants, monks, prostitutes, and thieves. Charudatta, a ruined merchant, falls ardently in love with Vasantasena, a courtesan, who deeply and sincerely reciprocates his passion. Their mutual devotion falls within a code of courtly love. Charudatta is happily married and has a child; but his wife is a model of patience and understanding and sacrifices her one remaining necklace to make good the theft of a precious jewel casket which Vasantasena had left in Charudatta's possession. The courtesan, in her turn, pays touching homage to the wife, conceiving herself to be the husband's slave. The crisis occurs when a villainous courtier, frustrated by Vasantasena's consistent rejection of his advances, strangles her. The murderer goes to court and puts the blame on Charudatta, who is convicted on circumstantial evidence and very nearly executed. At the eleventh hour he is cleared of blame and Vasantasena is led in—alive. She has been revived by a compassionate monk. The lovers are reunited.

MEN (*25; doubling possible*): 1 is an old man; 2 2-man "bullocks" (ox suits); the others range from youth to adulthood. WOMEN (*7*): 1 is elderly and fat. BOY: 5–6. SETS: 5 locales are suggested, with a neutral outside area. A 2-mansion unit set with a "platea" between is one solution. Arena production possible. COSTUMES: Indian, 4th century A.D.; middle-class merchants; citizens; servants; thieves, gamblers; prostitutes; courtiers; and court of justice officials. DIFFICULTIES: Creating a presentational style of movement and speech to match the text. Traditional music and dance would much enhance the effect. Suggested instruments: sitar, esraj, tabla.

ROYALTY: Apply Samuel French. TEXT: Arthur William Ryder trans. (Theatre Arts).

Japanese

THE HOUSE OF SUGAWARA (*Sugawara Denju Tenarai Kagami;* 1746) TAKEDA IZUMO, MIYOSHI SHŌRAKU, and NAMIKI SENRYŪ. Kabuki.   A melodramatic saga of tragic intensity, this play deals with the exile of Sugawara no Michizane, a tenth-century poet and statesman who fell victim to the unmerited jealousy of a powerful political rival, Fujiwara. (Michizane was the foremost literary figure of his time, and a master calligrapher. Tradition has made him a god.) The play also concerns the effect of his exile on the lives of three brothers, one of whom (Umeōmaru) was his royal retainer and another (Matsuōmaru) served his worst enemy. The popularity of the play is based on the next-to-last act (*Terakoya:* "The Village School"), which is often played independently. Michizane's only son has been hidden away in a remote village school, but Fujiwara has tracked him down and demands his life from the terrified schoolmaster. Matsuōmaru is sent as envoy to identify the corpse. In an intensely affecting scene Matsuōmaru repents of his allegiance to the villainous Fujiwara and determines to rescue Michizane's heir by sacrificing his own son in his stead. The heartbreaking moment when the bereaved father receives his child's head and affirms it to be the son of Michizane is perhaps the high point of all Kabuki.

MEN (*52, 34 speaking roles; doubling possible*): 16 are 20–25; 3 are 25–30; 11 are 30–40; 11 are 40–55; 2 are 55–60; 2 are 60–70; 7 are 25–50 (minor). WOMEN (*13*): 2 are 16–20; 1 is 20–25; 1 is 25–30; 4 are 30–35; 1 is 40–45; 1 is 65–70; 3 are 20–50 (minor). SETS: The traditional Kabuki stage is very wide (90 feet), with massive, realistic sets, a revolving stage, and *hanamichi*—a bridge passing from the back wall of the auditorium, through the audience, to the stage. Adaptation to a simultaneous setting or arena stage is possible, but risks a loss of theatricality. Bank of the Kamo River; outer room of Sugawara's palace, shifting (without break) to inner room, and subsequently to the palace gate (by means of revolving stage); Domiyo temple; interior of a thatched hut; interior and exterior of a village school. Costumes: Tokugawa period or 10th century, depending on interpretation: court; middle-class; peasant; 2 2-man "bullocks" (ox suits); maids; palanquin bearers; guards; and samurai. Difficulties: Kabuki is avowedly a professional theatre, and it is hard for Western amateurs to achieve anything like the explicit stage form, which is the drama. Physical characterization and make-up are highly stylized.

Royalty: Apply publisher. Text: Louis M. Steed and Earle Ernst trans. in *Three Japanese Plays* (Grove).

MISCELLANEOUS EUROPEAN
DRAMA

Austrian

HERO AND LEANDER (*Des Meeres und der Liebe Wellen;*
1831) FRANZ GRILLPARZER. Tragedy.   At the goddess' shrine
in Sestor, Hero takes a vow to become a virgin priestess of
Aphrodite and renounces Hymen and Eros in her desire to
live a life of calm withdrawal. When Leander, a youth from
Abydos, follows her into a grove forbidden to men, she rejects
him but cannot banish him from her mind. That night, Leander swims through the Hellespont and enters her room. The
succeeding love scene has no equal in German literature. The
pure, trembling girl is irresistibly attracted to the shy yet ardu-
ous Leander; she flees—and then returns. Their first night of
love is to be their last. In the guiltless serenity of supreme
happiness, Hero fails to conceal her secret under questioning.
The next night the Grand Priest extinguishes the light Hero
had set to guide Leander through the stormy sea. In the
morning his body is washed up on the shore. Hero dies at
Leander's side. Grillparzer's characters lack the heroic grandeur of the Greek mythological prototypes; they are warm-
blooded human beings with diversified individual traits. In
contrast to the hesitant, nervous Leander, his friend Naukleros
is thoroughly uncomplicated. The stern, ascetic Grand Priest
is not inhuman.

MEN (5): 2 are 18–22; 3 are 30–50 (1 minor). WOMEN
(3): 2 are 17–20; 1 is 40–50 (minor). EXTRAS: Servants;
people. SETS: Aphrodite's shrine in Sestos; a grove in front of
Hero's tower; Hero's room; in front of Leander's hut at
Abydos. Arena production possible. COSTUMES: Greek mythological style. DIFFICULTIES: Many of the verse-tragedy's
more beautiful passages are to be found within monologues
of considerable length.

ROYALTY: Apply publisher. TEXT: Henry H. Stevens trans.
(Register Press).

THOU SHALT NOT LIE! (*Weh dem, der lügt!;* 1838) FRANZ GRILLPARZER. Comedy. Leon, the enterprising, resourceful kitchen-boy of the Gallo-Roman bishop Gregory of Chalons offers to rescue the bishop's nephew, Atalus, from the barbaric Germans. The saintly bishop consents on the condition that Leon proceed with absolute truthfulness. The boy sets forth over the Rhine and arrives at the fortress of the Frankish chieftain, Count Kattwald, where Atalus is held as hostage. There Leon manages to have himself sold as a slave to the brutish count, and, outwitting the barbarians by promising them the culinary delights of a superior culture, he soon dominates the entire household. By his very truthfulness—and with the aid of Kattwald's unbarbarically charming daughter Edrita —he succeeds in his mission. All the characters are refreshingly healthy and fairly uncomplicated. The serious problems beneath the surface of this lively, swiftly moving comedy concern the relativity of truth and the limits of human perfection.

MEN (*13*): 2 are 18–22; 9 are 20–40 (8 minor); 2 are 40–60. GIRL: 16–18. EXTRAS: Soldiers; poor people. SETS: Garden of Bishop Gregory; courtyard in Kattwald's primitive fortress; pasture; Kattwald's bedroom; forest; riverbank; outside the ramparts of Metz. Sets should be imaginative and colorful but not realistic. Arena production possible. COSTUMES: Relatively refined garments of Christianized Gauls; bearskins of barbaric Franks, early Merovingian era. DIFFICULTIES: The characters of Kattwald and of his prospective son-in-law, the imbecile Galomir, lend themselves to overacting, which must be avoided to preserve the smooth and elegant comedy style.

ROYALTY: Apply publisher. TEXT: Henry H. Stevens trans. (Register Press).

—o—

THE STRONG ARE LONELY (*Das Heilige Experiment;* 1943) FRITZ HOCHWÄLDER. The Jesuit theocracy in the immense South American forests was an unparalleled historic phenomenon. This play dramatizes the conflict of power that led to its downfall. In 1767 the King of Spain, to whom the Jesuits owed allegiance in temporal matters, sends an envoy to Buenos Aires to investigate charges brought against the Order by the jealous Spanish colonists. In a theatrically great inquest scene the Father Provincial disproves the accusations of profiteering and treachery; there are no hidden treasures, and the fathers have armed the natives only to protect them against the slave-driving "Christians." Against the Spanish Crown the Father Provincial is ready to defend the liberty of the Paraguayan Indians by force; yet, since the very success of the missions jeopardizes the survival of the entire Order, he brokenheartedly obeys the command of the Father General in Spain and abandons the Holy Experiment. Led by the dominating, idealistic, tortured Father Provincial, the all-male cast includes several impressive parts—among them the authoritative though sympathetic royal envoy; a plainspoken Dutch trader; a militant, rebelling Jesuit; a hypocritically pious bishop; and the implacable legate from the Father General, who has to remind the Provincial that this world is not the Kingdom of God.

MEN (*20*): 11 are 20–40 (8 minor); 9 are 40–60 (2 minor). EXTRAS: Jesuit fathers; Spanish soldiers; Indians. SET: Large room in the Jesuit College at Buenos Aires. Realistic scenery not necessary. Arena production possible. COSTUMES: Apparel of Spanish planters; officers and soldiers in the second half of the 18th century; Jesuit cassocks; Indian serapes. DIFFICULTIES: The spiritual agony of the Father Provincial, following the dramatically effective scenes of political struggle, will appear anticlimactic if this part is not portrayed by a powerful, experienced actor.

ROYALTY: $35, Samuel French. TEXT: Samuel French.

— o —

EVERYMAN (*Jedermann*, 1910) HUGO VON HOFFMANNS-THAL. In using the title of the famous anonymous English morality play, Hofmannsthal declares himself more indebted to this version of the *Rich Man's Summoning* than to any other of the numerous medieval treatments of the same theme. Half of the play is devoted to the hero's earthly life. Everyman is merciless with his debtors and indifferent to the poor; evading the mild pleading of his concerned mother, he indulges in a life of luxury with his sycophantic friends and his voluptuous paramour. At the height of a lavish banquet scene, Death appears and puts his icy hand over Everyman's heart. Deserted by his friends, ridiculed by the Mammon he adored, Everyman goes through a nightmare of agony until his Good Deeds (a pale creature on crutches) and Faith come to his side. They help him regain strength in a full repentance, protect him from the Devil, and escort him on his last journey. Hofmannsthal succeeded in preserving the poetic simplicity of the old morality play (see page 52) while strengthening its dramatic impact.

MEN *(18; doubling possible)*: 20–40 (12 minor). WOMEN *(8)*: 7 are 20–35 (4 minor); 1 is 50–70. EXTRAS: Guests; servants; boys; musicians; angels; a monk. The age and sex of several allegorical figures is unspecified. SET: A banquet hall in Everyman's house. No background scenery required. Suitable for arena. COSTUMES: Rich medieval or Renaissance clothes for Everyman and his guests; costumes of allegorical figures in the stylization of the same period.

ROYALTY: Apply publishers. TEXT: George Sterling trans. (Primavera Press, 1936; out of print) or John Reich trans., Goodman Memorial Theatre, Michigan Avenue at Adams Street, Chicago, Ill.

—o—

LIBERTY COMES TO KRÄHWINKEL *(Freiheit in Krähwinkel,* 1848) JOHANN NESTROY. The strife for liberty that swept over Europe in 1848 led to the March Revolution in Vienna and, according to the "Viennese Aristophanes," even to the uprising in Krähwinkel, "Caw-Nook." This is a little town of political and social caricature, a stronghold of patriarchal despotism, represented by pompous politicians, cobwebbed bureaucrats, iron censors, and slimy Jesuits. The leader of the suppressed citizenry is Gerhard von Ultra, a liberal journalist who outwits the reactionary authorities and succeeds in manning the barricades. Nestroy's sharp, satirical wit, flair for comic situations, and clearsightedness in exposing human failings have prevented his comedies, fantasies, and farces from appearing outmoded, in spite of his use of nineteenth-century Viennese dialect. In the English adaptation this political satire is considerably abbreviated. With the elimination of numerous allusions and details, understandable to Nestroy's contemporaries, some of the characteristic Viennese local color has also been lost.

MEN *(16; doubling possible)*: 6 are 20–40 (4 minor); 10 are 40–60 (5 minor). WOMEN *(9)*: 4 are 18–25 (2 minor); 5

are 40–60 (4 minor). EXTRAS: Soldiers; townspeople. SETS: Offices; rooms; taverns and streets in Krähwinkel. Simple, caricatural scenery. Arena production possible. COSTUMES: Apparel of Viennese citizenry, 1848; uniforms of 1 officer and 3 or more soldiers. Costumes need not be authentic.

ROYALTY: Apply publisher. TEXT: Sybil and Colin Welch adap. in *The Tulane Drama Review*, Summer 1961.

— o —

ANATOL (1893) ARTHUR SCHNITZLER. Comedy. Seven vignettes exposing the romantic idealism of seven affairs of the heart. Each vignette could be played as a one-act, but without the whole, the savor of the subtle interrelationships would be lost. Anatol appears in each scene, and his friend Max appears in all but two. Only the women change, one for each scene. The implicit humor of sex is light and frothy, in the tradition of romantic Vienna; it is never ribald or grotesque. Characterization is the essence of the comedy. The intricacies of the male-female "fencing" have not become dated with time, nor has the male vanity revealed by Anatol's intense desire to regard himself as the motive force in all his affairs.

MEN (4): All are 20–40 (2 minor). WOMEN (7): All are 20–40. SETS: Anatol's bachelor apartment; a Viennese street; Max's apartment; Emilie's room; a private dining room in a Viennese restaurant. Settings can be imaginatively realistic. Arena production possible. COSTUMES: Fashionable Vienna, 1900. DIFFICULTIES: Humor depends on facility with the spoken word.

ROYALTY: $50, Samuel French. TEXT: Grace Isabel Colbron trans. in *Sixteen Famous European Plays* (Random).

— o —

LA RONDE (*Reigen;* 1896–97) ARTHUR SCHNITZLER. Comedy. In ten scenes Schnitzler depicts the game of sex and seduction in a variety of moods. In the manner of a "round dance," one partner in each scene is handed on to the next in a chain that finally links the last encounter to the first. Each vignette has its own shading and tone, animal joy, sophistication, pathos, and satirical bite as the play ranges through the various levels of society that are all brought at last to the same basis.

MEN (5): 3 are 20–40; 2 are 40–60. WOMEN (5): 18–40 (a 6th woman appears only briefly and can be played by one of the major characters). SETS: There are 10 scenes, exteriors and interiors, such as a bridge over the Danube, a place near an amusement park, a drawing room, a private dining room in a café, and so on. They need not be realistic, but some of the settings should depict more than one part of the locale. A turntable set with real doors and props augmented with projections on a cyclorama could prove a good solution. COSTUMES: Clothing from various classes of Viennese society in the 1890s; 2 military uniforms, 1 for a common soldier and the other for a captain of Dragoons. Must have elegance and high style. DIFFICULTIES: Restraint, taste, and style are required of the actors, who might otherwise be tempted to emphasize the obviously sensational qualities of the play.

ROYALTY: Apply publisher. TEXT: Eric Bentley trans. in *The Modern Theatre* (Doubleday), Vol. II; Keene Wallis trans. in *From the Modern Repertoire* (Indiana), Ser. I; or Frank and Jacqueline Marcus trans. (as *Merry-Go-Round*, Weidenfeld and Nicolson Ltd., 20 New Bond St., London W 1).

— o —

THE GREEN COCKATOO (*Der grüne Kakadu;* 1898) ARTHUR SCHNITZLER. The days preceding the French Revolution provide the inspiration for this play, which is peopled with characters who confuse illusion with reality. Prospere has devised a unique entertainment for the nobility who patronize his wine cellar. Actors are employed to play at thieves and villains, whores and revolutionaries. The metaphysical juxtaposition is brought into focus by the leading actor, Henri, who after a seven-year courtship has married Leocadie, an actress who is the favorite of the men. The Duc de Cadignan has been Leocadie's most recent lover, a fact not known to Henri. Henri improvises a scene in which he claims to have discovered the Duc in the arms of his bride and to have killed the Duc. Henri learns the truth of his improvisation; and when the Duc enters, Henri falls on him and stabs him just as the stormers of the Bastille arrive to celebrate their victory. This is a long one-act play.

MEN (*16, plus extras*): 1 is 17; 1 is 24; 3 are 20–25; 4 are 25–30; 2 are 30–35; 2 are 35–40; 2 are 40–45; 1 is 50. WOMEN (*5, plus extras*): 2 are 18–21; 1 is 20–25; 1 is 25–30; 1 is 30. SET: The Green Cockatoo wine cellar. Setting should be selectively realistic. Arena production possible. COSTUMES: French, 1789; peasant and fashionable nobility. DIFFICULTIES: Plays less than 2 hours.

ROYALTY: Apply Samuel French. TEXT: Ethel Van der Veer trans. in *Thirty Famous One-Act Plays* (Random).

Belgian

BARABBAS (1928) MICHEL DE GHELDERODE. Ghelderode
elected to treat the events of the Passion indirectly, in its re-
flection as experienced by the populace of Jerusalem. The
central figure in this treatment of the Passion story is the
murderer who was preferred to Jesus when the mob, incited
by the priests, was given the traditional privilege of choosing
a prisoner to be released at Passover. Barabbas, a coarse, untamed brute, whose provocative braggadocio fails to conceal
his mortal terror, is confronted with Jesus three times. Once,
in the prison; once, in front of Pilate's palace facing the cheer-
ing and jeering crowd; and finally on a hollow fairground,
overshadowed by the crosses of Calvary. When Christ dies in
fulfillment of his mission, Barabbas is knifed and dies—for
nothing. While creating the character and destiny of his protagonist according to his dramatic concept, Ghelderode por-
trays numerous biblical figures such as Pilate, Herod, Caiaphas,
The Magdalen, the two thieves, and the Apostles with a minimum of poetic license. Jesus appears but never speaks. In its
blending of Flemish folklore with religious history, the drama
achieves a robust and naïve liveliness, reminiscent of the
medieval Mystery Play. *Barabbas* was written in response to a
request by the Flemish Popular Theatre to provide a play that
could be performed during Holy Week.

MEN (*23; doubling possible*): 17 are 20–40 (12 minor);
6 are 40–60 (3 minor). WOMEN (*3*): 20–35. EXTRAS: Soldiers; beggars; the crowd (possible to place the crowd off
stage). SETS: Prison; entrance to Pilate's palace; fairground in
the shadow of Calvary. Blending of biblical and medieval
styles, as in the paintings of Hieronymous Bosch. Not recommended for arena production. COSTUMES: Biblical-medieval.
DIFFICULTIES: Of Act III Ghelderode demands: "In this act
the actors will be as though in a cistern, and since every-

thing is strange and panic-stricken during this act, they will behave like madmen or sleepwalkers."

ROYALTY: Apply Dr. Jan van Loewen, Ltd.* TEXT: George Hauger trans. in *Michel de Ghelderode, Seven Plays* (Hill and Wang).

—— o ——

PANTAGLEIZE (1929) MICHEL DE GHELDERODE. Pantagleize, a man "who has kept the treasure of his childhood in his heart," decides that "What a lovely day!" will be the phrase with which he greets the people he meets on a certain day that starts out as any other. Unfortunately for Pantagleize, his phrase is the signal awaited by an odd assortment of revolutionaries, and Pantagleize is caught up in a round of extraordinary events that leave him at one moment in possession of the key to the revolution, and finally dead. The revolution has failed. The play is a combination of the absurd and the satiric, increasingly tinged with the macabre. The satire is most evident in the scenes with General Macboom, who guards the conservatives' treasure; the absurd dominates the relationship of Pantagleize and his Negro servant Bamboola and the apprehension of Pantagleize by Creep, a policeman. "A Farce to Make You Sad."

MEN (*24*): The play may be acted with fewer and also with more characters; 14 of the men, varying in age and type, are recognizable as characters, the others are extras. WOMEN (*2*): 1 is a small part; more could be used in crowd scenes. SETS: 10 scenes, only 2 of which take place in same setting. Sets must be simple and unrealistic. COSTUMES: Modern fantastic, indicated by Pantagleize's first outfit, "Flowery dressing gown, trousers too short, seaman's white and blue sweater." DIFFICULTIES: A technically difficult show, replete with practicable units, light effects, many props, and sound cues of various natures. The acting needs the precision of vaudeville.

ROYALTY: Apply Dr. Jan van Loewen.* TEXT: George Hauger trans. in *Michel de Ghelderode, Seven Plays* (Hill and Wang).

—— o ——

PÉLLÉAS AND MÉLISANDE (1892) MAURICE MAETERLINCK. Golaud, well past middle age, and his young half-brother, Pélléas, are princes of Allemande. Lost in the forest,

Golaud discovers the beautiful Mélisande weeping beside a well. He leads the weakly resisting girl to his castle as his bride. When Pélléas and Mélisande meet, they fall in love. Gradually they arouse Golaud's suspicion until he finally surprises them in each other's arms. Pélléas dies by his brother's hand, Mélisande from a broken heart. The external action with all the clichés of romanticism—the dark forest, the gloomy castle, the golden crown, the golden ring, the maiden with the golden hair—is transcended by the inner conflict of forceful though inarticulate emotions. The characters drift in a world of unreality. Their language follows the abrupt, repetitive, irrational pattern of the stream of consciousness. Maeterlinck's play consists of a mosaic of loosely connected, fragmentary scenes, some of which unobtrusively suggest a symbolic meaning. They are saturated with a mysterious air of impending doom.

MEN (5): 1 is 18–25; 3 are 40–60 (2 minor); 1 is about 100. WOMEN (12): 1 is 17–21; 1 is 40–60; 10 are 20–70 (minor). BOY: 6–8. EXTRAS: 3 old beggars; servants; children. SETS: Forest; cave; numerous locations in and outside of a medieval castle. Romantic scenery. Large stage and huge sets recommended. Esthetically unsuitable for arena production because of the imaginary barrier between audience and stage. COSTUMES: Apparel of medieval royalty.

ROYALTY: $25, Samuel French. TEXT: Richard Hovey trans. in *Twenty-Five Modern Plays* (Harper).

—o—

SISTER BEATRICE (*Soeur Beatrice;* 1901) MAURICE MAETERLINCK. Sister Beatrice, a nun in thirteenth-century France, falls in love with Prince Bellidor. She begs the image of the Virgin to give her a sign if she is to stay in the convent, but receiving none, she goes. The image comes to life and takes her place. The other nuns are at first suspicious of the changes in Beatrice, but when a miracle fills the chapel with light and flowers, they accept her as a saint. Twenty-five years later the true Beatrice, fallen into misery and disgrace, returns to the convent to die and finds herself revered, in her dying hour, by the others who never realized she had been gone. The characters are thinly drawn, but the lyric power of the play is great. Maeterlinck's gentle poetry softens and suffuses the simple miracle play of the thirteenth century.

MEN (2): 1 is 20–30; 1 is 40–60. WOMEN (9): 2 are 20–25; 7 are 15–40 (all of these but 1—the Virgin—age 25 years between Acts II and III). GIRL: 5–10. BOY: 5–10 (no lines). EXTRAS: A crowd of beggars and pilgrims. SET: A corridor in a 13th-century French convent. COSTUMES: Early Gothic; religious and peasant; several rich robes.

ROYALTY: $25, Samuel French. TEXT: Bernard Hall trans. (Samuel French).

—o—

THE EGG (*L'Oeuf*; 1956) FELICIEN MARCEAU. To shut out the hardships of life, it is advantageous to penetrate "inside the egg," but only those who discover the system find access. Émile Magis is one of the few, and he confides the secret to the audience. He narrates his development from a charming, innocent young man to a still charming, cynical scoundrel, and he illustrates it in a succession of sketchy scenes in which he proves that love and righteousness are negligible since everything happens by chance. His first petty theft leads to his seduction by an elderly spinster; his double-crossing of a friend secures a husband for his sister. As he seeks not work but employment, he chooses the career of a civil servant. He becomes a respectable family man who adds to his prosperity by blackmailing his wife's lover. In the end he commits murder and, of course, gets away with it. The numerous characters who are all inadvertently instrumental to Émile's progress into the egg are lucidly observed and their petty weaknesses presented with tongue-in-cheek humor. They are too human to be caricatures.

MEN (*19; reducible by doubling to 8*): 8 are 20–40 (5 minor); 11 are 40–60 (8 minor). WOMEN (*14, reducible by doubling to 8*): 6 are 18–24 (4 minor); 4 are 30–40 (3 minor); 4 are 40–60 (2 minor). SET: Variety of exterior and interior locations in a big city, can be suggested by simple means; quick and smooth transitions from narration to scene are essential. Arena production possible. COSTUMES: Contemporary street clothes.

ROYALTY: Apply Alexander S. Ince or publisher. TEXT: Robert Schlitt trans. (apply Alexander S. Ince, 234 W. 44 St., N.Y., N.Y.) or Charles Frank trans. (Faber and Faber).*

Czechoslovakian

R.U.R. (1920) KAREL ČAPEK. Harry Domin is the general manager of a factory which produces robots. (*Robot* in Czech means "worker".) Helena Glory is the first woman to visit the ideal factory of robot workers and human managers. When Helena discovers that the robots have no souls, she persuades Dr. Gall to alter the robot formula, thereby remedying the deficiency. The robots of the world unite and destroy all but one human, but the formula for robot reproduction has been destroyed. While attempting to rediscover the formula, the surviving human recognizes that two of Gall's robots with souls also seem endowed with the capacity for reproduction, and the play ends on a note of hope. Čapek's concern here is primarily with the destructive and debilitating force of the machine on human individuality and initiative. He also reflects the post-World War I thinking regarding the selfish and irresponsible motivation of industrial magnates to promote war.

MEN (*13*): 7 are robots 20–30 (4 minor); 6 are human 30–60. WOMEN (*4*): 2 are robots 20–30; 2 are human: 1 is 20–40, 1 is 40–60. (10 years pass between Acts I and II.) SETS: The office of a factory of the future; Helena's drawing room; a laboratory. Sets need not be realistic, but expressionistic distortion should not be carried to an extreme. COSTUMES: Business contemporary for humans; contemporary working clothes of a distinctive uniform cut and color for robots. DIFFICULTIES: Avoidance of science fiction stereotypes in design and acting.

ROYALTY: $25, Samuel French. TEXT: Paul Selver and Nigel Playfair trans. (Samuel French).

— o —

THE INSECT COMEDY (*Ze Života hmyzu;* 1921) KAREL AND JOSEF ČAPEK. Comedy. This play bares the petty and selfish motivations of mankind in an ironic comedy which superimposes these motivations on creatures of the insect world. In the first-act world of the butterflies, we see the pettiness of love; in the second-act world the rivalries of family and existence as lived by the beetle, cricket, and ichneumon fly; in the third act, the tendency to war is illustrated by the ant world. Bracketing the insect world is a prologue and epilogue, populated by humans, to emphasize the life cycle. The human element in the world of the insects is adroitly conceived and selected. The level of comprehension is necessarily on an adult level only.

MEN (*26, plus numerous extras*): Only 1, about 60, plays the entire show. WOMEN (*16, plus numerous extras*). Ages for all characters variable; primarily insects with typed human characteristics. SET: Single set; imaginative forest setting with variable acting areas. Scrim. COSTUMES: Imaginative; varied possibilities. Insect costumes can be contemporary dress with suggestion of dominant insect characteristics, or they can be representative of insects. DIFFICULTIES: Extremely large cast. Some choreography. Not a fantasy.

ROYALTY: $25, Samuel French. TEXT: Owen Davis adap. (Samuel French).

— o —

ADAM THE CREATOR (*Adam stvořitel;* 1927) KAREL AND JOSEF ČAPEK. Adam, dissatisfied with the world God has created, destroys all living creatures but himself with his Cannon of Negation. The Voice of God speaks to Adam and charges him to make a better world, if he can, with the clay of creation which lies at his feet. Adam's efforts at creation only repeat the complexities and irrationalities of the world he had destroyed. Then, having re-created the world, Adam is relegated by his creations to the position of symbolic figurehead with no voice in the administration of government. Disillusioned, Adam once more contemplates the destruction of man, but he is deterred from doing so and, with the echo of the Voice of God, agrees to leave the world as it is. There is implicit hope in this play: Man must stand squarely before his problems and actively cope with their resolution.

MEN (*22; doubling possible*): Ages variable, predominantly 20–40 (1 requires an outstanding actor, 18 minor). WOMEN

(3): All are 20–40. CHILDREN (6): Varying ages and both sexes (minor). SETS: An exterior with a slum; slum removed; a hut added; a 2nd hut added; the exterior with 2 modern cities on the horizon; the same with scaffolding in the foreground. The slum must be removed from the exterior during a blackout with Act I. New characters are supposedly molded by Adam from the mound of clay of creation in the foreground. COSTUMES: Modern dress and representation of the classic dress of Adam and Eve.

ROYALTY: Apply publisher. TEXT: Dora Round trans. in *Dramas of Modernism* (Allen and Unwin, Ruskin House, 40 Museum St., London WC 1).

Dutch

THE GOOD HOPE (*Op Hoop van Zegen;* 1900)   HERMAN
HEIJERMANS. Tragedy.   In a Dutch fishing village which
looks to the sea for life as well as for death, attention is fo-
cused on the agonized waiting endured by the women for the
return of their men from each voyage. The young men of the village must choose the sea or be considered cowards in the
eyes of the village. The true tragedy of this fateful struggle is
somewhat weakened by the melodramatic characterizations of
the shipowner, Bos, who orders the unseaworthy *Good Hope*
to sea, and his daughter, Clementine, who learns of the existence of evil through this action of her father. It is impossible
not to be aware of the similarities between this play and John
Millington Synge's 1904 one-act *Riders to the Sea.* Where the
two differ most is in the resignation to fate in Synge's play
and in the struggle with fate in Heijermans' play.

MEN (*11; doubling possible*): 5 are 18–30 (3 minor); 6
are 50–70 (1 must play the fiddle). WOMEN (7): 5 are 20–40;
2 are 50–60. SETS: Poorly furnished room in Kniertje's fisherman's cottage; the working office of Bos. Realistic. Arena
production possible. COSTUMES: 1900; primarily peasant;
upper-middle class; 2 coast guard uniforms.

ROYALTY: $25, Samuel French. TEXT: Lilian Saunders and
Caroline Heijermans-Houwink trans. (Samuel French).

Hebrew

THE DYBBUK (1914) S. ANSKY. This most famous of modern Jewish dramas, is a kind of dark fairy tale with religious and mystic overtones. A poor young student, Channon, loves Leah, the daughter of the rich Sender. He feels that she is predestined to be his bride; her father will not agree, and he begins to experiment with the magic of the Kabala to win her. She is betrothed to a rich suitor and Channon dies. On the wedding day, however, as the bridegroom approaches, the dead man enters as a *dybbuk* (evil spirit) into the body of the maiden. On appeal from Sender, the wise Rabbi Azrael undertakes to cast out the demon. During the course of the ceremony, it is made clear that Channon did have rights to Leah because of an old promise of Sender's to his father. Sender denies that he knew Channon was the rightful bridegroom. The Rabbi weighs the issues and orders the dybbuk to leave the young girl. Finally, it does so, and she returns to her sanity. Before the delayed wedding can take place, however, Leah hears the voice of her lover calling her. She goes toward his love and to her death.

MEN (*21; doubling possible*): 2 are about 30; 2 are 40–60; other ages unspecified. WOMEN (*13; doubling possible*): 2 young and 2 old; and 1 hag; others unspecified. SETS: Synagogue; street and square; the rabbi's house. These need imaginative, unrealistic treatment. COSTUMES: Contemporary, with some distinct Jewish touches such as prayer-shawls and phylacteries. DIFFICULTIES: Style required to emphasize the mystical weavings of the plot.

ROYALTY: Apply publisher. TEXT: Henry G. Alsberg and Winifred Katzin trans. in *Twenty Best European Plays on the American Stage* (Crown).

444

THE TRAGEDY OF JOB (500–300 B.C.) ANONYMOUS.
The adaptation by Horace Meyer Kallen takes the form of
Greek tragedy, retaining the text of the American Revised
Version of the Bible. He has broken up some of the long
speeches by assigning passages to the chorus or to another
character. When God speaks proudly to Satan of his perfect
and upright servant, Job, Satan reminds God that Job has
been protected and blessed; he challenges God to test Job's
faith by taking away that protection. When Job has lost home,
possessions, and children, three friends arrive to comfort him.
Each argues from his particular viewpoint: that Job has
sinned, else he would not be punished; that God is just; that
Job must acknowledge his sins and repent. Job questions the
justice of his suffering and protests his uprightness. Young
Elihu sets forth his argument that sin itself is corrective. Finally comes the Voice out of the Whirlwind to reassert the
orthodox view and to remind Job of God's omnipotent dominion over the earth and man's dependence upon him. Job
answers in humility, "Behold I am of small account. . . . I
recant my challenge and am comforted." The Epilogue narrates the story of God's restoration to Job of family, home, and
possessions. (Compare the same theme in MacLeish's *J.B.;*
see p. 354.)

MEN (5): 1 is 25–35; 4 are 50–60. WOMEN (*1, 2, 3 or
none*): Prologue, Epilogue and Voice out of the Whirlwind can
be played by either men or women: CHORUS: Preferably 15, but
may be reduced; men or mixed. SET: A village on the edge of
the Arabian desert. COSTUMES: Ancient Hebrew. DIFFICUL-
TIES: Similar to those in training a chorus for a Greek play
in unison and individual speaking. Movement less choreo-
graphic than in Greek tragedy.

ROYALTY: Apply publisher. TEXT: Horace Kallen adap.
(Hill and Wang), or in *A Treasury of the Theatre* (Simon
& Schuster).

Hungarian

LILIOM (1909) FERENC MOLNÁR. The story of Liliom, the carousel barker, and his star-crossed lover, Julie, is well known both in the original and in *Carousel*, the musical adaptation by Rodgers and Hammerstein. The brutal yet gentle Liliom is unable to find the motivation to provide for his wife, Julie, until he discovers that she is going to have a child. Then he blunders into an attempted robbery with his friend Ficsur and chooses suicide rather than capture and imprisonment. He appears before a police-court magistrate in heaven and is told to contemplate his sins for sixteen years, when he will be permitted to return to earth for one day to redeem himself. When Liliom returns to earth he does the nicest thing that he knows how to do—he brings his daughter a star he has stolen from heaven. The poignancy of this love story captures the depth sometimes seen in even the most seemingly shallow individuals.

MEN (*18*): 12 are 20–40; 6 are 40–60 (doubling possible). WOMEN (*9*): 7 are 18–25 (4 minor); 2 are 40–60. SETS: Amusement park with carousel; a park; a room in a cottage with tintype equipment; a railroad embankment; a heavenly courtroom; before Julie's cottage. Sets need not be realistic. There are 7 scenes and a prologue; shifts should be rapid. COSTUMES: Hungarian peasant; police uniforms.

ROYALTY: $25, Samuel French. TEXT: Benjamin F. Glazer trans. (Samuel French).

—— O ——

THE SWAN (*A hattyú;* 1914) FERENC MOLNÁR. A wistful spirit of romance underlies this story of Princess Alexandra, her suitor, Prince Albert, and the family tutor. Alexandra, who is seemingly ignored by Prince Albert, becomes involved in a scheme devised by her mother to permit the young scholar to exceed the bounds of his social position by paying court to the Princess. It is hoped that the romantic inclinations of the Prince will be aroused. The scheme gets out of hand, however, when the tutor insults the Prince and the Princess defends the tutor's action. The confusion of the midsummer eve is restored the following morning when the Princess comes to realize that, by virtue of her position, she must always remain the majestic swan, floating in the royal pond, for if she comes out of her element onto the land of the commoners, she can only waddle awkwardly through life. Possible levels of comprehension make this play suitable as either a children's or an adult show.

MEN (*10*): 6 are 20–40 (4 minor); 4 are 40–60. WOMEN (*8*): 4 are 20–30 (3 minor); 4 are 40–60. BOYS (*2*): 16 and 17. SETS: A formal garden in the castle of the Princess Beatrice. COSTUMES: Fashionable costumes of about 1830; servants' livery.

ROYALTY: $25, Longmans Green. TEXT: M. P. Parker trans. (Longmans Green).

— o —

THE PLAY'S THE THING (*Játék a kastélyban;* 1925) FERENC MOLNÁR. Comedy. Sandor Turai, a famous dramatist, and his collaborator, Mansky, arrive unannounced at a Riviera castle with their composer protégé. They overhear a love scene between the composer's fiancée and an aging actor. To restore the composer's faith in his fiancée, Turai writes a play which includes the dialogue that has been overheard. Much of the humor in the play depends upon the not-so-subtle *double entendres* and in the spoofing of dramatic technique. As for the latter, the characters provide background details directly, thereby supposedly dispensing with the conventional means of exposition; and the rehearsal of Turai's play within the play sharply exposes many other dramatic conventions, including the means at the dramatist's disposal to take revenge on the actor.

MEN (*8*): 3 are 20–30 (2 minor); 5 are 40–60. WOMAN: 25–35. SET: A room in a castle on the Italian Riviera. Realistic. Arena production possible. COSTUMES: Fashionable contemporary.

ROYALTY: $50, Samuel French. TEXT: P. G. Wodehouse adap. (Samuel French).

Swiss

THE MARRIAGE OF MR. MISSISSIPPI (*Die Ehe des Herrn Mississippi;* 1952) FRIEDRICH DUERRENMATT. Comedy. A public prosecutor who believes fanatically in the fierce retributive justice of Moses has managed to obtain 350 executions in his attempt to purify society. His childhood friend believes equally fanatically that salvation lies in adherence to the precepts of Karl Marx, in spite of the bad example offered by "the vodka-drinking nation to the east." A third reformer is completely devoted to the concept that by telling the exact truth at all times some mysterious alchemy will correct all wrongs and mend all broken hearts. Each of these men is frustrated by his own blindness and the wiles of a woman who is "not a liar, but always a different person . . . [For her] what *is* will always be stronger than what *was* and what *will be* will always defeat the present." At the end of the play each of the reformers has failed and the future of the nation is in the hands of a fatuous time-serving politician. The apparent simplicity of the plot is not matched by the form of the play. Characters step out of the play to address the audience; exposition is accomplished with film, pantomime, or a series of photographs; the temporal sequence of the play is often broken to emphasize some point in the plot; and many modern shibboleths of both theatre and society are pitilessly pilloried.

MEN (*7–12*): 3 must be mature and 1 younger (to play the romantic). The others can be of any age. Doubling possible. WOMEN (*5–8*): Only 2 female parts are speaking roles: Vanessa, who must correspond roughly to the age of the prosecutor (mature), and the maid, whose age is unimportant. COSTUMES: Modern, with 2 sets of evening clothes; a suit in rags; a prosecutor's robes. SET: 1 nonrealistic interior, with specified vistas through 2 windows; numerous technical effects. DIFFICULTIES: Most of these will be technical.

448

ROYALTY: $50, apply Kurt Hellmer.* TEXT: Apply Kurt Hellmer.

—o—

THE VISIT (*Der Besuch der alten Dame;* 1958) FRIEDRICH DUERRENMATT. The impoverished town of Güllen in central Europe hopefully awaits a visit from Claire Zachanassian, an eccentric elderly billionairess who was once a local resident. The townspeople accept as charming such peculiarities as her sleek pet panther, the cigars she smokes, and the coffin she carries about with her. They rejoice when they learn of her beneficent plan—to give Güllen a billion marks to revive its fortunes. But she has a story and conditions. In her youth she was seduced and disgraced by Anton Schill. Eventually a brothel inmate, she was visited and finally married by the wealthy Zachanassian. Now she wants to buy justice; when Schill's life is taken, the town will get its money. The citizens express pious horror, but they all make heavy purchases on credit—the police chief, the minister, even Schill's own family. Following a town meeting, the citizens close in around Schill on a dark lane. When they pull back, Schill is dead—of heart failure, say some; of joy, say others.

MEN (*22; doubling possible*): 1 is teen-age; 2 are 20–30; 3 are 30–40; 10 are 40–50; 5 are 50–60; 1 is 70–80. WOMEN (*5; doubling possible*): 1 is teen-age; 4 are 50–60. GIRLS (*2*): 5–10. SETS: The railway station; interior of the inn; street across from the inn; exterior and interior of Anton's shop; balcony of the inn; the burgomaster's office; exterior (no setting required); interior of church; interior of barn; forest scene; the town hall. Settings are many and complex. COSTUMES: Contemporary middle class—overalls for painter; formal clothes, including top hat for burgomaster; uniforms for conductor, policeman, butler. DIFFICULTIES: The author's directions call for imaginative, complex procedures, changing sets while the show is in action.
ROYALTY: Apply Samuel French. TEXT: Maurice Valency trans. (Random).

—o—

THE CHINESE WALL (*Die Chinesische Mauer;* 1955) MAX FRISCH. Exploring man's chance to prevent total destruction by the atomic bomb, the author turns to the past. A modern intellectual, the Contemporary, combining the functions of chorus and participant, introduces and interrelates the sketchy, kaleidoscopic presentation. Time is suspended: the action, though taking place in China during the completion of the Great Wall, is pervaded with significant historical and fictional figures. Napoleon, Brutus, Romeo and Juliet, Pilate, Columbus, Cleopatra, Don Juan, Philip of Spain, and the Unknown Woman of the Seine, mingle and exchange their messages of what is to each essential in life. The author interpolates passages from such great writers as Confucius, Shakespeare, and Schiller; he also refers to the dramatic works of such contemporaries as Bertolt Brecht, and even refers to his own work. *The Chinese Wall* is an attempt to hold up time, to dam up history. The Contemporary is forced to conclude that he cannot stem the tide of history. A farce that offers a warning, not a solution.

MEN (*17, doubling possible*): 10 are 20–49 (5 minor); 7 are 40–60 (3 minor). WOMEN (*7*): 6 are 17–24 (2 minor); 1 is 50. EXTRAS: Soldiers, mandarins, waiters, eunuchs, journalists. SET: Chinese Imperial Palace. (A throne; a few modern chairs.) Set can be very simple. It must be unrealistic, suggesting timelessness. Arena production possible. COSTUMES: Ancient Chinese robes; uniforms. Apparel of historical and fictional figures of various periods. Costumes need not be authentic but must be recognizable.

ROYALTY: Apply Kurt Hellmer.* TEXT: James L. Rosenberg trans. (Hill and Wang).

Welsh

UNDER MILK WOOD (1956) DYLAN THOMAS. This play was originally written for radio, with the subtitle "A Play for Voices." It is an extended series of vignettes, linked by a narrator, which give a kind of poetic glimpse into the life of a Welsh town from dawn to dark of one day. The play focuses on the activities and thoughts of various townspeople throughout the day: blind Captain Cat, who pulls the town hall bellrope to announce the day, dreams of his mates long lost at sea and listens to children at their play; Mrs. Willy Nilly, the postman's wife, steams open mail to keep tabs on the long-standing romance of Myfanwy Price, the dressmaker and sweetshop keeper, and Mog Edwards, the draper; and, toward evening, Mr. Waldo, in a corner of the local pub, sings as he has a few drinks before going off to a rendezvous with Polly Garter, the town tart.

MEN (*29, doubling and tripling possible and some can be cut*): 1 is 16–20; 2 are 20–30 (minor); 10 are 30–40 (5 minor); 14 are 40–55 (1 should have a good singing voice; 4 minor); 2 are 55–70. WOMEN (*28; doubling and tripling possible and some can be cut*): 1 is 17; 7 are 20–30 (1 should have a good singing voice; 2 are minor); 16 are 30–45 (10 minor); 3 are 45–55 (2 minor); 1 is 85. BOYS (*6; doubling possible and some can be cut*): 7–10. GIRLS (*5; doubling possible and some can be cut*): 7–12. SET: Attempt at symbolic representation of locale possible but not necessary; a black drape background or a white cyclorama (lighted to indicate time of day or mood of scene) is best to insure quick pace and fluidity of transition between scenes. Arena production possible. COSTUMES: Modern, appropriate to a small Welsh town; or evening dress for all with no attempt to use costumes to aid characterization. DIFFICULTIES: The large cast creates problems in casting and costuming. Movement of

451

characters in and out of playing areas must be carefully planned. Amount of visual spectacle to create for the audience is also a problem.

ROYALTY: $50–25, Samuel French. TEXT: New Directions or Samuel French.

DIRECTORY OF AGENTS AND PUBLISHERS

The following list includes the addresses of agents, other than publishers, within the United States, to contact for text or royalty information. Also included are the addresses of publishers and agents outside the United States. If an agent or publisher is referred to only once in the book, the address is included with the play.

The Actors and Authors Agency
234 W. 44th Street
New York, New York

A. D. Peters
10 Buckingham Street
Adelphi, London WC 2
England

American-Scandinavian
   Foundation
127 E. 73rd Street
New York, New York

Brandt & Brandt
101 Park Avenue
New York, New York

Curtis Brown, Ltd.
575 Madison Avenue
New York, New York

Dramatic Publishing Company
179 N. Michigan Ave.
Chicago 1, Illinois

Faber and Faber Ltd.
24 Russell Square
London WC 1, England

International Copyright Bureau
   Ltd.
Suite 8D
26 Charing Cross Road
London WC 1, England

Dr. Jan van Loewen Ltd.
81-83 Shaftsbury Avenue
London WC 1, England

Kurt Hellmer
52 Vanderbilt Avenue
New York, New York

Marie Rodell and Joan Daves,
   Inc.
15 W. 48th Street
New York, New York

Madame Ninon Tallon-Karlweis
57 W. 58 Street
New York, New York

Secker and Warburg Ltd.
7 John Street
London WC 1, England

Theatre Guild, Inc.
23 W. 53rd Street
New York, New York

Willis Kingsley Wing
24 E. 38th Street
New York, New York

INDEX

459